D1789244

Bird of Many Plumes

Studien und Texte zur Geistesgeschichte des Mittelalters

Begründet von

Josef Koch

Weitergeführt von

Paul Wilpert, Albert Zimmermann
und Jan A. Aertsen

Herausgegeben von

Andreas Speer

In Zusammenarbeit mit

Wouter Goris, Kent Emery, Jr.
und Georgi Kapriev

BAND 139

The titles published in this series are listed at *brill.com/stgm*

Bird of Many Plumes

*Conceptions and Applications of Authority in the
Thought of William of Saint–Thierry*

By

Delphine Conzelmann

BRILL

LEIDEN | BOSTON

The open access publication of this book has been published with the support of the Swiss National Science Foundation.

The Library of Congress Cataloging-in-Publication Data is available online at https://catalog.loc.gov
LC record available at https://lccn.loc.gov/2025014042

Typeface for the Latin, Greek, and Cyrillic scripts: "Brill". See and download: brill.com/brill-typeface.

ISSN 0169-8028
ISBN 978-90-04-72941-4 (hardback)
ISBN 978-90-04-73087-8 (e-book)
DOI 10.1163/9789004730878

A.M.D.G.

∵

Contents

Acknowledgements

> To read, study, and embrace William's teaching is to set out on a
> spiritual journey that is an ascent into the Trinitarian mystery of
> Christ.[1]
>
> THOMAS X. DAVIS

∵

Over the past years, I had the great privilege of experiencing the truth expressed in these words. As I have dedicated myself to the study of the works
of William of Saint–Thierry, a world of spiritual depth, monastic commitment, and deep reverence for the history of the Christian church has
opened its doors to me. My doctoral studies have, therefore, not been exclusively academic but also a spiritual endeavor that has allowed me to explore
my faith in a more meaningful way. My first expression of thanks is therefore owed to William himself and the many scholars who, throughout history, have been concerned with the transmission and interpretation of his
texts. They constitute a source of Christian spirituality, the value of which is
far from exhausted. With impressive and relatable honesty, they speak
about the dynamics of the human relationship with God. According to my
experience, reading and studying them challenges not only one's intellect
but one's heart and soul. Thus, I will continue to be grateful beyond my doctoral studies.

Furthermore, there are many people to whom I would like to extend
my gratitude and without whom I would not have been able to finish this
project. This is, first and foremost, my doctoral supervisor, Prof. Dr. Ueli
Zahnd (Institut de l'Histoire de la Réformation, Geneva), who has supported my ideas and my hopes for this project from the very beginning. I
would like to especially thank him for always connecting me with scholars,
calling my attention to conferences, and alerting me to lines of thought

---

1   Thomas X. Davis, "The Trinity's Glorifying Embrace: *Conscientia* in William of
    Saint–Thierry," in *A Companion to William of Saint–Thierry*, ed. F. Tyler Sergent (Brill,
    2019), 132.

with which I was not yet familiar. This has been incredibly beneficial for my academic growth.

One of the people with whom he connected me is my second supervisor, Dr. John T. Slotemaker (Fairfield University, Connecticut), who has shown much care and enthusiasm for this project. I was always able to discuss central questions, possible issues, and even controversial ideas with him. Particularly in the last phase of writing my dissertation these conversations have inspired and encouraged me, and his comments have certainly improved my writing and expanded my knowledge in the field.

This dissertation is also the result of three years during which I had the privilege to work, study, and research at the University of Basel. I want to thank the Theological Faculty of Basel for providing the means and circumstances that allowed me to finish my project at this time. I am very grateful to my colleagues and my superiors for supporting me with helpful advice, sympathetic ears, and support whenever I needed it. In particular, I would like to thank my colleague, Prof. Dr. Michael Bangert, with whom I was always able to share my research, and whose curious inquiries and creative approaches have been very much appreciated.

I also want to thank some of the experts in the field who have graciously welcomed me into the academic community. They are namely Prof. Dr. Rozanne E. Elder (Western Michigan University), Dr. Aage Rydstrøm–Poulsen (emeritus, University of Greenland), and Dr. Tyler Sergent (Berea College, Kentucky), who have offered their help and assistance regarding research and translation work, and whose excellent scholarship I relied on a lot during my studies. Dr. Sergent, in particular, provided tremendous insight while I was working on the publication of the work, and his help was invaluable.

Exceptional gratitude goes to the series editors who have made the publication of this project possible, especially Associate Editor Marcella Mulder, who has guided me through the publication process with patience and professionalism at every step of the way.

Of course, I could hardly have finished this project without the support of my personal friends and family, who have been very patient with me, even if I had little more to talk about than my dissertation or could not make much time for them. Their words of encouragement and prayers allowed me to continue to research, write and revise until the end. Finally, my partner and my parents have ceaselessly supported me throughout the highs and the lows of this process, and I am more grateful to them than I could put into words.

Introduction

> According to the poet's fable, we have majestically clothed our
> little bird with the colors and feathers of a variety of birds. If
> each of them came and took away what they believed to
> be theirs, our little crow would remain nude and stripped of
> everything.[1]

∴

With these words, William of Saint–Thierry prefaces his Commentary on
Romans. He likens it to a bird adorned with the feathers of others. These
others, as he explains, are the Church Fathers, whose spiritual and theological insights left their mark on William's thought; so much so, he claims, that
they are the actual authors of his work. Initially, this could be taken as a
particularly poetic and hyperbolic attempt at displaying humility. Yet, it is
also a testimony to how William wants his audience to understand the work
and task of a Christian author. Exegesis and theological reflection should
not serve to glorify the author's ego. Their value does not hinge on the
author's brilliance or the incomparability of his ideas. Rather, every contribution that relies on individual innovation alone, William declares, stands
naked and stripped of its colors. What constitutes the beauty of Christian
thought, he believes, is the harmony of tradition as a whole.

Yet, the 12th century was a time when the value of tradition was under
heavy consideration, and the notion of traditional Christian thought both
lost old and gained new meaning. The world of medieval monasticism
burst wide open, and the increasingly conflicting attitudes toward the past
would set the course of Christian discourse for centuries to come. Historio-
graphically, the 12th century was often understood as a turning point for
the course of the Middle Ages; the 'bosom' of the gothic movement, the

---

1 Expositio super Epistolam ad Romanos (Corpus Christianorum Continuatio Mediaevalis
86), praef., linea 16: *Secundum poeticam fabulam auiculam nostram diuersarum plumis
auium et coloribus sollemniter uestiuimus quae si uenerint et abstulerint singulae quae re-
cognouerint sua, nuda uel nulla remanebit nostra cornicula.* The Corpus Christianorum
Continuatio Mediaevalis will hereafter be abbreviated as cccm. All the translations from
William's primary sources, unless otherwise specified, are my own.

resurgence of mystic spirituality, and, of course, the dawn of scholasticism.[2] The dichotomy between monastic and scholastic thought is in itself more than controversial, and to apply it as such to the 12th century would be anachronistic. Still, the developments of later centuries point to the un-solved problem at the heart of the 12th-century discourse: the role of au-thority. In this book, I will discuss the conceptions and the significance of authority in work and thought of William of Saint–Thierry, one of the early authors of the Cistercian order. Before discussing the central question of this study, I will briefly offer an overview of William's life and works.

1   William's Life and Work

Very little is known about William's early life. The testimony closest to his lifetime is the *Vita Antiqua*, a hagiographical work written several decades after William's death.[3] While it is neither an entirely credible work, as its author did not know William personally, nor preserved in its entirety, it served as the primary source for anecdotes and legendary descriptions of William as a person. The text states that Willim was born in Liège (in pres-ent-day Belgium) and of noble parentage (*clarus genere*).[4] It also mentions an early companion named Simon – possibly a brother, although the exact nature of their relationship is not specified – who later became the abbot of Saint-Nicholas aux Bois. Yet the vita tells us little more about William's early years and contains no concrete dates. With few literary indications, the conjectures regarding William's date of birth range from 1075 to 1080.[5]

---

2   In his history of medieval piety, Arnold Angenendt refers to Friedrich Ohly's characteriza-tion of the 12th century as a century of 'incomparable creative vigour' (citing Ernst Frie-drich Ohly "Die Kathedrale Als Zeitenraum. Zum Dom von Siena," in *Schriften Zur Mittelalterlichen Bedeutungsforschung* (Darmstadt: Wissenschaftliche Buchgesellschaft, 1977), and considers it an indisputable fact that the 12th century introduced entirely new kinds of intellectual and emotional expression into the European Middle Ages (Arnold Angenendt, *Geschichte Der Religiosität Im Mittelalter*, 4th ed. (Darmstadt: WBG (Wissen-schaftliche Buchgesellschaft, 2009), 45).

3   An English translation is available in David N. Bell, "The Vita Antiqua of William of St Thierry," *Cistercian Studies Quarterly* 11 (1976).

4   Brian McGuire, however, has raised the question of whether this is truly a claim about William's provenance or simply a hagiographical formula (Brian P. McGuire, "A Chronol-ogy and Biography of William of Saint–Thierry," in *A Companion to William of Saint–Thierry* (Leiden: Brill, 2019), 12).

5   This range has been determined by Ludo Milis in "William of Saint Thierry, His Birth, His Formation and His First Monastic Experiences," in *William, Abbot of St. Thierry: A Colloquium at the Abbey of St. Thierry.*, trans. Jerry Carfantan, Cistercian Studies 94 (Ka-lamazoo, MI: Cistercian Publications, 1987), 20. Paul Verdeyen defends 1075 as his

William and Simon left Liège for Reims at an unspecified age, where the two companions likely studied the liberal arts at the local cathedral school.[6] Brian McGuire points out that William's education ought to be contextualized in the radically changing intellectual context of the transition between the 11th and the 12th century:[7] "We concentrate today, especially on the 'schools' of Laon and Chartres, but virtually every cathedral had its own masters and often ambitious reforming bishops. It must have been an exciting time to be alive for a young man who was curious about learning and at the same time felt attracted to the monastic life".[8] William certainly was. Probably around 1105, he joined the monastery of Saint Nicaise,[9] where he completed his monastic formation.[10] He was likely already about 40 years old when he encountered a figure who would fundamentally shape the rest of his life:[11] Bernard of Clairvaux (1190–1153). William accompanied the abbot of Saint Nicaise on his visit to the young Cistercian monastery of Clairvaux. William's encounter with Bernard and the community at Clairvaux kindled his interest in the Cistercian reform movement.

---

definite date of birth (Paul Verdeyen, "La Chronologie Des Œuvres de Guillaume de Saint–Thierry," *Ons Geestelijk Erf* 82, no. 3 (September 2011): 190), yet the evidence is not entirely sufficient to be certain.

6   Milis, "William of Saint Thierry," 23–25.

7   The concept of the 12th century as a period of a fundamental intellectual shift has been discussed extensively ever since the 19th century. The term of the "12th-century Renaissance" was coined by Jacques Antoine Ampère (1800–1864) (see: Jacques Antoine Ampère, *Histoire Littéraire de La France Avant Le Douzième Siècle*. 3 vols. (Paris: L. Hachette, 1839). Other notable contributions to the concepts and its critical discussion are: Robert Louis Benson, Giles Constable, and Carol Dana Lanham, eds., *Renaissance and Renewal in the Twelfth Century*, Cambridge: Harvard University Press, 1982); Charles H. Haskins, *The Renaissance of the Twelfth Century*, (Cambridge: Harvard University Press, 1971); Jacques Verger, *La Renaissance du XIIe siècle* (Paris: Éditions du Cerf, 1996); Robert Norman Swanson, *The Twelfth–Century Renaissance* (Manchester: Manchester University Press, 1999); Christian Speer, *Die entdeckte Natur. Untersuchungen zu Begründungsversuchen einer "scientia Naturalis" im 12. Jahrhundert*, Studien und Texte zur Geistesgeschichte des Mittelalters (Leiden: Brill, 1995), 45. Notable is also the more recent volume: Peter Dinzelbacher, *Structures and Origins of the Twelfth–Century "Renaissance."* Monographien Zur Geschichte Des Mittelalters (Stuttgart: Anton Hiersemann, 2017). More information on the historiography of the concept can be found in Cédric Giraud, "Schools and the 'Renaissance of the Twelfth Century,'" in *A Companion to Twelfth–Century Schools*, ed. Cédric Giraud, trans. Ignacio Duran, A Series of Handbooks and Reference Works on the Intellectual and Religious Life of Europe, 500–1800 88 (Brill, 2019).

8   McGuire, "A Chronology," 15.

9   Paul Verdeyen, "Introduction," in *Guillelmi a Sancto Theodorico Opera Omnia, Iv: Meditationes Devotissimae.* CCCM 89 (Turnhout: Brepols, 2005), viii.

10   McGuire, "A Chronology," 16.

11   McGuire, "A Chronology," 16.

In 1121 William became abbot of the Benedictine monastery of Saint–Thierry, but his contact with the reform order's way of living awoke his desire to become a simple monk at Clairvaux – a wish that Bernard would deny him for years. Despite not being entirely content with his situation at Saint–Thierry, the 1120s were an incredibly productive literary period for William. His first significant work was *De contemplando Deo*, written between 1121 and 1124,[12] which is often paired with *De natura et dignitate amoris*, composed around the same time.

Central both to his relationship with Bernard and his own literary development was William's stay at the infirmary of Clairvaux during a period of illness. Bernard, himself sick at the time, had invited him to convalesce alongside him. For weeks, the two friends read and interpreted the Song of Songs together. It was likely during this time, around 1124,[13] that the *Brevis commentatio* was produced, either by William alone or in cooperation with Bernard. William's interest in the Song of Song was intensified after this exchange, leading him to compose florilegia of Patristic interpretations of the text during 1124 and 1125:[14] The *Excerpta de libris beati Ambrosii*, collected from the works of Ambrose of Milan, and the *Excerpta ex libris sancti Gregorii super Canticum canticorum*, a compilation of exegetical statements by Gregory the Great.

During his time as the abbot of Saint Thierry, William also began composing his *Meditativae Orationes*, a series of twelve literary prayers and meditations that are the product of his contemplation of the Psalms. The meditations are a beautiful reflection of William's spiritual unrest. Yet William was not occupied exclusively with articulating his relationship with God but continued to react to the theological and ecclesial developments outside his monastery. In 1127, William wrote his first polemical work, *De sacramento altaris,* a critique of the Eucharistic theology of Rupert of Deutz.[15]

---

12   Verdeyen, "La chronologie des oeuvres," 200.

13   According to Paul Verdeyen, this convalescence took place in 1124 (Verdeyen, "La chronologie des oeuvres," 193) while Stanislaus Ceglar places it four years later, in 1128 (Stanley [Stanislaus] Ceglar, "The Date of William's Convalescence at Clairvaux," *Cistercian Studies Quarterly* 30 (1995): 30–31).

14   Verdeyen, "La chronologie des oeuvres," 199.

15   Verdeyen, "La chronologie des oeuvres," 198. However, an alternative date has been provided in John van Engen, "Rupert of Deutz and William of Saint–Thierry," *Revue Bénédictine* 93, no. 3–4 (1 January 1983): 327–336.

In 1132, William composed the *Responsio abbatum* in the name of the chapter of Benedictine monks at Soissons, defending them against the criticism voiced by Cardinal Matthew of Albano. In it, William made clear that he and his combatants did not adhere to the customs of Cluny but the Benedictine rule.[16] His engagement in the controversy between reform-oriented Benedictines and Cluniac traditionalists was followed by a personal life change, marking the fulfillment of his longstanding wish. In 1135, William retired from his abbacy at Saint Thierry and entered the Cistercian monastery of Signy.

William's desire for seclusion accompanied him throughout his life and eventually led to his retirement. That does not mean that William's productivity and engagement with the world outside the monastery of Signy diminished. On the contrary, having been relieved of his abbatial duties, William could devote more time to intellectual reflection. His *Expositio super Epistolam ad Romanos*, which he had already begun in 1130 in Saint Thierry, came to fruition in 1137.[17] His second sizeable exegetical work, the *Expositio super Canticum canticorum*, was also composed during that time, between 1137 and 1139.[18] It could be considered the pinnacle of William's long-standing fascination with the Song of Songs.

William did not shy away from controversy during his later years despite his retired status. Most notable is his pamphlet attacking several theological assertions by Peter Abelard, the *Disputatio Adversus Petrum Abelardum*, written as a letter to Bernard in 1139.[19] The *Disputatio* was one of the core texts leading to the condemnation of Abelard at the Council of Sens in 1141. It would not be the last of William's polemical texts, as he composed another letter to Bernard in 1143, this time condemning the theology of William of Conches, the *Epistola de erroribus Guillelmi de Conchis*.[20]

During his later years in Signy, William also put forth some of his most significant spiritual works. Shortly following one another, William composed both the *Speculum Fidei* and the *Aenigma Fidei* from 1142 and 1143.[21] In 1145 he finished writing *De natura corporis et animae*.[22] These three

---

16 McGuire, "A Chronology," 23.
17 Paul Verdeyen, "Introduction," in *Guillaume de Saint–Thierry, Exposé Sur l'Épître Aux Romains. Livres I–III*, Sources Chrétiennes 544 (Paris: Les Éditions du Cerf, 2011), 11.
18 Verdeyen, "Introduction," in *Exposé Sur l'Épître aux Romains*, 11.
19 McGuire, "A Chronology," 23.
20 Verdeyen, "La chronologie des oeuvres," 195.
21 Verdeyen, "La chronologie des oeuvres," 194.
22 Verdeyen, "La chronologie des oeuvres," 195.

works contain systematic expositions of William's core theological and spiritual concepts. Around 1145 William composed the Golden Epistle, the *Epistola ad fratres de Monte Dei*, for the Carthusian community of Mont Dieu. It is one of William's central pastoral works, containing theoretical and practical reflections on monastic life.[23]

His last work was composed from 1145 to 1148, the *Vita prima Sancti Bernardi*. It is one of the most influential early hagiographies of Bernard of Clairvaux, drawing both on the *Fragmenta* of Geoffrey of Auxerre and William's own experience with his close friend.[24] It was the last of William's endeavors, and he died on 8 September 1148.[25]

2   State of Research

The experience I had most often, sharing my research on William of Saint Thierry, is somewhat representative of his historiographic fate. While few people, even in the field of church history, are aware of his name, the association with his fellow Cistercian Bernard of Clairvaux lets them nod in understanding. Indeed, William was destined to live in the shadow of his famous friend for centuries. Several of his works, notably the Golden Epistle, were long misattributed to Bernard, causing William's name to disappear progressively from the list of influential 12th-century authors.[26] The history of research on William shifted once these works were rediscovered as his.[27] Yet, interest in William's texts gained significant traction no earlier than a century ago, prompting Brian McGuire to state that "William is very much a product of 20th-century scholarly research".[28] According to Tyler Sergent, one of the leading scholars on William today, the history of William scholarship can be roughly divided into two periods: the earlier period from the

---

23   Verdeyen, "La chronologie des oeuvres," 194.
24   McGuire, "A Chronology," 31.
25   McGuire considers this the possible "single date in the life of William of Saint–Thierry which is more or less certain" (McGuire, "A Chronology," 11).
26   I will discuss this historiographic issue in more detail in the chapter "6.1. A History of Misattribution".
27   Notable in this regard is the relatively early claim of Bernard Tissier, who discovered William to be the author of the Golden Epistle in the 17th century. However, it was not until the early 20th century that André Wilmart corroborated Tissier's conjecture. (McGuire, "A Chronology," 11).
28   McGuire, "A Chronology," 11.

late 19th century up until the 1950s and the more recent period up to the present.[29]

The scholars editing and translating William's original texts from Latin to – in most cases – French had made great strides in the early period to which modern scholarship is highly indebted.[30] The first notable edition was part of the *Patrologia Latina* produced by J.–P. Migne. However, this edition still operated with some long-held misattributions, which André Wilmart corrected in the 1920s.[31] As Paul Verdeyen recounts in his overview of William scholarship,[32] improved editions and translations were notably put forth in the 1950s and 1960s by Marie–Madeleine Davy,[33] Jacques Hourlier,[34] and Robert Thomas.[35]

The most comprehensive and commonly used edition of William's writings was edited from 1989 to 2011 in the *Corpus Christianorum Continuatio Mediaevalis*. These editions were produced by some of the most prominent William scholars: Stanislaus Ceglar, Jean–Marie Déchanet, and Paul Verdeyen.[36] Verdeyen has published most of the more recent editions,

---

29 F. Tyler Sergent, "Introduction," in *A Companion to William of Saint–Thierry*, ed. F. Tyler Sergent (Brill, 2019), 5–6.

30 So far, some of William's works have also been translated into English and very few into German and Italian.

31 see Sergent, "Introduction," in *Companion to William*, 5–6. He references in this context André Wilmart, "La Série et La Date Des Ouvrages de Guillaume Dé Saint–Thierry," *Revue Mabillon* 14 (1924).

32 Paul Verdeyen, "En Quoi La Connaissance de Guillaume de Saint–Thierry a–t–Elle Progresse Depuis Le Collogue de 1976?," *Revue Des Sciences Religieuses* 73 (1999): 17–20.

33 Davy, M.–M., ed. and trans. *Guillaume de Saint–Thierry, Deux Traités de l'amour de Dieu*. Paris: J. Vrin, 1953, and Davy, M.–M., ed. and trans. *Guillaume de Saint–Thierry, Deux Traités Sur La Foi*. Paris: J. Vrin, 1959.

34 Jacques Hourlier, ed. and trans., *Guillaume de Saint–Thierry, La Contemplation de Dieu, L'Oraison de Dom Guillaume*, 2nd ed., Sources Chrétiennes 61 bis. (Paris: Les Éditions du Cerf, 1959), and Jacques Hourlier, ed. and trans., *Guillaume de Saint–Thierry, Oraisons Méditatives*, Sources Chrétiennes 324 (Paris: Les Éditions du Cerf, 1985).

35 Thomas, Robert, ed. and trans. *Commentaire Sur Le Cantique Des Cantiques*. Pain de Cîteaux 9–12. Roybon, France: Abbaye de Chambarand, 1961; Thomas, Robert, ed. and trans. *Oraisons Méditées*. Pain de Cîteaux. Roybon, France: Abbaye de Chambarand, 1964; Thomas, Robert, ed. and trans. *Nature et Dignité de l'amour*. Pain de Cîteaux 24. Roybon, France: Abbaye de Chambarand, 1965, and Thomas, Robert, ed. and trans. *Prière de Guillaume, Contemplation de Dieu*. Pain de Cîteaux 23. Roybon, France: Abbaye de Chambarand, 1965.

36 The three of them, often in cooperation with one another, and with the contribution of other scholars have edited six volumes in total: Verdeyen, Paul, ed. *Guillelmi a Sancto Theodorico Opera Omnia, i*. Corpus Christianorum Continuatio Mediaevalis 86.

providing the most referenced study on the chronology of William's works.[37]

Ceglar has contributed seminal studies, particularly regarding the dates and circumstances of William's biography.[38] Jean–Marie Déchanet, on the other hand, was one of the first scholars to turn to William's thought more integrally, publishing one of the first monographs on the subject, entitled "Guillaume de Saint–Thierry, l'homme et son oeuvre."[39] He also paid particular attention to the question of William's sources and influences and has put forth controversial yet still influential theories on William's reception of Eastern thought.[40]

Based on the editorial and biographical efforts of all of these scholars who have made William and his writings more accessible, the study of William has accelerated significantly during the last decades. As Sergent points out, many articles and papers have been published, yet only a few monographs and larger volumes.[41] Without the aspiration to be exhaustive, I would like to mention some of the studies that have been particularly helpful for my research.

Turnhout: Brepols, 1989; Verdeyen, Paul, Stanislaus Ceglar and Antony van Burink, eds. *Guillelmi a Sancto Theodorico Opera Omnia, ii*. Corpus Christianorum Continuatio Mediaevalis 87. Turnhout: Brepols, 1997; Verdeyen, Paul, and Stanislaus Ceglar, eds. *Guillelmi a Sancto Theodorico Opera Omnia, iii*. Corpus Christianorum Continuatio Mediaevalis 88. Turnhout: Brepols, 2003; Verdeyen, Paul, ed. *Guillelmi a Sancto Theodorico Opera Omnia, iv*. Corpus Christianorum Continuatio Mediaevalis 89. Turnhout: Brepols, 2005, and Verdeyen, Paul, ed. *Guillelmi a Sancto Theodorico Opera Omnia, v*. Corpus Christianorum Continuatio Mediaevalis 89A. Turnhout: Brepols, 2007.

37   Verdeyen, "La Chronologie des oeuvres".

38   Ceglar, "The Date of William's Convalescence"; Stanislaus Ceglar, "William of St.-Thierry: The Chronology of His Life with a Study of His Treatise On the Nature of Love, His Authorship of the Brevis Commentatio, the In Lacu, and the Reply to Cardinal Matthew," Ph.D. diss. (Washington, D.C., Catholic University of America, 1971), and Stanislaus Ceglar, "William of Saint Thierry and His Leading Role at the First Chapters of the Benedictine Abbots (Reims 1131, Soissons 1132)," in *William, Abbot of St. Thierry: A Colloquium at the Abbey of St. Thierry*, trans. Jerry Carfantan, Cistercian Studies 94, (Kalamazoo, MI: Cistercian Publications, 1987).

39   Jean–Marie Déchanet, *Guillaume de Saint–Thierry, l'homme et Son Oeuvre* (Bruges: Charles Beyaert, 1942).

40   Jean–Marie Déchanet, *Guillaume de Saint–Thierry, Aux Sources d'une Pensees* (Paris: Beauchesne, 1978); Jean–Marie Déchanet, *Aux Sources de La Spiritualité de Guillaume de Saint–Thierry. Premiére Série d'études* (Bruges: Charles Beyaert, 1940), originally published as: "Aux Sources de La Doctrine Spirituelle de Guillaume de Saint–Thierry: 1, Saint Grégoire de Nysse," *Collectanea O.C.R.* 5 (1938–39): 187–198, 262–78; and Jean–Marie Déchanet, "Guillaume et Plotin," *Revue de Moyen Age Latin* 2 (1946).

41   Sergent, "Introduction," in *Companion to William*, 7.

In the 1970s, John Anderson contributed to the line of research initiated by Jean–Marie Déchanet with his study on William's potential Eastern sources.[42] David N. Bell has pursued the same question, albeit with very different results.[43] Bell's monograph on William's reception of Augustinian thought and material is notable in this context. Sergent identifies it as one of the "only two original English language books" published in recent decades. The second one to which he refers is the collection of essays published in honor of Rozanne E. Elder in 2015 entitled *The Unity of Spirit: Studies on William of Saint–Thierry*.[44] Rozanne Elder deserves a special mention as she has dedicated herself to studying the Cistercian context and spirituality and published several studies on William's Christology[45] and spiritual experience.[46] Her research positions William as one of the most significant and influential early Cistercians, alongside Bernard of Clairvaux and Aelred of Rievaulx.

Two of the contributing editors of the *Unity of Spirit*-volume are prominent William scholars in their own right,[47] who deserve special mention: Aage Rydstrøm–Poulsen, on the one hand, who has in recent years contributed significantly to the study of William's thought, particularly his Augustinian influences and his conception of the human soul.[48] And on the other

---

42   John D. Anderson, "The Use of Greek Sources by William of St Thierry Especially in the Enigma Fidei," in *One Yet Two: Monastic Tradition East and West.*, ed. M. Basil Pennington, Cistercian Studies 29 (Kalamazoo, MI: Cistercian Publications, 1976), 242–253.

43   David N. Bell, "Greek, Plotinus, and the Education of William of Saint–Thierry," *Cîteaux – Commentarii Cistercienses* 30 (1979); David N. Bell, "The Alleged Greek Sources of William of St. Thierry," in *Noble Piety and Reformed Monasticism. Studies in Medieval Cistercian History VII.*, ed. E. Rozanne Elder, Cistercian Studies 65 (Kalamazoo, MI: Cistercian Publications, 1981), and David N. Bell, "William of St Thierry and John Scot Eriugena," *Cîteaux – Commentarii Cistercienses* 33 (1982).

44   F. Tyler Sergent, Aage Rydstrøm–Poulsen, and Marsha L. Dutton, eds. *Unity of Spirit: Studies on William of Saint–Thierry in Honor of E. Rozanne Elder*. Cistercian Studies 268. Collegeville, MN: Cistercian Publications, 2015.

45   E. Rozanne Elder, "The Christology of William of Saint–Thierry," *Recherches de Théologie Ancienne et Médiévale* 58 (1991); E. Rozanne Elder, "The Image of the Invisible God: The Evolving Christology of William of Saint–Thierry." Ph.D. diss., University of Toronto, 1972, and E. Rozanne Elder, "William of Saint Thierry and the Greek Fathers: Evidence from Christology," in *One Yet Two: Monastic Tradition East and West*, ed. M. Basil Pennington, Cistercian Studies 29 (Kalamazoo, MI: Cistercian Publications, 1976).

46   E. Rozanne Elder, "The Influence of Clairvaux: The Experience of William of Saint–Thierry," *Cistercian Studies Quarterly* 51.1 (2016).

47   The third editor of the volume is Marsha L. Dutton, who is not a William scholar per se, but has published significant studies on Cistercian spirituality and Aelred of Rievaulx in particular.

48   Aage Rydstrøm–Poulsen, "The Way of Descent: The Christology of William of Saint–Thierry," in *Unity of Spirit: Studies on William of Saint–Thierry in Honor of E. Rozanne*

hand, Tyler Sergent has focused in his research on retracing the sources and possible originality of William's spiritual and anthropological ideas – a line of study that has provided much of the foundation on which this book stands.

Sergent has also notably edited Brill's *Companion to William of Saint–Thierry*, the publication of which has fatefully fallen into the period of formation of this volume.[49] Although Sergent did not self-referentially mention the Companion when he discussed existing publications, it is notable here as the third "original English language book" in the past decades. I would argue that it also marks another shift in the study of William, hopefully initiating the third phase of scholarship and inspiring scholars from various areas of study to turn their attention to William. The Companion reflects the main areas of interest within scholarship on William so far: his anthropological deliberation, his conception of the soul's relationship with God, and consequently, his thought on the Trinity. Within English-speaking scholarship, less but still notable attention has been paid to William's conflicts, particularly with Peter Abelard,[50] and his role within the Cistercian and broader monastic context of the time.[51]

Although the bulk of French scholarship on William was written in the era of Davy and Déchanet, William still appears in several French-speaking publications.[52] His writings receive notably less attention in German- and Italian-speaking scholarship, and the published studies and articles are few.

Elder, ed. F. Tyler Sergent, Aage Rydstrøm–Poulsen, and Marsha L. Dutton, Cistercian Studies 268 (Collegeville, MN: Cistercian Publications, 2015); Aage Rydstrøm–Poulsen, "The Humanism of William of Saint–Thierry," in *A Companion to Medieval Christian Humanism. Essays on Principal Thinkers*, ed. John P. Bequette, Brill's Companions to the Christian Tradition 69 (Brill, 2016); and Aage Rydstrøm–Poulsen, "The Human Person in the Trinity – William of Saint Thierry's Trinitarian Mysticism," *American Benedictine Review* 61 (2010).

49   F. Tyler Sergent, ed., *A Companion to William of Saint–Thierry*. Brill's Companions to the Christian Tradition 84 (Brill, 2019).

50   Notable are several studies by Constant Mews, as well as the research presented by Steven Cartwright. Both scholars' works will be referenced in the chapter "2. Authority as Tool and Topic in William's Conflicts".

51   For instance, Adriaan Bredero, "William of Saint Thierry at the Crossroads of the Monastic Currents of His Time," in *William, Abbot of St. Thierry: A Colloquium at the Abbey of St. Thierry.*, trans. Jerry Carfantan. Cistercian Studies 94 (Kalamazoo, MI: Cistercian Publications, 1987).

52   Another French William scholar is Yves–Anselme Baudelet, who has published the influential study: Yves–Anselme Baudelet, *L'Expérience Spirituelle Selon Guillaume de Saint–Thierry* (Paris: Les Éditions du Cerf, 1985).

However, scholars have recently discovered the texts of German mystics as sources to study the reception history of William's thought. This area could open a field for more research in future years.[53] Given the relatively recent rectification of misattributions in William's corpus, many of the later medieval texts that have formerly been believed to have been influenced by Bernard should be re-examined. Such studies would also fill one of the few fields of William-scholarship that has largely been ignored so far, namely the reception history of his works. In light of the increased attention William has received in the last century, this volume can rely on a solid foundation.

3   Main Question, Structure, and Methodology

The question of authority in Christian scholarship is fascinating, particularly as it relates to the context of the 12th century, a period of significant intellectual and cultural change. Heretofore Patristic authority served as a bulwark of orthodoxy, a defense against heretical opinions that threatened the simplicity of the Christian faith – both in the past and the present. The doctrinal authority of the Fathers and the ecclesial authority that exerted its power in the concrete structures of the medieval church were, in their ideal form, expressions of the same values and insights. Authority as a concept was thus fundamentally ahistorical. An observation made by Richard William Southern describes this notion poignantly: "Few people in ad 1000 would have expected the world to last another 1,000 years, and probably no one another 2,000 years. The end was in sight almost as clearly as the beginning, and history was the story of a tight and compact world, of which the main outlines could be grasped without any disturbing uncertainty [...]. History was monolithic and what men knew they knew without ambiguity".[54] History unfolded as a coherent narrative that could be systematized without awkwardly incorporating diverging points of view. In this context, the significance of authority can hardly be overestimated.

---

53   The issue has received prominent attention in Glenn E. Myers, "Manuscript Evidence of the Golden Epistle's Influence in the Sermons of Johannes Tauler," Cistercian Studies Quarterly 48.4 (2013).

54   R. W. Southern, "Hugh of St. Victor and the Idea of Historical Development," in *History and Historians. Selected Papers of R. W. Southern*, edited by R.J. Bartlett (Malden, MA: Blackwell Publishing, 2004), 31.

While this was still true for most authors of the 12th century, the kind of theology developed at the emerging urban schools more heavily emphasized other aspects of authority, raising the question of the role that human *ratio* (reason) could fulfill in the pursuit and definition of truth. It is tempting to conceptualize rational reflection as a counter notion to authority itself, yet this is not necessarily the case in the early days of the scholastic method. Rather, the use of *ratio* queued up with the writings of the Fathers and the declarations of Scripture as yet another source of knowledge. Rational insight too was considered authoritative in its right. Depending on its particular application it could serve the purpose of unraveling and systematizing Patristic statements, supporting their claims, or – as a last resort – challenging their authoritative status.[55] As Marie-Dominique Chenu puts it: "Reason, by introducing 'well ordered arrangement' (*artificioso successu*) somehow entered into the structuring of the faith itself [...]."[56]

It is tempting to assign the faith in Patristic and ecclesial authority to the monastic, and the trust in rational reflection to the scholastic stream of thought. Yet that would be reductive and fail to grasp the intertwined nature of these two aspects of medieval intellect, especially in the context of the 12th century.[57] I propose to highlight that both approaches share the intention and desire of pursuing truth, and thus are not to be thought of as mutually exclusive. Whether it is through careful reading and analysis of the Church Fathers' texts, or dialectical inquiry, the authors of the 12th century hoped to advance deep into the mysteries of Christianity and to ensure that what they discovered was both morally and intellectually true. The pursuit of truth was both at the center of the methods taught at the theological schools and the life lived in the confines of the monastery. It also lies at the heart of William of Saint–Thierry's life and work.

The title of this book, *Bird of Many Plumes*, applies to William in a variety of ways. On the one hand, it describes the character of William's literary works. His treatises and commentaries emerge from the vast sea that is

---

55   On the concept of ratio in the 12th century, see Constant J. Mews, *Reason and Belief in the Age of Roscelin and Abelard*, Variorum Collected Studies Series (Aldershot: Routledge, 2002).

56   Marie-Dominique Chenu, *Nature, Man, and Society in the Twelfth Century: Essays on New Theological Perspecitves in the Latin West*, ed. Jerome Taylor, transl. Lester K. Little (Toronto: University of Toronto Press, 1997), 280.

57   Constant Mews provides a brief historiographic overview and critique of what he calls the "monastic/scholastic binary" in Constant J. Mews, "Rethinking Scholastic Communities in Latin Europe: Competition and Theological Method in the Twelfth Century," *Medieval Worlds* (2020): 13–14.

his knowledge of tradition. They rely greatly on the *auctoritas* of the early Church Fathers in their defense of orthodox thought, and they are clothed in the evocative words with which these Fathers had expressed their love for God. Yet, William himself as a thinker deserves the designation as much as his works: given his hand in the thoughtful choice of "plumes" he collected, he too could be considered a bird of many facets. For decades he was notorious as an enemy of the inexorable rise of scholasticism – a conservative thinker, unable to recognize theology's prospects. On the other hand, William acted alongside Bernard as a spearhead of monastic reform, challenging the habits and the liturgical practice of the Benedictine monasteries of his time and contributing to developing such revitalized communities as the Cistercian and the Carthusian order. Meanwhile, he desired little more than the life of a contemplative recluse.

What these different, even seemingly conflicting, contexts of his life have in common is that they were all expressions of William's desire to pursue truth. His conflicts with Peter Abelard (1079–1142) and William of Conches (1080–1154) were, in essence, William's attempts to defend the truth contained in orthodox beliefs against their impending contamination with what he perceived to be heretical ideas. His commitment to the Cistercian reform was fundamentally about restoring authentic monastic life to an order he considered to have become lazy and morally corrupted. On the other hand, his exegetical and speculative works reveal that he sought to understand truth deeply and intellectually; he was applying analytic and systematic methods to explore the mysteries of faith. Lastly, the contemplative writings he composed as an abbot and monk for his community are reflections of his aspiration to live as best he could according to the truth that he had expounded in his doctrinal works.

His different endeavors all display an incredible versatility regarding the use of *auctoritas*. This volume's central purpose is to recreate, comprehend and systematize William's various concepts of authority, as they are fundamentally reflective of how he understands his role as a Christian author. The first necessary step to trace the meanings of authority in his works is thus to define what kind of authority will be central to my research. As Wolfgang Hessler once pointed out, the word *auctoritas* is so difficult to translate accurately that one would do well to refrain from even attempting to do so.[58] What he expresses with this admonition is the knowledge that the German term "Autorität" (and consequently also the English term

---

58   Wolfgang Hessler, "Auctoritas Im Deutschen Mittellatein. Eine Zwischenbilanz Im Mittellateinischen Wörterbuch," *Archiv Für Kulturgeschichte* 47 (1965), 255.

"authority") does not cover the broad range of meaning of the Latin *auctoritas*. The study at hand, however, does not intend to examine the usage of the term *auctoritas* in William's work, but focus instead on expressions of authorship as they relate to figures, institutions, and ideas of authority. Even though "authority" is such a versatile notion throughout the Middle Ages, medieval authorship as such is defined inherently by authority. As Jan Ziolkowski points out, "[r]ather than being a cultural monolith, medieval auctoritas is a vast edifice that was constructed year by year, century by century, by the cooperation and interaction of texts and readers."[59] Using William's works as grounds to contribute to the definition of literary authority in the 12th century, rather than approaching his texts with a preconfigured classification, is methodologically vital. It allows us to view authority as a dynamically changing and developing presence in the mind of medieval authors.

A first and crucial aspect, especially regarding the development of Christian thought, is Patristic authority. Theological and spiritual works of the Middle Ages cannot be accurately studied without listening intently to the voices of the Church Fathers that speak through the text. To a certain extent, the conflicting 12th-century attitudes toward the emerging scholastic method could be framed as differences in the attitude toward intellectual authority, such as the authority of the Fathers.[60] Retracing the presence of a variety of Church Fathers through William's commentaries and treatises reveals that he did not consider Patristic authority as a singular force but attributed different purposes to different authors. Observing William's flexibility and adaptiveness regarding his Patristic sources contributes to a clearer understanding of his role within the Christian tradition. Discussing the explicit and implicit ways in which the Fathers are received in William's works allows us to explore both how authorities shaped his thought and the places where the absence of their influence is conspicuous. Do such instances point, for example, to medieval originality?

---

59 Jan M. Ziolkowski, "Cultures of Authority in the Long Twelfth Century," *The Journal of English and Germanic Philology* 108, no. 4 (2009): 423.

60 Bernard McGinn seems to argue for such a position in his discussion of the scholastic and monastic approaches to Christology. While the thinkers of the schools were interested in solving "technical questions", using the Fathers' perspectives on these questions to different degrees, the "monks were original in the ways in which they revitalized patristic christological teaching and even deepened it [...]" by their spiritual emphasis on love (Bernard McGinn, *The Growth of Mysticism: Gregory the Great Through the 12 Century*, vol. 2. The Presence of God. A History of Western Christian Mysticism (New York, NY: Crossroads, 1996), 277–78).

Originality, as much as authority itself, is controversial and multifaceted when applied to medieval texts.[61] William was very critical of innovation or people who presented themselves as innovative thinkers (Abelard comes to mind most prominently). Yet there are undeniable elements in his works that go beyond what he found in Patristic texts and contribute aspects and ideas that influenced his readers. Whenever the term originality is used within the context of 12th-century thought, it has to be done with caution and distinction: are we discussing medieval authors' speculative originality[62] or the creative elements in their handling of traditional ideas? Are they displaying philosophical or literary originality, and how do they evaluate their contributions? As a 21st-century admirer of medieval texts, one is tempted to attribute a relatively high degree of originality to highlight their exceptional value. However, it is essential to note that originality and innovativeness are virtues in modern academia but were not necessarily something medieval authors themselves pursued. This fine line is easier to walk when one sets the idea of originality in relation to the variable of *auctoritas*. In other words, William's relative independence from tradition can more accurately be specified by examining his reception of Patristic thought.

Meanwhile, the Church Fathers and their legacy are not the only force in the matrix of authority within which William operated. Particularly in the context of Cistercian spirituality, the aspect of clerical and ecclesio-political authority played a significant role. As a proponent of monastic reform, there is an inherent tension in William's approach to clerical and monastic authority. His critical stance towards specific Benedictine authority figures of the time – and even some hierarchical structures – is contrasted by his reverence of the Early Fathers, whom he considers the determining authorities of monastic life. Discussing *auctoritas* in terms of theoretical questions and daily practice expands the definition of authority beyond that of a set of

---

61 The conceptional web of terms, such as originality, creativity, and intellectual discovery, and their possible use as criteria of literary analysis of medieval texts is discussed very well in Marianne Borch, "The Semantics of Originality as Indicator of the Cultural Paradigm Shift from Medieval to Modern," in *Origins as a Paradigm in the Sciences and in the Humanities*, ed. Paola Spinozzi (Göttingen: Vandenhoeck&Ruprecht, 2010).

62 Francesco Del Punta, for instance, uses the term in "The Genre of Commentaries in the Middle Ages and Its Relation to the Nature and Originality of Medieval Thought," in *Was Ist Philosophie Im Mittelalter? Qu'est–Ce Que La Philosophie Au Moyen Âge? What Is Philosophy in the Middle Ages? Akten Des X. Internationalen Kongresses Für Mittelalterliche Philosophie Der Société Internationale Pour l'Etude de La Philosophie Médiévale, 25. Bis 30. August 1997 in Erfurt*, Miscellanea Mediaevalia 26 (Berlin, Boston: De Gruyter, 1998).

doctrinal statements. In monasticism, authorities function as moral examples, as members of an extended community that transgresses the physical
sphere and encompasses both past and present relationships.

More theoretical and practical kinds of authority share a central element:
the interdependence of teaching and learning. Approximating the concept
of authority in the works of William entails examining how he envisions the
actual student-teacher relationship, both in the context of the monastery
and the schools. As an abbot, he integrated pedagogical concerns into his
works while remaining a lifelong student regarding his spiritual journey.
The tension between acting as a monastic authority while subjecting himself to the authority of his teachers and brothers reveals the issue's complexity: *auctoritas* is not an abstract concept but a lived reality. The different
dimensions of authority in William's work correlate directly with the concrete milieus in which he lived and wrote.

Thus, I have structured this book according to three distinct environments and the problems that arose from them, respectively. The first is that
of the 12th-century schools. Having studied at Reims, one of the leading
schools of the time, William was familiar with and yet critical of the methods developed in these new intellectual centers. He was particularly ske-
ptical of theology as a systematic subject that would use philosophical
methods and dialectic tools. The first of the three parts of this book, entitled "William's Engagement with School Theology" discusses William's self-
conception regarding the intellectual environment that gave rise to scholasticism. Here William's dissociation from certain intellectual tendencies is
most pronounced and leads to conclusions regarding the way he wanted
Christian thought to be pursued. Two of his works serve as primary sources
for this part of the analysis: *Expositio super Epistolam ad Romanos* (1137)
and *Disputatio adversus Petrum Abelardum* (1139) on the other. This first
sets William's self-conception as an exegete and his reaction to proto-scholastic notions of the theological task into dialogue and asks in what way
differing approaches to authority contributed to the tension in question.

The second part shifts the focus away from the broader intellectual scene
of the 12th century and enters the world of the Cistercian monastery. Cen-
tering on one of the core texts of Cistercian spirituality, the Song of Songs,
this second part, entitled "Mapping William's Exegetical Process: Receptivity
and Originality in his Reading of the Song of Songs," explores the relationship between Patristic and original thought in William's works. Set against
the backdrop of his literary self-conception examined through the lens of
his Commentary on Romans, his various works dealing with the Song reveal
how he practically applied his ideal and in which ways he deviated from it.

Importantly is his relationship with Bernard of Clairvaux (1090–1153) fueled his interest in the Song more than any other source of inspiration. Arguably one of the most prominent authorities of the 12th century, Bernard's role in William's life was not merely that of an authority figure but that of a friend. Examining their exegetical cooperation elucidates the differences and commonalities between the status William assigns to past authorities and contemporary thinkers.

The second aspect of William's treatment of the Song of Songs is reflected in his two florilegia: the *Commentarius in Canticum canticorum e scriptis S. Ambrosii* and the *Excerpta ex libris Sancti Gregorii super Canticum canticorum* (both composed around 1128). Here William compiled Ambrose's and Gregory the Great's interpretations of the Song, respectively. The 12th century was no longer the high point of florilegia but the period during which other more systematic and creatively independent genres emerged. William's compilations, therefore, give reason to contextualize William's relationship with Patristic sources not only in contrast to his contemporaries but also in comparison to the traditions that preceded him. Given its remarkable contribution to florilegia literature, the early medieval period and its attitudes towards authority will serve as an interesting reference point. The central questions arising in this context are how William directly relates to earlier models of Patristic reception and whether his compilations reflect the spirit of traditional florilegia or display a sense of autonomy that distinguishes them.

The third and pivotal focus within the discussion of William's reading of the Song is his exegesis, presented in his *Expositio super Canticum Canticorum*. As one of his most notable works, it opens up perspectives on his exegetical process, his concrete reception of Patristic thought, and the features of his spirituality that could be deemed original in a broader sense. A closer look at how Origenist material was molded in William's hands and shaped into ideas will reveal that his deep appreciation for the Fathers' observations and extraordinary creativity go hand in hand. Based on his Commentary, it is possible to study William's conception of authority as a practical element of his writing.

The third and last part of this volume broaches the issue of William as a monastic reformer and an influential voice of ecclesio-political, practical change. Entitled "William's Vision for the Cistercian Community", this part focuses on one of William's most famous pastoral texts: *Epistula ad Fratres de Monte Dei* or *Epistula aurea*. Addressed to the Carthusian monks of Mont Dieu, the text is both a spiritual and a practical guide to life in the monastery. It reflects most explicitly the ideals of reform and renewal, which William believed to be the foundation of Christian monasticism. At the same time, it introduces new aspects of the theme of *auctoritas* into our study, namely the practical dimensions of a monastic community. Their hierarchical structure, contrasted with the values of humility and mutual love, reveal a notion of authority that goes beyond mere principles and constitutes the core of monastic living. This practical context also allows for a verification of William's theoretical ideals based on his implementation of values into the communities over which he presided: how do the figures of the abbot and the author encounter and complement each other in the person and work of William?

Throughout these three parts, I hope to present William as a representative of a *Schwellenzeit* – a time of fundamental change. Neither he nor any of his contemporaries could have foreseen how decisive the outcome of their controversies would be for the following centuries of Christian thought. William could not have possibly understood himself as the last defender of an outdated model of Christian intellectuality, seeing that the success of scholastic theology was yet to be determined. The fervor he applied to his time's theological, spiritual, and ecclesio-political issues is all the more notable. Rather than describing William's role in the 12th-century 'renaissance' as already clearly defined, either by himself or by his contemporaries, the tripartite structure allows for exploration of his voice as polychromatic.

Sherri Olson has raised the theory that while 'individuality' is a difficult concept to apply to medieval people, the Middle Ages might have been more individualistic, given that "they were not exposed to the homogenizing effects of modern 'mass culture' and the pressure to conform which it creates".[63] This notion is beneficial when dealing with a period such as the 12th century, the historiography of which often focuses on broad movements and trends. Remembering the awareness, or relative unawareness, of medieval monastic authors of some of the more significant cultural streams is essential. It allows us to view them as authors with particular positions rather than merely the proponents of later identified tendencies. Studying William's texts as the works of a critical, multifaceted, and sometimes even self-contradictory thinker helps to transcend the clichés surrounding 12th-century authorship that are often difficult to avoid.[64]

---

63   Sherri Olson, *Daily Life in a Medieval Monastery* (Santa Barbara: Greenwood, 2013), 38.
64   As pointed out by Eileen Sweeney in "Rewriting the Narrative of Scripture: 12th-Century Debates Over Reason and Theological Form," *Medieval Philosophy and Theology* 3 (1993): 2.

However, I would like to supplement and possibly counterbalance this idea with Caroline Walker Bynum's crucial observation that the question of individuality should be approached in light of the "self-conscious interest in the process of belonging to groups and filling roles"[65] arising in the 12th century. Indeed, William's expressions of originality and receptivity should be viewed in relation or in contrast to the groups with which he was interacting. Rather than characterizing him as a 'mystic' opposing 'scholasticism', it is helpful to set him into concrete dialogue with those whose methods he criticized and to contextualize his notion as arising from his school education and a personal fascination with monastic scholarship. Similarly, his exegesis of the Song can neither be read as originating from a vacuum of ideas nor as a typical expression of 12th-century spiritual writing. Both approaches fail to grasp that he deliberately pursued the kinds of relationships and influences that would shape his thought. Thus, the Cistercian context has to be understood not as one he coincidentally belonged to, but as one he deliberately sought out as his sphere of creativity. The roles he consciously fulfilled or avoided within the different aspects of his life directly shaped the content of his works. My study, therefore, explicitly takes William's communities – the worlds in which he moved – as a starting point.

My goal is to create a dialogue between William's own words and the existing narratives about him and the century in which he lived. Instead of presenting a biographical study that centers on chronology and bibliography, this volume intends to explore the ways in which William navigates faithfulness to authority and intellectual originality. What comes to mind is the image Marinus Pranger used to describe his study of Bernard of Clairvaux: "[...] I intend to stick to the Bernardine text as closely as possible. In doing so, I hope to be able to describe one single image in an unlimited variety of configurations, just as the buildings of the monastery make up one single Church and one single cloister."[66] As a result, using William's relationship with the Church Fathers, his contemporaries, and the monastic structures in which he lives as a prism through which to consider his life and work reveals a variety of perspectives and contributes to a complex narrative portrayal of William as a 12th-century author.

---

65   Caroline Walker Bynum, "Did the Twelfth Century Discover the Individual?," *The Journal of Ecclesiastical History* 31, no. 1 (January 1980): 3.

66   Marinus B. Pranger, *Bernard of Clairvaux and the Shape of Monastic Thought: Broken Dreams,* Brill's Studies in Intellectual History (Leiden: Brill, 1994), 14.

PART 1

William's Engagement with School Theology

∵

Introduction to Part 1

Before pursuing a monastic life, William had enjoyed a thorough education at one of the best schools of his time: the cathedral school of Reims. His studies endowed him with philosophical knowledge and logical skills and enabled him to write complex speculative works. Moreso than many of his fellow monks, including his friend Bernard, he was equipped to understand the nuances and the consequences of the intellectual debates taking place all around him. Yet these very debates and controversies also aroused in him a deep skepticism toward the emerging subject of *theologia* and its increasingly dialectical methods, which he found personified in Peter Abelard. His critique of Abelard was not merely a matter of doctrinal disagreement but concerned a fundamental question of Christian thought: what is the purpose of Christian authorship, and what are its limitations? William's critique of the Abelardian approach and his own self-conception are therefore necessarily intertwined. I have selected two works that ideally represent this connection and elucidate both William's understanding of his own role as an author and his worries regarding the attitudes and methods he witnessed in 12th-century scholarship. These works are, first, his *Expositio super Epistolam ad Romanos* (1137) and second, his *Disputatio adversus Petrum Abelardum* (1139).

The latter is his polemic against Abelard, in which he names what he considers Abelard's transgressions against orthodoxy. In it, he employs authority strategically: with the aid of the Church Fathers and some of their most critical anti-heretical writings against what he considered the heresies of his own time. It is the work in which he reveals his concerns for the future of Christian scholarship by specifying clearly what he is rejecting. On the other hand, his Commentary on Romans is an example of what he does envision as appropriate Christian thought. As the only type of commentary or treatise he shares with Abelard, it exemplifies how he understands the task of a Christian author. Unlike Abelard, who presents himself as a brilliant *theologus*, William implicitly and explicitly characterizes himself as a humble reader of Scripture, simply following the Fathers' guidelines.[1] This first part of the book sets William's self-conception as an exegete and his reaction to the developing notion of 'theology' into

---

1 William's rejection of the name *theologus* and the method of *theologia* will pose a methodological issue for the study, that I will discuss at the outset of the first part.

dialogue and asks in what way differing approaches to authority contributed to the tension in question.

One of the central issues of such an endeavor is the terminology used. William's relationship with a form of 12th-century theological reflection that can only anachronistically be characterized as 'scholastic', and even the term proto-scholastic suggests an awareness of future developments that neither William nor the scholars he criticized could have had. The juxtaposition of William's and Abelard's respective approaches to doctrinal and Biblical questions will reveal that there are indeed significant differences between their basic assumptions and methodologies. Yet, William could not have considered himself anti-scholastic at that point in history; attempting to do so from a modern perspective would superimpose a binary of thought that did not yet, or possibly ever, exist.

The idea of scholasticism and monasticism being two fundamentally opposing principles has been heavily criticized within the study of medieval thought for quite some time now, and rightfully so. There is a significant number of authors who blend the rational analysis of theological questions, pursued in medieval universities, with the profound spiritual experience, as it was facilitated in monastic communities. While I will weave some considerations on the relation between typically scholastic and typically monastic lines of thought into the chapter at hand, and the terminology is not altogether avoidable when discussing distinctive lines of thoughts and methods, it is essential to acknowledge the limitations of such language.

Beyond the stereotypical distinction, between scholastic and monastic, alternative terminology exists, to differentiate William's methodological approach from the ones he criticizes. An important term in this regard is that of 'theology' itself. William, as we will see, rejects the label of theologian and the description of his task as theological. Only in the 13th century did the title of 'master of theology' (*magister theologiae*) assert itself over the former 'master of the sacred page' (*magister in sacra pagina*), demonstrating, as Beryl Smalley pointed out, "the increasing importance of speculative theology and doctrine and their separation from lectures on Scripture."[2] During the 12th century, however, *theologia* was not yet a general and widely accepted descriptor of Christian scholarship.[3] Abelard understood

---

2   Beryl Smalley, *The Study of the Bible in the Middle Ages* (Notre Dame, IN: University of Notre Dame Press, 1964), 271.

3   Although, of course, attempts have been made in the 12th century to define *theologia* as a more encompassing mode of Christian science (see Martin Grabmann, *Die Geschichte Der Scholastischen Methode*, vol. 1 (Basel: Schwabe, 1961), 255).

theologia as the "refutation of objections to the Trinity" on doctrinal grounds.[4] It hence poses some difficulty to apply the term theology, which from a modern standpoint more generally describes Christian scholarship and reflection about God, to the authors presented in this chapter without transgressing or misinterpreting their self-conception to a certain degree.

There are different possible solutions to this problem. It is very tempting, for example, as Jean Doutre did, to describe William as a "theologian and mystic" and Abelard as a "theologian and philosopher".[5] It is a way to acknowledge that William and Abelard, educated in the same intellectual climate, shared a common ground and interest yet emphasized different aspects (particularly methodology). Another possibility is to describe Abelard as a theologian but William instead as a spiritual or mystic author. While there is, as we will see, certain truth to such a distinction, it carries the danger of minimizing William's speculative thought and ability to systematize complex doctrinal ideas by focusing exclusively on the experiential aspects of his work.

In the following, I will attempt carefully not to call William a theologian, based on his overt rejection of the term, which I will discuss in the context of his *Disputatio* against Abelard. Rather than simply characterizing him as a mystic, a radically different brand of thinker than Abelard, I will use his self-descriptions and the implicit ways in which he reflects on his task and its limitation as a basis to approach a more precise definition of William's thought. I will first analyze the categories of William's readership and authorship as they appear in his Commentary on Romans to get a sense of the ethical and hermeneutical principles that underlie his exegetical writing. In the next stage, I will bring those principles in dialogue with his critique of Abelard, deriving from this chapter a better understanding of William's vision and fears for the future of Christian scholarship.

---

4   Fiona Robb, "Intellectual Tradition and Misunderstanding: The Development of Academic Theology on the Trinity in the Twelfth and Thirteenth Centuries," PhD. diss (London: University of London, 1994), 55.

5   Jean Doutre, "Romans as Read in School and Cloister in the Twelfth Century: The Commentaries of Peter Abelard and William of St. Thierry," in *Medieval Readings of Romans*, ed. William S. Campbell, Peter S. Hawkins, and Brenda Schildgen, Romans through History and Cultures Series (New York: T&T Clark, 2007), 57.

CHAPTER 1

The Use of Authority in William's *Lectio Divina* of Romans

William's *Expositio super Epistolam ad Romanos* was a project he had already started during his time in Saint–Thierry (around 1130) but was able to finish no earlier than during his retirement in the Abbey of Signy, about 1137.[1] His study of the Pauline theology thus took place in a context of personal reclusion, borne from a desire to grow closer to God in understanding and love. William shows particular interest in applying Pauline theology – the theology of divine grace – to the concrete monastic life. Revolutionary in its context, William was the first Cistercian author to show interest in the Epistle to the Romans.[2] His work is an appropriate reference point to understand how William conceptualizes his role as a monastic exegete over and against the ideals of Christian authorship that circulated in the context of school theology.[3]

While his Commentary marks a pivotal point for the tradition of Cistercian exegesis, it also does so in his literary biography. William wrote his Commentary after he had written a large part of his treatises on spiritual experiences, such as *De contemplando Deo, De natura et dignitate amoris,* and his *Meditativae orationes.* He also had already compiled his florilegia on Ambrose's and Gregory's reading of the Song of Songs, having spent extensive time with Patristic principles of exegesis.[4] The *Expositio* on Romans was the first of his biblical commentaries. In it, William brings his perspective as an exegete to the fore. Here, he formulates the hermeneutical principles and authorial ideals he would later apply to the Song of Song in his magnum opus, the *Expositio super Canticum Canticorum.*

---

1   see McGuire, "A Chronology," 25. Verdeyen claims that William resumed his work on the Commentary because he was, due to his age and health, no longer able to participate in the manual labor of monks, enjoying instead the privilege of dedicating his time to study (Verdeyen, "Introduction," in *Exposé sur l'Épître aux Romains,* 11).

2   Verdeyen, "Introduction," in *Exposé sur l'Épître aux Romains,* 16.

3   Very different kinds of treatments of Pauline thought during that time could be found, for example, in the exegetical works of Anselm of Canterbury, Peter Lombard, or Petrus Comestor.

4   see Verdeyen, "La chronologie des oeuvres,"

These principles and ideals of exegetical work relate fundamentally to William's cherished devotional practice of *lectio divina* as the inspired reading of Scripture. William discusses the principles of the *lectio* in his later work, the Golden Epistle. Yet, we will see in the discussion of the *Expositio* that they are crucial for his understanding of an exegete's task and appropriate habitus. The Commentary on Romans is, first and foremost, a commentary on Paul. But it is also a literary testimony to the shared and private monastic practice of the *lectio*. It reveals just as much about William's spiritual practice as it does about his theoretical considerations on authorship and the purpose of Christian writing. Therefore, we find, therefore, in the Expositio a fascinating dynamic between William as a monk in pursuit of intimacy with God and William as an author in the quest for concrete social and even political goals.

This becomes especially apparent if the *Expositio* is read, as Steven R. Cartwright suggests, as the "doctrinal foundation with which he opposed Peter Abelard",[5] shortly after its completion. I will discuss the *Disputatio adversus Petrum Abaelardum* – the charges of heresy William had raised against Abelard – at length in chapter 2.3. It is, however, important to note that the *Disputatio* contains little original content on the level of theological assertions. Instead, it functions mainly as an application of Patristic standards against the Abelardian innovations. The *Expositio* provides the intellectual framework necessary to understand William's strategy in his conflict: here, he reveals his understanding of faithful Patristic reception and his general notion of the intellectual limitations of Christian thought. We can understand his work as an exemplification of William's theoretical ideals of author– and readership, according to which he would later assess and judge Abelard's theological work. It will serve us well to read the Disputatio against the backdrop of William's Commentary, especially given that the reading of the Pauline Epistle is the only literary genre the two vastly different authors ever shared.[6]

It is important to note that William's exegesis, while it provides the grounds for methodological comparisons, is at the same time a self-sufficient piece of theological insight. As Lesley Smith points out, "there is

---

5   Steven R. Cartwright, "The Romans Commentaries of William of St. Thierry and Peter Abelard: A Theological and Methodological Comparison," Ph.D. diss., Kalamazoo MI: Western Michigan University, 2001, 20.

6   Their respective exegetical works on Romans was the only literary genre these two very different authors had in common over the course of their lives' works (Cartwright, *The Romans Commentaries*, i).

a tendency, associated perhaps with historians of medieval philosophy, to assume that commentary is the simpler way, springing from contemplative monasticism, and merely a preparatory step to the study of isolated theological issues or practical morality";[7] a perspective she is correct to dismiss. Rather than providing a stepping stone for further and somehow more relevant theological inquiry, the *Expositio* allows William to expound theological concepts. I will argue in the following that it is not out of intellectual inability that he refuses to apply the theological (or rather dialectically informed) method of his opponents to the doctrinal questions that emerge from the biblical text. Instead, I assume that his methods and principles arise from a categoric and confident decision: in his *Expositio*, he defines what he believes to be a faithful and appropriate pursuit of knowledge[8] and develops a Christian epistemology, which eliminates such intellectually curious projects as Abelard proposes them.

In the chapter at hand, I will map out the different dimensions of author- and readership as I find them reflected in William's work. A primary question will concern the very object of all exegetical endeavors: the biblical text. In this context, it will prove fruitful to touch upon 12th-century notions of the nature and function of Scripture, differing theoretically and pragmatically from modern definitions. In a second step, I will discuss the methodology of reading, examining the already mentioned practice of *lectio divina*. Considering this monastic reading process in the context of other aspects of the devotional life, such as prayer and meditation, will be essential. This entails questions of attitude and intentionality, with which the reading task is undertaken in the first place. Thirdly, the persona of the reader itself deserves specific attention. The 'reading subject' appears in William's work on several levels. We find, for instance, an explicit discussion of readership and self-conception in the preface of the *Expositio*. This will prove to be a vital source to understand how William desires his work to be received by his audience.

---

7 Lesley Smith,*What was the Bible in the Twelfth and Thirteenth Centuries? Neue Richtungen in der hoch- und spätmittelalterlichen Bibelexegese* (München: Oldenbourg Wissenschaftsverlag), 2009, 1.

8 This is the sentiment Smith hopes to express when she characterizes monastic vis à vis scholastic conceptions of authorship: "The apparent division between writers of commentary and writers of treatises on theological questions is said to make its appearance after the work of Abelard or, in theology, with Peter Lombard. Thenceforward, scholars are divided into the speculative or practical theologians and those – purer or simpler – souls, the exegetes who study the Bible. I have argued elsewhere that this is a false dichotomy, not because writers did not have preferences or specialties but precisely because they did." (Smith, *What was the Bible?*, 14).

Lastly, it will be important to take note of the specific Cistercian context in which and for which William is reading and writing. Readership in 12th-century monasteries are inherently communal in nature. I will attempt to illustrate two separate yet interconnected dimensions of the 'reading community', first presenting the introduction of the Church Fathers as co-readers into the concrete, monastic setting of his readership and second, the pedagogical concern of William's exegesis. This canvassing will hopefully provide a clearer image of William's self-conception in the face of authority and pastoral responsibility. These considerations will prepare us to examine William's conflict with Abelard, a conflict for which concepts of literary freedom were of central importance.

1   Exegesis of Romans in the Context of 12th-Century Education

Understanding William's approach to Christian authorship, especially as it relates to the establishment of what can only tentatively be called early scholastic theology, with its own authorial ideals, requires us to first take a look at the educational landscape of the 12th century. Although for William and many of his contemporaries theological education was monastic or clerical in nature, monasteries had already started to lose their educational monopoly status around the beginning of the 11th century.[9] Meanwhile, cathedral schools continued to gain significance as 'intellectual centers' of the time.[10] Their rise did not mark the elimination of the spiritual and the communal elements that had defined Christian education over centuries,[11] but their institutionalization enabled the accessibility of education for pupils who were not pursuing the priesthood.[12] By the 12th century, cathedral

---

9   Beryl Smalley notes Bec under the guidance of Anselm and Lanfranc as the one notable exception to this trend (Smalley, *The Study of the Bible*, 46).

10   These schools derived their political weight and growing social importance from a combination of canonical and episcopal power in urban environments (Haskins, *The Renaissance of the Twelfth Century*, 48).

11   Sita Steckel says about the early phase of medieval thought (defined as ca. 800–1150) that "it is religion and not intellectuality which lied at the core of this period's culture of knowledge" (Sita Steckel, "Charisma and Expertise Constructing Sacralized Mastership in Northern and Western Europe, c. 8000–1150," in *Schüler und Meister*, edited by Andreas Speer and Thomas Jeschke, Miscellanea Mediaevalia 39. (Berlin, Boston: De Gruyter, 2016), 641).

12   Sidney L. Jackson, "The Twelfth Century in the West, Its Libraries, and Hugh of St. Victor's Classification of Knowledge," *The Journal of Library History* (1966–1972) 2, no. 3 (1967): 188.

schools were flourishing along with Benedictine culture,[13] and centers of intellectual and spiritual growth were founded throughout Europe.[14]

Famous French schools in particular – Tours, Orléans, Lyon, Reims, or Chartres, to name a few – were producing great minds in the fields of exegesis and Christian doctrine.[15] These institutions and the way in which they conceptualized knowledge centered principally on traditionalist ideals. Knowledge was not yet defined as a product of human reason but as a valuable good passed on through generations of Christian thinkers. Intellectual progress was fundamentally relational, as it was defined by the close relationship between teachers and pupils and the transhistorical relationship between the ancient Fathers of the faith and their medieval followers.[16]

The early days of Cathedral school education were thus primarily determined by prolific figures who established learning communities based on their authoritative status and social visions.[17] Examples of this are William of Champeaux (1070–1121) and Hugh of St. Victor (1097–1141), with their respective Parisian collectives emphasizing rigorous scholarship and spiritual discipline.[18] The realities of the monasteries and of the schools respectively

---

13   While there is an evidential connection between Benedictine communities and the flourishing of Western intellectual life, these medieval monasteries did not by their very nature prioritize education: "A monastery might be a refuge for travelers, an economic center, a lamp of architecture, an exchange of ideas and information, a source of new types in music and literature; but it was all or any of these things only incidentally and by no means necessarily." (Haskins, *The Renaissance of the Twelfth Century*, 34).

14   In addition to monastic and Cathedral schools, it is important to point out the role of private teachers in the development of the 12th-century intellectual landscape. Thierry Kouamé highlighted this aspect poignantly: "[...] the 12th century is distinctive because it saw the significant growth of urban schools run by private masters in response to social demand; these, in turn, engendered debates and doctrines" (Thierry Kouamé, "The institutional Organization of the Schools," in *A Companion to Twelfth-Century Schools*, ed. Cédric Giraud, trans. Ignacio Duran (Leiden: Brill, 2019), 30).

15   "France, on the whole, was more important, with its monks and philosophers, its cathedral schools culminating in the new University of Paris, its Goliardi and vernacular poets, its central place in the new Gothic art" (Haskins, *The Renaissance of the Twelfth Century*, 11).

16   Grabmann, *Geschichte der Scholastischen Methode, vol. 1*, 180.

17   Although this was by all means nothing new. Sita Steckel points to the mid-eighth century as the source of what she calls "professional often life-long masters (described as *magister/magistra, institutor, caput scholae* and eventually *scholasticus/a*) attached to larger churches and monasteries" (Steckel, "Charisma and Expertise," 651–52).

18   Paul Rorem calls their models of scholarship "integrated learning and life" (Paul Rorem, "Bonaventure's Ideal and Hugh of St. Victor's Comprehensive Biblical Theology," *Franciscan Studies* 70 (2012): 387).

were overlapping and mutually informative.[19] Thus the conceptualization of communal life and scholarship depended in its particularities on the founders and teachers of a school.[20] Many of the great minds of this period cannot be categorized easily into the long-held categories of 'mystic' or 'scholastic', and thus the practiced educational concepts equally defy generalization.[21] It is noteworthy that the two intellectual spheres were compatible on many levels. All shared the image of Christ as *magister* of wisdom;[22] those who understood the extent of magisterial authority within the intellectual contexts of the schools and those who pursued truth through practical and spiritual *imitatio Christi*.[23] Thinkers who were spiritually oriented and intellectually curious could simultaneously be fluent in both languages, or rather, the two dialects of a single language.

Both within the context of the monasteries and the schools, learning was primarily receptive, and its productive element took place within a framework of a shared tradition. Christian thought was as institutionalized now as it had never been before, both in terms of content and pedagogical method. It is thus essential to note that, while this previsionary form of 'scholastic' education produced authors who could not seem more distinct – William and Abelard being representative examples – they shared most of their foundational knowledge in matters of Scripture, Patristic literature, and Christian history.[24] Whichever direction their thought would go, their

---

19   Frank Rexroth discusses the similarities and interactions between the monastic and the scholastic sphere under the heading of "habitual closeness" (Habituelle Nähe) (Frank Rexroth, *Fröhliche Scholastik: Die Wissenschaftsrevolution des Mittelalters*, 1st ed. (München: C. H. Beck, 2018), 257–261).

20   Sita Steckel says about the intellectual developments of the 12th century, that "experiments with new intellectual methods seem to have been accepted much more easily where they were embedded in older, strongly sacralized cultural patterns of teaching and learning – and where well-functioning social networks among masters, students and ecclesiastical superiors generated enough support for innovation" (Steckel, "Charisma and Expertise," 670–71).

21   Jackson notes "the danger of bracketing the Bernards and the Hughs, without qualification, as 'mystics'" (Jackson, "The Twelfth Century in the West," 188).

22   This image had already been determinative for scholars in the 9th century, as can be seen, for instance, in the texts of Smaragdus of St. Mihiel (Steckel, "Charisma and Expertise," 653).

23   Michael A. Signer, "Rabbi and Magister: Overlapping Intellectual Models of the Twelfth–Century Renaissance," *Jewish History* 22, no. 1/2 (2008): 116. Bernard used this image to instruct the monks under his care regarding the proper relationship between the monastic and scholastic context, reiterating the Benedictine sentiment that the monastery was itself a *dominici schola servitii*. (Pierre Riché and Guy Lobrichon, *Le Moyen Age et la Bible* (Paris: Beauchesne, 1998), 167).

24   Cartwright, *The Romans Commentaries*, 39.

shared context of learning left them with an inevitable appreciation for those who had determined the course of doctrinal development in the past.[25] The study of history and historically developed thought started to take a more prominent part in the work of Christian authors.[26] The emphasis on past authorities is not a sign of the period's lack of originality but marks its special character.[27]

We can thus speak both of a recovery of early thought and an intellectual revolution of sorts when discussing 12th-century academia. The unquestionably high status of the Fathers no longer meant that faithful reflection had to remain confined to Patristic statements in a literal or rigid sense. The school of Anselm of Canterbury would become exemplary for a new intellectual ideal that demanded a deeper analysis and understanding of traditional doctrine rather than mere reiteration. The great exegetes of the period modeled a creative reading of Scripture and the authorities that continued to inspire much of their writing. Noteworthy is undoubtedly the approach of Hugh of Saint Victor, whose reception of Augustine transcended the collection and presentation of quotations and attempted to embody the Augustinian spirit.[28]

---

25 As Clara McMahon points out: "The twelfth century as a whole reflected a deep interest in history and historical writing, to such an extent that Haskins calls it one of the greatest periods of medieval historiography." (Clara P. McMahon, "The Teaching of History in the Twelfth Century," *History of Education Quarterly* 2, no. 1 (1962): 47). Indeed Haskin's study "The Renaissance of the Twelfth Century", which has been a great inspiration to me, has proven that the 12th-century fascination with the past stands in no way contrary to its innovative character but rather facilitated it.

26 This process, albeit slow, is well illustrated in R.W. Southern's paper "Hugh of St. Victor and the Idea of Historical Development," in *History and Historians. Selected Papers of R. W. Southern*, edited by R.J. Bartlett (Malden, MA: Blackwell Publishing, 2004). Here he claims that after the contributions to a self–reflecting Christian 'historiography' made by the Venerable Bede (627–735), it was not until the 12th century that further strides in the field of historical study were made (Southern, "Hugh of St. Victor," 33).

27 Haskins defines the period's distinct characteristics as follows: "While it is true in general that 'each succeeding mediaeval century, besides inheriting what had become known in the time immediately preceding it, endeavored to reach back to the remote past for further treasure,' the twelfth century reached out more widely and recovered more." (Haskins, *The Renaissance of the Twelfth Century*, 16). R.W. Southern has pointed out the particular influence of Benedictine monasteries and their scholars in the development of a written sense of 'history', ingeniously calling their compilatory efforts their "most original contribution to literature" (R.W. Southern, *The Making of the Middle Ages* (New Haven, CT: Yale University Press, 1961), 192).

28 see Martin Grabmann, *Die Geschichte Der Scholastischen Methode*, vol. 2 (Basel: Schwabe, 1961), 89. Franklin Harkins argues in his study on Hugh's use of liberal arts and his view of salvation that "in maintaining and teaching that liberal arts study is both partially restorative in its own right and propaedeutic to the study of Sacred

With a broadening understanding of what Patristic reception ought to look like, the reader's role changed as well. The process of reading increasingly demanded active participation. Scripture was no longer a text that simply exerted its inherent spiritual power over those who heard its message. Moreso, its message required the willingness and worthiness to understand the words' often hidden meanings. The meaning of *lectio* shifted from the act of meditative, spiritual reading to the notion of a lesson or a course curriculum.[29] While exegetes took on a more productive role themselves, the Bible turned from a living, breathing document into an object of their studies. Especially for early 12th-century authors, this did not mean a devaluation of Scripture's authoritative status.[30] On the contrary: all kinds of intellectual reflections on divinity were biblical theology. A noticeable pause in the medieval study of the Bible during the Ottonian period came to an end in the 11th century, when many thinkers addressed exegetical problems with a newfound fervor.[31]

The academic institutionalization of theological thought led principally to the emergence of new genres,[32] such as the *commentatio* or *expositio* orthe gloss.[33] Authors were no longer exclusively interested in 'simply'

Scripture, Hugh presents and represents a synthesis of the early and late Augustine"; a synthesis, Harkins claims, that justifies Hugh's reputation as the *secundus Augustinus* (Franklin T. Harkins, "Secundus Augustinus: Hugh of St. Victor on Liberal Arts Study and Salvation," *Augustinian Studies* 37.2 (2006): 221).

29   Verdeyen, "Introduction," in *Exposé sur l'Épître aux Romains*, 15.

30   The study of the Bible did not only concern future theologians but also canonists and political theorists. Ecclesio-political matters, such as church reform, as well as wide-reaching warfare, were grounded on biblical interpretation (Aryeh Grabois, "The Hebraica Veritas and Jewish–Christian Intellectual Relations in the Twelfth Century," *Speculum* 50, no. 3 (1975): 613).

31   Sita Steckel, *Kulturen des Lehrens im Früh- und Hochmittelalter: Autorität, Wissenskonzepte und Netzwerke von Gelehrten* (Köln: Böhlau Verlag, 2011), 700. Steckel ties this observation back to Beryl Smalley's assertion that the Cluniac interest in liturgy had overshadowed the exegetical tradition: "Creative energy went to the invention of liturgical poetry and drama, to chronicles and lives of saints of the Order" (Smalley, *The Study of the Bible*, 45).

32   This applies to 12th-century academia even beyond the boundaries of theology and exegesis, with the development of biographies, memoirs, court annals, and city chronicles, as Haskins points out (Haskins, *The Renaissance of the Twelfth Century*, 7). A detailed study of the emergence of genres and their respective features, focusing on the elements of *lectio, disputatio*, and *predicatio* is offered in Cédric Giraud, "The Literary Genres of Theology,'" in *A Companion to Twelfth-Century Schools*, ed. Cédric Giraud, trans. Ignacio Duran, A Series of Handbooks and Reference Works on the Intellectual and Religious Life of Europe, 500–1800, 88 (Brill, 2019).

33   In turn, medieval academia revolved significantly around the study of the Bible "with scholars working as copiers, glossators, commentators, exegetes, and translators."

presenting the exegetical observations of the Fathers, and collecting them in a systematized way – as was the primary theological task in the golden age of florilegia[34] – but desired to discuss the biblical text themselves, employing all scholarly and literary tools at their disposition.[35] The schools, whether their philosophy was influenced by monastic spirituality or the dialectic pursuit of truth, were therefore concerned with developing hermeneutical systems for reading and interpreting Scripture.[36]

During this high time of exegetical productivity, the Pauline corpus was commentated extensively by exegetes and theologians[37]. Paul's Epistle to the Romans was a vital part of the exegetical training Cathedral schools were offering, leading to an abundance of commentaries that, in turn, became objects of intense study for younger students.[38] This is primarily due to the spiritual and theological importance of the figure of Paul. He was considered by many of the early scholastics "their own predecessor in the interpretation of Scripture and expositor of doctrine".[39] With the establishment

---

(Brenda Schildgen and Peter S. Hawkins, "Introduction," in *Medieval Readings of Romans*, ed. William S. Campbell, Peter S. Hawkins, and Brenda Schildgen, Romans through History and Cultures Series (New York: T&T Clark, 2007), 1).

34   The early medieval tradition will be the subject of more detailed discussion in the following chapter.

35   R.W. Southern summarizes this development as follows: "Everywhere the Biblical text was commented on, and became the starting point for discussions of many kinds–grammatical, dialectical, theological and historical. The twelfth-century schools were not centers of research into the mystical senses of Scripture of the kind which St. Augustine had urged scholars to undertake. But they made the Biblical text in all its many meanings more familiar than ever before" (Southern, *The Making of the Middle Ages*, 218).

36   The Bible was commonly referred to as *bibliotheca*, especially within monastic scholarship (Haskins, *The Renaissance of the Twelfth Century*, 79). Thus, Scripture was considered a source for various themes and questions and a composition of texts that took a lifetime of study without being exhausted.

37   see Schildgen and Hawkins, "Introduction," in *Medieval Readings of Romans*, 1.

38   Notably, one of the most researched Commentaries on Romans of the time was often attributed to Bruno of Cologne and supposedly written during his time at Reims. It is, however, questioned whether the Commentary was, in fact, his (as argued by Beryl Smalley in *The Study of the Bible*, 48) or composed by a member of his 'school' (as argued by Arthur Michael Landgraf in *Einführung in die Geschichte der theologischen Literatur der Frühscholastik: unter dem Gesichtspunkte der Schulenbildung* (Gregorius–Verlag, 1948), 53–54). It is clear, however, from the extensive studies of A.M. Landgraf and others that the Romans commentaries of magistri such as Bruno were often used as an exegetical textbook of sorts to introduce young students to the art of Biblical interpretation (Riché and Lobrichon, *Le Moyen Âge et la Bible*, 174).

39   Schildgen and Hawkins, "Introduction," in *Medieval Readings of Romans*, 6.

of a theological method, one looked to the Fathers to justify one's scholarly treatment of the Bible and the intellectual reflection of doctrinal thought. Within this perceived 'history of theology', medieval scholastics thought of Paul as the prototype for theological work as they envisioned it.[40]

But even for the growing Cistercian tradition and their ideal of the monk's figure, Paul served as an example. Among the first generation of Cistercian authors, Paul was admired for his wisdom and ability to put his faith into words and practice. For William, as we will discuss, Paul was the first exegete and preacher of the New Testament message. Aelred of Rievaulx emphasized Paul's willingness to join the lowly,[41] and Bernard revered him as a rhetorical master[42]. Thus, Paul not only explicitly influenced these authors' theology but also guided their self-conception and method. Paul's mastery of the Latin language and his understanding of a faithful life were pivotal to how these monastic writers defended their mission against an increasingly theoretical and intellectualized understanding of the theological task.

Furthermore, Paul was a moral icon for Christian communities throughout the Middle Ages. As we will later encounter in William's texts, he functioned as a personification of a variety of virtues, such as kindness and humility.[43] He also encompassed all theological virtues and intellectual abilities that started to differentiate themselves with the institutionalization of academic theology. The Church Fathers, in turn, were considered predecessors of particular specializations, such as doctrinal study or contemplative authorship.[44] 12th-century authors did not yet adhere necessarily to the

---

40   The Pauline Epistles, along with the Psalms, provided the most intriguing material for the logicians and theologians of the time (Schildgen and Hawkins, "Introduction," in *Medieval Readings of Romans*, 6).

41   Schildgen and Hawkins, "Introduction," in *Medieval Readings of Romans*, 8.

42   Schildgen and Hawkins, "Introduction," in *Medieval Readings of Romans*, 8.

43   Schildgen and Hawkins, "Introduction," in *Medieval Readings of Romans*, 5.

44   In the 13th century, Bonaventure would go on to assign particular doctrinal roles to the Church Fathers, and systematize what authors in the 12th century (and possibly before) had already implicitly included in their patristic reception: "Therefore, the whole of sacred Scripture teaches these three truths: namely, the eternal generation and incarnation of Christ, the pattern of human life, and the union of the soul with God. The first is concerned with faith; the second with morals; and the third, with the ultimate goal of both. The effort of the doctors should be aimed at the study of the first; that of the preachers, at the study of the second; that of the contemplatives, at the study of the third. The first is taught chiefly by Augustine; the second, by Gregory; the third, by Dionysius. Anselm follows Augustine; Bernard follows Gregory; Richard follows Dionysius. For Anselm excels in reasoning; Bernard, in preaching; Richard, in

differentiation of fields and disciplines within the theological realm. The distinction between different theological subjects was not primarily the fragmentation of the Christian task, as it would later nonetheless occur, but the
systematization of an intact holistic body of thought.[45]

The self-conception of the authors I will discuss has to be viewed, therefore, within a more extensive and generally integrative understanding of exegesis and theology. While Abelard and William clearly emphasize different
aspects and questions in their work and display different methodological
approaches, they operate within a much more cohesive general context.
Exegesis, doctrinal theology, and practical spirituality were necessarily considered to be dependent on each other, and different specializations were
not defined by rigid boundaries but by individual interest and intellectual
curiosity.

Apart from the systematizing and unifying tendencies within the field of
theology itself, the academic revolution of the 12th century did know forces
of separation and distinction.[46] Contemplative and philosophic thought
started to drift farther apart from each other, both in method and content.
While the relationship between faith and reason remained a complex question for scholars in both areas, it became clear that the juxtaposition of the
two entities could become grounds for insurmountable differences.[47] The
texts I will discuss are not yet representative of opposing front lines and
should not be read as examples of clearly 'mystic' or 'scholastic' theology,
especially if one thinks of them as mutually exclusive.

However, they display an early instance of the conflicts that would continue throughout the Middle Ages and even the Reformation, with its critics
and defenders of the scholastic method.[48] This is such an exciting part of

---

contemplation. Hugh excels in all three" (Bonaventure. *St. Bonaventure's on the Reduc-
tion of the Arts to Theology (English and Latin Edition)*. Translated by Zachary Hayes.
New York: The Franciscan Institute, 1996, 199), as cited in Rorem, "Bonaventure's
Ideal," 386).

45   This is well exemplified by the work of Hugh of St. Victor, as Paul Rorem characterizes
      it: "Hugh understood the unity of theology, namely God's works of restoration as en-
      countered in scripture, according to the architectural metaphor of constructing a
      building" (Rorem, "Bonaventure's Ideal," 389).

46   R.W. Southern intertwines the observation that in the 12th century "scholars begin to
      feel comfortable about their command of the achievement of the past", and that it
      consequentially "became possible at this time to envisage the consolidation of great
      tracts of knowledge in systematic form" (Southern, *The Making of the Middle Ages*,
      204).

47   Jackson, "The Twelfth Century in the West," 187.

48   This rather large and complex topic has been presented extensively and from vari-
      ous perspectives in Willem J. van Asselt and Eef Dekker, eds., *Reformation and*

doctrinal history, not because the frontiers of opposing positions were already solidified but precisely because they were not yet delineated. The following considerations will provide insights into the variety of 12th-century thought, its diverse tendencies, and forms of critical dialogue.

2   Scripture in the 12th Century

To understand William's self-conception as a reader and exegete of Scripture, some preliminary remarks on the significance of the biblical texts in the 12th century are appropriate. I will discuss this, as far as it pertains to the study of William and his contemporaries, and will therefore focus on a few central images that suitably express their understanding of the text with which they were working. In her extensive study on the usage of Scripture in the Middle Ages, Beryl Smalley generally prefers the terms *sacra scriptura* or *sacrae paginae* to the term *biblia*,[49] as she believes this accurately reflects the terminology the medieval authors themselves used.[50] As Lesley Smith points out, the avoidance of the term 'Bible' contains two significant aspects of the medieval conceptualization and usage of Scripture. Smith associates the semantic choice with the Jeromeian imagery of the biblical text as a *bibliotheca* and refers to the practical dimension of the biblical texts in the Middle Ages: rather than dealing with a compact, single-volume book, these authors read and discussed the biblical texts as distinct sources. While all of them deserved the attribution sacrum, their common message unified them and not their literary coherence. As Smith puts it, rather poetically, Scripture "was not an untouchable relic, but a living, changing, usable library".[51]

While William was undoubtedly familiar with Scripture, he was acutely aware of the differences between biblical texts' literary genres and their historical contexts. He was fully conscious that, while reading the Word of God, he was also reading the spiritual expressions of distinct human authors and considered their concrete intentions when interpreting their testimony. This is especially noteworthy regarding William's exegesis of Romans: as I will later discuss, he displays a particular interest in the historical figure of Paul and his personal relations with the community in Rome.

Scholasticism. An Ecumenical Enterprise. Texts and Studies in Reformation and Post–Reformation Thought (Grand Rapids, MI: Baker Academic Press, 2001).

49   An overview of the differences in terminology is provided also in Riché and Lobrichon, *Le Moyen Âge et la Bible*, 164–165.

50   Smalley, *The Study of the Bible*.

51   Smith, *What was the Bible?*, 2.

However, this notion of Scripture as a variety of very different texts only speaks to one side of the coin. While it was not uncommon for medieval exegetes to recognize the historical human writers of the biblical texts as *auctores*, they knew that these *sacrae paginae* had two authors by nature.[52] Scripture was the Word of God, yet it was so in the form of human expression. This twofold conceptualization is also the basis for understanding the truth contained in Scripture. William himself gives voice to this sentiment when he offers his definition of Scripture and its role:

> In the Holy Scriptures, that is, the ones that are edited for the fixed and stable memory of all, held to have been [inspired] by the Holy Spirit.[53]

The biblical texts were written, transmitted, and ultimately presented as an authoritative corpus for all future generations because they were received from the Holy Spirit. William acknowledges both aspects mentioned above: divine inspiration as the source of texts' insight on the one hand, and on the other hand, the ecclesial, and thus human role in their formation and propagation. While the message contained in Scripture is divine and inspired, the text through which these monastic exegetes would access it had gone through many human hands. Most likely, William has in mind in this passage the earliest readers of the texts, who were responsible for their canonization. However, his acknowledgment of the significance of the editing and transmission process points to his more extensive awareness, that the reader of Scripture contributes fundamentally to understanding what Scripture is and how it should be used.

Scripture and its reader stand in a close, possibly inextricable relationship. On the one hand, the biblical texts determine the particularities of the Christian life as the ultimate authority. On the other hand, the human reader – not merely in representative ecclesial functions, but even the individual believer – participates actively in establishing Scriptural authority and influence. The reader sets herself in relation to Scripture, and her willingness to subject herself to the biblical narrative determines whether Scripture speaks to her. This is beautifully illustrated in William's remarks on Paul's addressee in Romans:

---

52   Alastair Minnis, *Medieval Theory of Authorship: Scholastic Literary Attitudes in the Later Middle Ages*, 2nd ed. (Philadelphia: University of Pennsylvania Press, 2010), 36.

53   Expositio super Epistolam ad Romanos (CCCM 86), Lib. I, linea 48: *In scripturis sanctis, hoc est ad fixam et stabilem omnium memoriam editis, a Spiritu sancto habitis.*

He speaks to the People of God, to the church of God. He writes to the Romans, yet he speaks to the universal church. He speaks to the wheat, not the bale; to the hidden grain, not the visible straw so that everyone might know in their own heart whether they belong to it [the People of God].[54]

Every reader has to determine 'in their heart' (*corde suo*) if the insight and admonition Paul offers apply to them. The reader chooses whether she desires to enter into an intimate relationship with Scripture. Thus conceptualized, exegesis takes on the character of a personal dialogue rather than a rationally accessible analysis of a static text. Scripture, or rather, its human and divine authors, function as active interlocutors, who continue to address the reader directly, even centuries after the text had first addressed its original recipients. William acknowledges this biblical potential for actualization when he says that while Paul was *writing* to the Romans, he was *speaking* to the Catholic Church as a whole.

This twofold definition of the biblical text as a written and historically developed testament, on the one hand, and a timeless source of divine revelation, on the other, gives voice to the inherent tension that accompanies every attempt to define the nature of Scripture. Beryl Smalley called on Claudius of Turin (ca. 780–827) and his understanding of the biblical texts to exemplify this notion: "The Word is incarnate in Scripture, which like man has a body and soul";[55] a distinction that was coined by Patristic exegetes and became central for the tradition of affective mysticism, with which William (alongside Bernard) is often associated. Scripture meant the literal text's historical growth and the inspired truth expressed in the text.[56] The latter aspect often resulted in a blurred demarcation between canonic and Patristic writings: the Fathers, who interpreted and handled the inspired Word, participated in its authority. Conversely, medieval authors' usage of the term 'Fathers' could often include the authors of the New Testament as well. This could be read as an awareness of the gradual and complex canonization process or as an emphasis on what Claudius of Turin calls the

---

54   Expositio super Epistolam ad Romanos (CCCM 86), Lib. v, linea 47: *Populo Dei dicit, ecclesiae Dei dicit; Romanis scripsit, sed uniuersae ecclesiae dixit. Tritico dixit, non paleae; massae latenti, non stipulae apparenti. Vnusquisque in corde suo cognoscat si ad eum pertineat.*

55   Smalley, *The Study of the Bible*, 1.

56   Such a broad conception is not unique to medieval exegesis but has already appeared in Patristic hermeneutical concepts. Augustine, for instance, has not differentiated between Scripture and the Catholic tradition as foundations of Bible study (Smalley, *The Study of the Bible*, 27).

'word's soul', as the biblical and Patristic authors shared their purpose of propagating the messages of the Holy Spirit. It becomes clear from this hermeneutical premise that the exegetical tradition of the church shaped medieval readings almost as much as the explicit wording of the biblical texts.[57]

Furthermore, the question regarding the nature of Scripture was not merely a theoretical issue for medieval exegetes but had significant consequences for their practical use of the texts. Practical problems, such as the accessibility and the quality of the texts with which they were working, informed the concept of Scripture for William and his contemporaries. The early 12th century did not yet know a standard Vulgate version, which would not be established until the 16th century. Instead, the authors of the time worked with various accounts produced for distinct contexts of the Christian, or more specifically, the monastic life. Biblical texts had no particular *Sitz im Leben*: different transmissions existed for the liturgical, the academic, or the pastoral use. As Steven Cartwright observed, William made use of a plurality of sources. His study, comparing the Charleville MS.49.10 (and its glossed text of the Pauline epistles) with the quotations William used in his *Expositio*, showed that, although he used the text, it was not his primary source. To reconstruct all of his sources is, however, a near-impossible undertaking, as it is very likely that William often quoted Scripture from memory, allowing for a certain degree of divergence from the explicit wording of the medieval variations.[58] In this context, the role of liturgy in the transmission of Scriptural knowledge can hardly be overstated. As Chrysogonus Waddell points out: "It is remarkable, the extent to which biblical texts used by Cistercian preachers, were taken not directly from the Bible but from the Bible as utilized by the liturgy."[59] It follows that the understanding and transmission of Scripture was shaped as much by the oral, liturgical tradition, as by its written tradition.

This observation of William's practical work with the biblical text shows that Scriptural authority was not tied to literal reiteration; what was considered authoritative was the meaning the biblical authors had intended to convey.[60] Differing from a theological position that considers the text

---

57   Lesley Smith remarks in this context the fact that Hugh of St. Victor considered conciliar decrees to be tantamount components of the scriptural corpus. She understands this, I believe rightfully so, as Hugh's acknowledgment of the "truth of tradition in the Church." (Smith, *What was the Bible?*, 12).

58   Cartwright, *The Romans Commentaries*, 44.

59   Chrysogonus Waddell, "The Liturgical Dimension of Twelfth-Century Cistercian Preaching," in *Medieval Monastic Preaching* (Leiden: Brill, 1998), 347.

60   Elucidating in this context are several quotations that Giles Constable offers in his discussion of medieval plagiarism. He references, for instance, Simon of Tournai's

inherently holy, in an almost sacramental way, the readers and the audience of Scripture up until the early 12th century were much more concerned with the words' content and the way it affected their thought than they were with particular wording.[61] Following another of William's statements about the Bible and its role, we could say that it offers a hermeneutical principle to understand life itself: *non debet videri absurdum, quia nec in scripturis est insolitum*,[62] or in other words, 'let us not reject, what Scripture accepts'. While William does appreciate and defend the irrefutable authority of the Bible in this statement, he conceptualizes it as dynamic rather than static. Scripture's unique role lies in its ability to interact with its reader. It wields its power not by providing an assemblage of objective information but by subjectively defining the human condition.

Although Scripture theoretically had a universal claim for truth, the obvious limitation of this universality deserves mentioning. The accessibility of texts in the Early and High Middle Ages was limited mainly to the monastic elite, setting the practice of reading necessarily in the context of a spiritual and intellectual elite. Even more so, the medieval concept of literacy was not primarily that of secular education of socio-economic potential but was instead a distinctly spiritual category. Laypeople (the 'uninitiated') were mostly considered illiterate in both a proper and a spiritual sense. Without access to the linguistic and thematic wealth of Scripture, they were deemed

---

evaluation of the Augustinian idea that the Father is the "beginning of the entire Trinity", in which he states that this Patristic notion "was true not from the sense of the words, since He is not the beginning of divinity but rather divinity itself, but from the sense in which the words were made by the author" (Simon of Tournai. *Les Disputationes de Simon de Tournai: Texte Inédit*. Edited by Joseph Warichez. Spicilegium Sacrum Lovaniense: Études et Documents 12, 1932, 32 (Disp. v, 3), as quoted in Giles Constable, "Forgery and Plagiarism in the Middle Ages," *Archiv Für Diplomatik* 29, no. JG (1 December 1983): 24, fn. 120). Similarly, he quotes Hilary of Poitiers's statement: "Heresy flows not from the words used but from the user's intention or interpretation of the words" (Nikolaus M. Häring, "Commentary and Hermeneutics," in *Renaissance and Renewal in the 12th Century*, ed. Robert L. Benson, Giles Constable, and Carol Dana Lanham (Cambridge: Harvard University Press, 1982), 196, as quoted in Giles Constable, "Forgeries and Plagiarism," 24, fn. 120). Both these examples show that the intention and, thus, the moral integrity of an authority was integral to their credibility.

61   However, it was a genuine concern for the early Cistercians to avoid "jarring discrepancies between the chants and the lections to which the monks were accustomed and those in their new lectern Bible" (Diane Reilly, *The Cistercian Reform and the Art of the Book in Twelfth–Century France. The Cistercian Reform and the Art of the Book in Twelfth–Century France*, Knowledge Communities 5 (Amsterdam: Amsterdam University Press, 2018), 65). This attests to the fact that the primary locus of Scripture in the lives of monks was the daily liturgy rather than a linguistic study of the biblical text.

62   Expositio super Epistolam ad Romanos (CCCM 86), Lib. I, linea 102.

spiritually uneducated and unable to understand the depths of their relationship with God. Conversely, the monks could justify their spiritually ele-
vated status by their access to and understanding of the biblical texts.[63]
This understanding of Scripture as the source of knowledge for the intellectually gifted and literate few goes back to Augustine: Augustine had asserted
that "reading nature is for the unlearned, while the Bible is for scholars".[64]
This dual epistemology remained influential throughout the Middle Ages.
The 12th-century circle of Cistercian authors considered Scripture a status
symbol of sorts – the hallmark of an exclusive community. Appropriately,
monastic art has employed the symbol of the book to "affirm the literate
status of the privileged monk".[65]

The purpose of this last observation was undoubtedly not to attempt a
critique of 12th-century social hierarchies. Instead, it might offer insight into
the kind of reader William had in mind when writing his *Expositio*: he is
both an author and himself a reader within a monastic, and thus an elite
context. Therefore, his concept of the practice of reading is connected to a
notion of spiritual literacy. In the following chapter, I will take a closer look
at William's understanding of readership as a practice and how Patristic, ecclesial and communal authority contributed to it.

3   The Monastic Practice of *Lectio*

The *Expositio*, as much as it is representative of William's exegetical method, contains little theoretical reflection on the practice of reading the
Bible and does not make the methods of *lectio divina* a subject of discussion. To acquire a working definition of William's concept of readership, we
will first have to take a look at the monastic tradition of *lectio divina* with
its 12th-century proponents and then consult one of William's later works,

---

63   Conrad Rudolph, "Inventing the Exegetical Stained–Glass Window: Suger, Hugh, and a
        New Elite Art," *The Art Bulletin* 93, no. 4 (2011): 406.

64   Constant J. Mews, "The World As Text: The Bible and the Book of Nature in
        Twelfth–Century Theology," in *Scripture and Pluralism: Reading the Bible in the Reli-
        giously Plural Worlds of the Middle Ages and Renaissance*, ed. Thomas Hefernan and
        Thomas E. Burman, Studies in the History of Christian Traditions 123 (Leiden: Brill,
        2005), 102.

65   Conrad Rudolph mentions the example of the Life of Benedict window in the crypt at
        Saint–Denis that shows two monks witnessing the deification of Benedict while each
        is holding a book; according to Rudolph a clear sign of their distinctive identity. Ru-
        dolph, "Inventing the Exegetical Stained–Glass Window," 406.

the *Epistola ad fratres de monte Dei*,[66] to see how his understanding relates and differs from the classical scheme. *Lectio divina* is a spiritual practice that traces back to the Patristic age and describes a contemplative approach to Scripture. Classically, the scheme consists of four stages: reading (*lectio*), meditation (*meditatio*), prayer (*oratio*), and contemplation (*contemplatio*),[67] contemplation being the ultimate ambition of the process. Although it constitutes the first stage and thus the foundation of the practice, the physical act of reading is to lead to the following non-literal forms of exegesis.

The Fathers themselves, Saint Jerome, for instance, had yet to differentiate as clearly between the steps as the later monastic tradition did and had conceptualized *lectio* and *oratio* in closer union. He understood *lectio* as a crucial part of the spiritual ascent, whereas 12th-century monastics tended to emphasize the need to transcend the physical stage of reading, to ascend to divine truth.[68] In such later conceptions, the act of reading strives to gather the information, which can then be synthesized, systematized, and harmonized in the following stage of *meditatio*.[69] Traditionally, the process of meditation served to imprint the information collected from one's reading onto the *memoria* or, to put it more simply, the biblical text is inscribed on the reader's mind during meditation.[70]

Early in the history of *lectio divina*, the practice went through several variations. Eucher of Lyons had introduced the stage of *disputatio* into the scheme to synthesize the more contemplative approach he found in Cassian, and the more philosophical aspects, which Jerome had emphasized.[71] This adaptation would find notable supporters in the future, particularly toward the end of the 12th century. One was Peter the Chanter, who understood Scriptural study to rest on three main points: *lectio*, *disputatio*, and *praedicatio*. While he did not depreciate the contemplative aspects of *lectio*

---

66   Verdeyen, Paul, ed. *Guillelmi a Sancto Theodorico Opera Omnia, Iii: Epistola Ad Fratres de Monte Dei*. Corpus Christianorum Continuatio Mediaevalis 88. Turnhout: Brepols, 2003.

67   In this traditional fourfold form, the process is prominently recorded in John of Salisbury's *Metalogicon* (Duncan Robertson, *Lectio Divina: The Medieval Experience of Reading* (Trappist, KY: Cistercian Publications, 2011), 205).

68   Smalley, *The Study of the Bible*, 282.

69   Boyd Taylor Coolman, "'Pulchrum Esse': The Beauty of Scripture, the Beauty of the Soul and the Art of Exegesis in Hugh of St. Victor," *Traditio* 58 (2003): 198.

70   Riché and Lobrichon, *Le Moyen Âge et la Bible*, 263.

71   Smalley, *The Study of the Bible*, 29.

divina as a whole, his definition reveals conceptual reorientation: certain elements of reading Scripture that had always been tied to the monastic world would now be applied in a new, scholarly context.[72] The third aspect in Peter's characterization, however, was one the cloisters would continue to share with the schools and emerging universities, one that had already been a central part of the *lectio divina* the Fathers had envisioned: teaching.

As Beryl Smalley put it: "We learn by sharing our learning".[73] As we will later witness in William's work, pedagogical interest often lies at the core of contemplative practices. All the stages of *lectio divina*, from reading to prayer and even contemplation, took place in the concrete monastic routine. From their very origins, monastic rules – most prominently Benedict's – incorporated the proper engagement with Scripture into their rules. This entailed the physical act of reading but was not necessarily bound to it. Throughout the day, monks and nuns would regularly hear Scripture read out loud in various liturgical contexts.[74] The spoken word, often more so than the written word, would inform their meditation.[75] In a universe permeated by the messages and images of Scripture, the classical concept of *lectio divina* should not exclusively be understood as a theoretical instruction but also as a schematization of the life that took place in cloisters daily. In a way, even the visual artistry and craftwork, which would later flourish particularly in female monasteries, could be considered a form of meditation on Scripture and thus an application of *lectio divina* in a broader sense.

As mentioned above, William presents his ideal of good readership in his *Epistola ad fratres de monte Dei*. This is an unsurprising source for such a theoretical conception: the Golden Epistle provides William's idea of a practical application of the Benedictine Rule to the newly founded Cistercian and Carthusian communities.[76] This necessarily includes direction on the reading and processing of biblical texts. However, the Golden Epistle is not merely the 'instruction manual' for spiritual practices, as Cistercian communities have used and understood it for centuries. While this is undoubtedly a crucial aspect of the work, and William did indeed write the Epistle for the sake of his brothers' education, the work's medieval readers generally overlooked the fact that it contains significant autobiographical elements.

---

72   Riché and Lobrichon, *Le Moyen Âge et la Bible*, 194–95.
73   Smalley, *The Study of the Bible*, 27.
74   Riché and Lobrichon, *Le Moyen Âge et la Bible*, 141.
75   Smalley, *The Study of the Bible*, 28-29.
76   I will discuss the relationship between Cistercian and Carthusian culture or practice in regard to the Golden Epistle in the chapter "6.2. Two Perspectives on Reform".

This is significantly due to the Epistle's history of misattribution: shortly after William's death, the work was understood as a Bernardine admonition, setting the interpretive focus on the famous abbot's authority.[77] However, acknowledging that William uses the Golden Epistle to reflect on his literary legacy allows us to view his concept of readership as simultaneously practical and theoretical. William imparts here the wisdom he had acquired and applied throughout his life and dedicated five paragraphs (§120–124) of the Epistle to the practice of reading Scripture. While these paragraphs belong to a larger educational context – discussing, for instance, the necessity of discipline and the promotion of virtues in a monk's life – the few paragraphs on the practice of *lectio divina* are so concise and rich in content that they should suffice at this point to give an account of William's 'fundamentals of readership'.

A significant question concerns his assessment of the concrete act of reading. As mentioned above, *lectio* could be viewed both as a closely interwoven part of meditation or simply as a first step, which ought to lead to higher stages and is more physical than spiritual in nature. The monasticism of the 12th century tended to favor the latter notion.[78] While *lectio divina* was considered a distinctly spiritual practice, *lectio* was considered a physical and sensual process. Reading is an act that operates on the 'animal' level of the human mind.[79]

In her study on female medieval readership, Helen Solterer emphasizes the sensual and carnal aspects of reading.[80] She bases significant parts of her argument on William's Golden Epistle. I assume that it was the following statement that aroused her particular curiosity in our author: "From this regular reading, we ought to draw affection" (*Hauriendus est de lectionis serie affectus* [...]).[81] She interprets the short, albeit rich passage as follows: "Insofar as reading is understood to stimulate feelings, it is designated a function of human carnality. Visually, and aurally, reading engages the

---

77   I will discuss the topic in detail in the chapter "6.1. A History of Misattribution".

78   Smalley, *The Study of the Bible*, 282.

79   Both William and Bernard differentiate between the animal (*animalis*), the rational (*rationalis*), and the spiritual (*spiritualis*) state, through which the human mind ought to progress. This distinction is not identical but analogous to many such threefold schemes, such as the *katharsis–photismos–teleios* conception of Dionysius Areopagita, or the Augustinian *caritas inchoata – provecta –perfecta* scheme (see Heinrich Stirnimann, *Unio–communio: Dimensionen mystischer Erfahrung* (Freiburg, CH: Universitätsverlag, 1995, 197).

80   Helen Solterer, "Seeing, Hearing, Tasting Woman: Medieval Senses of Reading," *Comparative Literature* 46, no. 2: 129.

81   Epistula ad fratres de Monte Dei (CCCM 88), Lib. I, par. 123.

major sensory organs; and judging by Thierry's (sic) metaphor of savoring food, it involves taste and touch as well. [...] Since reading entices readers to dwell on the ensuing pleasures, indeed to become fully engrossed in them, in Thierry's (sic) it brings out the 'beast' in them."[82]

Solterer admits that this kind of reading might overstate the case of a 'carnal reading', given William's monastic propensity for discipline and general ideal of subordination of the senses. William does not advocate for an erratic unleashing of bodily desires. Instead, his statement in the paragraph on prayer continues and contextualizes how he envisions these *affectus* as a part of the ultimately devotional and spiritual practice of *lectio divina*:

> From this continuous reading, we shall draw loving affection and let it form our prayer, which shall interrupt our reading. This interruption shall not as much impede our reading as purify our spirit so that it might understand continually what it is reading.[83]

William acknowledges the human reality of the reader and the fact that the act of reading itself can provoke aspects of the 'animalistic'. However, he does not simply condone this reality but instructs his brothers to pursue reading in a structured and disciplined way, to submit it to the process of ascent. Reading Scripture – but only if it is done correctly – can be incorporated into the spiritual life. For this reason, he ultimately assigns the act of reading to the 'spiritual' state as well (rather than exclusively to the 'animal' state) in his organization of devotional practices.[84] In its ideal form, the reader opens herself up to divine guidance and inspiration, and her practice is transformed from a physical act into a spiritual one. While Solterer is right to observe that "the process itself is set in motion by the sensibilities of the body", William essentially calls his brothers to 'sober up' and subject their senses entirely to God in the process.[85] This twofold notion of acknowledging the physical aspect of reading on the one hand and yet urging

---

82   Solterer, "Seeing, Hearing, Tasting," 130.

83   Epistula ad fratres de Monte Dei (CCCM 88), Lib. I, par. 123: *Hauriendus est de lectionis serie affectus, et formanda oratio, quae lectionem interrumpat, nec tam impediat interrumpendo, quam puriorem continuo animum ad intelligentiam lectionis restituat.*

84   Expositio super Epistolam ad Romanos (CCCM 86), Lib. III, linea 972: *Spiritualis est in lectionis studio et meditationis, et maiorum doctrina, conueniens eis quibus dominus dicit:Vobis datum est nosse mysterium regni Dei.*

85   William describes those, who find themselves in the spritual stage of ascent as *sobrium sensum.* (Expositio super Epistolam ad Romanos (CCCM 86), Lib. III, linea 972).

the reader to overcome it on the other might play into the fact that William continues to speak about the act of reading and interpreting in pronouncedly sensual ways. He does so beautifully in the *Expositio* when discussing Paul's usage of the name of Jesus:

> Or, what appears more credible, the name of Jesus was sweet on Paul's lips because the love of Jesus burned in his heart, and it seemed sweet to him to submerge his sayings and writings with the frequent mention of His name. Even the pronouns of his name, like "in whom", "through whom", and "in him" or "through him" he seems to use so often everywhere and in awkward (*importune*) places. This could seem tedious to the reader if it were not for the passion it incites in the writer himself.[86]

The name of Jesus, William believes, must have tasted sweet on Paul's lips, a sensory experience that allowed the apostle to grow deeper in his love for Christ.[87] Paul metaphorically consumed Jesus and, in turn, was consumed entirely by Christ's love. This is an ideal example of how William idealizes the subjection of all senses to a spiritual good while appreciating the depth and concreteness of sensual imagery. He describes the Pauline authorship as one that is fundamentally experiential and affective. Only if it is understood as such, and Paul's passionate love for Christ is taken into consideration, will the reader succeed in understanding the Apostle's texts. If not, William warns his brothers, they might risk dismissing them as dull and miss the significant spiritual insights they contain.

Following the tradition of monastic rules, William hopes to prevent misuse of the practice of reading by instilling detailed instructions for the time and sequence of individual study of Scripture. First, he advises his brothers against a haphazard or random reading of Scripture. Just as the monks' devotional ordinance follows a firm regiment, so too should they structure the

---

86   Expositio super Epistolam ad Romanos (CCCM 86), Lib. I, linea 112–116: *Vel quod credibile magis uidetur, dulce quiddam Paulo nomen eius sapiebat in ore, cuius ei amor ardebat in corde; et suaue ei erat dicta seu scripta sua, quae de illo erant, crebra nominis ipsius commemoratione respergere. Sed et pronominibus nominis ipsius, sicut est: "in quo, per quem, in ipso, per ipsum" tam crebro ubique et importune uti uidetur, ut nonnumquam taedium legenti facere uideatur, si non cogitetur scribentis affectus.*

87   The sensual dimension of the spoken name of Jesus will reappear as a motive in the later chapter "5.5. The Breasts of God: William's sensual spirituality", where I will focus more on the *Expositio super Cantica Canticorum.*

time they devote to Scripture. Rather than reading Scripture whenever their religious schedule allows it, they should appoint fixed hours (*certis horis*) for their study. Rather than simply perusing the biblical corpus, they should assign particular texts (*certae lectioni*) for themselves.[88] William wants to discourage his brothers from taking this part of their spiritual life too lightly:

> A random and varied reading, to which one returns almost serendipitously, does not edify the spirit but renders it volatile. Starting lightly, it will also easily withdraw from memory. Instead, one is to dwell on certain authors to habituate the spirit.[89]

The goal of *lectio divina*, as he mentions it here, is spiritual edification (*aedificatio*). To this end, scriptural knowledge should not merely be acquired but internalized. It should enter the monks' *memoria* and assume a permanent place in their minds. Casual reading will not prepare the mind to retain the deep spiritual insight the texts offer and result only in fleeting and void discoveries that pass as soon as they come. William believes that the human mind requires a period of adjustment to 'get used' (*assuefaciendus*) to the spiritual world it encounters in Scripture. This entails, of course, intense focus on the part of the reader. External circumstances, such as the aforementioned reading schedule, can support such a state of mental concentration. William, additionally, suggests narrowing one's focus to a particular biblical author (*certis ingeniis*) for a certain amount of time.

As discussed earlier, William makes it clear, at this point, that he does not consider Scripture a mere document but a personal counterpart. The biblical author addresses the reader directly. The reader, in turn, as soon as he begins his exegetical endeavor, enters a relationship with the author and his work. Considering the aspects of time and devotion, which William stresses, Eileen Sweeney characterizes this relationship as a "friendship rather than mere acquaintance".[90] As one would with a close friend, the monk must spend ample time with Scripture. It does not suffice that he

---

88   Epistula ad fratres de Monte Dei (CCCM 88), Lib. I, par. 120.

89   Epistula ad fratres de Monte Dei (CCCM 88), Lib. I, par. 120: *Fortuita enim et uaria lectio, et quasi casu reperta, non aedificat sed reddit animum instabilem, et leuiter admissa leuius recedit a memoria. Sed certis ingeniis immorandum est, et assuefaciendus est animus.*

90   Sweeney makes this observation based on William's statement that 'there is the same gulf between attentive study and mere reading as there is between friendship and

devotes himself intensely to a biblical text once and then moves on to another. Instead, a text and its meaning should be pondered daily for a more extended period. William employs here the imagery of physical digestion and conceptualizes the reading monk as a spiritually ruminant species:[91]

> But from the daily reading, something ought to be fed daily to the stomach of memory so that it will be more faithfully digested and, when recalled, get ruminated more often: a thought that is in accordance with our proposition, that benefits our intention, and that detains our spirit, so that nothing foreign to us may be thought.[92]

Scripture accompanies a monk throughout his day. It continues to sink deeper into his mind while he fulfills his chores. The biblical words he is 'chewing' (*ruminetur*) keep his mind fixated on God while he follows his occupation.[93] William does not use the term *meditatio* to describe this aspect of the practice, yet one is reminded of the meditative stage in the classical scheme of *lectio divina* as he describes the importance of memorizing and internalizing Scripture.

However, William's focus on how the mental study of the Bible is to accompany the monk in his everyday chores might suggest that he also has a further stage of *lectio divina* in mind. Hugh of Saint-Victor had adapted the classical scheme by adding a fifth element:[94] *Operatio*. It could be translated with 'application', as it embodies the importance of carrying one's reading into one's everyday life and putting the biblical words into action. The

---

acquaintance with a passing guest, between boon companionship and chance meeting' (Sweeney, "Rewriting the Narrative of Scripture", 7).

91   The early medieval understanding of reading is often associated with the terms *ruminare* or *ruminatio*. These associations conceptually represent "a 'chewing' of a text, rereading it (just as animals chew the cud)" (Mariken Teeuwen, *The Vocabulary of Intellectual Life in the Middle Ages*, vol. 10, Études Sur Le Vocabulaire Du Moyen Âge (Turnhout: Brepols 2003), 292). Such 'alimentary metaphors' are especially common in 12th-century conceptions of the meditative practice. (Robertson, *Lectio Divina*, 205).

92   Epistula ad fratres de Monte Dei (CCCM 88), Lib. I, par. 122, linea 869: *Sed et de cotidiana lectione aliquid cotidie in uentrem memoriae demittendum est, quod fidelius digeratur, et sursum reuocatum crebrius ruminetur; quod proposito conueniat, quod intentioni proficiat, quod detineat animum, ut aliena cogitare non libeat.*

93   The practice of 'rumination' of biblical texts ties back to early Egyptian monasticism (Giraud, "The Literary Genres," 254).

94   On the particular role of Hugh of Saint Victor in the schematization of lectio divina see Giraud, "The Literary Genres," 255–258.

insights gained from the classical steps of *lectio divina* thus become the basis for one's behavior in the world.[95] *Operatio* can be woven into different places of the sequence and is therefore not necessarily an additional step but more of an intention that accompanies the reader through the spiritual process. In this regard, William's and Hugh's notions of readership reveal notable similarities, as both models are not systematically bound to the classical steps. Reading, meditating, praying, and working are not phases that supersede one another but aspects that simultaneously and cooperatively establish a life permeated by Scriptural truth. For William and Hugh, it is not the adherence to a scheme but a particular *habitus* of the reader that distinguishes *lectio divina* from any other kind of readership.

This becomes clear in William's understanding of *oratio*. More so than a step that follows *lectio* and *meditatio*, he conceptualizes prayer as a posture the reader should assume to make his reading practice spiritually fruitful. At its core, prayer is the active request for God to enter and transform human activity. The reading monk ought to let God creatively interrupt his practice. Throughout the *Expositio*, William utilizes prayer in a sense that seems aligned with this notion of divine interruption. Rather than asking for illumination at the beginning of his work, he addresses God throughout the Commentary – for instance, at the beginning and end of thematic sections –, to draw the reader's and his own attention back to the divine source of insight.

William makes it abundantly clear, whether in the *Expositio* or throughout his literary corpus, that he believes in the importance of a reader's attitude. The state of a reader's heart and mind determines to a high degree if Scripture will reveal its secrets to them or not. William makes this understanding a norm for monastic readership, as he dedicates the fifth and last paragraph of the Golden Epistle's account of *lectio divina* to the question of intentionality:

> Reading serves the intention. If someone truly seeks God in their reading, then everything they read will cooperate in them to that extent. It will capture the sense of the reader and subjects every understanding of what is read to the servitude of Christ. If the reader's sense, however, deviates in any way, then he draws all things after himself: nothing sacred and pious will be found in the Scriptures that [the reader] could not through vain glory, a distorted sense, or a

---

95   Christine Valters Painter, and Lucy Wynkoop, *Lectio Divina: Contemplative Awakening and Awareness* (Mahwah, NJ: Paulist Press, 2008), 8.

wrong understanding apply to their malice and vanity. The beginning of all reading of Scripture ought to be the fear of God, that in it the reader's intention may be solidified, and that from it a structured understanding and sense of what is read will emerge.[96]

Scripture is by no means self-explanatory. It does not simply reveal its secrets to the apt mind; it is not permeable for mere reason. Only the heart of one who longs for God will hear God's voice speaking from the biblical verses. William's hermeneutics bears a resemblance to his sacramental theology. In his disputation against Rupert Deutz, he stresses the spiritual reception of the Eucharist. While everyone can receive the elements physically, the spiritual benefits can only be reaped by the pure of heart.[97] William follows the Scriptural tradition that warns against negative consequences for those who receive the Eucharist in a sinful state.[98] Nathaniel Peters points out that "William equates meditation and Eucharistic reception" to a "shocking" extent.[99]

The parallels between his sacramental theology and his understanding of *lectio divina* are, in consequence, similarly striking: just as the effect of the Eucharist is dependent on the spiritual purity of its receiver, so the edifying power of Scripture is only accessible to those who read it with a pure heart. In turn, those who approach Scripture with a sinful mind might face a similar spiritual danger as those who illegitimately receive the Eucharist. If one is to attempt exegetical understanding with false intentions, they might garner falsehood from their *lectio*. 'False intentions', according to William, are essentially all desires that deviate from a pure love of truth.[100] The sole

---

96   Epistula ad fratres de Monte Dei (CCCM 88), Lib. I, par. 124, linea 878: *Intentioni enim seruit lectio. Si uere in lectione Deum quaerit qui legit, omnia quae legit cooperantur ei in hoc ipsum, et captiuat sensus legentis, et in seruitutem redigit omnem lectionis intellectum in obsequium Christi. Si in aliud declinat sensus legentis, omnia trahit post semetipsum; nichil que tam sanctum, tam pium inuenit in scripturis, quod seu per uanam gloriam, seu per distortum sensum, seu per prauum intellectum, non applicet suae uel malitiae uel uanitati. In omnibus enim scripturis legenti initium sapientiae debet esse timor Domini, ut in eo primo solidetur intentio legentis, et ex eo exurgat et ordinetur totius lectionis intellectus uel sensus.*

97   McGuire, "A Chronology," 20.

98   Nathaniel Peters, "The Eucharistic Theology of William of Saint–Thierry," in *A Companion to William of Saint–Thierry* (Brill, 2019), 174.

99   Peters, "The Eucharistic Theology," 181.

100   "L'amour (ou la charité) de la vérité' (I, 25 et 54; V, 63) est l'amour de l'homme pour Dieu tendant à la contemplation de son objet divin, tandis que la 'vérité de la charité (ou de l'amour)' (V, 63) est l'amour du prochain, sans lequel il n'y a point de véritable amour pour Dieu (VII,40). Leur présence simultanée chez le croyant constitue un

purpose of reading Scripture should be to seek out God for God's sake: any hope for reward, be it intellectual or physical, will taint the process and preclude the potential for divine inspiration.[101] Intention determines what the reader receives. A heart full of love will gain insight into the mysteries of the 'highest love'. A deceitful heart, however, will find itself deceived by what it reads.

Although it might seem as though William focuses entirely on human responsibility rather than divine revelation, his discussion of a reader's intent must be considered in the context of the traditional last step of the *lectio divina: contemplatio*. Human intention matters insofar as it affirms the reader's willingness to subject herself to God entirely. As the reading mind ought to strive for God, reading itself will ideally lead to the enjoyment of beatific vision. God is both the source and the aspiration of the monastic reader. It is helpful to remember at this point that William understands Scripture as a work conceived by two authors: an inspired human author on the one hand, and a divine author, desiring to reveal Godself on the other. Biblical authorship and devotional readership alike resemble a continuous conversation with God.

This, however, necessarily introduces the notion of divine *Unverfügbarkeit* into the process of reading. Biblical truth is never revealed once and for all; it remains hidden for those undeserving of such a gift. William's notion of Scriptural truth is not objective in a classical sense but derives its status and meaning from the subjective relationship with the divine. Although, as we will see, William values the interpretive authority of the Fathers and is heavily concerned with matters of orthodoxy, the mere reiteration of doctrines and Patristic statements does not exhaust what he means by understanding Scripture. Insight is directly dependent on what God reveals to the reader. To give voice to this notion, William returns to a position of prayer:

> Open, Lord, your Scriptures only to those that seek you [...] and in this solve for us the sign of the most high sacrament. For no one has been found worthy of the solution, neither in the heavens nor on earth nor below the earth, save for you, who carries the key of David.[102]

---

critère de discernement spirituel, car l'authenticité de la contemplation se mesure au service fraternel qui en découle". (Verdeyen, "Introduction," in *Exposé Sur l'Épitre aux Romains*, 49).

101 Expositio super Epistolam ad Romanos (CCCM 86), Lib. I, linea 253.

102 Expositio super Epistolam ad Romanos (CCCM 86), Lib. IV, linea 657–661: *Aperi, domine, scripturas, quae de te sunt, non nisi te quaerentibus in eis; [...], et in ea huius*

The fundamental process of reading is conversational and intimate. It takes place between God and the reader. God's revelatory role, however, does not relieve the reader from the responsibility to enter the relationship. Only those who search for God in Scripture will recognize it as a source of divine insight. To read, in the first place, means to ask God for understanding and hope for a gracious answer. In the framework of William's monastic vision, it is an integral part of the prayerful life. Conversely, the reader's spiritual life affects his potential for insight: only the worthy (*dignus*) will enjoy the disclosure of the innermost biblical mysteries. Since, according to William, no one – neither in the heavens nor on earth – has been deemed worthy of such a revelation, this aspect of William's hermeneutics remains a hopeful plea.

Acknowledging the obscure character of the biblical texts necessarily affects the self-conception with which a reader may approach his task. To anticipate insight confidently would mean to overestimate the human role in the revelatory process, yet, to look for God in Scripture necessitates a certain degree of hope on the human part. The Christian reader is simultaneously assured of her relationship with God and humbly grateful, as she knows it is not by her own achievements that she enjoys this relationship. To acquire a better understanding of William's own self-conception, both as a reader and an author of exegetical commentaries, we will now have to turn to the way he presents himself in the *Expositio*.

4   William's Self-Representation in the *Praefatio*

As with many medieval commentaries, the preface of William's *Expositio* is one of the most informative parts regarding his understanding of his authorial role. Here he reflects on the task he is setting out to fulfill and the limitations he faces. As Alastair J. Minnis shows in his constitutive study on medieval authorship, academic prologues are fruitful sources when determining an author's sense of purpose. A medieval writer's self-conception was, however, not only linked to his thoughts and ambitions but closely intertwined with his understanding of authority. Prologues were often used to give voice to the "medieval veneration of the past":[103] How the past and its

---

maxime sacramenti signaculum resolue nobis. Quod qui resolueret, nemo dignus inuentus est neque in caelo, neque in terra, neque sub terra, praeter te, qui habes clauem Dauid.

103   Minnis, *Medieval Theory of Authorship*, 9.

influential figures were portrayed contributed significantly to a work's authoritative claims and literary freedom. Whether in terms of literary quality
or doctrinal reliability, the *auctores* of antiquity provided the highest standard, and the reception of their work was crucial to establish one's authority
and credibility.

12th-century academic authors had different 'types' of prologues at their
disposal. Literary templates allowed them to present the work they were
reading and discussing. One of the more simplistic types that was known
and established up to that point was the threefold structure that Fathers
like Gregory (540–604) and Bede (672–735) employed. It focused on three
aspects of the work and its *auctor* and contextualized them according to the
categories of *persona, locus,* and *tempus*: who was the author, and where
and when did he write the work in question? This practice was based on
the ancient rhetorical emphasis on the *circumstantiae*. Minnis calls this
'type A' (in reference to Richard William Hunt's literary theory),[104] noting
that scholars who employed it were free to add specific questions to their
inquiry, such as a discussion of the ideological and academic material the
auctor had used.[105]

This minimalist approach experienced less and less reception in the 12th
century. Although Hugh of Saint Victor used it pervasively in his biblical
commentaries, he is the rule's exception.[106] According to Minnis, the shifting requirements of 12th-century scholarship and the variety of academic
disciplines had given rise to the 'type C' prologue, a method of inquiry reflecting the decline of the rhetorical arts in favor of a dialectical point of
view. This literary template was based on Boethian theory, introducing aspects of intention and reception into the considerations of *auctoritas*. Following this type of prologue, most 12th-century commentators included the
following elements in their discussions of ancient works: the title of the
work in question (*titulus*), the author's name, and the work's authenticity
(*nomen auctoris*), the author's objective (*intentio auctoris*), the work's subject-matter (*materia libri*), the didactic method the author had employed

---

104   Minnis refers here to the theory Hunt proposed in an article in 1948 (most currently
        published as Richard William Hunt, "The Introduction to the 'Artes' in the Twelfth
        Century," in *The History of Grammar in the Middle Ages: Collected Papers* [*by Richard
        W. Hunt*], ed. Geoffrey Leslie Bursill–Hall (Amsterdam: John Benjamins Publishing
        Company, 1980).
105   Minnis, *Medieval Theory of Authorship*, 16–17.
106   Minnis, *Medieval Theory of Authorship*, 17.

(*modus agendi*), the work's usefulness for its readers (*utilitas*) and the branch of philosophy it belonged to (*cui parti philosophiae supponitur*).[107]

These categories, especially how medieval authors understood them, display a growing interest in secular literature or controversial *auctores*. For instance, the questions concerning the intentio auctoris or the work's utilitas were headings under which commentators discussed the validity of their inquiry: "The commentators were more interested in relating the work to an abstract truth than in discovering the subjective goals and wishes of the individual author. The *intentio auctoris* – the intended meaning 'piously expounded' and rendered unimpeachable – was considered more important than the medium through which the message was expressed".[108] Receiving pagan philosophers or Christian authors of disputed orthodoxy was not an unquestioned right for medieval theologians. Discussing an author's intention was a means of defending a work's claim to authority, whether by arguing for an implicit but unknown faith in the author or by identifying a moral project in the work itself that aligns with the more profound objectives of Christian teaching. Including such a specifically apologetic concern in the typology of a prologue shows that it was not designed for the reception of the Fathers or, more importantly, the exegesis of Scripture. While there were indeed biblical commentaries that employed the structure of the 'type C' prologue, it required much modification.[109] The Bible could not be treated like any other book; thus, the methods needed for its interpretation could not simply be borrowed from other disciplines but had to be uniquely developed.

This is especially the case if one considers that the central question all types of ancient and medieval prologues raised – the authority of the work's *auctor* – is, as such, not applicable to a work that claims to be divinely inspired. If God is considered at least one of the biblical authors, the issue of authority does not arise, or at least not in the same way as it would with a human author. How then, do the human writer's context and personality influence the theological content, and how far does it call for consideration? Minnis describes the 12th century as a time of methodological change for Christian scholarship, which simultaneously called for a clear

---

107   Minnis, *Medieval Theory of Authorship*, 19–22.
108   Minnis, *Medieval Theory of Authorship*, 21.
109   The category of *intentio* was used in Commentaries on the Pauline Epistles to systematically analyze the author's motives and objectives in composing the biblical text (Riché and Lobrichon, *Le Moyen Âge et la Bible*, 174).

distinction of the unique role of the biblical text and its authorship: "It would seem, then, that twelfth-century exegetes were interested in the *auctor* mainly as a source of *auctoritas*: the human writer of Scripture was important in proportion to the extent to which he had provided (perhaps unwittingly) part of the vast pattern of meaning supposed to lie behind the literal sense of Scripture. It was this pattern, which the exegetes strove to describe, not the individual contribution of any human *auctor*."[110] The *auctoritas* of the human author and, subsequently, the spiritual truth of the biblical text come from God.

Not all 12th-century authors shared this notion with fervor and consistency. Still, those who did had to take the premise to its logical conclusion: literary observations on the author's *circumstantiae* or his motives could only provide interpretive insight if embedded in a framework of divine guidance. This understanding impacts the literary structure of a prologue and the exegetical project. If the timelessness of divine nature determines a work's veracity, its historical and literal dimensions must take a backseat. Instead, the allegorical and the moral sense become the ones that carry Scriptural authority.

While the *auctoritas* of the biblical author and his text experienced a consolidation, the *auctoritas* of the medieval reader and the orthodoxy of his claims remained an issue that needed to be resolved differently from case to case. The apologetic concern addressed in non-biblical commentaries under the headings of *intentio auctoris* or *utilitas* had to shift towards discussing the exegete's trustworthiness. Therefore, the prologue of a biblical commentary increasingly had to entail aspects of self-reflection. Whether an author gave a more detailed account of his method, his points of reference in tradition, or his spiritual emphasis, it is clear that medieval commentators of the Bible had to clarify their role for their readers. This concern speaks clearly from William's preface to his *Expositio*, as he explores his own work's potential authority from several perspectives.

First, it is essential to note that the preface does not lack strategic motives. It was common throughout antiquity and the Middle Ages to garner one's readers' favor with a *captatio benevolentiae*: the author presents himself in a humble light to seem compliant in the eyes of his audience. In pursuing this strategy, William was undoubtedly no exception among his contemporaries, given that the standards of medieval authorship not only tolerated but expected such literary expressions of humility. His ideas, he

---

110   Minnis, *Medieval Theory of Authorship*, 72.

claims, are not his own but were initially developed by the Fathers, who in turn provide his claims with authority and reassurance of orthodoxy. Rather than simply trusting his words, his readers should trust the opinions of the Fathers, of which the *Expositio* is a mere compilation – or so he assures them.

If one were to trust his *praefatio*, the work could no longer be considered a personal exegetical project but an anthology of Patristic interpretations of Romans. He explicitly excludes his interpretive efforts from his general intention:

> We have undertaken the study of Paul's Epistle to the Romans, a text riddled with many diverse and complex questions. Not to explain it, which would exceed our capabilities, but to compile in a single work some of what the Fathers, and especially Saint Augustine, have thought and written about it in their books and works.[111]

The Pauline Epistle, according to William, is a text of such complexity that no medieval author alone – and indeed not himself – could attempt to understand its depths. William's goal is, therefore, not to expound the meaning of Scripture through his theologically apt mind but rather to expound the meaning of the Fathers' interpretations. This, however, raises the question of the *auctor* anew: who is the author whose work William is referencing? Is it Paul, as the genre of a biblical commentary would suggest, or might it be Augustine, and a variety of Patristic authors, thus making the *Expositio* an anthology of sorts? At this point, it is important to note that it was common among William's contemporaries – or generally between the 10th and 12th centuries – to make little distinction between the New Testament and the Patristic writings.[112] Yet it is interesting that William, instead of focusing in his *praefatio* on Paul's Epistles to the Romans, seems to show particular

---

111   Expositio super Epistolam ad Romanos (CCCM 86), Praef., linea 2: *Epistolam Pauli ad Romanos multis et uariis et difficillimis quaestionibus inuolutam suscepimus, non ut exponamus, quod supra nos est, sed ut aliqua sanctorum patrum, et maxime beati Augustini, sensa in eam uel scripta ex libris eorum et opusculis hinc inde collecta in unum hoc opusculum compingentes [...]*.

112   Riché and Lobrichon, *Le Moyen Âge et la Bible*, 180. Hugh of St. Victor, for instance, had understood the *patres* as a part of the New Testament (Cornelia Linde, "Twelfth–Century Notions of the Canon of the Bible." In *Reading the Bible in the Middle Ages*, ed. Jinty Nelson and Damien Kempf, Studies in Early Medieval History (London: Bloomsbury, 2017), 12).

interest in the Fathers' interpretations of Romans. In that regard, he does not view himself as an exegete in the first place but rather as a student and interpreter of exegetes. This self-portrayal is fascinating in the context of 12th-century education. Students did not participate in a standardized educational system that provided the same opportunities and contents to all. Instead, the medieval student was his master's student in particular; different schools of thought formed and stood in competition with one another.[113] Education meant entering personal relationships that determined the method and content of learning to a high degree. The student's status correlated directly with that of his respective master(s). This includes, of course, the student's sharing in magisterial authority. Referring to one's teacher could significantly enhance one's authority and support one's trustworthiness.[114]

William makes use of this effect, as he expands the circle of his teachers beyond that of his Cathedral school: the Fathers themselves take on the role of his masters, imparting on him a near unquestionable authority. However, his insistence on Patristic influence in his *praefatio* is not primarily a matter of exegetical substance. It is a calculated way to introduce authority as a determining factor in the relationship he establishes with his readers, whose trust he hopes to gain by denying any personal responsibility for the trustworthiness of his claims:

> This interpretation shall be all the more appreciated by the readers, as no presumption of novelty or vanity can be found in it. Instead, it commends itself by the great authority of the great Doctors: Saint Augustine in particular, as mentioned, as well as Ambrose, Origen, and some other Doctors, and even some of the masters of our own time who, as

---

113   "The vitality of intellectual life in the twelfth century owed much to this competition between rival masters and rival student communities, often exacerbated by competing political loyalties" (Constant J. Mews, "The Schools and Intellectual Renewal in the Twelfth Century: A Social Approach," in A Companion to Twelfth–Century Schools, ed. Cédric Giraud, trans. Ignacio Duran, A Series of Handbooks and Reference Works on the Intellectual and Religious Life of Europe, 500–1800 88 (Brill, 2019), 28).

114   This did, however, not place any authors beyond reproach. Berengar of Tours († 1088), for instance, was a student of the orthodox and respectable Bishop Fulbert of Chartres († 1028). However, this did not protect him from receiving allegations of heresy and critique from his contemporaries (see Sita Steckel, "Submission to the Authority of the Masters: Transformations of a Symbolic Practice during the Long Twelfth Century," in *A Companion to Twelfth–Century Schools*, ed. Cédric Giraud, trans. Ignacio Duran (Brill, 2019), 81–82).

we have verified, do not go beyond the limits the Fathers have set up for us in any way.[115]

William's reference to the Fathers is juxtaposed to novelty (*novitas*) and vanity (*vanitas*), two characteristics – or rather vices – he seems to witness in certain works of his contemporaries. Novelty, an attribute that might well be considered a positive quality by today's standards, inherently runs the danger of heterodoxy if William's definition is taken into account. Orthodoxy is not an ever-growing and developing concept, but a corpus of thought whose limits had long been defined by the sum of Patristic opinions. Thus, introducing new content into Christian thought necessarily results in a transgression of these boundaries.[116] Not the potential veracity of an assertion, but its source determines its orthodox (or heretical) nature. A thought that had arisen from the intellect alone, rather than a *lectio* of Christian authorities, bases its claim to truth on nothing but human *vanitas*.

As for William, he gives a clear account of his sources precisely to counter such possible accusations: he bases all of his thought, so he claims, on Augustine, Ambrose, Origen,[117] and, under particular circumstances, the contemporaries who, in turn, follow their theological guidelines. One could rightfully ask what qualifies the orthodox Fathers as such if one were to evaluate them by the content of their works rather than their ecclesiastically attributed authority. As we will later see, Abelard attempted to solve this problem by applying his dialectic methods. William, however, established an inner-Scriptural hierarchy of meaning: an orthodox exegesis emphasizes divine grace over human achievement. While the Pauline Epistle lends itself exceptionally well to the topic of grace, it is a criterion that

---

115   Expositio super Epistolam ad Romanos (CCCM 86), Praef., linea 8: *Quae tanto debebit gratior esse lectoribus, quanto eam non nouitatis uel uanitatis praesumptio adinuenit, sed magnorum doctorum magna commendat auctoritas, praecipue, sicut dictum est, beati Augustini, deinde uero Ambrosii, Origenis et nonnullorum aliorum doctorum; aliquorum etiam magistrorum nostri temporis, de quibus certum habemus non praeterisse eos in aliquo terminos quos posuerunt patres nostri.*

116   On this notion and its more general application to medieval authorship, see Edward M. Peters, "Transgressing the Limits Set by the Fathers: Authority and Impious Exegesis in Medieval Thought," In *Limits of Thought and Power*, Varium Collected Studies Series 721 (Aldershot: Ashgate Publishing, 2001).

117   Although Origen's doubtful orthodoxy and the consequences for his reception in the Middle Ages will be discussed at a later stage (in the chapter "5.1. Origen as an (il)legitimate Source"), it is notable that William includes him here in the chorus of Church Fathers he gladly received.

William applies to Christian tradition. William considers Paul the upholder of grace against the Jews, taking up an anti–Jewish trope common in the history of exegesis, and he considers the Fathers the 'defenders of grace' against the heretics of the early church.[118] Their effort to protect the value of *gratia* qualifies them as trustworthy and, ultimately, as authorities of orthodoxy.

William is sensible about the importance of historical contextualization. While Paul's mission was rooted concretely in the idiosyncrasies of the ancient Roman congregation and its cultural discourse of 'Jewish' and 'pagan' Christians, and many of the Fathers had stood in biographical and theological conflict with a variety of heretical groups, his role differs from theirs. William does not assume responsibility for establishing the 'true' Christian faith but instead can rely – in the context of a medieval Christian society – on what these ancient authorities had already put into practice. William is not a *propugnator* of the message of divine grace, for it had already been preached for centuries before. Although its purpose aligns with the tradition he refers to, his mission is different from the Fathers'; rather than carrying the gospel out into a world dominated by darkness, he tries to illuminate the darkness within those who had already heard it. Grace, which the early church had to defend against those it considered its enemies, now needs to come to fruition within the believers themselves:

> The Apostle, the most courageous defender of grace, has maintained it with apostolic authority and wisdom against the Jews; the holy Fathers have defended it against heretics everywhere. Yet we desire that it may engrave itself into our hearts and lead us to perfect humility and pure devotion.[119]

William is out to convert hearts rather than people. At a time when the idea of crusades and the fight for religiopolitical domination had just emerged within Latin Christianity, William's theology took a distinct turn inwards. Historically, William recounts, divine grace had acted as the force of predestination and allowed for the justification of the converted. Now – and this is

---

118   Expositio super Epistolam ad Romanos (CCCM 86), Praef., linea 21.

119   Expositio super Epistolam ad Romanos (CCCM 86), Praef., linea 21: *Quam in tota epistola hac constantissimus propugnator eius apostolus apostolica auctoritate et prudentia defendit contra Iudaeos; sancti patres ubique contra haereticos; nos autem ad plenae humilitatis affectum et purae deuotionis effectum nostrorum cordibus desideramus inscribi.*

where he places himself and his readers by changing the grammatical *tempus* – it will ensure the glorification of the grateful from within.[120] The purpose of William's *Expositio* is thus not a theological defense of grace, in the sense of an anti-Pelagian discourse, but rather that of a spiritual guide. The theoretical concept of grace, well known to his readers, shall now actualize itself in their devotional attitude.

Here again, the lines between the writer's and the reader's roles become blurred. The work can be understood both as William's meditation on grace and as an invitation to his readers to follow him on the path of contemplation. Neither he nor his audience would do justice to the book's subject if they tried to engage with it on a merely intellectual level. Considering that the work is a biblical commentary, the exegetical work it entails is less that of dissecting the text and its implied theological meaning, but rather that of letting the kind of grace the text speaks of operate in oneself.

William translates this 'inward turn' into a literary structure, as he ends his *praefatio* with an extended prayer of his own. It reflects his Scriptural hermeneutics in a poetic and personal way: not the text itself, on a literal level, is the object of meditation, but the Word of God, spoken through it. *Gratia* cannot be extrapolated from the biblical verses, but she reveals herself uniquely to everyone willing to subject themselves to the biblical narrative as a whole. In consequence, the exegetical task too is distinctly personal:

> Heretofore this grace resounds from your words in the ears of those it has reached before so that it will not reach the ears of others, calling those that are not as those that are. This grace teaches the proud to be wise, for they are men, and to subject themselves to the humble, for they are brothers. It teaches them to ablate the shame of which they are suspect. It exhilarates the hearts of the humble and renders the faces benevolent that have been created but not abducted into foreign ground.[121]

---

120 Expositio super Epistolam ad Romanos (CCCM 86), Praef., linea 31: *Gratia enim priusquam essemus, cum nichil essemus, nos praedestinauit; auersos uocauit; conuersos iustificauit; iustificatos, si ingrati non fuerimus, glorificabit.*

121 Expositio super Epistolam ad Romanos (CCCM 86), Praef., linea 54: *Haec usque hodie quiddam sonans in uerbis tuis ad aures eorum quos praeuenit, quod ad aures aliorum non peruenit, uocat ea quae non sunt, tamquam ea quae sunt, superbos docens sapere quia homines sunt et humilibus consentire quia fratres sunt, et amputare opprobrium*

Grace, in a word, is relational. It is the means through which God creates, not only metaphysically but morally; grace carries the potential to change human nature from within. Whereas this sentiment lies at the heart of many theological traditions, not least the Augustinian doctrine of original sin, William puts it into decidedly practical terms: grace, speaking through the biblical words, admonishes every one of her students precisely in what they are lacking in. She teaches humility to the proud and reassurance to the humble. She is audible, not to all, but only to a few, making her message all the more precious to receive. Finally, she is not a philosophical principle, acting on her terms, but spoken directly from the mouth of God. Therefore, while William understands Paul as the defender of the divine Word, its author remains Godself. Reading – that goes for William as a reader of the biblical source, as much as for the readers of his *Expositio* – is at its core relational, deriving its essence from the relationship between the subject and the author of Scripture.

A question that arises for modern readers of the text is to what extent William's professions of humility conceal or distort his actual literary originality. In this regard, discussing William's moral judgment of such values as originality and innovation in Christian authorship is beneficial. One particularly curious passage reveals that William viewed literary originality rather critically. Here, he defends himself against criticisms of authorial theft or 'plagiarism' (to the extent to which this category applies to medieval discourse):[122]

> Lest anyone accuses us of theft: we admit it ourselves. According to the poet's fable, we have majestically clothed our little bird with the colors and feathers of a variety of birds. If each of them came and took away what they believed to be theirs, our little crow would remain nude and stripped of everything.[123]

---

quod de se suspicati sunt; humilium exhila\rans corda et facies gratificans, qui sic sunt, sicut creati sunt, nec in aliena abducti sunt.

122 Giles Constable offered a concise overview of the ideas of forgery and plagiarism in the Middle ages. He makes clear that the concept of plagiarism in a modern sense appeared only in the 17th century and that there was "no sense of literary or creative property" in the Middle Ages that would have allowed for such a term (Constable, "Forgery and Plagiarism," 27). Yet he concedes that a "sense of literary individuality is reflected in the accusations of stealing that were increasingly brought against authors in the twelfth and thirteenth centuries" (Constable, "Forgery and Plagiarism," 32). Thus, William likely did not conjure imaginary accusations but faced or witnessed them in his surroundings.

123 Expositio super Epistolam ad Romanos (CCCM 86), Praef., linea 15–16: *Nemo ergo furti nos arguat: ipsi nos prodimus. Secundum poeticam fabulam auiculam nostram*

William, instead of defending his creative genius, leans into the critique. Theft of intellectual property (*furtum*), or, if one were to put it in favorable terms, faithful reception is not the negation of his literary self-conception but an integral part of it.[124] In an explicitly poetic reference, he defends his work as a *cornicula* who would remain naked if it were not for the feathers of others. William receives this image almost literally from one of the Epistles of Horace.[125] He refers to his source as a fable (*fabula*), which could indicate that he did not know the source in its original but instead received the tableau from different Christian writers, who had used it devoid of its context, leaving William with the mere knowledge of its author. Yet, the sentiment William expresses with his strategically placed quotation unfolds such a subversive significance that the reader is enticed to believe that William understood all dimensions of the Horatian context.[126] The image is cited from Horace's letter to the young but relatively unknown author, Julius Florus. In it, Horace offers advice and stern critique to his friends, whose talents he feels are wasted amidst Florus' questionable life decisions. Florus appears to have had an entourage of other writers whom Horace deemed less talented and possibly "not up to the task of writing poetry".[127] One of these friends, explicitly mentioned in the letter, is a certain Celsus, probably referring to Celsus Albinovanus, to whom Horace had later addressed another letter. Celsus does not get off lightly in Horace's critique: he uses the image of the featherless bird to humiliate the author. According to the poet, Celsus' penchant for imitation goes so far that if stripped of all his sources, he would be left a laughing stock.[128]

---

     diuersarum plumis auium et coloribus sollemniter uestiuimus quae si uenerint et abstulerint singulae quae recognouerint sua, nuda uel nulla remanebit nostra cornicula.

124   Whether contemporaries had raised accusations of 'plagiarism' against William based on prior works of his or like-minded authors is unclear. Attacks against this patristically grounded exegesis from Peter Abelard or William of Conches, in an attempt to defend their own methodology, are certainly possible but lack textual evidence.

125   Epistolae Liber I,3 (Horace. *Satiren / Sermones. Briefe / Epistulae.* Edited by Gerhard Fink. Translated by Gerd Herrmann. *Satiren / Sermones. Briefe / Epistulae.* Sammlung Tusculum. De Gruyter, 2011, 158–160).

126   It is absolutely possible, and even likely, that William was familiar with the text in its original context. Latin authors and poets were read widely by medieval authors and were appreciated for their literary style (Haskins, *The Renaissance of the Twelfth Century,* 99).

127   Jeanne Neumann O'Neill, "Florus and the 'Commendatio Ad Gloriam' in Horace 'Epistles' 1.3.," *Phoenix* 53, no. 1/2 (1999): 84.

128   Epistolae Liber I,3, 158): *quid mihi Celsus agit – monitus multumque monendus, privatas ut quaerat opes et tangere vitet scripta, Palatinus quaecumque recepit Apollo, ne, si forte suas repetitum venerit olim grex avium plumas, moveat cornicula risum furtivis nudata coloribus – ?*

Horace opposes one's 'own property' and 'borrowed goods' when it comes to literary products, clearly favoring the former as the defining characteristic of a true poet. His notion of authorship thus stands in stark contrast to William's self-conception. However, William uses this discrepancy creatively and turns a traditional vice of antiquity into a distinctly Christian virtue. More so than the passages in which he refuses to take intellectual ownership of his work, the Horatian image allows him to describe his authorial ideal in moral terms. First, William characterizes the act, which Horace disparagingly calls 'borrowing', as a 'solemn adornment', offering a new and positive connotation to an approach, formerly considered shameful. Second, while Horace describes the 'removal of plumes' and the subsequent humiliation of the author as an adverse event, the idea of humiliation does not invoke the same negative associations for William. Humiliation, in the context of monastic theology, is instead a part of spiritual progress. It is a means by which the proud can achieve the desirable humility.

While the *praefatio* allows us to catch a glimpse of William's self-portrayal and the ideal he upholds, it raises the question of whether or not he does justice to it in his work. Whether humility and faithfulness to the Fathers are mere literary strategies to convince his readers of the orthodoxy of his claims or whether they are sincere values and principles of his writing can only be determined in a closer reading of the *Expositio* itself. In the following chapters, I will discuss William's use of Patristic works and his explicit and implicit treatment of humility in the Commentary.

5   Reading (alongside) the Fathers

As he has already suggested in the preface to his work, William considers the Fathers his teachers in a 12th-century context of learning. For him, this does not merely entail the schools and their particular student-teacher relationships but also the monasteries and their hierarchies.[129] The monastic notion of Fatherhood, represented especially in the figure of the abbot, significantly affected how William conceptualized Patristic authority and

---

129   As Blaise Dufal pointed out, the Fathers were conceptualized in the context of kinship, within which they "were at the centre of the practices of communication by different social agencies from the twelfth century on." (Blaise Dufal, "The Fathers of Scholasticism: Authorities as Totems," in *Individuals and Institutions in Medieval Scholasticism*, ed. Antonia Fitzpatrick and John Sabapathy (London: University of London Press, 2020), 56).

influence.[130] The Church Fathers share in his Cistercian vision of communal faith and serve as theological teachers and concrete examples for the devotional practices that William encourages his readers to pursue. He is interested in reiterating the doctrinal insight of his Patristic role models and discussing the methods through which they had come to those insights. For instance, he simultaneously presents the Fathers as teachers of exegesis and practical examples for the practice of *lectio divina*:

> There is, however, no piety without the activity of grace and no activity of grace without knowledge of grace. Meditating upon this often, they [the Saint Fathers] have become the blessed poor in spirit to whom the kingdom of God belongs and whose spirit is entrusted to God in its entirety.[131]

The meditative principle of *lectio divina*, so his argument goes, is not simply his methodological preference but is deeply ingrained in the history of biblical interpretation. Divine inspiration is the defining factor of authority, scriptural and ecclesial. The personal statements of the Fathers are expressions of this divine inspiration. As such, and by the church's sanctioning of their orthodoxy, they also become authoritative for the medieval reader. Thus, William can use Patristic texts as valid sources for his exegetical work. William instructs his readers to seek knowledge from a place of prayer because the earliest and most prominent thinkers of the church had done so, establishing a moral and epistemological example. Adhering to the same principles of meditative reading, which the Fathers had applied, will lead the medieval reader to theological insight into the Fathers' spirit and, therefore, to doctrinally acceptable knowledge.

Orthopraxis and orthodoxy are closely interconnected in this framework. William believes that Scripture ought to be read with the aid of those who stood closer to the lifetime of Christ than himself, those who had actively furthered the cause of the church when Christianity had still faced persecution and self-destructing controversy. Just as Paul, the early Fathers had

---

130 Dufal calls these conceptualizations of 'spiritual fathers' in the monastic context "institutionalizing totems" (Dufal, "The Fathers of Scholasticism," 68).

131 Expositio super Epistolam ad Romanos (CCCM 86), Praef., linea 28–29: *Pietas autem nulla est sine gratiarum actione; gratiarum actio nulla sine gratiae agnitione. Hoc enim crebro meditantes, efficiuntur | beati pauperes spiritu, quorum est regnum Dei, quorum cum Deo totus spiritus creditus est.*

'defended' the cause of grace,[132] and with their intensity, sense of calling, and devotional attitude in the face of divine activity, the medieval reader should apply herself to the cause of grace entirely. Participating in the Father's intentions in such a way will guarantee, in turn, the accuracy of theological assertions made in their spirit.

Although William concedes that even in his own time, certain but few individuals might receive direct inspiration from God – a possibility that constitutes a theoretical premise of mysticism – he deems the Patristic texts necessary sources for the 'ordinary reader'.[133] They inspire devotional affection in the readers' hearts, support them in developing a hermeneutical sensory, and, most importantly, safeguard the orthodoxy of their thought. The Fathers, William notes in his *preaefatio*, had set up the limitations (*termini*) of Christian thought; fundamental statements of faith, which cannot be transgressed.[134] Any theological proposition has to be evaluated according to the doctrinal perimeters the Fathers had established. Although the references to medieval authors are few, he clarifies that this practice is only permissible regarding works that are in line with the more authoritative voices of the Patristic canon:[135] Augustine, Ambrose, Origen, and 'various doctors' of the church.[136]

The fact that William understands the Fathers principally as warrantors of sound doctrine and faithful exegesis begs the question if William himself adheres to the kind of unquestionable authority for which he seems to advocate. While he owes significant elements of thought to his Patristic sources, a certain degree of uniqueness and innovation is nonetheless indisputable. As William Campell puts it: "Fidelity to the Fathers does not mean a simple repetition of what they said. In the twelfth century, the rediscovery of the Fathers was accompanied by a vitality that, in the case of William, sets the theological foundations of what will become known as affective theology."[137] To understand how William truly understood and

---

132   Expositio super Epistolam ad Romanos (CCCM 86), Praef., linea 21.

133   On the medieval views of 'giftedness' and 'talent', and their shift of meaning in the late eleventh century see Steckel, "Charisma and Expertise," 664.

134   Expositio super Epistolam ad Romanos (CCCM 86), Praef., linea 8: [...] *aliquorum etiam magistrorum nostri temporis, de quibus certum habemus non praeterisse eos in aliquo terminos quos posuerunt patres nostri.*

135   For instance, as Jean Doutre points out (Doutre, "Romans as Read in School and Cloister," 36): "[William] actually accepts Abelard's ideas, as long as they do not transgress his own sense of the limits set by the Fathers."

136   Expositio super Epistolam ad Romanos (CCCM 86), Praef., linea 8.

137   Doutre, "Romans as Read in School and Cloister," 53.

realized his authorship in the *Expositio*, we need to understand William's concrete adaptation and usage of the Fathers' views.

In our later discussion of William's Commentary on the Song of Songs, I will focus on Origen as a possible source and the relationship between William's usage of Eastern and Western material. I will also touch on his use of Origenist ideas in the following, but mainly concerning how they relate to Augustine's predominant and overpowering influence and his doctrine of grace. Augustine's role in the *Expositio* – and possibly in the medieval exegesis of the Pauline epistles in general – is exceptional and singular. On the one hand, this is the case statistically, as the quantitative volume of Augustinian quotations dramatically exceeds that of any other Patristic sources, drawing from over twenty works of the Bishop of Hippo[138]. On the other hand, William makes sure his readers acknowledge Augustine's ideological prominence when he singles him out as the primary source for the Patristic compilation in which he presents his work.[139] His reception is, he claims, a tapestry of Augustine's biographical, ecclesio-political and theological legacy: Augustine becomes a multifaceted Doctor of Grace.

William's veneration of Augustine is, of course, no oddity in his day and age[140] and certainly not within the monastic tradition in which he stands. As Grabmann says, "[die] mächtige Gestalt Augustins hat mit solcher Zaubergewalt das wissenschaftliche Leben und Streben des abendländischen Mittelalters beherrscht und bestimmt, dass daneben die Einwirkungssphäre der früheren lateinischen Väter als eine beschränkte erscheint".[141] Reflecting

---

138 Thomas P. Scheck, *Origen and the History of Justification: The Legacy of Origen's Commentary on Romans* (Notre Dame, IN: University of Notre Dame Press, 2008), 127.

139 Expositio super Epistolam ad Romanos (CCCM 86), Praef., linea 2: [...] *unam continuam non nostram, sed ipsorum texamus explanationem.*

140 Among William's contemporaries, Hugh of St. Victor, Anselm of Canterbury, Rupert von Deutz, and Peter Lombard come to mind as the most prominent readers of Augustine. However, their applications and usages of Augustinian thought are very distinct, with different emphases on doctrinal or exegetical elements of his writing (M.W.F. Stone, "Augustine and Medieval Philosophy," in *The Cambridge Companion to Augustine*, ed. Eleonore Stump and Norman Kretzmann, Cambridge Companions to Philosophy (Cambridge: Cambridge University Press, 2001), 255).

141 Grabmann, *Geschichte der Scholastischen Methode, vol. 1*, 116. It is this sentiment that is voiced as well in Jaroslav Pelikan's famous claim that the medieval history of thought and Christian practice could be read as "a series of footnotes to Augustine" (Jaroslav Pelikan, *The Christian Tradition: A History of the Development of Doctrine, Volume 1: The Emergence of the Catholic Tradition (100–600)* (Chicago, IL: University of Chicago Press, 1971), 330). However, it is important to note with M.W.F. Stone that "[m]ost medieval thinkers were in one sense or other influenced by some of Augustine's theories, but their actual ideas cannot be said to be completely dependent on his work" (Stone,

this historical, cultural development on the level of authorship, the Augustinian concept of grace emerges pervasively throughout William's works. He is not merely cited, albeit often, to answer specific questions. Instead, Augustine provides the overarching framework of thought within which William develops his ideas. This is especially the case in his reading of Romans since the theological and spiritual themes commonly associated with this particular text are also known, throughout early medieval exegesis, as essentially Augustinian themes. This includes Trinitarian and sacramental theology, concepts of predestination and foreknowledge, particularities of a devotional life, and, of course, the dynamics of sin and grace.[142]

William's interest in Patristic texts is not fueled by historical curiosity but by the notion that their authors impart the inspiration they had received through them. Augustine is, therefore, not only William's favorite Christian author but possibly a spiritual 'Father'. William's thought, like that of most Western monastic authors, is steeped in Augustinian insight. When he professes to offer a reiteration of Augustine's Romans exegesis, he does not intend to compile a *florilegium*. Instead, he attempts to assume the Augustinian perspective more fundamentally as the perspective of an author who had particularly profound insight into the mysteries of grace.[143] More importantly than the theological content, the Bishop of Hippo determines the Christian readers' ideal attitude towards its Scriptural object. Whether Augustine could or should be understood as a mystic – or maybe one of the first mystics of Western Christianity – is a controversial question within scholarship on Augustinian reception and monastic spirituality. While I cannot answer it satisfactorily in this volume – and do not intend to try – Augustine's potential mystical tendencies are essential to note for discussing Patristic reception in the 12th century. His work carries many elements that would later constitute the

---

"Augustine and Medieval Philosophy," 253). A comprehensive work on 'Augustinianism' and the reception of Augustine throughout the history of Christianity is provided for instance in Allan D. Fitzgerald, ed., *Augustine Through the Ages: An Encyclopedia* (Grand Rapids, MI: Eerdmans Publishing, 1999).

142   Cartwright, *The Romans Commentaries*, 102.

143   William applies this same concept to the historical Paul, considering him "a mystic who can teach the monk about grace because of his own experience with God" (Doutre, "Romans as Read in School and Cloister," 52). Franklin Harkins contextualizes the role of Augustine in medieval theology within a historical narrative "spanning from the debate on free will and predestination that spanned from the Second Council of Orange (529) to the mid–seventeenth–century condemnation of Jansenism" (Harkins, "Secundus Augustinus," 219).

mystical nature of medieval authors. Although William certainly did not consider himself a mystic, he did endorse his role model's exegetical and pastoral intentions.

William uses the term 'mystical', to refer to certain notions of Christ's passion and resurrection. William differs from most medieval authors insofar as he does not equate the mystical with the allegorical sense of Scripture. Yet, mysticism functions as a hermeneutical principle of sorts: discovering the mystical sense in the biblical account enables the reader to conform to Christ in his self-sacrificing position.[144] It is a reading that requires spiritual participation in and personal experience of grace rather than an intellectual understanding of the workings of grace. Therefore, Augustine's authority as the Doctor of Grace is, as well, not an intellectual one but one that is based on the Father's own spiritual experience and relationship with God. His extraordinary life as a Christian thinker and the inspiration he has received throughout qualify him as a reliable voice.

This notion determines the concrete process of reading Patristic texts and, more importantly, what it means to transmit them faithfully. Although William might suggest so in his preface, the *Expositio* is not a compilation of direct and literal quotations. As Cartwright had analyzed in his study on the text, three-fourths of the work are original to William.[145] Significantly, the passages that constitute the "heart of William's teaching on the third and fourth stages" (referencing the four human states mentioned earlier), namely chapters seven and eight, contain very few quotations from Augustine and Origen and are otherwise composed by the author himself.[146] While the Fathers can be understood as guides through the biblical narrative, William shows reverence to them without losing sight of his primary task: he is not an exegete of Patristic texts but an exegete of the Bible. While the latter is sacrosanct by nature, the former is not. As much as he is influenced by Patristic theology, William does not cling to the Fathers' words, cites freely, and is even willing to adapt their positions to fit his overall exegetical scheme.

---

144   Cartwright, *The Romans Commentaries*, 71.
145   Cartwright, *The Romans Commentaries*, 98. As Scheck mentions justly, the fact that "no more than one fourth of William's commentary draws on patristic sources, a point that has been neglected by some secondary sources." (Scheck, *Origen and the History of Justification*, 107). This negligence possibly contributed to a historiographical bias that presented William as a conservative and less productive author, in the face of Abelard's innovative genius.
146   Cartwright, *The Romans Commentaries*, 98.

Regarding the *Expositio*, a central question is to what extent William based his exegesis on Origenist material and how far he deviated from it. The debate is embedded in a more considerable controversy surrounding the influence of Eastern authors on William's thought.[147] William himself names Origen among other Fathers after whose reading of Paul he intends to fashion his Commentary. Paul Verdeyen has even attributed the beginning of a 12th-century renaissance of Origenist thought to the *Expositio*[148] and believed that the work was heavily indebted to the Alexandrian, or rather, the translations of Rufinus.[149] The idea of a direct and extensive reception of Origen has been vigorously defended by Jean–Marie Déchanet and Jacques Hourlier but was also heavily critiqued by scholars who believed the Eastern influence to be exaggerated.[150] William is – as has been rightfully insisted upon in response to efforts of recovering possible Greek influences – a thoroughly Augustinian author. J. D. Anderson, for instance, has taken the stance that William is a "Latin writer in the Latin West drawing upon the Latin heritage which admittedly includes some translations from the East";[151] some of the themes emerging in his works thus being coincidentally rather than explicitly Eastern.

I find the strategies to be most intriguing that believe in some coexistence of both Fathers in William's works. Louis Bouyer, for instance, has claimed that William provided an original synthesis between Greek and Latin ideas.[152] Rozanne Elder, having researched the manuscripts that might

---

147   The history of the controversy and its various contributors are well summarized by
        F. Tyler Sergent in "William of Saint–Thierry's Sources and Influences: Ratio Fidei and
        Fruitio," in *A Companion to William of Saint–Thierry*, ed. F. Tyler Sergent, 35–66 (Brill,
        2019). I will present other aspects of this debate in the chapter "5.3. 'Know Thyself'
        William's spiritual anthropology and his understanding of image–likeness", because it
        unfolded particularly in regards to William's exegesis of the Songs and the possible
        Eastern themes represented in his Commentary on the Song.
148   Verdeyen, "La chronologie des oevres," 197.
149   Verdeyen, "Introduction," in *Exposé Sur l'Épitre aux Romains*, 19.
150   This has notably been David N. Bell with his critical article "The Alleged Greek Sources
        of William of St. Thierry," in *Noble Piety and Reformed Monasticism. Studies in Medieval
        Cistercian History VII.*, ed. E. Rozanne Elder, Cistercian Studies 65 (Kalamazoo, MI: Cistercian Publications, 1981), and his study *The Image and Likeness: The Augustinian Spirituality of William of St. Thierry*, Cistercian Studies 78 (Kalamazoo, MI: Cistercian
        Publications, 1984).
151   Anderson, "The Use of Greek Sources," 253.
152   Louis Bouyer, *The Cistercian Heritage*, trans. Elisabeth A. Livingstone (Westminster,
        MD: The Newman Press, 1958), 110–11.

have been available to William in Saint–Thierry, and Signy,[153] has noted that William's "enthusiasm" for Greek thought – even if his access might have ultimately been limited – is detectable.[154] This kind of enthusiasm describes William's use of Origenist material throughout the *Expositio* rather well. He displays here a particular admiration for Origen's exegetical talent and originality. The Alexandrian provides William with creative imagery, with which to illustrate theological notions, and with the cultural and etymological knowledge necessary better to understand the intentions of the ancient biblical writer. William appreciates Origen especially for the deep understanding of the Greek text's subtleties, to which he would otherwise have little access.[155]

In the context of the debate surrounding William's sources, there is a slight tendency to play off Augustine and Origen against each other. To avoid that, it is important to note that the principles that William applies to his reading of Origen differ from those he uses when reading Augustine. Thomas Scheck, for instance, has proposed the theory that William interprets Origen through the lens of his Augustine, essentially integrating Origenist ideas into a principally Augustinian framework.[156] This is a surprising and daring thesis given that a traditional reading of these authors has emphasized their fundamental disagreements, especially in discussing the

---

153   She concludes that the works of at best nineteen Greek authors could have been available to William in their Latin translations (Elder, "William of Saint Thierry and the Greek Fathers," 258).

154   Elder, "William of Saint Thierry and the Greek Fathers," 266.

155   William refers to an Origenist observation in his discussion of predestination, when he mentions that the 'truth of the Greek translation' (*secundum Graecae translationis veritatem*) speaks of Christ as 'destined to arrive' (*destinatus est* [...] *et venit*), rather than pre–destined, as he wants to leave no doubt that Christ had always been God (*qui Deus semper erat*) (Expositio super Epistolam ad Romanos (CCCM 86), Lib. I, linea 71). In her recent article on the reception of Origen in the works of William and Abelard, Carmen Cvetković provides a detailed list of themes, for which William consults Origen in his *Expositio*: "In terms of content, William used Origen's commentary as a convenient source for clear distinctions and useful definitions of key terms found in Paul's epistle on the Romans, following Origen in his explanations of grace and apostleship,[54] Jew and Greek,[55] anger,[56] faith and works,[57] keeping the law and perfecting the law,[58] stages of conversion,[59] and so forth. William also followed Origen when speaking of justification, the new life of dying to sin, and conformity to Christ. However, he makes no use of Origen in his treatment of the Trinity, the sacraments or predestination" (Carmen A. Cvetković, "Conflict and Authority: William of Saint-Thierry and Peter Abelard as Readers of Origen," *Open Theology* 7, issue 1 (October 2021), accessed November 29, 2022, https://doi.org/10.1515/opth-2020-0181, 539).

156   Scheck, *Origen and the History of Justification*, 8.

themes crucial to William's exegesis: sin and grace. A strict reading of Augustinian soteriology classically suggests that any notion, including the potential for human participation, must be dismissed entirely out of a deep and all-encompassing concern for divine grace. It is an understanding that views Augustine's theology primarily through the lens of his anti-Pelagian efforts.[157] While there is positive value in stressing the importance of divine grace over and against a possibly harmful over-assessment of human agency, such a reading, runs the danger of suspecting most anyone of Pelagianism who does so much as broach the human role in the soteriological process. The reformational rejection of Origen is undoubtedly part of the problematic legacy of such theological hermeneutics.[158]

It would be straightforward to superficially categorize William as a pre-reformational campaigner for divine grace and against 'Pelagian' tendencies that resurfaced time and again throughout the Middle Ages. In his *Disputatio*, which I will discuss in more detail in chapter 2, he does make liberal use of the kind of anti-heretical terminology that was prominent throughout late antiquity, the term *pelagianus* in particular. The inference that his admiration for Augustine and his anti-heretical project would keep him from at least rejecting Origen's hamartiology thus seems evident. Such a conclusion would, however, lose sight of William's more general hermeneutic principle when it comes to Patristic theology, as he explicitly rejects the assumption of fundamentally opposing viewpoints among the Fathers.[159] A concept that conceives authority as a divine gift has to assume unanimity among those who have received it. Therefore, William's ideal of the Christian reader notes the importance of synthesis and harmony as the principle of any *lectio*.[160]

---

157   On the reception history of the Pelagian dispute, see Alexander Hwang, Brian Matz, and Augustine Casiday, eds., *Grace for grace: the debates after Augustine and Pelagius* (Washington, D.C.: The Catholic University of America Press, 2014).

158   Scheck, *Origen and the History of Justification*, 8–9.

159   As G.R. Evans notes, William "allows for the possibility that the Fathers sometimes treated their subject-matter 'more obscurely', sometimes 'more openly' (*modo obscurius, modo apertius*). But he is confident that their opinions will be seen to agree in faith". It is the spiritual authenticity and dependence of their thought on divine revelation that ensures their unanimity (G.R. Evans, *The Language and Logic of the Bible* (Cambridge: Cambridge University Press, 1985), 139).

160   Contextualizing the contestations against Abelard, Karl Morrisson speaks of a "belief in a tradition that was ever old and ever new, always and everywhere the same" (Karl F. Morrison, *The Mimetic Tradition of Reform in the West* (Princeton, NJ: Princeton University Press, 1982), 174).

William applies this theoretical notion practically, incorporating Origenist material into his thoroughly Augustinian framework. "Committed to the Augustinian doctrines of original sin, grace, and predestination",[161] William searches Origen's work for statements compatible with his theology. Scheck's description of William's literary process is that of 'glossing' Origen's exegetical insights with an Augustinian concern for grace to preserve Augustine's general doctrinal framework. His method allows him to use Origen's impressive rhetoric, his ethical and moral observations, and his vast linguistic knowledge without compromising his spiritual query, which remains throughout the Commentary decisively Augustinian. In other instances, of course, William rejects certain of Origen's statements. He does so, however, implicitly and without noting his deviation. Sometimes he even favors an Origenist thought over an Augustinian notion.[162] Although this is mostly the case with passages of minor theological significance, in certain instances, it reveals William's willingness to accept Origenist input, even when it comes to merit, forgiveness, and perfection.[163] The emphasis on the latter could be considered an attempt to counterbalance a theology that, in focusing entirely on divine action, runs the risk of suppressing human responsibility – a notion crucial to the monastic life in particular.

To provide an insightful reading of Scripture that gives voice to his spiritual experience, William has to consider the possibility of improving and revising Patristic insights – even Augustine's. This necessitates a great degree of methodical freedom in his reception of the Fathers. We can see this exemplified not only in the level of content but also in the *Expositio*'s literary structure. One of the ways in which William unfolds his exegesis is according to the four Augustinian stages (*gradus*) of human ascent.[164] The people of God, according to Augustine's narrative of salvation history, progress through these different states, standing first 'before the law' (*ante legem*), then 'under the law' (*sub lege*), thirdly 'under grace' (*sub gratia*). William, along with Augustine, detects these stages in the Pauline epistle and applies these stages to the process of individual salvation and spirituality.[165] To him, they are suitable categories, according to which he unfolds

---

161   Scheck, *Origen and the History of Justification*, 105–106.

162   Scheck, *Origen and the History of Justification*, 112.

163   Expositio super Epistolam ad Romanos (CCCM 86), Lib. II., linea 687–695.

164   Cartwright, *The Romans Commentaries*, 13–14.

165   Expositio super Epistolam ad Romanos (CCCM 86), Lib. II., linea 107: *Secundum has quatuor differentias, per totum corpus epistolae huius agitur, modo de homine Dei singulariter, modo de populo Dei generaliter.*

not only a theology of divine grace but also of humanity's reception thereof. William displays a sensibility to distinguish between Patristic propositions and guidance and the yet greater steadiness of Scripture herself.

While the theological emphasis he receives from Augustine helps him to develop his notion, he is cautious of overriding the biblical themes themselves. The Augustinian stages do not naturally fit the sevenfold structure of Romans. William consequentially does not force the fourfold order onto the biblical matrix but remains primarily true to the Pauline narrative. Where the thematic segmentation of his reading does not comply with the literary composition of the epistle, he either abandons or adjusts it, never favoring it to the biblical guidelines. However, while it demonstrates William's reverence for the different degrees of authority, his prioritization of Scriptural over Patristic themes does not end up stifling his creativity in the process. Subordinating the themes he receives from the Fathers, or even his contemporaries, to the biblical text brings his role closer to that of his non-scriptural authorities. Whether it is Augustine's reading, emphasizing the four stages of salvation or the distinction of the three human states (*animalis, rationalis,* and *spiritualis*) that several Fathers share, or even William's particular emphasis on the individual soul's ascent: all these approaches are equally submitted to the biblical voice, or spiritually defined the divine revelation that speaks through it. Within these parameters, William can combine perspectives and emphases flexibly and creatively without necessarily having to favor one over the other or playing them against each other. He can unfold themes as they emerge without adhering to them throughout his work.

What does the observation of relative freedom of reception tell us about William's self-conception as an exegete in his own right? Staying true to Patristic guidelines by no means suggests the practice of mere repetition. In fact, with Cartwright, we might understand William's 'flexible' reading of the Fathers, which allows for actualization and adaptation, as the "greatest compliment to his teacher", for he attempts to "use his thought as an important foundation of his own, but not to parrot him unthinkingly or quote him at every opportunity".[166] It is in this sense that we can also understand William's claim that his Commentary is not his own, but the Fathers': in subjecting himself to the same cause as theirs, pursuing the same literary intentions, and attempting to give an interpretation that corresponds to their spiritual mission, he can present his work as theirs in spirit. As William

---

166   Cartwright, *The Romans Commentaries*, 104.

offers his faithfulness to the Fathers in the context of humility, it will prove fruitful to explore his concept of intellectual humility in more detail in the following. First, I will contextualize William's *lectio* as one that takes place not only in a framework of past thinkers and saints but also within his actual monastic community.

6   Reading as a Communal Endeavor

Whether conceptualized as a personal, devotional practice or a public literary project – two dimensions present in the *Expositio* – reading necessarily entails communal considerations. Reading, as much as theological reflection, is never an end in itself but serves the spiritual progress of those who receive its insights. It is practiced with and for the community of spiritual brothers and sisters. William, throughout his Commentary, reveals that he has his own readers' interest in mind, valuing the comprehensibility of his work over theoretical complexity. Whenever William fears his discussion ventures into the abstract or could become unclear, he reiterates, as though to hold his reader's hand while guiding her through the text.[167] His usage of intricate rhetoric to reflect the spiritual beauty of Scripture further serves the purpose of making his discussion engaging and appealing to his readers. In doing so, William reveals himself to be a classic proponent of monastic writing. While the growing tradition of school theology displayed an increasingly dismissive attitude towards the rhetorical arts, William and his Cistercian contemporaries valued them as a means to elicit the reader's affection.[168] Theological thought that draws its inspiration from concrete ways of living and considers its purpose in dynamic relationships is best expressed in terms applicable to the environment from which it arises. William's context is the sensual world of the Cistercian monasteries. William

---

167   Expositio super Epistolam ad Romanos (CCCM 86), Lib. I., linea 486: *Sed quia haec ad declarandam rei seriem per transcursum dicta sunt, paululum ad superiora redeundum est.*

168   Steven Cartwright points out the following: "Jean Leclercq has especially distinguished between the writing styles of monks and schoolmen: monastic writers had a strong sense of beauty developed through their contact with classical and patristic writers and their participation in the liturgy, and monastic culture 'is more literary than speculative;' scholastic writers preferred dialectic to grammar and rhetoric, and clarity of thought and specificity to artistry in expression" (Cartwright, *The Romans Commentaries*, 133).

seamlessly introduced aspects of liturgical song, devotional art, and unifying
aesthetics into his exegetical reflection, demonstrating that his project is
neither individual nor purely intellectual.[169] Rhetoric is the device William
employs to make his own experiences tangible in his writing and thus to
fulfill the main subject of the *Expositio*: to aid the reader's spiritual progress.[170] He comprehends grace not only as the theoretical subject of his
work but intends for his readers to experience the activity of grace intimately. Understanding his exegetical writings as a shared *lectio divina*, the
devotional aspects of this reading assume an instructive character. Rather
than pursuing a contemplative state by and for himself, William hopes to
lead other monks to contemplate and experience divine grace.[171]

The reading audience is thus an integral part of William's (self-)concep-
tion of authorship too. Just as he shapes his understanding of a humble
reader vis–à–vis Paul, he also tailors his notion of the Christian writer after
the Apostle's example. William identifies the primary Pauline intention,
analogously to his vision, as a pedagogical one: Paul's sense of calling, tied
to his apostolic office, is not that of literary success or academic innovation
but rather the pastoral guidance of his fellow Christians. William emphasizes, therefore, that Paul's writing (as his own) reflects a high degree of
awareness regarding the needs and circumstances of his readers. While Paul
might not always be concerned with appearing incredibly eloquent or rhe-
torically apt – something William, in his strong sense of linguistic artistry,

---

169   It is, however, important to note that William does not condone an all too liberal use
      of visual art. As Conrad Rudolph notes in his study on the exegetical stained-glass win-
      dows at the abbey of Saint–Denis, William offers an elaborate critique of art, warning
      against an inappropriate use of visual means (for enjoyment or out of curiosity). But,
      as Rudolph continues, "even if properly used, [the use of art and architecture] is ex-
      plicitly restricted to the level of beginner, such an interaction being 'unforgivable' in
      the intermediate state of rational man. For even something devoid of imagery, such as
      monumental architecture, can cause the monk to regress in his spiritual ascent" (Ru-
      dolph, "Inventing the Exegetical Stained–Glass Window," 407). The sensual and artistic
      aspects of William's *Expositio* are therefore to be understood in a distinctly spiritual
      context.

170   Steven Cartwright explains that the rhetorical figures William uses go hand in hand
      with the spiritual progress that lies at the heart of his mission: "[...] in capable hands,
      such as those of William of St. Thierry, it expresses the beauty and power of divine
      truths, to the point that the hearer or reader, affected by the beauty and power of the
      exposito's words, is led into the experience described in those words" (Cartwright, *The
      Romans Commentaries*, 140).

171   Doutre, "Romans as Read in School and Cloister," 52.

notices – his efforts to ensure the appropriateness and effectiveness of his message is what truly distinguishes his work:

> Yet Paul has not omitted the following due to lack of eloquence but because he foresaw an even greater purpose in it. A wise donor of the Word, when he encounters the passages that seem to say something remarkable about the goodness of God, either expresses them in an obscure and short manner or passes over them in total silence, for he fears that the hope of pardon will render the lukewarm even more in-different. Therefore, after saying. 'just as sin entered the world through one man', he omits what should follow after, clearly leaving it to the wise and withholding it wisely from the imprudent. In all that, he re-veals that although justice and life have been brought to the people through one man, this does not occur immediately or indolently, but for those who, through much labor and study, seek what is hidden, knock on what is closed, and desire what is invisible.[172]

Following an Origenist distinction of the senses of Scripture and their asso-ciation with different stages of spiritual maturity, William detects in Romans a sense of prudence. Not all theological statements, even if they are accu-rate, are suitable for everyone to hear. The soul's relationship with God is dynamic and grows according to the believer's journey. While certain as-pects of the divine nature should be highlighted to encourage the individu-al's growth, others should remain undisclosed, lest the individual faces further obstacles. Although the Pauline Epistle is addressed to the church as a whole, William witnesses Paul's great care for the spiritual safety of his readers, revealing a lot about his ideals of pastoral care. To gain further in-sight into William's self-conception as an author, it therefore serves us to

---

172 Expositio super Epistolam ad Romanos (CCCM 86), Lib. III., linea 253–258: *Sed non hoc Paulo contigit ex defectu eloquii, sed aliquid in hoc prospexit utilitatis. Prudens enim dispensator uerbi, cum uenit ad ea loca quae de bonitate Dei eximium aliquid ui-dentur praeferre, aut obscurius et breuius ea solet proferre, aut silentio omnino subte-gere propter tepidiores, ne ex remissione spei faciat segniores. Vnde et hic cum dixisset: Sicut per unum hominem in hunc mundum peccatum intrauit, et siluit quae inferenda erant, prudentibus palam reliquit subintelligenda, et imprudentibus prudenter subticuit, simul et illud ostendens quod, etiam si per unum hominem iustitia et uita in omnes homines pertransiuit, tamen non hoc otiosis statim accidere, sed his qui multo labore et sudore potuerint quae occulta sunt quaerere, pulsare quae clausa, quae abscondita sunt desiderare.*

discuss his understanding of apostolicity and Christian instruction in the Pauline sense.

As Paul had received his office by divine grace, William grounds his understanding of the 'spiritual teacher' on various divinely bestowed charismata. The first aspect of apostolicity is its authoritative nature: the apostle had received the entitlement to 'correct those in need of correction' (*apostolatum in coercendo eos qui coercendi sunt*). However, this privilege comes with the ability to do so convincingly and lovingly, keeping in mind the social well-being and internal cohesion of the community. The apostolic authority is associated with a set of pedagogical qualities. Through divine wisdom, the apostle received 'the ability of discernment regarding worldly realities' (*per sapientiam in contemptum praesentium*). By grace, he received both the 'capacity for patience' (*gratiam ad laborum patientiam*) and the 'power of persuasion' regarding matters of importance (*gratiam in persuadendo ea quae persuadenda sunt*). These gifts are fundamental to sharing Scriptural and theological truth;[173] they express a deep concern for a conversational and caring approach to doctrinal instruction.

Christian authority and submission, teaching, and learning are two threads of a single fabric: the reception and dissemination of faith through grace. Some are called to apostolicity, others, through the apostolic work, to sainthood.[174] As one teaches the deep mysteries of faith, the other receives them as fundamental tenets for their own life. Both, however, are gifts of grace that ultimately depend on each other. William's pedagogy does not draw an exclusive distinction between authoritative figures and their disciples but interweaves these two threads designed to honor God. Rather than understanding apostolicity (representing the teacher) and sainthood (representing the student) as distinct responses to individual callings, both reflect the general human response to grace: an attitude of humility. In humility, the teacher and the student, the missionary and the convert, the apostle and the saint are connected both to one another and to God. This might sound like a poetic and somewhat abstract notion, but it is crucial to keep in mind that William develops it for his concrete context of monastic teaching and learning. Using Paul's exclamation of gratitude (*primum quidem gratias ago Deo meo*) as his exegetical basis, William describes in detail what he envisions a pedagogy of humility to look like:

---

173   Expositio super Epistolam ad Romanos (CCCM 86), Lib. I., linea 124.

174   Expositio super Epistolam ad Romanos (CCCM 86), Lib. I., linea 136: *Non primum uoca-tis sanctis et post|modum quasi pro sanctitate dilectis, sed primum gratuito dilectis et postmodum uocatis sanctis, uel etiam uocatis ut sancti sint, ut gratia sit gratia.*

Hence the psalmist says: worshipping, I invoke the Lord. Thus, the preacher of grace first thanks the one from whom all grace is expected and received; then and in due order follows the preaching of grace itself. What pleases the sovereign and good God in respect to our good is that God's gifts may be received not ungratefully, and God's goodness may be understood humbly and piously. What also pleases God is the sacrifice of fraternal love, expressed in the affect of the one who rejoices in his brother's progress towards God.[175]

While a *praedicator* could well be understood as a 'giver of sermons',[176] William generally talks here about someone sharing spiritual insight amongst brothers. This could include the traditional act of a sermon, lessons of any kind, and even individual intuition, as William's particularly monastic notion of education does not separate spiritual practice and intellectual knowledge. The type of knowledge that is to be pursued, and consequentially to be imparted on others, is knowledge of God, in the face of which love and intellect become one, requiring an equally 'holistic' method of pedagogy. This means that the student's and the teacher's attitudes towards their objects and the educational content itself have to harmonize: to teach and understand grace, one has to adopt a posture of gratitude.

In his humility and gratitude, Paul is the ideal personification of the Christian teacher. First, he demonstrates awareness that the knowledge he imparts to his students does not come from him but from God. Revealing his source of knowledge without concern for his vanity could be considered William's monastic version of 'academic integrity'. Second, Paul cares primarily about his students' spiritual progress: willing to sacrifice his authoritative status within the community, Paul delights in his pupils' educational success, sharing the gift of insight as freely as he had received. A pedagogy of humility, according to William, therefore, has to entail gratefulness, not only for one's knowledge but also for the progress of one's brothers.[177] If

---

175   Expositio super Epistolam ad Romanos (CCCM 86), Lib. I., linea 170: *Vnde psalmista: Laudans, inquit, inuocabo dominum; sic a praedicatore gratiae primo gratiae ei agantur, a quo gratia omnis speratur et accipitur deinde uero suo ordine gratia ipsa praedicetur. Placet enim summo et bono Deo in bonum nostrum in donis suis sensus accipientis non ingratus, et humilis ac pius intellectus diuinae bonitatis; placet ei multum de profectu fraterno ad Deum in affectu congratulantis fraternae sacrificium caritatis.*

176   *Praedicatio* and *sermo* can generally be understood as synonyms. (Teeuwen, "The Vocabulary of Intellectual Life in the Middle Ages. Vol. 10," 309).

177   Expositio super Epistolam ad Romanos (CCCM 86), Lib. I., linea 178: *Et sicut apud eum nullum peccatum maius deputatur quam gratiae eius esse ingratum, sic animo fideli et*

understood as an educational program, the attitude of humble gratitude ensures the continuation of doctrinal tradition.[178] Even more so, the concern for communal, rather than individual progress, accounts for an edifying mutuality that defines Christian relationships:

> Mutual edification of faith cannot be missing in either, for the students see in their master what they ought to imitate, and the master is encouraged by the students' progress to [pursue] even greater labors for the Gospel.[179]

Sharing knowledge, both ethical and intellectual, is a fundamentally reciprocal endeavor. As students grow and learn through *imitatio*, emulating their teacher's ways, the teacher, in turn, is encouraged by their progress to pursue an even higher degree of spiritual perfection. Witnessing the positive results of the student's efforts, the teacher is reassured in his aspirations and becomes even more eager in his pursuit.[180]

It becomes clear from his discussion of the apostolic task that William does not think of the acquisition and propagation of theological knowledge as a one-person operation. The individual believer is ever self-taught, no matter the degree of their spiritual insight. Christian teaching and learning are relational at their core: they derive their truth and authority from a relationship with their very source and flourish only in a community of mutual care. This allows conclusions to be drawn regarding William's self-conception, both as a teacher and a student of Christian thought. William's exegesis is not an abstract theological system but a literary reflection of communal living in Christ. Every insight he could claim for himself is therefore attributed primarily to God, and secondarily to the community that upholds God's grace and charity for one another.

---

      diuinarum fideliter assueto gratiarum, nil dulcius, nil iocundius est in profectu sui siue proximi ipsarum actione gratiarum.

178   Expositio super Epistolam ad Romanos (CCCM 86), Lib. I., linea 188: *Qui ergo gratus semper in his coram domino studet apparere, et in semetipso semper potiora dona accipere meretur, et dignus est et aptus etiam pro aliis interuenire.*

179   Expositio super Epistolam ad Romanos (CCCM 86), Lib. I., linea 288: *Nec enim deesse potest mutua ad alterutrum fidei aedificatio, cum et discipuli uident in magistro quod imitentur, et magister ex discipulorum profectu ad maiores pro euangelio labores animatur.*

180   Expositio super Epistolam ad Romanos (CCCM 86), Lib. I., linea 284: *Quos ergo apostolus ad perfectionis robur incitat, eis quae spiritus sunt impertiri praeoptat. Quod cum fit, et ipse accipit consolationem, opus suum in discipulorum profectu firmum uidens et stabile; et illi consolantur, qui participes fiunt apostolicae gratiae.*

William's ideal of Christian studies is inspired by his experiences of Cistercian monastic living, with its dynamic interplay of structural discipline and personal obedience. In contrast, he does not seem to reference his experience in Reims and the common pedagogical system of the Cathedral schools. William's disagreement with the methods of exegesis taught in the intellectual environments of the schools is mirrored, therefore, in a fundamentally different understanding of the objectives and parameters of education. The role of the Christian teacher, drawn from the apostolic ideal reflected in the person and work of Paul, is, for William, not a primarily intellectual one but entails responsibility for the student's spiritual well-being. This observation, however, begs the question of the general role William attributes to human intellect. Theological reflection and Scriptural study are, as we will see, embedded not only in the community of believers but also in an epistemological framework of humility. I will now turn to *humilitas* as an intellectual concept and central theme of the *Expositio*.

7   *Humilitas* and the Ideal Reader

As we have just seen, William conceptualizes his role as an author and thinker in a close relationship with his spiritual teachers. As they have, he strives to let his work be inspired by the Holy Spirit and thus in line with Christian orthodoxy. He did not merely consider the Church Fathers teachers and role models in such a concrete way but also the biblical authors themselves. Like many authors of his time, William did not explicitly differentiate between the text of the New Testament and early Patristic literature.[181] In the canon of both Patristic and biblical authors, the figure of Paul takes on a most prominent and exemplary role for William. Particularly in regards to the *Expositio*, Paul functions as William's spiritual and ethical teacher par excellence. William attempts to understand the Epistle's message through the lens of the Pauline faith. On a literary level, William frames Romans as Paul's faith journey. William's Commentary consequentially follows and retraces the stages of ascent displayed in Paul's Epistle. William and his readers are called to join Paul's spiritual path and experience it themselves.

---

181   This understanding was very common during the 10th to 12th century (Riché and Lobrichon, Le Moyen Âge et la Bible, 180).

William starts with an interpretation of the Epistle's first words: Paul's self-identification as the letter's author. *Paulus servus Christi Iesu* – Paul, a servant of Christ; a textual starting point that simultaneously corresponds to the beginning of the human journey towards God that William intends to discuss. Paul's biography itself exemplifies the redemption narrative that lies at the core of William's notion of human development. Once known as Saul, the persecutor of early Christians, the biblical author had experienced an encounter with divine grace that resulted in a change of name and, more importantly, a change of heart. Subsequently calling himself Paul, he became one of the first apostles of Christian history. To William, this personal experience of redemption symbolizes the juxtaposition of 'the humble' and 'the proud' within a single lifetime. It enables him to identify the characteristics of these two human states and explicate them as responses to divine intervention. Saul and Paul correspond to the presence of *superbia* and *humilitas* in the human soul. Starting with this biographical experience enables William to place himself and his readers alongside Saul and recreate the lowest spiritual state of humanity, which still awaits the redeeming action of grace.

William structures his reconstruction of spiritual growth in an Augustinian sense according to the three of the four human stages (*gradus*): *ante legem, sub lege*, and *sub gratia*.[182] Since William defines and articulates these stages only occasionally rather than systematically and consistently throughout the work, it is unclear whether Saul's state corresponds to the first state, *ante legem*. Although the literary structure he employs would suggest so, it seems unlikely that William, given his awareness of Saul's Jewish identity, would attribute to him a state 'before the law'. Rather, Saul's preredemptive state seems to be associated with the second *gradus* (*sub lege*). This could either mean that the first and the second state are closely connected on a conceptual level and that the second state could still be considered a part of the initial phase of human ascent. One could argue for such an assumption mainly because both the first and the second state lack the activity of and reliance on divine grace. Suppose one were to take the distinction of states seriously. In that case, however, the localization of Saul's soul *sub lege*, rather than *ante legem*, could suggest that his Jewish background provided him with a different spiritual starting point:

---

182   James Wetzel, "The Recovery of Free Agency in the Theology of St. Augustine," The Harvard Theological Review 80, no. 1 (1987): 108.

Living according to the flesh in the deepest shadows of ignorance with-out any resistance of reason, that is the first human state. Then, after the law creates awareness of sin, but the divine Spirit has not yet come to aid, one who desires to live according to the law is convicted and commits sin knowingly. The knowledge of committing sin causes con-cupiscence in humankind. A great number of transgressions are added according to what is written: the law was brought in so that the tres-pass might increase. This is the second human state.[183]

In this account, unlike the first, the second state performs a specific purpose for spiritual advancement. William's understanding of the law's function, es-pecially if it is considered an instrument that precedes the intervention of grace, resembles the *usus elenchticus legis*, as Luther had later explicated it in response to the Pauline theology. Here too, it is the human knowledge of the law that reveals the true extent of sinful desire; the law ensures human awareness of sin as a conscious and yet unavoidable act. The second stage, within William's framework, is, therefore, a necessary degree within the spiritual progression he believes Paul to have undergone.

Further, William associates *superbia*, the sin he most strongly identifies with the figure of Saul, not with the 'flesh', but rather with the illusion of security that stems from subjection to the law. This becomes apparent in his reading of Romans 2:17–20, in which he understands Paul's specific ad-dress to the Jewish Christians of Rome as an admonition against idle boast of the law:

What is more futile than boasting about what one does not have or preaching about what one does not do? This people languishes in the second state of the people of God, meaning according to the Law, and takes pride in what it has received without it having been accom-plished according to the flesh.[184]

---

183   Expositio super Epistolam ad Romanos (CCCM 86), Lib. II, linea 86–93: *Cum enim in altissimis ignorantiae tenebris nulla resistente ratione secundum carnem uiuitur, haec sunt prima hominis. Deinde cum per legem cognitio fuerit facta peccati, si nondum diui-nus adiuuat spiritus, secundum legem uolens uiuere, uincitur, et sciens peccat, id agente scientia peccati, ut peccatum operetur in homine omnem concupiscentiam, et cumulo praeuaricationis adiecto impleatur quod scriptum est: Lex subintrauit, ut abundaret de-lictum. Haec sunt secunda hominis.*

184   Expositio super Epistolam ad Romanos (CCCM 86), Lib. II, linea 135–136: *Quid enim tam inane quam iactare quod non habet, quod non facit praedicare? Languebat quippe populus ille circa secunda populi Dei, id est circa legem, de qua accepta superbiebat, nec tamen implebat eam uel carnaliter [...].*

Here, William draws a clear analogy between the Jewish converts, a group
Paul both addresses and belongs to, and the notion of religious *superbia*.
The Jewish people are identified in this passage with the 'second kind of the
people of God' (*languebat ... circa secunda populi Dei*), that is, the second
stage of humanity. William concludes that the assurance of the law entices
those who had previously received it to assume their spiritual superiority.
Relying on the redeeming ability of the law – misjudging the human inability to show obedience to it – is an expression of self-deceiving pride and
creates (or maintains) a distance between God and the human souls in
question. William notes the Pauline use of irony in this passage as a rhetorical device to humiliate the Jewish Christians he addresses.[185] While he acknowledges Paul's criticism of the 'pagan Christians' and discusses it at
length, humiliation is unique to his treatment of Jewish religiosity. The sins
Paul detects in the *pagani* are, according to William, best dealt with in the
form of a stern reproach or through the instilling of discipline. He attributes
the first human state (*secundum priorem statum*) to the concrete transgressions of 'pagan Christians' before they biographically came to know the
Judeo–Christian law. It is their 'Godless past' that is humiliation enough.[186]
The conjunction of *superbia* with the second stage of humanity *sub lege*,
however, demands both literary and veritable humiliation.[187] In the Epistle
to the Romans, Paul assumes this task as his own. In the case of Saul, however, it was God who had taken on the role of the *humiliator*.

Divine grace and the act of humiliation are seldom associated with one
another in the context of modern spirituality. Yet for William, and as he
understands, for Paul, grace operates within a believer according to their
nature. Thus, a different kind of human need reveals a different sort of gracious activity. Grace acts not as a general and abstract principle but aids the
progress of the individual believer by concretely entering their specific

---

185   Expositio super Epistolam ad Romanos (CCCM 86), Lib. II, linea 131: *Sciendum est
      omnia, quae hic quasi in laudem falsi Iudaei proferuntur, per ironiam prolata.*

186   Expositio super Epistolam ad Romanos (CCCM 86), Lib. I., linea 758: *Doctor egregius et
      mirae in euangelio prudentiae, et qui omnibus omnia fieri nouerat, gentium apostolus,
      ministerium suum semper sollicitus et aedificare et honorificare, postquam satis partem
      gentium secundum priorem statum depressit et humiliauit* [...].

187   Expositio super Epistolam ad Romanos (CCCM 86), Lib. VI., linea 597–600: *Cum enim
      peruigilem curam et iugem sollicitudinem erga doctrinam gentium apostolus gerebat et
      conuersationem earum probabilem exhibebat, uidentes hoc Israelitas ad aemulationem
      proficientium prouocabat.*
          *Et haec erat magna ministerii eius glorificatio: alterum per profectum alterius susci-
      tare ad profectum.*

situation. While the humble require divine reassurance and delight, the proud require humiliation that would remove the element of pride standing in the way of their spiritual advancement.[188] This is also the narrative William retraces within the Pauline biography. Saul's humiliation is framed as a divine act of mercy:

> You have humbled him like a wounded proud one, and with the arm of your force and the breath of your grace, you have made Paul out of Saul; the young Benjamin who, in a rapture of the spirit, penetrates the heavens and in God's paradise hears the mysterious words that a human may not speak; once a ravenous wolf he divides his prey in the evening.[189]

Pride is described here in terms of a wound that requires healing. Only in the wake of his healing does Paul receive insight into the divine mysteries. This is an essential passage, as it shows how humiliation is required, not only for spiritual progression as such but also for any human knowledge. Especially knowledge of God, which William closely links to a more affective human-divine relationship, is reserved for the humbled. Paul's identity as an apostle, who can speak from a place of divine authority and teach Christian truth, is grounded in his embrace of human lowliness.

Paul's internal experience is evidenced externally by his name change. William, falling back on a traditional Hebrew etymology, traces it back to Augustine. As he often does in his Commentary on the Song of Songs, he uses etymological insight to corroborate his interpretation. According to Augustine, the name Paul signifies puniness, humility, and composure (*quasi paululus humilis ac quietus*), a name, William states, which Paul had assumed to mark the significant shift of identity he had experienced.[190] The addition *Servus Christi Iesu* – with which Paul introduces himself to his audience – functions further as an explication of this name. It explains not only Paul's status as a *servus*, a designation epitomizing humility but also whom he serves.

---

188 Expositio super Epistolam ad Romanos (CCCM 86), Praef., linea 54.
189 Expositio super Epistolam ad Romanos (CCCM 86), Lib. 1., linea 6: *Tu enim humiliasti eum sicut uulneratum superbum et in brachio uirtutis tuae et spiritu gratiae tuae de Saulo fecisti Paulum, Beniamin adolescentulum in mentis excessu caelos penetrantem et in paradiso Dei audientem uerba arcana, quae non licet homini loqui*; lupum olim rapacem, sed ad uesperum praedam diuidentem [Gen 48,27].
190 Expositio super Epistolam ad Romanos (CCCM 86), Lib. 1., linea 15.

William displays yet again an impressive awareness of the Roman social context. As was the case in his reiteration of the Horatian image of the callow crow, William subverts classic Roman vices into Christian virtues. It seems as though William understands the significance of Paul's choice to self-identify as a *servus*, the lowest stratum of Roman society. A slave within the Roman system was exempt from citizenship and belonged to a class without rights. This attribution stands in juxtaposition to Saul's former social identity as the proconsul of Asia. Precisely this juxtaposition is reversed when viewed through the perspective of divine grace. Under the light yoke of Christ (*sub leve iugum tuum*), the identity of the slave receives its glory. More so, in explicit reference to the Roman system, the *servus Christi* becomes a proper citizen of the Kingdom of God (*regni tui provincialis*). Not the attitude of subordination alone, but subordination to Christ, constituting a change in 'allegiance', marks the subversive turn from Saul to Paul.[191]

As an ideal personification of humility, Paul does not only serve as an ethical ideal for William but as an intellectual one.[192] *Humilitas*, I will suggest in the following, is the core of William's distinction between appropriate and inappropriate and consequentially fruitful and futile intellectual endeavors. His *Expositio* presents a normative example of a faithful human quest for divine truth. Reflecting the principle he set up in his *lectio divina*, William stresses the importance of the human disposition to receive insight into divine truth. Humility lies thus at the center of his anthropology and concept of divine intelligibility. It becomes an epistemological category.[193]

---

191   Expositio super Epistolam ad Romanos (CCCM 86), Lib. 1., linea 27–31: *Seruitutis huius professio et humilitatis est, et gloriae, et auctoritatis eximiae, cum se seruum eius quasi gloriabundus profitetur, qui dicit: Magnum est tibi uocari seruum meum, cui, sicut ipse dicit, seruiebat in euangelio Filii eius. Christi Iesu.*

192   William also refers to the common medieval image association of humility with the figure of David, juxtaposing David's trust in divine support with Goliath's pride and self-confidence (Expositio super Epistolam ad Romanos (CCCM 86), Lib. 1., linea 230–231). He does so, however, merely in passing, while discussing the Pauline *humilitas* at length, exemplifying his exegetical ideal of reading the biblical text through the lens of their author.

193   In doing so, William is aligned with conceptions of learning present in the Early Middle Ages as Sita Steckel characterizes them: "Early medieval concepts of teaching emphasized the acquisition of religious virtues such as humility and piety, which were understood as prerequisites enabling the student to attain divine inspiration, and hence to understand scripture. But the presence of divine inspiration was imagined as momentary, or at least as contingent – it could not be learned or acquired as a permanent skill. Inspiration thus depended on a scholar's continued humble submission to Christian norms and values" (Steckel, "Charisma and Expertise," 663).

For these purposes, William establishes an elaborate distinction between 'natural knowledge' and 'humble knowledge'.

Acquiring natural knowledge, though possible to a certain degree, dismisses its divine source, and will eventually flounder in the face of its purpose. On the other hand, the pursuit of humble knowledge bases its methodology and intent on the acceptance of divine grace as both the origin and substance of insight. Instructing his readers to follow the model of a humble Christian thinker, as he finds it discussed and represented in the Pauline Epistle, William contrasts *superbia* and *humilitas* as opposing motives of readership. As he finds both kinds of readership represented in the present time and throughout the history of human thought, he illustrates the distinction according to the 'philosophers of this world' (*philosophi huius mundi*):[194]

> They have searched for God whom they should seek in humble piety through proud curiosity. They thought they could find the one who can only be found in the kingdom of charity and on the luminous throne of wisdom in the region of reason and in the secret of an esoteric science instead. Wisdom is not found through haughty loquaciousness but in the perfect charity of a pure heart, a good conscience, and faith without deceit.[195]

According to William, the philosophers' primary fault is not logical inconsistency in their teachings but their lack of humility.[196] The human thirst for knowledge stems either from humble piety (*humilis pietas*) – a genuine love for God and a subsequent desire for deeper understanding – or it contains an ulterior motive: proud curiosity (*superba curiositas*). Once the latter is the case, any intellectual project is bound to fail, no matter its logical clarity or dialectical complexity. Curiosity will ensnare the mind to look for God in

---

194   Expositio super Epistolam ad Romanos (CCCM 86), Lib. 1., linea 491. This term stands in the context of Rm 1,18–19. William here identifies the *philosophi huius mundi* as the objects of divine wrath (*ira Dei*), which Paul addresses in the pericope at hand.

195   Expositio super Epistolam ad Romanos (CCCM 86), Lib. 1., linea 542: *Quaesierunt Deum superba curiositate, quem quaerere debuerunt humili pietate, inueniendum arbitrantes in regione rationis, et recessu occultioris scientiae, qui non inuenitur nisi in regno caritatis et lucidissima sede sapientiae: sapientiae autem, non in loquacitate uentosa, sed in caritate perfecta, de corde puro et conscientia bona, et fide non ficta.*

196   Expositio super Epistolam ad Romanos (CCCM 86), Lib. 1., linea 541: *Quaesierunt uiam, sed eam perdiderunt, quia humiles esse noluerunt.*

the world of reason and within the depths of 'esoteric science' (*occultioris scientiae*) and therefore prohibit the mind from encountering the one who reveals Godself only in charity and wisdom. This argument is, however, more complex than it might seem at first sight and deserves a closer analysis.

William does not deny the possibility of intellectual insight outside the confines of a Christian moral framework. He has to acknowledge both the existence and value of natural knowledge, as he conceptualizes human reason as a divine gift to humanity. All human beings, albeit to different degrees, are not only capable of simple perception but of 'highest intelligence' (*rationem sublimioris intelligentiae capacem*).[197] This ability is deemed natural because it is not dependent on any decisions and intentions but is an ontological part of humanity. While the conceptual emphasis lies on the human rather than divine nature, it remains implicit that God bestows the capacity for natural knowledge.

This understanding allows William to praise the 'philosophers of this world' for their vast knowledge and brilliant genius (*magni studii, praeclari ingenii*)[198] without endorsing their lifestyles or faith. William does not name any of the authors he has in mind. Still, he does quote their reverence of Platonic thought, allowing the conclusion that he speaks of classic 'pagan' philosophers and contemporary thinkers alike, potentially even including Christian thinkers in his address.[199]

Acknowledging their gifts of reason, William admits that the accuracy of their more basic theological statements is undeniable, even from a distinctly Christian perspective. He declares, for instance, that it is entirely possible, through reason, to come to a series of conclusions regarding the nature of God and the world:

> They could see that God is eternal life, immutable, intelligible, intelligent, wise, and creating wisdom; irrevocable, stable, and never decaying truth; in whom everything was made that lives; in whom are all

---

197   Expositio super Epistolam ad Romanos (CCCM 86), Lib. 1., linea 580.
198   Expositio super Epistolam ad Romanos (CCCM 86), Lib. 1., linea 491.
199   Expositio super Epistolam ad Romanos (CCCM 86), Lib. 1., linea 550: *Vnde egregius eorum Plato: "Fugiendum, inquit, est ad clarissimam patriam, ubi Deus Pater est, et lucida ueritas"*. It is most likely that William received this Platonic thought through Augustine, himself quoting this statement in Civ. Dei 9,17, apparently from Plotinus' Enneads, who in turn cited from Plato's Theaetetus 176 A–B (see Déchanet, *Aux sources de la spiritualité de Guillaume*, 141–145).

the reasons of the things and creatures established for eternity or for a certain time.[200]

This catalog of theological principles seems impressive in volume and could thus easily be read as an appreciation of the contributions of Hellenistic philosophy to the foundations of Christian thought. This positive acknowledgment of such propositions and their methodological introduction into theological systems would be representative of the increasing theological reception of 'pagan' philosophy. Yet, William's approach to these statements is not that of enthusiastic implementation into his thought, but is instead, without dismissing their metaphysical truth-value, critical in nature. His rhetorical choice to list these distinct concepts without any further explanation or structure but merely in the form of a simple, summarizing catalog is deliberate: as examples of natural knowledge, these propositions are almost banal.[201] The complexity of philosophical reflection might seem impressive. Still, mere intellectual prowess is little to boast about, or as William puts it: *digni utique laude, si non eos iuste percuteret sermo ille propheticus: Accinxi te, et non cognovisti me.*[202] Even the highest insight achieved by reason alone will fail to recognize God's true essence. Although a basic understanding of divine attributes is possible even for a mind distant from God, the desire to be close to God is necessary to recognize God as Lord. In other words, while philosophic insight might be objectively accurate, it lacks the subjective component that constitutes truth in a mystic sense.

The main transgression of such worldly sages, as William characterizes them, is not intellectual but moral. Their curiosity has led them to some astonishing insights, yet they did not receive them with gratitude and glorification:

---

200 Expositio super Epistolam ad Romanos (CCCM 86), Lib. 1., linea 495: *Potuerunt etenim uidere Deum esse quamdam uitam aeternam, immutabilem, intelligibilem, intelligentem, sapientem et sapientes facientem, ueritatem fixam, stantem, indeclinabilem, ubi quod factum est uita est, ubi omnes rationes rerum et creaturarum sunt aeternaliter dispositarum uel euntium temporaliter.*

201 Expositio super Epistolam ad Romanos (CCCM 86), Lib. 1., linea 566: *Veritas Dei apud homines, vera et naturalis divinitatis cognition est, scilicet vere Deum esse; et curare res humanas, regere ac disponere quaecumque creatvit, ipsum qui creavit. Quod nulli homini dubium esse potest, penes quem ratio humana est, maximeque illis hominibus, quorum prefessio erat philosophia, quae rerum humanarum ac divinarum scientia est.*

202 Expositio super Epistolam ad Romanos (CCCM 86), Lib. 1., linea 491.

These people thank and glorify God through their knowledge of God. The wise of that age, as the Apostle says, had not done that: they have become vain in their reasonings. Calling themselves wise according to their efforts, they have been abandoned by grace, rejected from knowledge of God, and their foolish hearts have darkened; as it is said, they have lost on account of their vanity what they had received on account of their curiosity.[203]

Throughout his work, William understands pride, particularly intellectual pride, as a misattribution of insight to the human mind rather than divine grace.[204] Pride is primarily the belief that one is wise by virtue of one's mental capacity.[205] Such an attitude would ultimately result in an atheistic utterance, refusing not only the divine contribution in one's works but the existence of God entirely.[206] This failure to show reverence to the divine source of knowledge, in turn, renders the thus misconceived understanding unserviceable: following Romans 1:22, William associates *superbia* with *stultitia* and therefore dismisses the insight of the proud as 'folly'.[207] Nothing worthwhile could spring from the fount (*fons*) of hybris. A 'contaminated river' (*pestifer fluvius*) flows from it, of which the monks – William warns – ought to beware.[208] The idolatrous attitude of pride, which leads to a host

---

203 Expositio super Epistolam ad Romanos (cccm 86), Lib. 1., linea 624–625: *Et ipsi sunt qui cum cognouerint Deum, gratias agunt ei, et glorificant eum. Quod quia non fecerunt sapientes huius saeculi, de quibus ait apostolus: Sed euanuerunt in cogitationibus suis, dicentes semetipsos a semetipsis sapientes esse, a gratia deserti, et a facie cognitionis Dei proiecti sunt, et obscuratum est insipiens cor eorum; et, sicut iam dictum est, uanitate | perdiderunt idipsum quod curiositate didicerunt.*

204 He defines the notion for instance in his reading of Rm 9,22–24 and its parable of the two kinds of vases: *Sustinuit in multa patientia uasa irae apta in interitum, non quod illi essent necessaria siue angelica, siue humana peccata, cui nec iustitia cuiusquam est necessaria, sed ut notas faceret diuitias gloriae suae in uasa misericordiae, ne se in bonis operibus tamquam de propriis extollerent uiribus, sed humiliter intelligerent, nisi illis Dei gratia non debita sed gratuita subueniret, id fuisse reddendum meritis suis quod aliis in eadem massa redditum cernerent.* (Expositio super Epistolam ad Romanos (cccm 86), Lib. vi., linea 21).

205 Expositio super Epistolam ad Romanos (cccm 86), Lib. 1., linea 454: *Superbi enim facti sunt, dicentes se esse sapientes.*

206 Expositio super Epistolam ad Romanos (cccm 86), Lib. 1., linea 630: *In tantum quippe stulti facti sunt et insipientes, ut dicerent in corde suo, in corde fatuo et penitus a gratia derelict: Non est Deus; [...].*

207 Expositio super Epistolam ad Romanos (cccm 86), Lib. 1., linea 742: *Sorores quippe sunt indiuiduae stultitia et superbia, nisi quod tanto tolerabilior est stultitia, quanto nonnumquam sine superbia inuenitur; superbia uero numquam est sine stultitia.*

208 Expositio super Epistolam ad Romanos (cccm 86), Lib. 1., linea 719.

of sins and eventually an irreconcilable distance between the soul and God, requires a virtuous remedy: the return to humble faith.

Although William often discusses *superbia*, or the lack of faith (*infidelis*),[209] in either the Jewish or the Pagan context, his concept of faith and humility is not as preoccupied with external religious affiliation as with an internal attitude of the heart. Faith, for William, is less about social affiliation or public proclamation and more about an intimate relationship with God. Similarly, the kind of humility he has in mind does not derive its worth from public displays of poverty or grandiose religious gestures. A definition that places faith into the setting of personal spirituality rather than outwardly expressed religiosity is especially noteworthy in the context of 12th-century monasticism. While his exegesis indeed entails the themes of hierarchically imposed discipline, and even physical practice, as necessary aspects of a monk's practice, religious exertion is always secondary to the inward experience. William's introduction of *humilitas* into his concept of faith and knowledge is, therefore, not to be understood as a mere attempt to instruct his readers in asceticism. Humility is an inner response to the personal experience of divine grace, and hence precisely not a means to garner divine favor. William seems to be aware of this danger, as he warns his readers explicitly against taking the practice of humility too far:

> Just as the doctor of the church must be careful not to deter his audience with any semblance of pride, he should also not degrade the word of God in his mouth through too great a self-humiliation. This is why Samuel has said that he was sought out by all because the word of God is precious.[210]

The primary objective of a humble life is not the degradation of humanity but the glorification of God. Thus, if humility is to play a role in the pursuit and propagation of theological knowledge, the preciousness of God's word cannot be compromised by the self-abasement of those who proclaim it. In other words, the human soul ought not to claim her lowliness without simultaneously emphasizing God's reconciling work in her. While achieving a state of humility requires the human soul to subject herself, as

---

209   Expositio super Epistolam ad Romanos (CCCM 86), Lib. VI., linea 696.
210   Expositio super Epistolam ad Romanos (CCCM 86), Lib. VII., linea 968–969: *Doctori enim ecclesiae, sicut omnimodis cauendum est ne qua superbiae similitudine auditores a se deterreat, sic etiam ne nimia humilitatis remissione uerbum Dei in ore eius uilescat. Vnde de Samuele dicitur, cum ab omnibus requireretur, quia erat sermo domini pretiosus.*

the above-mentioned passages on the process of humiliation have shown, this subjection is never an end in itself but merely a necessary step in the process of ascent. Displaying humility for humility's sake would be an expression of *superbia*, for it would simply reveal the individual's reverence for human standards of ethical behavior, a danger especially prevalent in monastic communities that stress the importance of discipline. William's theology explicitly rejects meaningless religious routines as vain misconceptions of faith. True *humilitas* should reflect the desire to align the human will with God's, sometimes even at the expense of human morals or values. Virtues are only virtues if they are expressions of unconditional obedience, not to a set of worldly rules (even of the monastic kind) but to God.[211]

The inherent ambivalence of humility as a virtue poses a problem for most monastic authors. While humility is central to the tradition of Christian monasticism, its practical history has brought forth many perversions of the concept itself. Boasting about one's degree of humility defies the meaning of the term. Great monastic minds had always been aware of this spiritually dangerous irony, as they usually witnessed it occurring in the communities for which they were responsible. Later mystics, like Meister Eckhart, had developed the notions of *Gelassenheit* or *Abgeschiedenheit* to counter the two-edged implications of humility. The soul ought to let go, not only of worldly attachment but essentially of herself and any concern for her salvation.[212] Only in total *Abgeschiedenheit* can one overcome the last traces of *superbia*. However, this concept is not yet present in William's theological approach. To prevent the abuse of humility, he develops a distinctly affective concept based on the Augustinian notion of image-likeness.[213]

---

211 Expositio super Epistolam ad Romanos (CCCM 86), Lib. VII., linea 236.

212 View on the theme of Gelassenheit: Enders, Markus. *Gelassenheit Und Abgeschiedenheit: Studien Zur Deutschen Mystik*. Schriftenreihe Boethiana, Bd. 82. Hamburg: Kovač, 2008, and Wohlfart, Günter. "Gelassenheit: Die Mystische Intuition Als Moment Religiöser Und Ästhetischer Erfahrung." *Zeitschrift Für Religions– Und Geistesgeschichte* 42, no. 4 (1990): 353–364.

213 I have adopted the term 'image–likeness' from Nicholas Groves' study on the links between William of St. Thierry's Golden Epistle and the teachings of the tathagatagarbha (Nicholas Groves, "Image–Likeness and 'Tathāgatagarbha': A Reading of William of St. Thierry's 'Golden Epistle' and the 'Ratnagotravibhāga,'" *Buddhist–Christian Studies* 10 (1990)). Most secondary sources use the two Augustinian notions of image (*imago*) and likeness (*similitudo*) separately or as a conjunction, while Groves' coinage expresses accurately William's concern of a single, representative attitude.

As I have discussed, William differentiates between natural and humble knowledge, or in other words, between intellectual pursuits he believes rooted in pride and his ideal of a pious quest for God. The distinction centers on the question: *where* does the human mind attempt to find God? In a passage discussed above, William accuses the philosophers of this world of looking for God in the land of reason (*regio rationis*), a venture he believes to be doomed to fail from the start. He chooses the term region deliberately, alluding to the biblical theme of the 'foreign land'. He had already employed it in his *De natura corporis et animae* (§118).[214] In his reading of Genesis 4:16, he identifies the *terra Naim* (actually referencing the foreign land of Nod, where Cain flees to) as the *regio dissimilitudinis*. The latter term is a reference to the Platonic notion of *dissemblance*. It is not until his *Expositio* – with its critique of worldly philosophy – that he connects the 'land of dissemblance' to the idea of a misguided intellectual quest into the 'land of reason'. Quoting their own 'egregious Plato' (*egregius eorum Plato*),[215] William reveals what he believes to be the fundamental methodological (and moral) misunderstanding of those who believe to be pursuing the theological task in a philosophical sense:

> 'One has to flee towards the home of all clarity, where God the Father and the luminous truth can be found.' What is this fleet? What is this flight? Resemblance.[216]

The passage poses some difficulty to understand, as it requires the reader to connect the otherwise opposing concepts of flight (*fuga*) and homeland (*patria*). However, read in the context of William's intellectual critique, his associations become more evident. The human soul ought to flee from the foreign land – the *regio dissimilitudinis* – to return to her native country, the region of likeness. William receives this Platonic thought from Augustine's theology of human likeness to the divine and therefore uses it in an Augustinian fashion: only as we progress to a state of likeness and allow God to restore the *imago Dei* within us does knowledge of God become possible.[217]

---

214 Verdeyen, Paul, ed. *Guillelmi a Sancto Theodorico Opera Omnia, Iii: De Natura Corporis et Animae*. Corpus Christianorum Continuatio Mediaevalis 88. Turnhout: Brepols, 2003.
215 Expositio super Epistolam ad Romanos (CCCM 86), Lib. 1., linea 550.
216 Expositio super Epistolam ad Romanos (CCCM 86), Lib. 1., linea 550.
217 William's proper theology of image-likeness will be the main subject of the later chapter "5.3. 'Know Thyself'. William's spiritual anthropology and his understanding of

William unfolds his theology of the image-likeness most fully in his *Golden Epistle*.[218] The concept he develops there is analogous to his under-standing of humility in the *Expositio*, seeing that William understands like-ness primarily as a subjection of the human to the divine will. The obedient soul delights in that in which God delights. She strives toward sainthood, not as humanity defines it, but as God displays it.[219] Even though the corpo-rality of the temporal life still constricts her, she desires to liken herself, her *memoria*, her intelligence, and her love to the divine nature.[220] In the *Expo-sitio*, William uses the theme of dissemblance as a negative foil, warning his readers that knowledge is only possible from a place of spiritual closeness to God. Within this framework, *superbia* is no longer the mere unfavorable character trait of arrogance but instead the factor that, metaphysically, cre-ates distance between the soul and God. Pride is what holds humanity 'cap-tive' in her sinful state. Humility, on the other hand, is what frees the soul and leads her back home (*nec in aliena abducti sunt*);[221] humility guides the soul to God. As such – as the facilitator of human-divine intimacy and not as an ascetic practice – *humilitas* is the foundation of William's intellectual program and his self-conception as a Christian thinker.

8   Interim Conclusion

These considerations on the *Expositio* have provided us with some signifi-cant insights into William's understanding of readership and authorship. First, William understands his theological reflection not as an intellectual exercise but as a literary extension of his devotional practice. He presents his exegesis as primarily spiritual work.[222] As the monastic community is the central setting of medieval spirituality, the social aspect is also signifi-cant to William's literary endeavor. Reading Scripture is never an activity individuals can do in isolation, by and for themselves. William's dialogue with past and present authorities provides him with the necessary doctrinal insight to ensure the orthodoxy he believes to be vital for the communal

---

image-likeness" that discusses the concept in relation to William's reading of the Song of Songs.

218   I will devote an entire chapter to the application of the theme in the Golden Epistle in the chapter "7.4. Concepts applied: The monk's image-likeness".

219   Epistola ad Fratres de Monte Dei (cccm 88), Liber ii., par. 209.

220   Epistola ad Fratres de Monte Dei (cccm 88), Liber ii., par. 242.

221   Expositio super Epistolam ad Romanos (cccm 86), Praef., linea 54.

222   Verdeyen, "Introduction" in *Exposé Sur l'Épitre aux Romains*, 17.

life; his sense of responsibility as an Abbot towards his brothers introduces a sense of pedagogical concern into his project and, ultimately, his intimate relationship with God is the foundation for his thought. His theology is thus deeply relational, and his close relationships make his perspective one that is determined by a dynamic interplay of activity and passivity. Rather than separating his literary from his pastoral task, William displays a more holistic approach, as he directs all of his efforts toward the spiritual progress and wellbeing of the Cistercian community, to which he is entirely devoted. The guiding virtue of humility, therefore, guarantees social cohesion and monastic discipline on the one hand but also contributes significantly to the success of William's exegetical venture.

CHAPTER 2

Authority as a Tool and Topic in William's Conflicts

Now that we have established a sense of William's ideals regarding Christian authorship, it will be of value for our present study to analyze how William applied his theoretical concept over and against other contemporary notions of the theological task. This is, of course, best exemplified in the context of William's most prolific conflict concerning the theology of Peter Abelard. Every modern discussion of their dispute must first disclose that it is nearly impossible to avoid all the clichés and preconceived categorizations accompanying its historiography. Given both authors' respective forces of conviction that had made it seem as though their visions for the Christian life opposed each other, it is tempting to paint them as the proponents of a 'conservative, fideistic' monasticism on the one hand and an innovative, modern scholasticism on the other.[1] While such a characterization is undoubtedly too simplistic to be accurate, William and Abelard indeed function as defenders of different ideals. In the following analysis, I will discuss their differences in methodology and purpose and the points of contention that led to William's letter of accusations against Abelard. To this degree, notions of a monastic and scholastic opposition might act as intentional exaggerations to clarify the authors' respective standpoints.[2] However, appropriate classification of any observations made throughout the analysis will be indispensable.

Based on my previous discussion of William's *Expositio*, I will first offer a comparative reading of Abelard's Commentary on Romans and attempt to extract its notions regarding the role of the Christian exegete. This will entail specific considerations of its methodologies and relationships with

---

1   Sweeney, "Rewriting the Narrative of Scripture," 2.
2   The benefit of such blanket terms has been explained for instance by Thomas Renna, who stated that "[w]hile no two historians agree on definitions of monastic and scholastic – their chronology, content, or procedure – this typology can be useful in detecting shifts in fundamental attitudes in Christian Europe, including its ecclesiology." (Thomas J. Renna, "The Idea of Jerusalem: Monastic to Scholastic," in *From Cloister to Classroom. Monastic and Scholastic Approaches to Truth*, The Spirituality of Western Christendom III, ed. Rozanne Elder, Cistercian Studies 64 (Kalamazoo, MI: Cistercian Publications, 1986), 96).

Patristic and philosophic authorities. Understanding their diverging approaches to authorship will provide a necessary background for a closer analysis of the historical conflict leading up to the condemnation of Abelard at the Council of Sens in 1141. William's *Disputatio adversus Petrum Abaelardum* will function as the chapter's primary source, as it ideally demonstrates how William employs Patristic sources and their authoritative status to establish his claim to orthodoxy. It will prove fruitful to take a closer look at William's stakes in the dispute and the doctrinal and spiritual concerns that led him to alert Bernard in the first place to better grasp the original motives behind the conflict.

It is not the aim of this chapter, nor could it be, to give an exhaustive account of how William's accusations correspond to the reality of Abelard's claims or to provide a fair defense of Abelard's thought. Instead, the focus lies distinctly on William's perception of his adversary. This will necessarily amount to a one-sided account of the conflict, which should be interpreted neither as a normative judgment of Abelard's theology nor as an uncritical endorsement of William's position. The chapter will allow us to comprehend these authors' particular concerns and forays without assessing their validity. This is especially the case, as William reveals in his rejection of the Abelardian *theologia* a general distaste for the 'theological task' and, by implication, his hopes for the future of Christian thought. Standing at the cusp of the scholastic era, William's contestation of Abelard's approach represents the Cistercian stance on intellectuality quite well. What this distinctly Cistercian perspective entails is highlighted best through what it repudiates; the person and work of Peter Abelard exemplify the latter most impressively.

1   Reading Romans from Two Perspectives

Abelard's Commentary on Romans might be a less conspicuous representation of his innovative methodology if we compare it, for instance, to his epochal *Sic et Non. Yet*, there is ample reason to examine the work, as it differs from William's commentary of the same title in literary purpose and exegetical approach. First, the authors had turned to Romans simultaneously, albeit independently. Both commentaries were written around 1139 in the same cultural climate of the Reims region.[3] The dating of Abelard's

---

3 Jean Doutre suggests the two works were both written between 1133 and 1139 (Doutre, "Romans as Read in School and Cloister," 33). While this period might mark the lengthy

commentary depends heavily on the fact that William had made explicit use of the work in his *Disputatio*, which in turn was written around 1140, necessitating Abelard's work to be written prior.[4] Abelard's *Expositio* provides the basis for the doctrinal and methodological accusations that William and Bernard later raised against him, which is vital to an understanding of the dispute. In the light of this later application, William's commentary gains an additional dimension, as it allows us to retrace the kind of exegetical approach William would have hoped to see in his contemporaries; not only do we have his negative critique of Abelardian exegesis at our disposal, but also a positive 'alternative' from his point of view. Steven Cartwright has rightfully pointed out the value of such a comparison in his extensive study of the two works, offering the first exploration of the much-discussed conflict "via these commentaries, which are the only literary genre William and Peter had in common, and which deal directly with many of the Christian doctrines disputed by the two scholars."[5] My juxtaposition of these works will depend heavily on Cartwright's observations but focus more on the literary methods than doctrinal content.

Such a methodological comparison is fascinating, given the respective status the two authors enjoyed during the composition of their Romans commentary in their communities and the intellectual context of the schools in northern France. Abelard was, of course, a well-known author in academic circles, albeit mainly thanks to the controversial nature of his person and oeuvre. By then, William had also made a name for himself as an abbot and influential monastic author, even though he was (and remains) less widely known than his opponent.[6] They considered themselves representations of two slowly but steadily diverging worlds: the monastic

---

writing process for both authors – certainly for William, who had started his *Expositio* already in Signy – it should be noted, that the works could not have been finished much earlier than 1139. I would argue so, based on the noteworthy fact that William does not make use of Abelard's Romans exegesis in his own work (while not refraining from using other Abelardian works), suggesting that he did not yet know of it. Contrarily, Paul Verdeyen has noted two references to Abelard's work in William's own Commentary (in Verdeyen ed. "Exposé sur l'Épître aux Romains," namely: IV,21 and VII,59) concluding that William had known Abelard's commentary. However, these passages seem to me to be too few and too inconclusive, especially as William would have had to receive them entirely uncritically, which is rather hard to believe, given his intense negative discussion of the work in his *Disputatio*.

4   Cartwright, *The Romans Commentaries*, 26.
5   Cartwright, *The Romans Commentaries*, ii.
6   Cartwright, *The Romans Commentaries*, 39.

context, continuously emphasizing Patristic tradition and a mystical read-ing of the Bible, and the academic context of cities such as Paris, providing the ground for the scholastic era to come.[7] Yet, both Abelard and William had the distinct advantage of intellectual 'bilingualism'. Abelard had been both a theological teacher and a monk, and his thought had undoubtedly benefitted from this diversity of experience. As Luscombe points out, "his writings reflect both his scholastic and monastic experiences and commit-ments; so does his Biblical exegesis."[8] His later authorship mainly reflects a high degree of awareness regarding the requirements and circumstances of the monastic life, proclaiming the necessity for reform and the restitution of discipline.[9] William, on the other hand, while being primarily concerned with his monastic responsibility, had retained the scholarly education he had received at the Cathedral school in Reims all his life. His texts display a considerable concern for linguistic precision and an impressive knowl-edge of the dialectic method.[10] A lack of theoretical understanding, of which Abelard had accused many of his critics and of which Bernard's crit-icism of Abelard had later often been suspect, can indeed not be found in William's discussion of the matter. His and Abelard's ability to compre-hend each other's methods and concerns allows us to interpret their con-flict as the clash of two conscious and convinced visions for the Christian

---

7 Pietro Zerbi cites Jean Jolivet in his assertion that the conflict between Abelard and William "is a matter of the incompatibility of two cultures, of two mentalities, of two worlds: the old monasticism, on the one hand, and, on the other hand, the new fervor or urbanites". (Pietro Zerbi, "William of Saint Thierry and His Dispute with Abelard," in *William, Abbot of St. Thierry*, trans. Jerry Carfantan, 181–203, Cistercian Studies 94 (Kalamazoo, MI: 1987), 191). Rozanne Elder (Elder, "The Christology of William," 91), however, contrasts this citation with Châtillon's claim that William "already belonged to a different era", having already started "to detach himself from these fascinating and spellbinding modes of expression of the faith and of religious life in which monastic tradition had for so long taken delight" (Châtillon, Jean. "William of Saint Thierry, Mo-nasticism, and the Schools: Rupert of Deutz, Abelard, and William of Conches." In *Wil-liam, Abbot of St. Thierry. Actes Du Colloque*, 153–80, 1987, 168).

8 David Luscombe, *The Bible in the Work of Peter Abelard and of his "School"*, in *Neue Richtungen in der hoch– und spätmittelalterlichen Bibelexegese*, ed. Robert E. Lerner (München: Oldenbourg Wissenschaftsverlag, 1996), 81.

9 John Marenbon, "Life, Milieu, and Intellectual Contexts," in *The Cambridge Companion to Abelard*, ed. Jeffrey E. Brower and Kevin Guilfoy. Cambridge Companions to Philoso-phy (Cambridge: Cambridge University Press, 2004), 16.

10 Châtillon, "William of Saint Thierry, Monasticism and the Schools," 169: "Being a theo-logian of the schools, the abbot of Saint–Thierry spoke with the assurance of a man confident of the education he had received and of the methods by which he had been formed".

task rather than as a mutual misunderstanding. Their respective commentaries on Romans function thus as exemplifications of their visions, yet untainted by the public denunciations and the political appropriation of the dispute that would occur later.

Regarding a contrast of methodology, Eileen Sweeney's juxtaposition of Bernard's and Abelard's biblical hermeneutics provides a useful starting point. Although William's and Bernard's exegesis, in practice, is certainly not identical, their close collaboration and shared Cistercian framework make it possible for us to assume Sweeney's characterization of Bernard's exegesis as an approximate description of William's exegetical approach. Both share, for instance, the distinctive feature of *humilitas* as an epistemological prerequisite for exegetical insight. Sweeney describes the monastic ideal of humble reading as a "submission to [Scripture's] mode of expression" and a "complete submersion to the whole".[11] Humility becomes a hermeneutic principle: Scripture should determine a reader's faith in its narrative. William, hence, advises his pupils to "imbibe the spirit" of Scripture and immerse themselves fully in the biblical reality.[12] Sweeney deems this kind of hermeneutics 'narrative', as opposed to 'dialectical', the latter of which she identifies as the sort of reading for which Abelard and his students advocated.[13]

While 'narrative' is indeed an appropriate terminology, one might also say that this kind of reading reflects the hermeneutic principles of *lectio divina*, as I have earlier discussed them. It is accompanied by a meditative sense, as it treats the Scriptural narrative not as the object, but *de facto* as the subject of the process, to whom the reader is called to (more passively) listen. It is a continuous form of reading that lets Scripture unfold its narrative on its own time rather than prematurely attempting to extract truth from it. Methodologically, 'narrative' exegesis is content with retelling and 'imitating' the course of the biblical story to experience it anew.[14] Sharing its intention with the traditional practice of *lectio divina*, narrative reading pursues the soul's spiritual ascent. Whichever literary product results from such a reading necessarily entails the exhortations of its audience. In Bernard's case, his exegetical endeavor most often took on the form of sermons and devotional writings rather than theological tractates – a circumstance

---

11   Sweeney, "Rewriting the Narrative of Scripture," 10.
12   Sweeney, "Rewriting the Narrative of Scripture," 20.
13   Sweeney, "Rewriting the Narrative of Scripture," 3.
14   Sweeney, "Rewriting the Narrative of Scripture," 13.

mostly due to Bernard's education.[15] William, on the other hand, was able to present his narrative *lectio* in the form of systematic, doctrinally reflective works, such as biblical commentaries and treatises (such as *De contemplando Deo, De natura et dignitate amoris*, or *De sacramento altaris*). Yet, he and Bernard share their fundamental understanding of Scripture as a speaking, self-revealing document and the reader's role as a patient and humble listener. Their mutual hermeneutic principle is also a significant aspect of their conflict with Abelard, who is the leading proponent of the opposite 'dialectical' form of reading and whose works demonstrate apparent methodological differences from his Cistercian contemporaries.

To illustrate this contrast, Sweeney invokes a fitting image from Bernard's reflection on their discord: "[...] Bernard accuses Abelard of having divided and shredded the seamless tunic of Christ, a garment which, even if it could be resewn, would nonetheless be irrevocably changed".[16] What becomes apparent in this tableau is that Bernard, along with William, considers Scripture to be composed by the Holy Spirit. It speaks divine truth and is, therefore, a reflection of divine unity rather than a human compilation of discriminatory insight. What Bernard thus describes as the wrongful 'tearing apart' of this biblical garment could be understood as approaching the Bible with an analytical mind, attempting to separate different layers of authorial intention or extracting specific insight from a seemingly irrelevant fictitious background. Indeed, Abelard's own hermeneutic does not necessitate the treatment of Scripture as an indiscernible whole. Compared to the narrative understanding of biblical continuity, he "stops Scripture's own narrative order to ask questions from another order".[17] To derive doctrinal conclusions about the content the biblical authors present as truth, Abelard needs to apply external methodological tools to their texts.

The 'narrative' and 'dialectic' exegetical principles correspond to the monastic practice of *lectio* and the scholastic method of *disputatio*, respectively: Abelard consults the intellectual resources of his training in philosophy and dialectics[18] rather than being content with using the resources

---

15   Sweeney, "Rewriting the Narrative of Scripture," 6.

16   Sweeney, "Rewriting the Narrative of Scripture," 24.

17   Sweeney, "Rewriting the Narrative of Scripture," 3.

18   Abelard's most significant source for the specifics of dialectical and logical methodology is Boethius, whose intellectual project he largely follows (Cartwright, The Romans Commentaries, 30). If we would like to think, along with R.W. Southern, of Boethius as "the master of those who wanted to know" (in reference to Dante's claim about

Scripture itself is willing to provide.[19] He does not, therefore, humbly 'submit' himself to the biblical narrative, as Bernard and William demand, but wants to dismantle and penetrate it using reason. His reading is somewhat 'impatient', as he refuses to let Scripture reveal its truth over time. Still, the intellect can expose its hidden truths at any given time if trained sufficiently in the dialectic arts. As we will later see when discussing the accusations against Abelard, William and Bernard include this sense of hermeneutic impatience in their charge of Abelard's more general lack of humility.

It is, however, important to discuss Abelard's exegesis in his Romans commentary without yet viewing it exclusively through the lens of the doctrinal and methodological accusations he would later face. An interesting question is whether what Abelard presents with his Romans commentary is exegesis, and if so, what kind of exegesis. According to Éloi Marie Buytaert, Abelard's *Expositio* is a "literal interpretation of the Epistle as it was understood in those days"; however full of and interspersed with doctrinal and philosophical *quaestiones*. Rather than in his properly exegetical insights, the originality of the work lies in the questions he raises about the text.[20]

Asking questions was not merely a methodological device that structured his work but was foundational to how Abelard conceptualized intellectual understanding as such. Inquiry was for him the *prima clavis sapientiae*: only through thorough questioning could one hope to attain wisdom.[21] He believed this was already exemplified by Christ, who, even at twelve years old, had a penchant for questioning and debating doctrine.[22] While he resembled Augustine in his appreciation of critical

---

Aristotle), Abelard seems to be a fitting example of those "who wanted to know" (Southern, *The Making of the Middle Ages*, 174).

19   In order to justify the application of the dialectic method to the reading of Scripture, Abelard is able to refer to Augustine (Grabmann, *Geschichte der Scholastischen Methode, vol. 1*, 129).

20   As referenced in Luscombe, "The Bible in the Work of Peter Abelard," p. 88, citing É.M. Buytaert, ed., Petri Abaelardi opera theologica: Commentaria in epistolam Pauli ad Romanos Apologia contra Bernardum, cccm xi (Turnhout: Brepols, 2013), 16.

21   Eileen Frances Kearney, "Scientia and Sapientia: Reading Sacred Scripture at the Paraclete," in *From Cloister to Classroom. Monastic and Scholastic Approaches to Truth*, The Spirituality of Western Christendom iii, ed. E. Rozanne Elder, Cistercian Studies 64 (Kalamazoo MI: Cistercian Publications, 1986), 117.

22   Beryl Smalley, *Studies in Medieval Thought and Learning From Abelard to Wyclif* (London: Bloomsbury, 1981), 1.

questioning, he transgressed the Augustinian scheme by 'contenting himself' with the questions themselves rather than the development of answers.[23] Doctrines and philosophical conclusions did not necessarily re- solve his questions but revealed even deeper problems about which to ruminate.

It is telling that Abelard did not apply the traditional distinction between *sapientia* and *scientia* to his definition of intellectual achievement. Wisdom and science – passive reception and active pursuit of knowledge – are closely intertwined for him.[24] Thus, even the practice of *lectio divina*, which he discussed primarily in his writings for the monastic context, did not use the same elements William had used (*lectio, oratio, meditatio, and contem- platio*) but instead focused on aspects of exegetical exposition and complex interpretation.[25]

Although Abelard was not the first to apply the *quaestio*-method to Scripture, his exegetical work remains somewhat of a novelty, for he dared here to discuss the same claims he made in his systematic treatises as well. As a commentary, Abelard's *Expositio* embodies the synthesis of dialectic method and traditional exegetical methods, such as glossing, that would flourish throughout the scholastic age.[26] Abelard's readiness to apply the dialectical method to the Bible, which had traditionally been exempt from such critical inquiry, is rooted significantly in his biography.

In his *Historia calamitatum*, Abelard gives – while certainly acting as an unreliable narrator of his fate – a first-hand account of the literary inten- tions with which he approached the exegetical task. Here he explains why, even after becoming a monk in 1117/18, he remained an advocate for the study of dialectics and the so-called 'secular arts': following the example of Origen, he intended to teach them, to draw his philosophically inclined stu- dents into the study of Scripture.[27] While he concedes, in a rare instance of fundamental agreement with William and Bernard, that the ultimate aim of Scripture is exhortation,[28] a reader does not need to approach it with a meditative spirit. Although Scripture's divine message to its readers is, at its

---

23   Smalley, *Studies in Medieval Thought*, 8.
24   Kearney, "Scientia and Sapientia," 117.
25   Kearney, "Scientia and Sapientia," 117.
26   Charles H. Lohr, "Peter Abälard und die scholastische Exegese," *Freiburger Zeitschrift für Philosophie und Theologie* 28 (1981): 109.
27   Luscombe, "The Bible in the Work of Peter Abelard," 81.
28   Luscombe, "The Bible in the Work of Peter Abelard," 88.

core, ethical teaching, Abelard believes the reader can access this kind of moral insight via intellectual knowledge.

He reveals this methodological difference in his terminology when discussing the reading process. Whereas his monastic contemporaries and the authorities he refers to generally employ *meditare* as an umbrella term for faithful reading, he prefers to speak of *legere*, the connotations of which are distinctly intellectual.[29] This theoretical definition naturally impacts Abelard's reading practice, as it takes on literary form in his *Expositio*. In his comparative reading of William's and Abelard's Romans commentaries, Cartwright offers a detailed account of how the two authors cite and introduce biblical passages into their exegetical writing. It uncovers how they differ as individual readers of Scripture. As I have previously illustrated, William's fundamentally meditative view of the reading process has led to him profoundly assimilating the biblical reality. Knowing Scripture by heart, William can cite liberally and form complex associations. When it comes to his biblical citations, William's level of sophistication greatly exceeds Abelard's, as he creatively interconnects passages, "creating longer and more varied chains of quotations".[30] Living the life of a monk, devoted entirely to studying the biblical texts, it seems that Scripture was not merely a sourcebook or a basis for doctrinal thought to William but his *Lebensraum*. His reading of the biblical text perceives them as living, breathing companions, and as such, it differs from Abelard's reading of the same texts in theory and practice.

Abelard used Scripture as a tool. He cites passages deliberately rather than associatively and uses them to argue for and against certain doctrinal positions.[31] Hence, whenever he forms Scriptural links and chains, he does so not because a particular pericope's language invoked another passage's poetic emotion or narrative structure but because he identifies different passages discussing the same theological concept.[32] However, this argumentative use of Scripture necessitates the usage of dialectic distinction despite Scripture's authoritative role. Since, outside of their logical context, biblical passages can be used to "support contradictory positions, dialectic may still

---

29   Regina Heyder, *Auctoritas scripturae: Schriftauslegung und Theologieverständnis Peter Abaelards unter besonderer Berücksichtigung der "Expositio in Hexaemeron"*, (Münster: Aschendorff, 2010), 229.

30   Cartwright, *The Romans Commentaries*, 63.

31   Cartwright, *The Romans Commentaries*, 61.

32   Cartwright, *The Romans Commentaries*, 60.

be required to resolve the question under consideration".[33] For Abelard, applying dialectics is not simply advisable or beneficial but vital for an accurate understanding of the biblical texts, as Abelard asserts in his *Theologia "Summi Boni"*.[34] Dialectics, he claims, is synonymous with interpretation.[35] Understanding the logic of language is key to permeating biblical secrets.[36]

Only the dialectical tools enable a reader to probe the surface meaning of words and sentences and uncover their more profound meaning. This ties in with Abelard's basic assumption that divine truth is rarely revealed literally. Whether he addresses the texts of ancient pagan philosophers or the prophets of the biblical age, he calls the reader to "pierce behind the surface of the letter, behind its *integumentum*."[37] Using popular rhetoric, poetic style, or exemplifying 'similitudes' these authors appealed to their historical readers. Only the use of dialectic, however, could make the underlying message applicable to the contemporary reader, Abelard argued.[38] Whereas he recognized the importance of grammar and rhetoric as an educational foundation, he believes dialectic and logic[39] to be the subtle and advanced arts necessary to counteract the possible oversimplifications taught by grammarians.[40] As such, Abelard's approach can rightfully be called 'symptomatic' of its time and cultural context,[41] which with the rise of cathedral schools (and future universities) encouraged critical thought concerning all kinds of philosophical and theological sources.[42]

For Abelard, the authority of Scripture was undeniable and ineluctable.[43] Contrary to the accusations he would later face, Abelard did not introduce

---

33 Cartwright, *The Romans Commentaries*, 61.
34 Heyder, *Auctoritas scripturae*, 207.
35 Lohr, "Peter Abälard", 107.
36 Lohr, "Peter Abälard", 107.
37 Luscombe, "The Bible in the Work of Peter Abelard," 83–84.
38 Luscombe, "The Bible in the Work of Peter Abelard," 83–84.
39 'Dialectic' and 'logic' function, in the context of Abelardian thought, as close relatives or even synonyms (Klaus Jacobi, "Philosophy of Language," in *The Cambridge Companion to Abelard*, ed. Jeffrey E. Brower and Kevin Guilfoy. Cambridge Companions to Philosophy (Cambridge: Cambridge University Press, 2004), 126).
40 Jacobi, "Philosophy of Language," 131. Abelard was in good company with his assertion that the different disciplines support each other in the pursuit of truth. Hugh of St. Victor also believed that grammar, rhetoric, and dialectic all belonged to the logical arts and thus all served the philosophical task (Mews, "The World as Text," 111).
41 Verdeyen, "Introduction," in *Exposé sur l'Épître aux Romains*, 15–16.
42 Steckel, "Submission to the Authority of the Masters: Transformations of a Symbolic Practice during the Long Twelfth Century," 69.
43 Cartwright, *The Romans Commentaries*, 168.

the use of dialectics to dismantle biblical authority but to reinforce and defend it. The purpose of reason and logic within the field of theology is threefold: it aids the clarification and explanation of the Bible, the reinforcement of traditional doctrine, and the defense of the Christian faith. His primary concern is apologetic in nature.[44] While, according to his profession, he was concerned with defending traditional faith against logical attacks from pagan philosophy, he had to defend the legitimacy of dialectics within theology, making his apologetic endeavor dually necessary. Dialectics, according to Abelard, could help Christian theology to safeguard its doctrinal tradition against the 'sophistic objections' of those who pursue a schismatic intention.[45] Rather than understanding the rationally reflected faith as a substitute for revealed faith, an intellectual discussion of the latter provides a defense and comprehensible representation of individually revealed truth, which might otherwise remain obscure for a wider audience.[46]

It becomes clear from statements such as these that while Abelard's means and methods differ from William's approach, their intention is not as different as it might seem.[47] The notion that we find here two kinds of theologies clashing with one another, namely one that bases its thought on philosophy on the one hand and one that grounds in Scripture on the other, is an inaccurate representation of both. Despite rejecting Abelard's introduction of the dialectic arts into matters of faith, William's commentary shows analytic proficiency. He, too, as we have seen, is interested in a careful differentiation of meaning, as shown, for instance, in his discussion of the biblical author's historical context and intention. Although he hopes for his reader's spiritual ascent, his *Expositio* is, at the same time, a theoretical explanation of Scriptural themes, which demands the reader's rational participation.

Abelard's theology, conversely, would be misrepresented if it were reduced to the stereotype of a purely philosophical endeavor. First, despite its employment of external tools of thought, it remains biblically oriented in many ways.[48] Although read and interpreted differently, Scripture continues

---

44   Robb, *Intellectual Tradition and Misunderstanding*, 57.

45   Grabmann, *Geschichte der Scholastischen Methode, vol. 2*, 181.

46   Evans, *The Language and Logic of the Bible*, 109.

47   McGuire, "A Chronology," 29.

48   The Abelardian attempt at dogmatic systematization exemplifies this notion. The tripartite foundation of *fides, sacramentum* and *caritas*, as Rainer Berndt argues, arose from Abelard's reading of the Bible. *Fides*, as a fulfillment of the new covenant and its laws includes, for Abelard, the fulfillment of the Old Testament laws. *Sacramentum*, is

to be the foundation of theological reflection and still enjoys the highest authority.[49] Second, Abelard must acknowledge the presence and importance of a continuously unfolding narrative in Scripture to avoid self-contradiction. The process of learning is precisely that: a process. Truth, therefore, necessarily emerges along with the biblical story over time. Although he might have sometimes failed to highlight this aspect, he, too, could not have consciously denied the temporality of insight.[50]

Thus, when using Sweeney's distinction between a 'narrative' and 'dialectical' method, certain limitations must be considered. Sweeney's framework, as she states, illustrates the Bernardine and Abelardian approach "at their worst".[51] She asserts that the two approaches, if they were exasperated to the greatest degree, "share a desire for certainty that would make theology (and philosophy) either unnecessary or impossible"; Bernard, she claims, "demands a certainty of faith which makes inquiry unnecessary", while Abelard's "doubt is so pervasive and irremediable that it makes inquiry impossible."[52] Given this caveat, it is important to emphasize the fact that both Abelard and William often deviated from their ideals or the more extreme implementations of their principles. I find it, for instance, necessary to add that William does not take his 'desire for certainty of faith' to such extreme lengths as Bernard does.[53]

The underlying argument remains all the more true: neither approach could provide a viable long-term basis for Christian theology if it were not for the critical corrective function of its respective opposite. It is an argument that appears similarly in Martin Grabmann's pivotal history of the

---

the historico-temporal communication of the divine (and thus the foundation of human hope), followed by *caritas* as a necessary consequence of faith and hope. This theoretical structure is therefore a conceptual representation and reiteration of salvation history in its biblical account (Rainer Berndt, "Überlegungen Zum Verhältnis von Exegese Und Theologie in 'De Sacramentis Christiane Fidei' Hugos von St. Viktor," in *Neue Richtungen in Der Hoch– Und Spätmittelalterlichen Bibelexegese*, ed. Robert E. Lerner (München: Oldenbourg Wissenschaftsverlag, 1996), 73).

49 In fact, he identifies his own theological teaching with the discipline of 'sacra pagina', at least terminologically (Riché and Lobrichon, *Le Moyen Âge et la Bible*, 188).

50 Sweeney, "Rewriting the Narrative of Scripture," 21.

51 Sweeney, "Rewriting the Narrative of Scripture," 4.

52 Sweeney, "Rewriting the Narrative of Scripture," 4.

53 This tendency might be rooted in William's stronger emphasis on pneumatology and the significance of the Holy Spirit in all kinds of theological endeavors. I will discuss this difference between William and Bernard in more detail in the chapters regarding their readings of the Song of Songs.

scholastic method (*Die Geschichte der scholastischen Methode*). Bridging the traditional divide between what has been considered monastic (or 'mystic') and what has been deemed scholastic, Grabmann illustrates these two features not as opposing forces but as tendencies inherent to medieval theology that contribute equally and simultaneously to the growth of Christian thought. He compares the inevitable bloom of scholasticism to the course of a river. Just as a river depends on its banks, the scholastic desire for intellectual progress requires the monastic insistence on tradition.[54] Therefore, understanding how William and Abelard represent different aspects of medieval theology requires a closer analysis of their respective concepts of authority vis–à–vis innovation.

We have already seen that Abelard's penchant for novelty does not lead him to question the authoritative status of Scripture as such.[55] While this is true for the biblical corpus as a whole, it is especially noteworthy in the context of his Pauline exegesis. For Abelard, Paul acted not merely as an ethical role model but also as the earliest "(not to say magisterial) master of theology".[56] He reads the Pauline Epistles as expositions of Scriptural evidence and systematic treatment of theological concepts, such as divine grace and charity. Although it is apparent from Abelard's explicit reverence of Paul that he does recognize his authority and aims at unfolding a theology that methodologically and substantively follows the Pauline texts, his understanding of Paul decidedly differs from William's.

While Abelard seemingly bases his acceptance of apostolic authority on Paul's intellectual prowess and notable literary talent, William fundamentally bases his faith in authority on divine inspiration. Perceiving the historical figure of the apostle through the lens of his literary intentions (just as Abelard), William understands Paul as a mystical author whose interest for his readers would have been primarily contemplative and moral.[57] Paul's devotion and spiritual closeness to God determine the truth in his writings.

---

54   Grabmann, *Geschichte der Scholastischen Methode, vol. 2*, 108.

55   Regina Heyder explains that Abelard's theological 'biblicism' (*Biblizismus*) is not to be interpreted as a strategic safety net against possible accusations, but as the necessary counterbalance to the fragility he attributed to the Church Fathers (Heyder, *Auctoritas scripturae*, 243).

56   Schildgen and Hawkins, "Introduction," in *Medieval Readings of Romans*, 6. As Jean Doutre points out, this has to determine the way we as readers understand his Commentary on Romans: "We can now see the commentary as a reflection Abelard's own 'magisterial' role, for it considers Paul to be a master of theology" (Doutre, "Romans as Read in School and Cloister," 51).

57   Doutre, "Romans as Read in School and Cloister," 37.

Understanding Paul as a biblical author on the verge of the Patristic age, Abelard's and William's discrepancy, considering the reasoning for a text's authoritative status, pertains to their treatment of the Church Fathers even more so.[58]

Abelard's innovative treatment of Patristic citations is as infamous now as it was controversial then. The most prolific example of his willingness to apply dialectical critique to authoritative texts is his *Sic et Non*. Surprisingly, neither William nor Bernard made use of the work in their accusations against him.[59] Nonetheless, the *Sic et Non* is one of the clearest examples of Abelard's *quaestio*-method and will, as such, have to influence our discussion of the different approaches to some extent. First, it is important to note that Abelard presented his various explicit and implicit treatments of the Fathers within the 12th-century context of Patristic rediscovery. He was far from the only Christian author who went beyond the production of florilegia and used Patristic sources as inspiration and foundation for one's original thought.[60] Abelard's willingness to develop his theological ideas does not make him unique or suspect of heresy.

However, the most distinctive and controversial feature of his thought is his open discussion of apparent contradictions and logical inconsistency within the Patristic corpus. While Abelard's self-proclaimed intention is

---

58   Although the distinction between Scriptural and Patristic authority is structurally valuable for my analysis it does not necessarily translate to our authors' actual 12th-century context. I share Marcia Colish's important observation that "the twelfth-century scholastics are not interested in discussing the relations between scriptural and patristic authority, or in placing them in a clear hierarchy vis–à–vis each other. Rather, they see the Christian message as a message that was begun to be interpreted within the New Testament itself, a process which was then continued by the church fathers and by the theologians of successive ages. All the witnesses are seen as a part of a single organic conception of authority." (Marcia Lillian Colish, "'...Quae Hodie Locum Non Habent': Scholastic Theologians Reflect on Their Authorities," *in Proceedings of* the PMR *Conference 15*, 1991), 3–4). However, Abelard (in this case, as in many) is the exception to the rule. Following Augustine, he proposes a more strict differentiation between the authority of the Bible and that of later Christian authors (Heyder, *Auctoritas scripturae*, 241).

59   Grabmann, *Geschichte der Scholastischen Methode, vol. 2*, 203. William does indeed mention the work in the *Disputatio* asserting that he expects the work's doctrines to be as 'monstruous' as its title: *Sunt autem, ut audio, adhuc alia eius opuscula, quorum nomina sunt: Sic et non, Scito te ipsum, et alia quaedam de quibus timeo, ne sicut monstruosi sunt nominis, sic etiam sint monstruosi dogmatis* (Disputatio Adversus Petrum Abaelardum, CCCM 89A, par. 4, pag. 14, linea 75).

60   Doutre, "Romans as Read in School and Cloister," 52.

to harmonize and ultimately prove the Fathers' doctrinal consensus, his project contains a distinct aspect of skepticism, as he highlights the observation of contradiction in his presentation of the problem.[61] In proclaiming that these gaps in tradition could be solved, in part, by the use of dialectic, he simultaneously implied – or so his opponents understood him – that he could act as a rational judge in the matter.[62] The *Sic et Non* contains famously a collection of questions that should be asked in response to obscure or difficult passages.[63] Abelard warns, several issues of textual criticism that might stand between a reader and his proper understanding of a text. He mentions, for instance, titular misattributions,[64] mistakes in the transmission history of the text,[65] or a culturally differing use of vocabulary.[66]

More importantly, however, Abelard points out the importance of historical awareness.[67] Several of his proposed *quaestiones* address the author's

---

61 Grabmann, *Geschichte der Scholastischen Methode, vol. 2*, 205.

62 Grabmann, *Geschichte der Scholastischen Methode, vol. 2*, 53. Several of his proposed *quaestiones* demand the reader to make a personal judgment and give their own verdict on the matter, as Heyder points out: "Im zweiten Teil des Prologs befasst sich Abaelard dann mit 'offenkundigen Kontroversen' (*si manifesta sit controversia*), die ein Urteil des Lesers erfordern." (Heyder, *Auctoritas scripturae*, 239).

63 Abelard applies this method throughout his Commentary in Romans. For instance, he discusses at length the question of the Romans' conversion, which had already been discussed throughout tradition. Following his own set of critical quaestiones, he examines "the opinions of Eusebius of Caesarea, Pseudo–Jerome, Gregory of Tours, and Haymo of Auxerre" (Cartwright, *The Romans Commentaries*, 30). All citations from Abelard's *Sic et Non* are taken from: Peter Abaelard, Sic et Non. Centre Traditio Litterarum Occidentalium, CETEDOC., and Brepols (Firm). 2000. *Library of Latin texts. Series A. Series A.* [Turnhout, Belgium]: Brepols. http://clt.brepolis.net/LLTA/pages/Text Search.aspx?key=MABAESINO_ (accessed January 10, 2025).

64 Sic et Non, Prol. pag. 91, linea 56.

65 Sic et Non, Prol. pag. 92, linea 56–74.

66 Sic et Non, Prol. pag. 96, linea 185. Further, Abelard differentiates between statements that are made *iuxta opinionem hominum and secundum veritatem rerum*, displaying his awareness for linguistic development (Heyder, *Auctoritas scripturae*, 238, referencing Sic et Non, Prol. pag. 94, linea 135).

67 Carmen Angela Cvetković notes that in William's earlier work, *De Sacramento altaris*, he seems to apply a methodology not unlike that which Abelard presents in the prologue to the *Sic et Non:* "William's work also proposed a way to deal with the contrasting statements of ecclesiastical doctors, which focused only on the presence of Christ in the Eucharist, in line to the topic of his treatise. William observed that some of the ambiguities and inconsistencies in the writings of the patristic authors arose from the fact that they were written circumstantially, in order to refute heretical issues without going into explanations beyond what was absolutely necessary. As a result, some of

role in a text's significance. Did he revoke what he once said at a different point in his work?[68] How did its author intend a particular statement?[69] Does the passage address doctrinal matters that need to be believed in their literal sense, or is there room for interpretation and the reader's judgment?[70] Although his critics often failed to take note of Abelard's differentiation, his acknowledgment of mistakes (both in Scripture and the Patristic canon) is not synonymous with an insinuation of untruthfulness on the part of these authorities.[71] The possibility of an error on the part of the interpreter, be it due to spiritual or intellectual deficiencies, is one of the primary questions to consider in the case of seeming Patristic dissent.[72]

The reader's role lies at the heart of Abelard's discussion of authority: he deeply trusts in the human *ratio* and its fundamental ability – and consequentially, its responsibility – to discover truth through relentless questioning. A thorough process of critique and the employment of the dialectic method will then allow a reader to make his own decisions regarding controversial doctrinal issues. Should a reader, after having worked through Abelard's proposed catalog of questions, still find a Patristic passage to be unclear or even unbiblical, they are free to dismiss it from their theological deliberations. Abelard understood himself – and any rational and dialectically trained reader – to be a trustworthy judge in cases of unsolved theological problems.[73] However, the importance of critical questioning meant that Abelard's method dismantled the notion of a single and self-contained

---

their accounts remained incomplete and were highly circumstantial, so it comes as no surprise that they occasionally express conflicting views. Therefore, like Abelard, William suggested that such passages ought to be read contextually" (Cvetković, "Conflict and Authority," 536).

68 Sic et Non, Prol. pag. 92, linea 86. Augustine's *retractationes* were Abelard's primary example for Patristic self-repeal (see Cornelia Rizek–Pfister, "Die hermeneutischen Pinzipien in Abaelards Sic et non," *Freiburger Zeitschrift für Philosophie und Theologie* 47 (2000): 484).

69 Sic et Non, Prol. pag. 96, linea 177.

70 Sic et Non, Prol. pag. 101, linea 274.

71 Luscombe, "The Bible in the Work of Peter Abelard," 82. Abelard also warns his readers against a rash judgment of Patristic error. Rather than accusing the Fathers of deliberate deceit, a reader should assume their ignorance (Heyder, *Auctoritas scripturae*, 234). It is further important to note that Abelard does not deem it necessary for an authoritative text to be literally inspired and departs "from the assumption that the divine inspiration of Scripture extends to the minutests detail of the choice of words [...]" (Evans, *The Language and Logic of the Bible*, 138).

72 Sic et Non, Prol. pag. 89, linea 1–6.

73 Grabmann, *Geschichte der Scholastischen Methode, vol. 2*, 205.

Christian tradition. This is particularly the case because Abelard's understanding of tradition includes contemporary authors in a more explicit way
than William's does.

According to Abelard, it is the Holy Spirit who reveals a text's diverse
meanings, thereby letting the reader participate in the same process that
has inspired the text's author in the first place.[74] Although divine inspiration
is a significant aspect of both authors' hermeneutic systems, Abelard more
clearly associates inspiration with ecclesial authority. For William, as for
most pre-scholastic authors, Scripture and the Patristic corpus form an
authoritative standard by which to measure the orthodoxy of doctrinal
claims,[75] even the ones that are seemingly 'inspired'. Within the Abelardian
framework, however, authority is a much more dynamic concept and resembles a narrative that remains open for continuation.

This is not only the case regarding contemporary or future authors but
retroactively for the pre-Christian philosophic tradition. One significant aspect in which Abelard's practical usage of authority differs from William's is
that he accepts pagan authors as authoritative in the first place. In contrast,
William demands Patristic support for any theological opinion to be voiced.
For him, authority is not only pneumatological founded but also necessitates communal consensus and clerical agreement; it is simultaneously a
theological and a social construct. Accepting voices outside the church as
authoritative is thus a conceptual impossibility for him.[76]

Abelard, on the other hand, works with different parameters of definition.
For him, authority is a concept tied closely to an abstract notion of truth (as
it is rationally comprehensible and mediated by the divine spirit). It is not,
however, bound to an exclusive religious body. Abelard's understanding of
truth allows him to stipulate that it was attainable beyond the confines of
the church or, in pre-Christian history, beyond the confines of the Jewish
people.[77] He argues that even the mystery of the Trinity could have been
revealed to Pagan philosophers by the sovereignty of the Holy Spirit and

---

74   Heyder, *Auctoritas scripturae*, 244.
75   Heyder, *Auctoritas scripturae*, 236.
76   However, William is here not representative of most authors of his time. Hugh of St.
      Victor, for instance, is an important proponent of a distinctly Christian and thoroughly
      orthodox author, who nevertheless liberally received pagan thought (Mews, "The
      World as Text" 109).
77   In fact, according to Abelard's implicit hierarchy of authority, the statements of the
      philosophers were to be regarded in even higher esteem than the prophecies of the
      Old Testament (Doutre, "Romans as Read in School and Cloister," 34).

God's revelatory acts in creation.[78] In doing so, Abelard not only manages to justify the reception of pagan texts but also establishes their authorities, whose metaphysics and philosophy could contribute significant insight to all kinds of theological questions.

Whereas William concedes the truth value of specific Platonic observations but uses them as examples of the inadequacies of a purely philosophical approach, Abelard lets his systematic reflection take place within a philosophic framework. Suggesting that thinkers such as Plato, Macrobius, Virgilius, and Seneca knew the Trinitarian God rather than a mere notional definition of the divine, Abelard can connect philosophical concepts and traditional Christian doctrine. He relates, for instance, the platonic notion of the νοῦς to Christ as the Son of God or the idea of the *anima mundi* to catholic pneumatology.[79]

While Abelard's and William's approaches thus differ significantly in the kinds of authority they dare to receive, another distinctive feature of their understandings of authority lies in how they introduce them into their thought on a practical level. While Abelard's corpus of referenced Patristic authorities looks different from William's,[80] certain Fathers are essential to both authors. Yet, they appear differently in their respective works. This is quite prominently the case with Augustine. The Doctor of Grace, as we have seen in chapter 1.5., acts in William's *Expositio* as a significant guide regarding doctrinal questions, particularly his discussion of the Trinity.

As the entire work represents William's intricate interweaving of Patristic thought with his own, his usage of citations does not always necessitate literal accuracy. He refrains, for instance, from the identification of citations making his language appear to fuse with that of the Fathers.[81] As he focused on the underlying message of an Augustinian statement, or sentiment, generally regarding it as true, William could quote at times from memory or adapt the language to fit it into the context of his discussion. For Abelard,

---

78   Grabmann, *Geschichte der Scholastischen Methode, vol. 2,* 198.

79   Grabmann, *Geschichte der Scholastischen Methode, vol. 2,* 198.

80   The Fathers whose statements Abelard discusses in his Commentary on Romans include most importantly "Bede, Rhaban Maur and the commentaries of Pelagius (under the name of Jerome), the Ambrosiaster, and Aymon of Auxerre" (Peter Abaelard, *Expositio in Epistolam Ad Romanos: [Lateinisch – Deutsch] = Römerbriefkommentar / Abaelard,* trans. Rolf Peppermüller, vol. 26, 1–3, Fontes Christiani (Freiburg i. Br.: Herder, 2000), 21). Although these authors appear in William's *Expositio* as well, they do so only very selectively, and seem to be referenced casually, exerting little influence on his exegetical views.

81   Doutre, "Romans as Read in School and Cloister," 52–53.

however, whose use of authorities entailed dialectic analysis, the particular wording of a doctrinal statement was, in most cases, crucial. His usage of literal citations, rather than paraphrases, clearly displays his consideration of the scholastic context and its requirements.[82]

Further, Abelard uses Augustine, less so than William, as a doctrinal authority. His references to Augustinian theology appear mainly in his discussion of moral problems.[83] Clearly, if read comparatively, William's understanding of authority is defined primarily by a concern for safeguarding faith. In contrast, Abelard values the contributions of particular authors for their contributions to specific questions. This conception allows Abelard to transgress Augustine's thought when he felt his exploration of a certain matter did not fully expound it. This was the case, for instance, when Abelard felt that Augustine's contribution to Trinitarian theology did not offer sufficient consideration of the divine persons' characteristics.[84] At different times, he thought it was essential for the development of his theology to break with the Augustinian tradition altogether, as was the case with his concept of original sin.[85] While thus professing the authoritative status of Patristic works, Abelard does not attribute authority to the historical figure of a church father in blanket statements. The Fathers, albeit great theological minds, had their intellectual specialties and inadequacies.

The fact that Abelard believed the Fathers to err regarding specific questions did not undermine their authority as such, as many of his critics feared. However, Abelard's sense of authority was less universal than William's and, one could argue, less significant for his understanding of the Christian task. Abelard was well aware of the consequences such a relativization of authority could have, especially for his status and academic career. As we have seen, Abelard's critical appraisal of Patristic authorities and his undeniable appreciation of Scripture defend his theology against the accusation of being entirely rationalistic. Abelard was undoubtedly concerned with balancing *ratio* and *auctoritas*, which would later become the two forces of scholasticism.[86] Yet, many of Abelard's contemporaries

---

82   Cartwright, *The Romans Commentaries*, 126.

83   Cartwright, *The Romans Commentaries*, 121.

84   Cartwright, *The Romans Commentaries*, 247.

85   Doutre, "Romans as Read in School and Cloister," 52.

86   This reflects the judgement of Grabmann himself (Grabmann, *Geschichte der Scholastischen Methode, vol. 2*, 193). However, Grabmann differentiates two schools of thought that have dominated modern historiography on Abelard: "Die einen – es sei auf V. Cousin, Ch. de Rémusat, Stöckl, Haffner, G. V. Hertling, de Wulf, Bonwetsch,

were not as generous in evaluating his work. The debate regarding Abelard's methodology and the orthodoxy of his doctrinal statements was sparked way before William committed himself to the matter. Before going into a detailed discussion of William's *Disputatio*, I will offer a bit of context regarding Abelard's reputation in the academic and clerical circles of the time leading up to William's involvement.

2 Abelard's Early Critics

As I mentioned above, Abelard might not be the most reliable narrator of his misfortune.[87] His discussion of the accusations he faced naturally represents his thought in a favorable light while dismissing the critique of his opponents as personal attacks with little to no doctrinal basis. However, the *Historia calamitatum* is worth consulting even apart from its very apparent entertainment value:[88] It gives the most representative contemporary account of Abelard's interpersonal relationships and how he related, not merely to the concept of authority, but ecclesial and scholarly authority on a social level. Of course, the two forms of authority were closely intertwined, especially in the context of theological education, since the schools and monasteries, as places of theological formation, depended on firm hierarchical structures. This evident correlation between intellectual and institutional authority was a circumstance Abelard made sure to point out in his autobiographical defense. Indeed, institutional dynamics of power played a specific role in Abelard's early conflicts, which began when he was still a student. One of his first teachers, the prolific Anselm of Laon, would also become one of his fiercest critics, similarly the famous Alberich of

---

J.F. Muth, A. Ehrhard u. a. verwiesen – sehen in dem Peripatetiker von Palais einen grundsätzlichen Rationalisten, einen Verfechter des Grundsatzes 'Intelligo, ut credam', der Scholastik festgelegt hat. Die anderen finden hinter Abälards Auffassung des grundsätzlichen Rationalismus. Zu diesen zählen J. Bach, A. Harnack, J. A. Endres, E. Kaiser, Portalié, de Régnon und Th. Heitz" (Grabmann, *Geschichte der Scholastischen Methode, vol. 2*, 178).

87   see for a study on the careful literary composition: Chad Schrock, "The Proportion of His Purpose: Peter Abelard's 'Historia Calamitatum' as Sacred History," *Archives d'histoire Doctrinale et Littéraire Du Moyen Age* 77 (2010).

88   All Latin citations are taken from: Peter Abaelard. *Historia Calamitatum*. Centre Traditio Litterarum Occidentalium, CETEDOC., and Brepols (Firm). 2000. *Library of Latin texts. Series A. Series A*. [Turnhout, Belgium]: Brepols. http://clt.brepolis.net/LLTA/pages/TextSearch.aspx?key=MABAEHICA_ (accessed January 10, 2025).

Reims. As becomes apparent, in Abelard's account of his conflict with Alberich – only one of many detailed reflections on his controversial nature –
Abelard reveals that the antipathy was mutual:

> One day Alberich came to me with some of his students, intending to
> intimidate me. After some superficial conversation, he said he was sur
> prised about a passage he noticed in that book, namely that even
> though God begot God and there was only one God, I seemed to deny
> that God begot Himself. To that, I immediately responded: "If you
> want so, I can offer you a rational explanation (*rationem*) on this mat
> ter". "We do not care", he said, "about a human reason or your own
> thoughts on the matter, but only in the words of an authority". To this,
> I said: "Open up the page of the book, and you will find an authority".
> The book was close – he himself had brought it. I flipped the pages to
> the passage, which I knew and which he had overlooked, searching
> only for things that could hurt me. It was the will of God that I found
> quickly what I wanted. It was a sentence entitled *Augustinus De trini
> tate libro primo*: "Whoever believes that God has the power to beget
> Himself is mistaken, because not only is God not like this in kind, but
> no creature, neither spiritual nor corporal, is. There is no thing that
> can beget itself." [Alberich's] students, who were there and heard it,
> were amazed and embarrassed. To somehow protect himself, he said:
> "This is to be understood correctly." I, however, responded that this
> would be nothing new but would not contribute to the matter at hand
> since he was only interested in the words and not their meaning. But
> if he desired the meaning and reason, I would be ready to show him
> according to his statement that he himself had fallen into heresy,
> namely that the Father is His own Son.[89]

---

89   Historia calamitatum, pag. 84, linea 751: *Quadam autem die, Albericus ad me animo intemptantis cum quibusdam discipulis suis accedens, post quedam blanda colloquia, dixit
      se mirari quoddam quod in libro illo notaverat; quod scilicet, cum Deus Deum genuerit,
      nec nisi unus Deus sit, negarem tamen Deum se ipsum genuisse. Cui statim respondi:
      "Super hoc, si vultis, rationem proferam". – "Non cu|ramus, inquit ille, rationem humanam aut sensum vestrum in talibus, sed auctoritatis verba solummodo". Cui ego: "Vertite, inquam, folium libri, et invenietis auctoritatem;" et erat presto liber quem se cum
      ipse detulerat. Revolvi ad locum quem noveram, quem ipse minime compererat aut qui
      non nisi nocitura mihi querebat; et voluntas Dei fuit, ut cito occurreret mihi quod volebam. Erat autem sentencia intitulata Augustinus De Trinitate libro 1-o: "Qui putat ejus
      potentie Deum ut se ipsum ipse genuerit, eo plus errat, quod non solum Deus ita non est
      sed nec spiritualis creatura, nec corporalis. Nulla enim omnino res est que se ipsam*

The story bears an interesting resemblance to the gospel accounts of Jesus's temptation, as well as his discourse with the Pharisees, and seems to cast Alberich and his students in the role of the latter. He accuses them of malicious intent, suspecting a logical trap was set for him. Similar to the devil's strategy to entrap Jesus with Scriptural passages, whose authority he could not deny, Alberich's plan seemed to be, according to Abelard, to corner him with the demand for superficial Patristic citations. Abelard proceeds, he claims, to beat Alberich at his own game, citing an Augustinian reference for the opinion, which Alberich had dismissed as heretical. Alberich is left with no choice but to concede, unable to deprive Augustine of his authoritative status, which he had earlier established as a standard for orthodox belief.[90] Abelard's real point, however, was not the claim that all of his statements have a corresponding Patristic confirmation but that they do not need to. They are confirmed and justified by their rational coherence.[91]

This argument lies at the heart of his defense against various critics, including Anselm of Laon. It is simultaneously the clear implication that his opponents could not grasp his logical explanations, leaving them with no actual argument apart from authority for authority's sake. He believed it was not his doctrinal claims that sparked their accusations but their jealousy regarding Abelard's talents in the field of dialectics and philosophy.[92]

---

gignat". Quod cum discipuli ejus qui aderant audissent, obstupefacti erubescebant. Ipse autem, ut se quoquomodo protegeret: "Bene, inquit, est intelligendum". Ego autem subjeci hoc non esse novellam sed ad presens nichil attinere, cum ipse verba tantum, non sensum, requisisset; si autem sensum et rationem attendere vellet, paratum me dixi ei ostendere secundum ejus sententiam quod in eam lapsus esset heresim secundum quam is qui pater est sui ipsius filius sit.

90   Stephen Jaeger uses this particular anecdote to make a point about the relationship with Patristic authority, displayed by such teachers as Alberich: "Naturally, Abelard wrote the scenario for the confrontation, and he cast himself in the role of winner. But even if his version is badly skewed, it shows us the issues as Abelard conceived them. Alberic's entire support in that confrontation was the false and wholly irrational assurance that he would not be contradicted. In facing a master of rational disputation armed only with that conviction, Alberic committed a fundamental and representative error for any learning based on authority: he confused his personal authority with the authority of texts and ideas" (C. Stephen Jaeger, *The Envy of Angels: Cathedral Schools and Social Ideals in Medieval Europe, 950–1200*, (Philadelphia: University of Pennsylvania Press, 1994), 231).

91   see on Alberich's accusations against Abelard: Mews, "Bernard of Clairvaux and Peter Abelard," 146–47.

92   Historia calamitatum, pag. 66, linea 117: *Tunc Melidunum reversus scolas ibi nostras sicut antea constitui; et quanto manifestius eius me persequebatur invidia tanto mihi*

While it is difficult to assert today whether this rather emotional aspect played into his opponents' critical reading of his texts, it reveals more about Abelard. Believing in the superiority of the dialectic method, Abelard felt the biblical exegesis taught at the Cathedral Schools, with its emphasis on rhetoric, was insufficient and unworthy of the theological task. The conviction that he was one of the few thinkers in possession of adequate methodology prompted him to offer his lessons and become a magister in his own right, competing with the famous masters of the time.[93] Abelard took particular issue with the inaccuracy and simplicity of Anselm's theology, impelling him to ridicule some of Anselm's statements publicly. An example of this is the Anselmian 'river analogy', in which he relates the source, the stream, and the pool of the River Nile to the three persons of the Trinity. Abelard's open mockery of this image, which he believed to be an outrageous simplification of the logically complex Trinitarian question, would famously contribute to Abelard's condemnation at Soissons in 1121.[94]

However, the primary matter of the heresy proceedings of Soissons was Abelard's first explicitly theological work: his *Theologia "summi boni"* marked an important biographical turn in his life as he moved from purely philosophical questions to the treatment of sacred doctrine.[95] Two students

---

auctoritatis amplius conferebat juxta illud poeticum, Summa petit livor, perflant altissima venti.

93   Abelard showed himself especially disappointed in the exegetical education he himself received from Anselm, after he began studying at Laon in 1113 (Marenbon, John. "Life, Milieu, and Intellectual Contexts," 14). Abelard's first theological writings could therefore be read as an exegetical 'alternative to Laon', offering less of a harmonizing singular narrative, but more so an exposition of the various problems that emerge from the text (Heyder, *Auctoritas scripturae*, 196).

94   Robb, *Intellectual Tradition and Misunderstanding*, 48 and more extensively in M. T. Clanchy, "Abelard's Mockery of St Anselm," *The Journal of Ecclesiastical History* 41, no. 1 (January 1990): 5. Clanchy is arguing that Abelard is mocking Anselm's analogy in the following passage: *Ponit itaque praedictus archiepiscopus quasi tria eiusdem substantiae, fontem uidelicet, riuum et stagnum: fontem quidem ex quo est riuus quasi Patrem ex quo Filius, stagnum uero quod ex fonte et riuo prouenit quasi Spiritum qui ex Patre et Filio procedit. Posuit etiam riuum in fistula quasi Filium in carne humana, ac si riuum infistulatum dicamus Verbum incarnatum* (Theologia christiana, CCCM 12, lib. 4, cap. 83, linea 1214–1218). A historical evaluation of Abelard's relationship with Anselm can be found in David Luscombe, "St Anselm and Abelard. A Restatement," in *Peter Abelard and Heloise* (London: Routledge, 2018).

95   For an overview of the different versions (and names) of the *Theologia,* see Jeffrey E. Brower and Kevin Guilfoy, "Introduction," in *The Cambridge Companion to Abelard,* ed. Jeffrey E. Brower and Kevin Guilfoy. Cambridge Companions to Philosophy (Cambridge: Cambridge University Press, 2004), 9.

of Anselm instigated the accusations against its claims and the subsequent trial. Although the papal legate could not find proof of heresy in the content of Abelard's work, the political influence the school of Laon and its exponents held overturned the council's decision. Consequentially, Abelard's *Theologia* was condemned and burned. He was sentenced to be imprisoned at the monastery of Saint–Medard (although he was able to return to Saint-Denis shortly after).[96]

Regina Heyder observed in her study on Abelardian exegesis that Soissons did not leave Abelard or his theology untouched. After condemning his work, Abelard attempted an extensive revision of the text. The changes he made in the new version of his *Theologia*, especially regarding his terminology or instructive advice to his readers, demonstrate that among his opponents' accusations, Abelard did find aspects of constructive criticism, based on which he desired to improve his work. First, he renamed his project, now calling it the *Theologia christiana* – a titular profession to the catholic doctrine and the teachings of the church, rather than the philosophical and somewhat non–denominational affirmation of God as the 'highest good' (*summum bonum*).[97] Although the intention of the work remained intact, Abelard added a significant amount of Patristic evidence to support his argument[98] and his dialectic method.[99] He even included a more detailed presentation of the problem, which led to his conflict with Alberich in the first place, discussing both Alberich's and his argument. Not only did he intend to defend himself from the accusations of heresy but also to convict Alberich and his school of implicit Sabellianism.[100] Whereas his professed objective in the *Theologia "summi boni"* was to teach what is in line with Holy Scripture (*sacra scriptura*), leaving room to argue for his reading, he changed his wording in the *Theologia christiana*. Here he promised not to teach anything that would contradict the Christian faith (*sacra fide*), demonstrating a newfound concern for the traditional doctrines shared by the body of believers.[101] For the first time, Abelard concedes that he is willing to correct himself should he depart from the catholic expression of faith (*a catholica intelligentia vel locutione*).[102]

---

96 Marenbon, "Life, milieu and intellectual contexts," 15.
97 Heyder, *Auctoritas scripturae*, 197.
98 Robb, *Intellectual Tradition and Misunderstanding*, 55–56.
99 Grabmann, *Geschichte der Scholastischen Methode, vol. 2*, 183.
100 Robb, *Intellectual Tradition and Misunderstanding*, 68.
101 Heyder, *Auctoritas scripturae*, 202.
102 Heyder, *Auctoritas scripturae*, 202.

Nevertheless, Abelard was not able to redeem himself beyond doubt. The list of his contemporary critics shows that Abelard remained a controversial figure. The accusations ranged from theological disagreements and methodological allegations to reproaches of Abelard's character. Roscelin, for instance, took issue with Abelard's insufficient knowledge of the Bible, whereas Hugh of Saint Victor reprimanded Abelard for his arrogance and pride over his intellectual abilities.[103] Yet, among his students, there were admirers of his, such as John of Salisbury, who called his teacher *clarus doctor et admirabilis*.[104] Even though his contemporaries and later historians often disagree in their evaluations of the famous philosopher, his desire to reform the theological task is indisputable. It is also the fact that prompted William in 1141 to write his *Disputatio* against the innovator. In the following, I will offer an account of the arguments William invokes in the indictment and how their differing views of authority play a crucial role in the conflict.

3   Orthodoxy and Authority in William's *Disputatio*

In 1135 William, who had long harbored the desire to retreat from public life, was finally granted to resign his abbacy of Saint–Thierry and enter the Cistercian monastery of Signy.[105] Throughout his life, he had often voiced his belief that his true calling was to live as a simple reclusive monk rather than acting as a political representative of the church. While he shared a lot

---

103   Grabmann, *Geschichte der Scholastischen Methode, vol. 2,* 171.
104   Grabmann, *Geschichte der Scholastischen Methode, vol. 2,* 171.
105   For a long time, Bernard had discouraged his friend from retiring and reminded him of how important his duty as an abbot was to the community he served. This is evidenced, for instance, by one of Bernard's letters, where he advises his friend in the following way: "Therefore I say hold on to what you have got, remain where you are, and try to benefit those over whom you rule. Do not try to escape the responsibility of your office while you are still able to discharge it for the benefit of your subject. Woe to you if you rule them and do not benefit them, but far greater woe to you if you refuse to benefit them because you shirk the burden of ruling them." (Bernard of Clairvaux, *The Letters of St. Bernard of Clairvaux von of Clairvaux St.Bernard,* trans. Bruno Scott James (Kalamazoo, MI: Cistercian Publications, 1998), Letter 88, 128). But as Sherri Olson rightfully points out, the history of monasticism is full of such stories of "individuals who at heart were recluses but were forced to relinquish a life of retirement to serve the larger Christian society" (Olson, *Daily Life in a Medieval Monastery,* 17).

of beliefs and opinions with his spiritual brother Bernard, their sense of self could not have been more different. While Bernard was easily one of the most influential and prolific figures of the time and was involved in countless proceedings of all kinds, William preferred to devote his life to private study. However, his application to the *casus Abelardi* was not the first instance of William's involvement in matters of public concern. In the early 1120s, he was involved in a dispute with Rupert of Deutz concerning the latter's theological thoughts on the eucharist.[106] He also took on a significant role in defense of Cistercian reform efforts when issuing his *Responsio abbatum* to the papal legate, Cardinal Matthew, in 1132.[107] What is interesting, and perhaps surprising, about his decision to write against Abelard is that he did so at a point when he no longer held the responsibilities of an abbot, which seemed to have driven his earlier controversies. In 1140 he had already lived a secluded life for years, devoid of any social or communal pressure to get involved in yet another quarrel. Therefore, out of deep personal concern – a conviction that Abelard's theology endangered the catholic faith and the church's unity– he must have decided to compose his allegations. This becomes clear from the opening lines of the *Disputatio*, written as a letter to Bernard:

> When I see the faith of our communal hope, which Christ has consecrated with his blood; for which the apostles and the martyrs have fought to their death, and which the holy doctors have defended with hard labor and much sweat to transmit it with integrity and without corruption to our miserable times, corrupted in a grave and dangerous way, without anyone resisting or anyone speaking up, then I dwindle. My broken heart and the pain of my spirit force me to speak on a matter for which, if necessary and timely, I would be willing to give my life.[108]

---

106 William's role in the conflict is represented in the *Epistola ad Domnum Rupertum* and *De sacramento altaris,* both written consecutively between 1120 and 1123.

107 Sergent, "Introduction," in *A Companion to William,* 3.

108 Disputatio adversus Petrum Abaelardum, CCCM 89A, par. 1, pag. 13, linea 3: *Cum enim fidem communis spei grauiter nimis et periculose corrumpi uideo, nullo resistente, nullo obloquente, quam Christus suo nobis sanguine sacrauit, pro qua apostoli et martyres usque ad mortem pugnauerunt, quam sancti doctores duris laboribus suis et magnis sudoribus defensam, integram et incorruptam usque ad faeces temporum nostrorum transmiserunt, contabesco in memetipso, et a frixura cordis et dolore spiritus cogor pro ea loqui, pro qua, si necesse et opportunum, uellem etiam mori.*

William sees the 'communal hope', the doctrinal tradition of Christianity, threatened. The importance of authority is apparent in this passage, yet William employs it unusually. Rather than invoking an abstract concept of hierarchical authority to support his position, he presents an emotional appeal to notable historical figures, describing the admirable ways in which they had fought for their faith. Starting with the physical sacrifice of Christ and its emulation through the apostles and the martyrs, William moves on to the early doctors of the church, emphasizing their intellectual labors for the support of Christian truth. A certain romanticization of the past speaks from William's words. Up until his point in history, he believes, Christians had worked arduously for the unity of the church. Now, divisive and self–destructive forces emerge – from within. As William suggests, they attack traditional doctrine and those who had given their lives for it. He clearly defines what he believes to be an 'attack' on faith, or in other words, heresy. It is, plainly, the introduction of novelty. Given Abelard's efforts to innovate theological methods and education, he was, in William's eyes, the personification of heretical endeavors:

> Peter Abelard teaches new things and writes new things. His books cross the oceans and traverse the alps. His new statements of faith and his new doctrines are carried between provinces and realms. They are preached with celebration and defended freely, so much so that they are said to have authority even in the Roman Curia.[109]

A modern reader could understand this assessment as flattering. Indeed, William acknowledges the astounding success of Abelard's teachings and his literary output. Yet, his words should by no means be taken as praise; the fact that Abelard's writings seem to be celebrated throughout the intellectual world is all the more proof of the actuality of this threat. Abelard was famous for his teaching and had acquired quite a large crowd of pupils at this point. Abelard's professed aim, with his insistence on the importance of dialectics, was pedagogical.[110] Rather than presenting a fully developed

---

109   Disputatio adversus Petrum Abaelardum, cccm 89A, par. 1, pag. 13, linea 14: *Petrus enim Abaelardus iterum noua docet, noua scribit, et libri eius transeunt maria, transsiliunt Alpes, et nouae eius sententiae de fide, et noua dogmata per prouincias et regna deferuntur, celebriter praedicantur et libere defenduntur, in tantum ut in curia etiam Romana dicantur habere auctoritatem.*
110   Lohr, "Peter Abälard," 99.

opinion to his students, he wanted to instruct them in the arts that would aid them in finding the truth for themselves.

William's fear that Abelard's teachings would 'corrupt future generations' faith related directly to Abelard's intention. Truth, William believed, should not be considered a matter of individual discovery. To convince one's pupils of the idea that they could discover new truths through intellectual pursuit would be equivalent to instructing them in the arts of heresy. Within William's framework, truth should remain a fixed entity, apart from a student's understanding or lack thereof. Hence, innovation had no part to play in discussing Christian truth.

William's incessant reiteration of the word *novum* shows not that he appreciates Abelard's innovative talents but underscores his sheer disbelief at Abelard's audacity. William has already managed to establish a case of heresy against his opponent without addressing any doctrinal matters yet, for questions of content are of secondary importance.[111] What makes Abelard's claims so outrageous is not any specific case of theological inaccuracy but the fact that they are new. The *Disputatio*'s opening statement thus reveals less about Abelard's theology and more about William's definition of heresy and orthodoxy, respectively.

William's main issue is with Abelard's method of exegesis and his *habitus* regarding Scripture. This he states early on, explaining that it was already the title of Abelard's work that made him expectant ('I admit, the title made me curious').[112] He is speaking, as mentioned earlier, of Abelard's *Theologia "summi boni"*.[113] Although he does not discuss his perplexity any further, I would argue that he takes issue primarily with the term *theologia*.[114] The 'theological' task was just emerging as an academic discipline of its own. William himself had enjoyed studies in the liberal arts, including a particular focus on the discipline of *sacra pagina*. Christian education, as he knew

---

111 This is, however, not the case for all conservative critics of the early scholastic method (Grabmann, *Geschichte der Scholastischen Methode, vol. 2*, 118).

112 Disputatio adversus Petrum Abaelardum, CCCM 89A, par. 1, pag. 13, linea 26: *Fateor, curiosum me fecit titulus ad legendum.*

113 William's accusations as a whole are grounded both on Abelard's *Theologia and the liber sententiarum,* about which William asserts that they share their essential content (Constant J. Mews, "Bernard of Clairvaux and Peter Abelard," in *A Companion to Bernard of Clairvaux* (Leiden: Brill, 2011), 158).

114 This terminological critique can also be found in Bernard's accusations against Abelard (Wendelin Knoch, "Der Streit Zwischen Bernhard von Clairvaux Und Petrus Abaelard: Ein Exemplarisches Ringen Um Verantworteten Glauben," *Freiburger Zeitschrift Für Philosophie Und Theologie* 38 (1991): 306).

and defended it, was centered on the exegetical task. The kind of academic theology that included the application of logic and dialectic to doctrinal questions – *theologia* in a sense, in which it would dominate the scholastic era – had little to do with the task of a Christian thinker, as he understood it. Other than Abelard, William follows here the Augustinian terminology and understanding, which characterizes *theologia* as the discourse about the pagan gods, and preferred the term *divinitas* for the Christian studies that were founded on Scripture.[115]

This should not lead us to the conclusion that William rejected the notion of dialectics per se.[116] He was well versed in it. It was the blending of a philosophic method with reflection on biblical themes that he viewed critically. Abelard, he claimed, demonstrated a lack of respect and reverence towards Scripture, treating it essentially as he would treat any other tractate of Pagan philosophy and disregarding the unique status of the biblical text:

> As almost all the masters of church doctrine have, of course, disappeared, as into an empty void, the domestic enemy of the Church rushed in, considering himself its only master and acting regarding the divine Scripture as one ought only to act regarding dialectics, according to his own devices and annual innovations; as a censor of faith, rather than a student; an enhancer, not an imitator.[117]

William explicitly defines the ideal attitude of a reader towards Scripture, which he had attempted to exemplify implicitly with his reading of Romans. A reader should learn from the Christian faith what he does not yet understand and submit himself to the teachings of holy doctrine as a student to his master. Scripture ought to be imitated to the point of true understanding. What William sees in Abelard is the reversal of these roles: giving

---

115   Abelard, in turn, based his terminology on Boethius rather than Augustine (although he differed from Boethius in other areas, such as his interpretation of Aristotle) (Mews, "The World as Text," 102–103).

116   William's position is representative for most monastic authors of his time, as Cartwright points out: "Monks objected not to dialectic per se, but to its excessive use, to disputation, especially in questions of doctrine" (Cartwright, *The Romans Commentaries*, 239).

117   *Disputatio adversus Petrum Abaelardum*, CCCM 89A, par. 1, pag. 14, linea 38: *Emortuis quippe ex Ecclesia omnibus paene doctrinae ecclesiasticae magistris, quasi in uacuam rempublicam | Ecclesiae domesticus irruens inimicus, singulare sibi in ea magisterium arripuit, agens in Scriptura diuina quod agere solebat in dialectica, proprias adinuentiones, annuas nouitates; censor fidei, non discipulus; emendator, non imitator.*

himself the air of a 'critic of faith' (*censor fidei*), he believes he could improve upon (*emendator*) the doctrines established through the Scriptures and the Fathers. Shortly, he acts within the biblical narrative as one should only ever act in the realm of dialectics itself. This would later prove to be one of the accusations with which the Council of Sens did agree. While similar to the prior proceedings in Soissons, the trial at Sens found little substantive proof of dogmatic inaccuracies or errors in Abelard's corpus; it was the fact that Abelard failed to provide a clear 'line of demarcation' between his philosophical and his doctrinal considerations that would become his downfall.[118]

As Clare Monagle rightly observes, the criticism of the use of philosophy in doctrinal matters, which William was not alone in voicing, was rooted in a fundamentally different view of the world and the role of the Christian faith in it: "That is, the critics of the schools perceived in the dialectical methods of the schoolmen a refusal to accept unity per se, be it in relation to a sacrament, a mystery, or the ecclesia itself."[119] The analytic method of the philosophers was oriented towards differentiation and distinction. To apply it to God would amount to a denial of divine oneness and simplicity.[120] Considering the 12th-century intellectual climate and its proponents' particular interest in the problem of universals, it is plausible that the way

---

118   As Grabmann reconstructs, Abelard did not draw a clear line between philosophy and theology ("hat er doch tatsächlich in seinen wissenschaftlichen Arbeiten keine deutliche Demarkationslinie zwischen philosophischer und theologischer Arbeit gezogen"). He concludes that Bernard and William's critique of Abelard was legitimate insofar as it applies, not to his principles, but to his actual work ("wenn nich Abälards prinzipielle Auffassung, sondern sein praktisches und faktisches Arbeiten getroffen ist") (Grabmann, *Geschichte der Scholastischen Methode, vol. 2*, 196).

119   Clare Monagle, *Orthodoxy and Controversy in Twelfth–Century Religious Discourse: Peter Lombard's "Sentences" and the Development of Theology*, vol. 8, Europa Sacra (Turnhout: Brepols), 2012, 5.

120   The scholastic 'attack' on the simplicity of Christian faith is a separate and important aspect of William's accusations against Abelard. For instance, he denounces Abelard's christology of having distanced itself from the holy simplicity of Christian faith (*sanctam christianae fidei simplicitatem alienis*), thus revealing its obfuscating intention. (Disputatio adversus Petrum Abaelardum, CCCM 89A, cap. 3, pag. 24, linea 42). In Abelard's works, on the other hand, especially those concerned with his self-defense, *simplicitas* receives a negative connotation, as he believes the mindless faith of the *simplices* to be inadequate of Christian truth (Knoch, "Der Streit," 309). In fact, Abelard claims, these 'simple souls' present easy targets for heretics, who hope to entice them with their lies. This is a major argument in his campaign to justify the implementation of dialectics into Christian education (Grabmann, *Geschichte der Scholastischen Methode, vol. 2*, 185).

in which William's perception and definition of reality differed from Abelard's played directly into their conflict. On the one hand, Abelard's dialectic
worldview allowed him to differentiate between the terms he used to describe theoretical systems and the ontological foundation of the things he
discussed. The Cistercian understanding, which William shared with Bernard, tended towards a classical-realist position, emphasizing the reality of
abstract notions and ideas. Whereas Abelard could discuss different signs of
divinity without touching the holiness of God, William believed that any
theological statement would necessarily affect one's relationship with the
divine. As Monagle puts it, this monastic perspective entailed "a mystically
infused view of the world, where meditation upon the Word aroused and
nurtured the individual through a spiritual praxis".[121] Therefore, knowledge
of God could not be pursued as the mere intellectual exercise, as which William perceived the task of *theologia*.

William displays his methodological disagreement with Abelard on a
rhetorical level throughout the *Disputatio*. Whenever he refers to Abelard
personally, he calls him 'this theologian' (*hic theologus*) as though he
could dismiss his work solely by exposing Abelard's inappropriate self-
perception.[122] Abelard's attitude was, as mentioned before, a particular
bone of contention for many of his critics. His project was grounded on the
conviction that his intellectual abilities would qualify him to grasp, analyze
and explain the mystery of faith, threatening understandably the highly
treasured monastic belief in divine ineffability. For William, as for Bernard,
Abelard seemed to disregard God's unspeakable yet all-pervasive presence
in the world.[123] As I have illustrated before, discussing William's emphasis
on humility as the foundation for interpreting Scripture, William considers
superbia to be the sin that distorts a reader's relationship with truth and
impedes insight into the divine mysteries. Abelard's entire endeavor, as

---

121   Monagle, Orthodoxy and Controversy, 25.
122   Discussing Abelard's reflection on the Trinity, William associates the ascription 'theo-
       logian' with intellectual novelty: [...] *in eo quod novus hic theologus invenisse se gloria-
       tur, queritur intellectui suo numquam se sufficiens potuisse invenire eloquium* [...]
       (Disputatio adversus Petrum Abaelardum, CCCM 89A, cap. 4, pag. 35, linea 304). Rhe-
       torically beautiful is his presentation of Abelard's christology, calling it the *nova novi
       theologi theologia de Patre et Filio* (Disputatio adversus Petrum Abaelardum, CCCM
       89A, cap. 3, pag. 24, linea 42). Alternatively, but in a similar tone and intention, Wil-
       liam also refers to Abelard as *novus hic magister* (Disputatio adversus Petrum Abaelar-
       dum, CCCM 89A, cap. 2, pag. 19, linea 72). William shares this negative use of the term
       theologus with Bernard (Mews, "Bernard of Clairvaux and Peter Abelard," 134).
123   Robb, *Intellectual Tradition and Misunderstanding*, 60.

William understands it, is fueled by the invalid glorification of his dialectical skills. It is, therefore, he concludes, doomed to fail from its beginning. In this judgment, William seems to echo Bernard's famous critique of the academic world and its different motivations for intellectual aspiration:

> There are those who want to know, only for the sake of knowing; that is ugly curiosity. There are those who want to know, so that they may be known; that is ugly vanity. There are those who want to know, so that they may edify; that is charity. And there are those who want to know, in order to be edified; that is prudence.[124]

Intentionality is crucial in determining the moral value of an endeavor. Pursuing knowledge for its own sake or to prove one's intellectual prowess invalidates the task itself, as it stems only from human vanity. As we have seen earlier, William often associates *vanitas*, as well as *superbia*, both with the emergence of heresy and with the use of philosophy. Abelard, the 'philosopher' among Christian thinkers, is, therefore, the exemplification of illegitimate and vain curiosity. While it is evident that Abelard would have disagreed with William regarding this negative assessment of his character, it is interesting that he agreed with him regarding the rejection of pride and self-serving curiosity as motivations for theological work.

Heresy, he agreed, was less a consequence of ignorance but rather of the 'tenacity of boastful competition'.[125] However, this agreement between our two authors should not be overstrained. Abelard argues, implicitly against his opponent, that the Pauline *scientia inflat* ought not to be misunderstood as an argument for the demerit of philosophy as such. Whereas William considers the social element of intellectual communities and educational

---

124   Bernard of Clairvaux. *Sermones super Cantica Canticorum.* Centre Traditio Litterarum Occidentalium, CETEDOC., and Brepols (Firm). 2000. *Library of Latin texts. Series A. Series A.* [Turnhout, Belgium]: Brepols. http://clt.brepolis.net/LLTA/pages/Text Search.aspx?key=MBECLSC___ (accessed January 10, 2025), sermo: 36, par. 3, vol. 2, pag. 5, linea 25: *Sunt namque qui scire volunt eo fine tantum, ut sciant: et turpis curiositas est. Et sunt qui scire volunt, ut sciantur ipsi: et turpis vanitas est. Qui profecto non evadent subsannantem Satyricum et ei qui eiusmodi est decantantem: SCIRE TUUM NIHIL EST, NISI TE SCIRE HOC SCIAT ALTER Et sunt item qui scire volunt, ut scientiam suam vendant, verbi causa pro pecunia, pro honoribus: et turpis quaestus est. Sed sunt quoque qui scire volunt, ut aedificent: et caritas est. Et sunt item qui scire volunt, ut aedificentur: et prudentia est.*
125   Heyder, *Auctoritas scripturae,* 221.

contexts as a contributing factor to the sin of pride, Abelard seemingly re-
duces it to an individual question of character.[126]

The use of dialectics, Abelard believes, could never lead to heretical
claims, as dialectics is merely a tool to discover and explain logical truth.
Unsurprisingly, this argument did not convince his opponents, as it missed
the point of their critique. William does not question the logical accuracy of
the dialectical method. His main argument against its use in doctrinal matters is that the Christian faith defies the world's logic and is not suitable for
such reflection. This again presents an instance of terminological confusion
between the two systems of thought. Abelard's definition of faith was that
of the *exestimatio rerum non apparentium*.[127] Faith, he believed, should not
be a matter of habit or inculturation but a personal matter of insight. Authorities should not be trusted based solely on their ecclesial status but because the doctrines they teach are rationally comprehensible. From
Abelard's perspective, to consider faith an *exestimatio* amounted to a higher
appreciation of the concept, emphasizing the responsibility of the believer.

This is, however, not how William and Bernard perceived Abelard's definition: faith, within the mystical framework, is not an opinion but absolute
certainty. It is grounded in the authority of God, rather than the quarreling
opinions of human philosophers: *non est enim fides aestimatio, sed certi-
tudo*.[128] Faith, for William, is the confession to the Trinitarian God rather
than the theoretical explication of the Trinitarian formula.[129] The notion
that this terminological and conceptual difference between the two perspectives contributed significantly to the course of their conflict is evidenced by
the fact that William introduces the doctrinal part of his *Disputatio* with a
citation of Augustine's definition of faith, to contradict Abelard's:

> Blessed Augustine says: "Faith is not to be judged or decided in the
> heart by the one in whom it is, but is a certain science acclaimed by
> the conscience." Far be it that the Christian faith has as boundaries
> estimations, academic opinions, and the assessment of those whose
> tenet it is to believe nothing, know nothing, and guess everything.[130]

---

126   Grabmann, *Geschichte der Scholastischen Methode, vol. 2*, 184.

127   Robb, *Intellectual Tradition and Misunderstanding*, 58.

128   Robb, *Intellectual Tradition and Misunderstanding*, 306.

129   Disputatio adversus Petrum Abaelardum, CCCM 89A, cap. 2, pag. 18 linea 44: *Propter
       quod dicimus, quoniam cum in nomine Patris et Filii et Spiritus sancti a catholicis patri-
       bus diuinitas praedicatur, fidei est haec professio, non diuinitatis descriptio.*

130   Disputatio adversus Petrum Abaelardum, CCCM 89A, cap. 1, pag. 17 linea 9: *Absit
       enim ut hos fines habeat christiana fides, aestimationes scilicet siue opiniones*

What makes this use of Patristic authority particularly interesting is that William does not theologically or argumentatively add to the Augustinian quotation. He does not feel the need to improve upon it in terms of content nor explain and defend Augustine's position through his reasoning.[131] William's trust in the inspired notion of Patristic works and his authoritatively based understanding of faith allows him to rely on the Fathers' support in his conflict in an unmediated way. While this passage gives the impression of Augustine addressing Abelard directly, William's role in the conflict becomes that of making it seem this way. He does not explicate the details of the Augustinian statement, but he does give the reader the information he needs to identify Abelard as one of Augustine's targets. Abelard, he suggests, is proposing theological insights without believing or knowing, solely deriving them from guesses. This depiction allows the reader to fill in the blanks and view Abelard as actively opposing the Augustinian doctrine of faith.

In his *Expositio*, William claimed to pursue a different aim than Paul and Augustine before him – not defending catholic doctrine against heretics but facilitating the spiritual experience of true doctrine in the hearts of Christian believers.[132] Yet, in his *Disputatio*, he presents the Fathers as his brothers in arms, joining not only their general fight against heretical tendencies but against the very same kind of heresies against which they had written. One of the *Disputatio*'s main literary features is that the Fathers appear not as abstract authorities but as William's real, seemingly contemporary companions. As in the *Expositio*, Augustine takes on the leading role again, showing that William appreciated him for his exegetical talents and for his historical part in establishing doctrinal orthodoxy. Seamlessly introducing Augustinian arguments in a theological dispute of the 12th century does not, in this case, demonstrate William's lacking awareness of context.

---

academicorum sint aestimationes istae, quorum sententia est nichil credere, nichil scire, sed omnia aestimare. Sita Steckel discusses this passage as an indirect response to Abelard's conception of faith as an existimatio rerum non apparentium, and understands William's perspective as a recovery of earlier medieval conceptions which "assumed that extraordinarily gifted humans were indeed able to understand divine truth" (Steckel, "Charisma and Expertise," 669).

131 However, it becomes clear, as the text goes on, that William, following Paul, closely associates the concepts of *fides, spes,* and *caritas.* If faith is not trusted as the sole source of intellectual insight, it loses its quality, and with that, both Christian hope and love wither (Disputatio adversus Petrum Abaelardum, CCCM 89A, cap. 1, pag. 17, linea 13).

132 Expositio super Epistolam ad Romanos, Praef., linea 21: [...] *nos autem ad plenae humilitatis affectum et purae deuotionis effectum nostrorum cordibus desideramus inscribi.*

Instead, William's literary strategy was to demonstrate the surprising likeness of his and Augustine's circumstances, especially regarding their respective opponents. Heresy, he claims, does not die easily. The same arguments
the Fathers had to counter reappear throughout Christian history as one of
the symptoms of the sin of *superbia*. He paints Abelard's theology as yet another reiteration of the positions refuted centuries ago. From a modern
standpoint, William's dedication to this cause looks like he was attempting
to defend the last garrison of the 'old world' against an inevitable rise of
intellectual progress. His perspective was decidedly different. His position
had been proven right throughout conciliar history and, he believed, would
certainly be proven right again. It was not the scholastic era to come that he
believed to be his enemy, but Abelard, in particular, as one of the few dis-
senting voices within an educational and spiritual context that largely supported the conservation of orthodox doctrine and traditional method.

On a literary level, his *Disputatio* portrayed this perspective by drawing
a direct parallel between Abelard's teachings and Arian, Manichaean, Sa-
bellian, or Pelagian claims.[133] William structures his *Disputatio* according
to the dogmatic missteps he identifies in Abelard's *theologia*. Thirteen in
total, the accusations range from Trinitarian to hamartiological issues. Although the doctrinal particularities of these accusations shall not be central to the study at hand, they nevertheless deserve to be mentioned. The
Disputatio notes thirteen of Abelard's claims that William considers doctrinally problematic:

1. That he defines faith as the guessing of a thing that cannot be
seen.[134]

---

133   As R.I. Moore points out, "the myth of the medieval manichee was a creation of the
      period after the middle of the twelfth century" (R.I. Moore, "Literacy and the Making
      of Heresy c. 1000–1150," in *Heresy and Literacy 1000–1530*, ed. Peter Biller and Anne
      Hudson (Cambridge: Cambridge University Press, 1996), 23). While Moore cites Gui-
      bert of Nogent and his interrogation of Clement of Bucy, as one of the earliest cases of
      such an 'anachronistic' use of heresy accusations. As I am hoping to show, William too
      could be considered one of these early exponents of the trope.
134   Disputatio adversus Petrum Abaelardum, CCCM 89A, par. 3, pag. 14, linea 45: *Quod
      fidem diffinit aestimationem rerum quae non uidentur*. Ingo Klitzsch remarks that while
      Abelard had intended to differentiate the term existimatio (meant to be used in regard
      to the non-apparent things) and cognitio (meant to be used for present things), Wil-
      liam, as well as Thomas of Morigny interpreted Abelard's notion as a sign that he re-
      fused to accept certainty in matters of faith (Ingo Klitzsch, *Die "Theologien" des Petrus*

2. That he considers it improper to ascribe the names of the Father, the Son, and the Holy Spirit to God, but this description is of the fullness of the Highest Good (*summi boni*).[135]

3. That the father is full power (*potentia*), the Son some power, and the Spirit no power at all.[136]

4. Of the Holy Spirit, that it is not [in the same way] of the substance of the Father and the Son as the Son is of the substance of the Father.[137]

Abaelardus: genetisch–kontextuelle Analyse und theologiegeschichtliche Relektüre (Leipzig: Evangelische Verlagsanstalt, 2010), 436).

135 Disputatio adversus Petrum Abaelardum, CCCM 89A, par. 3, pag. 14, linea 46: *Quod impropria dicit esse in Deo nomina Patris et Filii et Spiritus Sancti, sed descriptionem hanc esse plenitudinis summi boni.* This accusation entails issues, both with the Abelardian conception of the Trinity, and related to the issue of Abelard's particular position in the nominalist controversy. Peter King summarizes the Abelardian stance, to which William likely refers in this claim, as follows: "The three Persons are essentially the same as one another, since they are all the same concrete thing (namely, God); they differ from one another in definition, since what it is to be the Father is not the same as what it is to be the Son or what it is to be the Holy Spirit. The three Persons are numerically different from one another, for otherwise they would not be three, but they are not numerically different from God: if they were there would be three gods, not one" (Peter King, "Metaphysics," in *The Cambridge Companion to Abelard*, ed. Jeffrey E. Brower and Kevin Guilfoy. Cambridge Companions to Philosophy (Cambridge: Cambridge University Press, 2004), 91). Read in such a nuanced way, the potential for heresy is not as apparent, as it would have been to William, who had understood Abelard's position to indicate that the three names of the Trinity did not arise from the divine substance itself, but were merely human descriptions of their experience with God.

136 Disputatio adversus Petrum Abaelardum, CCCM 89A, par. 3, pag. 14, linea 48: *Quod Pater sit plena potentia, Filius quaedam potentia, Spiritus Sanctus nulla potentia.* What William is referring to here is Abelard's teaching of the properties applied to the three persons of the Trinity. He ascribes *potentia* to the Father, *sapientia* to the Son and *bonitas* to the Spirit. William, however, seems to be unclear about Abelard's differentiation of categories between the properties and the substance of God (see an explanation of this very problem in King, "Metaphysics," 91).

137 Disputatio adversus Petrum Abaelardum, CCCM 89A, par. 3, pag. 14, linea 49: *De Spiritu Sancto, quod non sit ex substantia Patris et Filii, sicut Filius est ex substantia Patris.* The problem William is referencing here arises from a logical dilemma Abelard faced in his theoretical conception of the Trinity. As Jeffrey E. Brower puts it, Abelard had to reconcile the Oneness of God's substance with the fact that "as the names of the divine persons suggest, they are traditionally thought to possess different essential attributes: only the Father begets, only the Son is begotten, and only the Holy Spirit proceeds or 'spirates' from that of which it is the spirit. But no things, not even divine persons, can be both identical to and distinct from one another" (Jeffrey E. Brower, "Trinity," in *The*

5. That the Holy Spirit is the World's Soul (*anima mundi*).[138]

6. That by free will, without the help of grace, we can both will and act well.[139]

7. That Christ did not assume flesh and suffered, to free us from the Devil's law.[140]

8. That Christ, God, and man, is not the third person in the Trinity.[141]

9. That in the sacrament of the altar the form of the earlier substance remains in the atmosphere (*in aere*).[142]

     Cambridge Companion to Abelard, ed. Jeffrey E. Brower and Kevin Guilfoy. Cambridge Companions to Philosophy (Cambridge: Cambridge University Press, 2004), 224).

138   Disputatio adversus Petrum Abaelardum, CCCM 89A, par. 3, pag. 14, linea 51: *Quod Spiritus Sanctus sit anima mundi.* John Marenbon differentiates two phases in the thought of Abelard regarding the World Soul. In his Dialectica, he rejected the term and any identification of the Spirit with the *anima mundi*; in the *Theologia "summi boni"*, however, he embraces the very notion that Plato and the Platonists were describing the Trinity as Good, Intellect and World Soul. Further, he contextualizes the debate as a pressing issue of 12th-century theology, and the reception of classic ancient philosophy as such (Marenbon, "Life, milieu, and intellectual contexts," 35–36).

139   Disputatio adversus Petrum Abaelardum, CCCM 89A, par. 3, pag. 14, linea 52: *Quod libero arbitrio sine adiuuante gratia bene possumus et uelle et agere.* Rozanne Elder has discussed this problem at length, exploring William's conception of the *homo dissolutus* (Elder, "The Christology," 87–91).

140   Disputatio adversus Petrum Abaelardum, CCCM 89A, par. 3, pag. 14, linea 53: *Quod Christus non ideo assumpsit carnem et passus est, ut nos a iugo diaboli liberaret.* This accusation would go on to be a central issue in the eventual condemnation of Abelard after Bernard accused him of exemplarism and Pelagianism (see on this issue: Thomas Williams, "Sin, Grace, and Redemption," in *The Cambridge Companion to Abelard,* ed. Jeffrey E. Brower and Kevin Guilfoy. Cambridge Companions to Philosophy (Cambridge: Cambridge University Press, 2004), 259). This too has been a particular concern of study for Rozanne Elder, who has discussed the "the Reasons for the Incarnation" according to William, and identifies twelve reasons in total (Elder, "The Christology," 92–93). William's teachings on the 'new justice' established by Christ are, as Elder argues, as explicit as they are because he had to flesh them out in response to Abelard (Elder, "The Christology," 97).

141   Disputatio adversus Petrum Abaelardum, CCCM 89A, par. 3, pag. 14, linea 54: *Quod Christus Deus et homo non est tertia persona in Trinitate.* This too would become a central accusation in the Council of Sens, and a claim that other so-called 'new heretics' would also be confronted with. It touches on the problem of the nature of Christ, and the question of whether his assumed humanity truly makes him God and man (Nicholas M. Häring, "The So–Called 'Apologia de Verbo Incarnato'," *Franciscan Studies* 16, no. 1/2 (1956): 107).

142   Disputatio adversus Petrum Abaelardum, CCCM 89A, par. 3, pag. 14, linea 55: *Quod in Sacramento altaris in aere remaneat forma prioris substantiae.* This problem, like most of the concerns William had with Abelard's concept of the Trinity, relates back to

10. That the diabolical suggestions are caused in humans in a natural way (*per physicam*).[143]

11. That from Adam we do not drag the guilt of original sin, but the punishment.[144]

12. That there is no sin, except in consent to the sin and in contempt of God.[145]

13. That he says in desire, delight, and ignorance, no sin is committed, and that such things are not sin, but nature.[146]

William treats them all similarly, presenting first a straightforward account of Abelard's position and then countering it with a Patristic quotation. At times, this approach seems to give a judicial dialogue between the Fathers, as the plaintiffs, Abelard as the accused, and William as either clerk or

---

Abelard's stance in the nominalist controversy, and his position in regard to the distinction between accidents and substance.

143   Disputatio adversus Petrum Abaelardum, cccm 89A, par. 3, pag. 14, linea *57: Quod suggestiones diabolicas per physicam fieri dicit in hominibus.* Rozanne Elder argues that William did not have "much attachment to the devil's rights theory – never arguing it apart from the Disputation – but because Abelard so cavalierly dismissed the teaching of the Church Fathers and tradition" (Elder, "The Christology," 98). The real issue with this statement is, however, that he reads Abelard's account of Satanic power as relieving humanity of its responsibility; Satanic power, he argues, was brought upon humanity by choice, not God–given nature (Elder, "The Christology," 88).

144   Disputatio adversus Petrum Abaelardum, cccm 89A, par. 3, pag. 14, linea 58: *Quod ab Adam non trahimus originalis peccati culpam, sed poenam.* Abelard focuses in his soteriology on the term of eternal punishment and the consequences of that punishment in this earthly life, rather than on the fallen nature of humanity (Williams, "Sin, grace, and redemption," 267-68). William's soteriology, however, is firmly planted in a discussion of human nature and redemption, not just from punishment, but from sinfulness itself (Elder, "The Christology," 96–99).

145   Disputatio adversus Petrum Abaelardum, cccm 89A, par. 3, pag. 14, linea 59: *Quod nullum sit peccatum, nisi in consensu peccati et contemptu Dei.* William references here Abelard's notion that "to form an intention to do something is to consent to that thing", and his belief that the stage of consent is inherent to the definition of sin (William E. Mann, "Ethics," in *The Cambridge Companion to Abelard,* ed. Jeffrey E. Brower and Kevin Guilfoy. Cambridge Companions to Philosophy (Cambridge: Cambridge University Press, 2004), 285–86).

146   Disputatio adversus Petrum Abaelardum, cccm 89A, par. 3, pag. 14, linea 60: *Quod dicit concupiscentia et delectatione et ignorantia nullum peccatum committi et huiusmodi non esse peccatum, sed naturam.* William here likely references Abelard's critical reading of Augustine's *De libero arbitrio,* arguing that not all evil acts are the result of sinful desire. See on this problem and the differences between the Abelardian and the Augustinian conception: Mann, "Ethics," 282–285.

witness, depending on the charge. This is, for instance, observable as William addresses Abelard's theology of the Trinitarian names. First, William
presents his understanding of Abelard's error as it relates to the tradition of
the Catholic doctrine.[147] In the introductory passages, in which he refrains
from using the Fathers' authority, he bases the legitimacy of his position on
the *usus loquendi*:[148] Historical faith, as it has been practiced and preached
over centuries, participates in the authority of the church. William's argument of a traditional and thus binding use of language has to be read in the
immediate context of Abelard's consideration of linguistic logic.

Whereas Abelard uses the argument of *usus loquendi* to relativize the literal aspect of authoritative teachings, William uses it to enforce them. He
advocates for a practiced and experienced articulation of doctrine rather
than a purely theoretical one: how faith had been articulated by those who
had contributed to the growth of the church is just as theologically valuable
as the reflection of philosophically trained scholars. William's side–by–side
presentation of the Abelardian claims and the orthodox view, as he understands it, allows him then to introduce the Patristic quotation that forms his
central argument:

> Contrary to the one who says it is inappropriate to apply to God the
> names of the Father, the Son, and the Holy Spirit as if another mean-
> ing was reflected in those names, that is against Arius, the blessed
> Ambrose has said in his book on the Holy Spirit: "Hear the Son of
> God: either destroy [his] name or confess [his] nature."[149]

---

147   Rozanne Elder perfectly conveys the impressive extent of William's Patristic knowl-
      edge: "William could draw on considerable theological reserves to demonstrate his
      Chalcedonian – and Augustinian – orthodoxy, identifying and denouncing perceived
      Arianism, Sabellianism, Nestorianism, as well as unique Abelardianisms, defending the
      unity of the person of Christ and denouncing confusion of natures, attacking irrever-
      ence for mystery, and careless terminology, using accurately the vocabulary of homo-
      ousion, hypostases, theotocon, and quaternity, and quoting on the subject not
      Augustine, but Leo the Great, Gregory the Great, Origen – though less lavishly than
      some scholars would have had us believe –, Cyril of Alexandria and Boethius" (Elder,
      "The Christology," 88).
148   Disputatio adversus Petrum Abaelardum, cccm 89A, cap. 2, pag. 20, linea 95: *Non
      quod saepius in Scripturis et in usu loquendi et consuetudine tractandi, Patri non ascri-
      batur potentia, sapientia Filio, benignitas seu caritas Spiritui sancto, sed secundum ra-
      tionem fidei et intellectum pietatis, ut semper et quantum ad omnipotentiam efficiendi, et
      quantum ad benignitatem miserendi, | non tantum potens sed et omnipotens intelligatur
      Pater, omnipotens Filius, omnipotens Spiritus sanctus* [...].
149   Disputatio adversus Petrum Abaelardum, cccm 89A, cap. 2, pag. 21, linea 141: *Contra
      hoc | uero quod dicit impropria esse in Deo nomina Patris et Filii et Spiritus sancti,*

Having presented the content of Abelard's *Theologia*, William lets Ambrose draw the conclusion. Abelard's reflection on the Trinity is a reiteration of the Arian heresy and, thus, heretical in nature. Yet, William does not rely entirely on the dogmatic argument as such. His citation of the Bishop of Milan is chosen so deliberately that he makes it seem as though Ambrose had prophetically addressed the future issue of scholastic curiosity, as he lets him speak to Abelard directly:

"Why does it please you to be tormented by questions? I am allowed to know that the Son of God was born, but I am not allowed to know in what way (*quomodo*) he was born". That is: "These names are not empty, but operating as indices of virtue. The Father is not the Son, but between the Father and the Son, there is expressed a distinction of generation so that God is understood out of God."[150]

On the one hand, the Fathers had established the content of Catholic doctrines. On the other hand, perhaps more importantly, they had defined the boundaries of theological thinking. The wording of the Ambrosian quote is crucial: one is only to ask the questions one is allowed (*licet*) to ask.[151] For

---

    tamquam aliud significantia quam quod in nominibus ipsis sonat, hoc est contra Arianos beatus Ambrosius in libro De Spiritu sancto dicit: "Audis Filium Dei: aut dele nomen aut confitere naturam. [...]."

150 Disputatio adversus Petrum Abaelardum, CCCM 89A, cap. 2, pag. 21, linea 145–148: *Quid te quaestionum tormenta delectant? Mihi licet scire de Filio Dei quod natus est, non licet scire quomodo natus est. Item: "Non sunt nuda haec nomina, sed operatricis uirtutis indicia. Non enim ipse Pater qui Filius, sed inter Patrem et Filium generationis est expressa distinctio, ut ex Deo Deus intelligatur".*

151 John Slotemaker has kindly called my attention to a quotation from Peter Lombard, that seems to echo William's caution in regard to the questioning of divine activity. Lombard, referring to Augustine's *Contra Maximinum* states: *Quid autem inter nasci et procedere intersit, de illa excellentissima natura loquens explicare quis potest? Non omne quod procedit nascitur, quamuis omne procedat quod nascitur; sicut non omne quod bipes est, homo est, quamuis bipes sit omnis qui homo est. Hoc scio. Distinguere autem inter illam generationem et hanc processionem nescio, non ualeo, non sufficio.* (Peter Lombard, *Sententiae in Iu Libris Distinctae*. Centre Traditio Litterarum Occidentalium, CETEDOC., and Brepols (Firm). 2010. *Library of Latin texts. Series A. Series A.* [Turnhout, Belgium]: Brepols. http://clt.brepolis.net/LLTA/pages/TextSearch.aspx?key=MPELOSENT_ (accessed January 10, 2025), Lib. 1., dist. 13, cap. 3, par. 4, linea 1). This could reveal on the one hand, that William's sentiment was not as reactionary as it is often made out to be. On the other hand, Lombard's argument seems to be one that refuses to ask the question at hand in detail not out of moral obligation, but because he felt the human mind was not adequately equipped to answer it. William however, as the use of *licet/non licet* shows, believes in an ethical limitation.

William, this amounts to a Patristic rejection of the kind of theological pursuit for which Abelard advocated. Applying the dialectic methodology to Scripture (and the Patristic corpus) indicates a clear transgression of the boundaries the Fathers had set up for intellectual inquiry in William's eyes. With Ambrose, he provides a convincing reason for his position: logical analysis – and essentially a philosophical 'deconstruction' – of the divine attributes is inappropriate because theological assertions are not empty (*nudum*) formulas.

They are grounded in the reality of divine existence and affect human life in a very real way.[152] For William, Abelard's theoretical conception of divine nature relates directly to the personal God, in whom he believes: changing a doctrine would essentially amount to changing one's God. This becomes clear in his discussion of Abelardian pneumatology:

> I do not want to withdraw from the good name, in which I was baptized, in which I am elected as a Christian; I do not know exactly [how] to talk about God, but I know to listen, and that I do not understand anything regarding the names of the Father, the Son, and the Holy Spirit.[153]

This passage reveals the true chasm between Abelard's and William's respective contexts. For William, theological reflection does not occur in the sphere of the intellectual but in the sacramental sphere. Words are not spoken out of argumentative necessity but because they hold the power to change the human condition fundamentally. William's insistence on adherence to the traditional Trinitarian names is rooted in ecclesial practice. The believer is baptized and redeemed in the Catholic name of God. To retract the Trinitarian formula would mean to nullify its sacramental effect on the human soul.

---

152   Again, William is revealing his position in the 'universalia argument'. However, it is not his primary concern to enter the debate with explicit arguments, nor to fight Abelard's conceptualism. His realism shines through implicitly, as he discusses his issues with Abelard's method and his treatment of concepts, doctrines, and notably divine names. His usage of the term *nuda nomina* at this point in the argument could rather be read as a nod to Roscelin's claim that human terminology are merely *flatus vocis*, although this is purely speculation.

153   Disputatio adversus Petrum Abaelardum, CCCM 89A, cap. 4, pag. 28, linea 63: *Nolo ergo recedere a nomine bono, in quo baptizatus sum, in quo christianus sum designatus; nec prorsus loqui scio de Deo, sive audire, sive intelligere aliquid nisi in nomine Patris et Filii et Spiritus sancti.*

Concerning Abelard's doctrine of the Holy Spirit, William again refers to Patristic authority. Equating the Abelardian view with that of ancient Arians, a quotation of Augustine's rebuttal of the latter suffices as evidence against his opponent.[154] He pursues this literary pattern through several of his arguments. This should not imply that William did not care about the dogmatic issues; however, he felt it more appropriate to let those address them, who had already successfully eradicated growing heresies. The *Disputatio* depicts a raging conflict between authorities. As William calls upon the Fathers' voices, he accuses Abelard of relying on an entirely different kind of authoritative support: that of Plato. Platonist ideas act in the text as a counter-model to Patristic theology because they are presented as mutually exclusive. This was, of course, even in the 12th century, a far-reaching thesis since the history of Christian doctrine owed a great debt to Neoplatonist principles, and William himself was far from immune to their influence. Apart from Patristic arguments against specific Platonist notions,[155] which do not pertain to the issue of pagan sources as such, William attempts to illustrate that Abelard's adoration of Plato amounts to idolatry:

He is embarrassed of the gospel of God; the simplicity of the Christian faith is worthless to him. If only he read the gospel of God with the same benevolence with which he reads Plato.[156] [...].

---

154 *Quod non ego ex me, sed beatus Augustinus hoc dicit: "Deus etiam", inquit, "spiritus est"* (Disputatio adversus Petrum Abaelardum, CCCM 89A, cap. 4, pag. 29, linea 91), and further: *Vnde etiam legimus quia Ariani, cum olim principibus huius saeculi patrocinantibus siue fauentibus, Orthodoxorum fidei insultarent, de eo quod Filium natum de substantia Patris praedicarent, urgebant dicentes: "Si de Deo natus est, de intra Deum. Si de intra Deum non est, de Deo non est"* (Disputatio adversus Petrum Abaelardum, CCCM 89A, cap. 4, pag. 35, linea 287). In conclusion, William suggests that Augustine's *De Trinitate* directly pertains to Abelardian pneumatology.

155 Against Abelard's reiteration of the Platonist concept of a 'world soul', William simply states: *Sed sensum hunc de anima mundi legimus iam olim a beato Augustino reprobatum.* It is notable that William (like other contemporary critics of Abelard) misunderstood Abelardian pneumatology. He understood the *anima mundi* as a pagan analogy to the Christian doctrine in an attempt to redeem Platonist philosophy (Lohr, "Peter Abälard," 103–104), but did not draw the usual pantheistic conclusions from the concept (Grabmann, *Geschichte der Scholastischen Methode, vol. 2*, 194).

156 Disputatio adversus Petrum Abaelardum, CCCM 89A, cap. 7, pag. 43, linea 56–57: *Erubescit euangelium Dei; uiluit apud eum christianae fidei simplicitas. Qui utinam uel ea beneuolentia legeret euangelium Dei, qua Platonem legit.*

In thoroughly Augustinian fashion, although without quoting him at this point, William sets up the premise that loving anything or anyone but God in a way only God should be enjoyed is the very definition of sin. His account of Abelard's fascination with pagan philosophy thus paints a picture of blasphemous worship: instead of pursuing the *imitatio Christi*, Abelard attempts to imitate Plato.[157] Addressing the issue of his supposedly non-exegetical method, he reads Plato rather than Scripture. His misdirected veneration goes so far that he is 'ashamed of the Gospel' (*erubescit evangelium Dei*), personifying the antonym of the Pauline ideal.[158] For William, this is not simply a matter of intellectual error but moral wrongdoing. Believing in Plato and, consequentially, Plato's notion of the divine means rejecting the Christian conception and denying Christ's redeeming power.[159]

This evokes the question of the inner necessity of certain Catholic doctrines. William assumes, along with the Fathers, one harmonious biblical narrative of creation, fall, and redemption. Its inherent coherency guarantees its authoritative nature. It cannot be segmented into individual claims, which one can then question individually without attacking its entirety. Abelard's approach calls this understanding of orthodox faith into question, as he no longer accepts inner necessity as an argument for doctrinal truth.[160] Dialectical reflection demands a logical justification for a doctrinal

---

157   Something he does, as Thomas Ricklin pointed out, not very accurately, given that even Plato had shown more reverence to the divine mystery (see Thomas Ricklin, *Plato Im Zwölften Jahrhundert: Einige Hinweise Zu Seinem Verschwinden,* in *The Platonic Tradition in the Middle Ages,* ed. Maarten J.F.M. Hoenen and Stephen E. Gersh (Berlin: De Gruyter, 2002). Ricklin refers to the following passage: *Vtinam et in hoc imitaretur Platonem, quem amat, quod ille cum de Deo agit, caute ac prudenter edicit quod ipso reuelante aestimando de creatura Creatorem, de eo sentit uel intelligit, caetera cum philosophica reuerentia patienter ignorans, inquirentes mittit ad ideas, quas esse dicit in mente summi Dei* (Disputatio adversus Petrum Abaelardum, CCCM 89A, cap. 7, pag. 43, linea 62).

158   William here alludes to Rm 1, 16.

159   Disputatio adversus Petrum Abaelardum, CCCM 89A, cap. 7, pag. 44, linea 91: *Amplecteretur certe et hic communis salutis effectum, nec tam temere uel curiose scrutaretur saluandi modos, si credendo et amando tantum deferret Christo mundi Saluatori, quantum Plato aestimando detulit Deo mundi Creatori.*

160   The argument of necessity is especially important for William, as for Bernard, in the context of christology: "The love of Christ for humankind manifested in his death stirs a subjective response in the human breast, Abelard thought, enkindling the love, which alone can obliterate contempt for God – the Abelardian definition of sin (and another of Abelard's errors in Williamvs eyes. After reading this, William delated Abelard to Bernard, and Bernard Abelard to the world, for saying that Christ died for nothing (*gratis*)" (Elder, "The Christology," 94).

claim to be accepted as true. For William, this demand is tantamount to a rejection of Patristic authority altogether:[161]

> "So, as the doctors say, it is necessary that the Son of God became incarnate because mankind could not be delivered rightfully from the law of the devil in any other way than through the death of an innocent. But, as it seems to us (*ut nobis videtur*), the devil's law has no claim on mankind save with the permission of God. Thus as a jailor, and not the Son of God, he took on flesh, to liberate mankind."[162] Is something we assert therefore better than what the doctors after the apostles have agreed on? Is what has been revealed to him, or what he has discovered, better than what those who have been taught by God have told us? Surely wisdom is deeper? Surely understanding is sharper? Surely life is more holy? Surely authority weighs heavier? "It doesn't seem so to us" (*nobis non videtur*), he says. What if it seems like it through the wisdom of God? What if it seems like it to Paul and other apostles?[163]

Abelard, William fears, asserts himself as a judge of spiritual insights and their accuracy. If a specific theological claim is not evident to him, it must not be apparent to anyone – *nobis non videtur*. This is where William's

---

161   This passage pertains to William's accusations against Abelard's view of the devil's rights. The respective theological arguments have been discussed at length by Rozanne Elder, demonstrating that William, although hoping to present an orthodox view, was not necessarily in line with the common 12th-century understanding: "But he differed from many of his contemporaries in believing that man, not God, had given evil power over himself [...]. The devil, he thought, simply provided the opportunity. Man deformed himself by the free exercise of his will and lost the freedom of choosing and acting on that choice" (Elder, "The Christology," 88).

162   Rozanne Elder, has named this a "non–solution" in William's eyes (Elder, "The Christology," 115).

163   Disputatio adversus Petrum Abaelardum, CCCM 89A, cap. 6, pag. 42, linea 19: *Ideo, sicut dicunt doctores, hac necessitate incarnatus est Filius Dei, ut homo qui aliter liberari non poterat, per mortem innocentis iure liberaretur a iugo diaboli. Sed, ut nobis uidetur, nec diabolus umquam in homine habuit ius aliquod, nisi forte Deo permittente, sicut carcerarius, nec Filius Dei, ut hominem liberaret, carnem assumpsit. "Vt nobis", inquit, "uidetur". Melius ergo ipse aliquid asseret nobis, quam in quo omnes doctores post apostolos conuenerunt et consentiunt? Melius ne aliquid ei reuelatum est, uel ipse per se adinuenit, quam quod nos docuerunt qui a Domino didicerunt?Num sapientia ei profundior? Num sensus acutior? Num uita sanctior? Num auctoritas grauior? "Nobis", ait, "non uidetur". Quid si ipsi sapientiae Dei hoc uisum est? Si apostolo Paulo et caeteris apostolis hoc uisum est?*

understanding of intellectual *superbia* becomes tangible: Abelard's belief
that every kind of insight needs to be logically comprehensible for him to
be valid lacks a sense of *humilitas* that would allow him to ascribe knowledge to the Fathers, in which he does not participate. A dialectically consistent system leaves little room for the mystic possibility of individual
revelation or spiritual experience as a source of knowledge.

Although there are real and practical implications to the doctrinal errors
William locates in Abelard's work, his criticism is primarily methodological;
Abelard's fallacious *habitus* as a reader of Scripture and an author of theological work would inevitably lead him into an entire field of heresies. William addresses a long list of instances in which this has already happened,
yet it is not William's primary objective to point out the nature of Abelard's
heretical claims. Instead, insisting on Abelard's participation in ancient heresies proves a more pragmatic point: given that Abelard's 'new' method
yields theological discoveries that closely resemble the long-refuted claims
of ancient heretics, William concludes that his project is futile.

There is a tension inherent to William's twofold critique of Abelard's pursuit of 'old heresies'[164] on the other. It can only be resolved if Abelard's
claims are understood to offer mere illusions of novelty. Just as William
uses *theologus* as a provocative term rather than an expression of respect, I
am inclined to understand his liberal use of the term *novus* as a rhetorical
side blow against Abelard's supposed arrogance. While the Fathers, on a
literary level, reveal Abelard's doctrinal errors,[165] William focuses on the
more general critique of Abelard's intention and the validity of a *theologia*,
such as his.

Ultimately, the *Disputatio* is not a dogmatic analysis but a passionate
plea. It is William's expression of deep concern for the future of Christian
thought, as he envisioned it in the context of the Cistercian reform movement. The accusations William raised against Abelard reveal not only the
differences between the two authors but also show their similarities. Both
were, in their respective fields, engaged visionaries on the verge of a significant cultural shift. While Abelard dedicated his work to the flourishing of
the his theological method and attempted to free Christian thought of

---

164   Disputatio adversus Petrum Abaelardum, CCCM 89A, cap. 3, pag. 26, linea 125: *Sed*
      haereses istae antiquae et uetustissimae ueterum sunt.
165   Disputatio adversus Petrum Abaelardum, CCCM 89A, cap. 6, pag. 39, linea 34: *Contra*
      quam quantis librorum uoluminibus, quantis tractatibus a sanctis doctoribus, Augustino,
      Hieronymo multis que aliis pugnatum est, et quomodo iam olim ab ecclesiae liminibus et
      fidelium cordibus anathematizata est, neminem arbitror ignorare qui uel leuiter | diuino-
      rum librorum familiarem habuerit lectionem.

certain boundaries, William hoped for a period in which exegesis would become more profound and experiential. Both had clear expectations for the Christian world to come and shared a certain idealism. I would thus argue that theologically and methodologically, a comparative reading of Abelard's and William's works is in some ways more fruitful than a juxta-position of Abelard's and Bernard's ideas. Yet, the latter pair would go down in history as the most famous intellectual opponents of the 12th cen-tury. At the same time, William often receives not so much as a sub-clause in the conflict's historiography. To evaluate not only the intent but also the actual consequences of William's *Disputatio* and its importance for the course of Abelard's heresy trial, it is thus vital to consider Bernard's politi-cal implementation of the text, of which he was – bear in mind – the ini-tial addressee.[166]

4   Bernard's Involvement and the Council of Sens

The Council of Sens owes its recent historiography in large part to the in-sightful and thorough work of Constant Mews.[167] His study on the trial's date and broader context has introduced the consideration of the political factors that contributed to Abelard's condemnation, which had been lacking in earlier studies.[168] My following account of the council's history is thus heavily indebted to Mews' discoveries. They present a shift of interpretation in the conflict between Bernard and Abelard, which had been portrayed as a battle between tradition and innovation for centuries.[169] While this

---

166   The letter was addressed to Bernard of Clairvaux, as well as to Geoffrey of Lèves, Bishop of Chartres (E. Rozanne Elder, "William of Saint–Thierry and the Renewal of the Whole 'Man'" in *A Companion to William of Saint–Thierry* (Brill, 2019), 111).

167   Constant J. Mews, "The Council of Sens (1141): Abelard, Bernard, and the Fear of Social Upheaval," *Speculum* 77, no. 2 (2002).

168   Wim Verbaal reconstructs the Council's reception history poignantly: "For far too long, understanding of what happened was firmly based on the account given by Bernard's biographers, in the first place his secretary (and adoring admirer) Geoffrey of Auxerre who related the confrontation between Bernard and Abelard in his contribution to the hagiographical biography of the Abbot [...]. The ensuing Age of Enlightenment broke definitively with the traditional interpretation. Since then the roles have been re-versed. Abelard is henceforth the innocent victim of a plot woven by the anti–intellectual Bernard" (Wim Verbaal, "The Council of Sens Reconsidered: Masters, Monks, or Judges?," *Church History* 74, no. 3 (2005): 460–61).

169   As Constant Mews says: "It is also difficult to say that Bernard and Abelard typified two distinct strands of theology, when many different modes of thought and pedagogy

theological aspect of the argument plays a significant role, as I have attempted to illustrate in my account of William's doctrinal accusations, the
trial and its outcome were not determined by matters of content or methodology. Bernard's involvement in the conflict was guided by various political
motives, concerning not only the claims of Abelard but also his relationships and social ties.[170] While Bernard's reiteration of the accusations
against Abelard heavily depends on William's work,[171] his reasons for raising
them differ from William's motivation.

Bernard's perspective naturally differed from his friend's. As we have
seen, William had written the *Disputatio* when he had already retired from
his public responsibilities. Bernard was still at the height of his prominence
and performed his diplomatic duties throughout 12th-century Europe. His
engagement and counsel were sought by political and ecclesial leaders of
the time, and it can be said, without dismissing William's literary and intellectual capabilities, that it was Bernard's rather than his judgment that
would carry the most weight. William was aware of his friend's prominent
role, and although he wished to live the life of a simple monk, he was not
averse to using Bernard's influence. The *Disputatio* was addressed to Bernard because William – wisely – did not believe he had enough power to
win the battle he was instigating.[172]

Yet, Bernard did not react to William's plea immediately. He was hesitant
to introduce himself into the conflict, even making light of his inadequacy
in such complex doctrinal distinctions.[173] When he finally got involved, it

---

emerged during the medieval period, both within and outside of monasticism" (Mews,
"Bernard of Clairvaux and Peter Abelard," 134).

170   Constant Mews recounts the social and intellectual environment (particularly around
the figure of William of Champeaux) within which both Bernard and Abelard were
raised and that has shaped their respective perspectives on matters of authority and
the theological method in Mews, "Bernard of Clairvaux and Peter Abelard," 135–143.

171   Bernard's treatise to the Pope was, however, as Constant Mews states, a simplified account of the arguments raised by William. Instead of reiterating all 13 points of accusation, he focused on only two: Abelard's disparaging conception of divine omnipotence
and the role he attributed to Christ's redeeming power (Mews, "Bernard of Clairvaux
and Peter Abelard," 162).

172   "He [Bernard] was drawn into these and other controversies, sometimes inadvisedly,
through the insistence of alarmed friends, who saw him as heir to the doctrinal authority that passed from Anselm of Canterbury to the School of Laon and its masters, Anselm of Laon and William of Champeaux" (Evans, *The Language and Logic of the Bible*,
131).

173   E. Rozanne Elder, "Bernard and William of Saint Thierry," in *A Companion to Bernard
of Clairvaux* (Brill, 2011), 121.

was not out of benevolent agreement with his friend William but because Bernard found the question pressing beyond protecting theoretical ortho-doxy.[174] Bernard was concerned with the practical implication of doctrinally problematic claims for the unity of the church, which found itself internally and externally challenged. The fear of schismatic forces was deeply instilled in him, and not without reason. In 1130 the papacy of Pope Innocent II had been threatened by the efforts of Anacletus II, who asserted himself anti-pope, evoking an eight-year-long schism; a matter that had also required Bernard's involvement.[175] To compare the papal schism to the doctrinal is-sues to which William alerted his friends is not inappropriate, given that Bernard himself drew the analogy. While he considered the claims of Ana-cletus II to the papacy, "the roar of Peter the Lion, occupying the seat of Simon Peter", he believed that Abelard – 'Peter the Dragon' – posed a simi-lar threat to the church, "attacking the faith of Simon Peter".[176] He consid-ered Abelard's theology to be divisive, not merely due to its content and the methodological risks he was taking, but also because he feared its progres-sive claims could be received and exploited by the enemies of Rome. One of these politically problematic figures Bernard most probably had in mind was Arnold of Brescia (1090–1155).

Arnold, whom pope Innocent II had expelled from Italy in 1139 due to his attacks on the church's involvement in the political government of Bres-cia,[177] fled to Paris, where he initiated a friendship with Abelard. Arnold was drawn to Abelard's philosophic ideas of progress and reform. While it is questionable to what extent Abelard had supported Arnold's radical po-litical interests, the argument of their opponents was their shared interest

---

174 It is also notable that William's report was not the first accusation against Abelard that Bernard had received. Already in the 1120s Hugh of St. Victor had written to Ber-nard about the dangers of Abelard's teachings (Mews, "Bernard of Clairvaux and Peter Abelard," 150). Bernard also had his own minor conflict with Abelard in 1131, concern-ing Abelard's adaptation of the Lord's Prayer for the Paraclete (Mews, "Bernard of Clairvaux and Peter Abelard," 150).

175 On Bernard's involvement in the Investiture Controversy and its aftermath see Karl F. Morrison, *Tradition and Authority in the Western Church, 300–1140. Tradition and Au-thority in the Western Church, 300–1140* (Princeton, NJ: Princeton University Press, 2015), 334–339.

176 Mews, "Council of Sens," 344.

177 A more recent biography of Arnold of Brescia and his involvement in political and ecclesial struggles is: Phillip D. Johnson, *Arnold of Brescia: Apostle of Liberty in Twelfth–Century Europe* (Eugene, OR: Wipf & Stock, 2016).

in the scrutiny of authority:[178] Abelard's theoretical interest in the status of doctrinal authority vis–à–vis the use of logic translated, especially in his later works, into his ethical concerns for reform and his calls to address the issue of corruption within the church.[179] Calling Arnold Abelard's 'shield-bearer', Bernard pointed out the dangerous influence the two could exert together, demonstrating that he believed discord to be Abelard's primary intent.[180] Suppose one considers Bernard's involvement in the conflict a re-action to Abelard's known association with Arnold. In that case, one could even consider more remote analogies between theological errors and politi-cal forays, such as Abelard's alleged questioning of divine omnipotence, more precisely the omnipotence of the Holy Spirit, potentially relating to a critique of ecclesial power.[181] Either way, the debate became distinctly po-litical only when Bernard got involved.[182]

When William sent his *Disputatio* to Bernard, along with the very sources of his concern – Abelard's *Theologia*, extracts from his teaching on faith, the sacraments, and charity. Initially less unsettled by the situation than Wil-liam, Bernard most likely did not read the works thoroughly but relied on his friend's intellectual analysis. His own *Disputatio*, which he addressed to Innocent II,[183] is built mainly upon William's arguments. It is suggested that

---

178 "Theological speculation, in particular, encouraged the questioning of sacred mystery, which was better left undisturbed. It was equivalent to Arnold of Brescia's threats of physical violence upon the papacy, in that it, too, threatened the unity of the Church" (Monagle, *Orthodoxy and Controversy*, 31).

179 "While Abelard never addressed himself to the specific issue of ecclesiastical privileges or the theory of the commune, he was merciless in his Ethics about prelates who abused their power of binding and loosing, a power, he argued, that had been given to the apostles personally and that was lost by prelates who abused their authority. Such arguments, even if expressed by Abelard with more subtlety than in popular anticleri-cal preaching, were political dynamite in a situation in which episcopal power was being directly challenged" (Mews, "Council of Sens," 363). Of course, it is ironic that of all things the one cause he shared with William and Bernard – monastic discipline and reform – would be used against him, by those very same people (see Marenbon, "Life, milieu and intellectual contexts," 26). However, it was largely the question of means, with which to pursue reform achievements, on which they disagreed.

180 Mews, "Council of Sens," 365.

181 Mews, "Council of Sens," 360, relating to William's concrete accusations against the alleged Abelardian claim: *Quod Pater sit plena potentia, Filius quaedam potentia, Spiri-tus Sanctus nulla potentia* (Disputatio adversus Petrum Abaelardum, CCCM 89A, par. 3, pag. 14, linea 48).

182 Meanwhile, Bernard was not the only one to worry. Abbot Suger of Saint–Denis was a driving foce behind the attempt to weaken Arnold by eliminating Abelard. The crucial approach of avoiding a scholastic debate at the Council and focussing entirely on ju-ridical actions was planned primarily by Suger (Verbaal, "The Council of Sens," 489).

183 Most likely Letter 330 (Verbaal, "The Council of Sens," 485).

Bernard ordered Thomas of Morigny to compose a second list of accusations, known as the *Capitula Haeresum XIV*.[184] The latter was more accurate in its accusations than William's *Disputatio* and more careful not to misquote Abelard.[185] Bernard's approach certainly had practical and administrative reasons. Yet, it also shows that he, other than William, had experience with the politics and proceedings of a 12th-century heresy trial and was highly aware of the necessity of precise evidence.[186] Yet it also shows that it was not primarily Bernard's theological council that was sought, given that both William and his assistant had received thorough training in the liberal arts that made them much better equipped to identify heretical claims. As Constant Mews puts it very directly: "He never understood what Abelard was saying at a technical level, but he was aware of the ramifications that could flow from challenges to ecclesiastical authority".[187] And he had the rhetorical power and the social standing to convince others of the reality of this threat.[188]

Bernard's first course of action was not the initiation of a heresy trial but an effort to solve the conflict bilaterally. In the winter of 1140, Bernard initiated meetings with Abelard, during which he urged him to revise specific passages of the *Theologia*. According to Geoffrey of Auxerre, this was part of Bernard's adherence to canonical procedure,[189] granting Abelard

---

184 Buytaert, E. M., ed., "Capitula Haeresum *Petri Abaelardi,*" in *Petri Abaelardi Opera Theologica.* CCCM XII (Turnhout: Brepols, 1969). On the Capitula, their composition and their contant see Mews, "Bernard of Clairvaux and Peter Abelard," 164–165. A helpful juxtaposition of the text with William's Disputatio can be found in Klitzsch, *Die Theologien,* 402–411.

185 Mews, "The Council of Sens," 367.

186 Not only was Bernard versed in the particularities of heresy trials, but "played a key role in the development of the council as a tool in the repression of heresy [...]" (Michael Frassetto, "Precursors to Religious Inquisitions: Anti–Heretical Efforts to 1184," in *A Companion to Heresy Inquisitions,* ed. Donald Prudlo (Brill, 2019), 60).

187 Mews, "Council of Sens," 368.

188 Bernard applied the same rhetorical force – the same biting sarcasm – to the attacks on Abelard, as he did in his critique of the Cluniac wealth and artistic sophistication (Pranger, *Bernard of Clairvaux,* 29). Thomson and Winterbottom put it very poignantly, stating that "Bernard was not a literary satirist by vocation, but he was Europe's best and best-known writer of satirical invective" (M. Winterbottom, M and R. M. Thomson, "Introduction," in *For and Against Abelard: The Invective of Bernard of Clairvaux and Berengar of Poitiers,* xi–xxxii, ed. and trans. R.M. Thomson and M. Winterbottom (Woodbridge: Boydell & Brewer, 2020), xii).

189 Following the initial instigation (in this case presented by William in his *Disputatio*), Bernard pursues further inquiry (*quaestio/inquisitio*), in order to verify the accusations. Only after collecting necessary evidence does he meet with the defendant for private admonition (*privata correptio* and possibly *privata denuntiatio*). Then he addresses the defendant's students (*publica correptio*). Lastly, he denounces the defendant's teaching

the opportunity to repent and withdraw his heretical claims.[190] However, Geoffrey also maintains that Abelard refused this offer, an assertion that is not historically accurate. Two revisions of the *Theologia "summi boni"* survived, as well as fragments of more extensive revisions in a 14th-century manuscript.[191] It is likely, therefore, that Bernard's proceeding was a lot less patient and benevolent than his hagiographer would have us believe. Bernard, in the course of a strategic campaign, compelled Abelard to denounce his heretical teachings and have them condemned by the Pope. Abelard attempted to turn the tables on his opponent, accusing him of slander and forcing him to either pursue the condemnation publicly or retract his accusations.[192]

This Abelardian effort proved futile. According to Abelard's pupil Berengar of Poitiers (*1120), Bernard had arranged an episcopal assembly on the eve of the Council, where he publicly read Abelard's works and had them condemned. As he had suggested in his first letter to Innocent ii, Bernard tried to avoid openly debating Abelard, whose dialectic abilities he must have feared to a certain extent.[193] Berengar's account is written as a satire and aims at ridiculing Bernard and his followers.[194]

However, he does not question the legitimacy of such a meeting without the defendant's presence but instead contents himself with deriding their intellectual capabilities.[195] And indeed, the Council proceedings and the arguments that led to its outcome were those of a political lawsuit, more

---

to ecclesiastical authorities (*publica denuntiatio*). This procedure, basing its legitimacy on the Pauline ideal of communal discipline, is also known as *denuntiatio evangelica* (Verbaal, "The Council of Sens," 482).

190   Marenbon, "Life, milieu and intellectual contexts," 17.
191   Mews, "Council of Sens," 371. The earlier mentioned study of Regina Heyder, references these alleged meetings with Bernard as a potential reason for the revisions, which primarily reflect an increasing importance of Scripture for Abelard (Heyder, *Auctoritas scripturae*, 228).
192   Marenborn, "Life, milieu and intellectual contexts," 17. Abelard's opinion of Bernard had already been shaped by the mid–1120s, as Constant Mews points out, stating that: "Bernard's support for Alberic of Reims in 1126 may well have provoked Abelard to identify him as one of two 'new apostles' stirred up against him by his former rivals" (Mews, "Bernard of Clairvaux and Peter Abelard," 148).
193   Verbaal, "The Council of Sens," 485–86. This approach took its cure from earlier proceedings against heretical scholars (Frassetto, "Precursors to Religious Inquisitions," 62).
194   On Berengar's arguments and his literary style see Winterbottom and Thomson, "Introduction," in *For and Against Abelard,* xv–xxv.
195   Verbaal, "The Council of Sens," 467.

so than those of a theological dispute.[196] The official condemnation of Abe-lard's work was then, similar to the course of the Council of Soissons, founded on a formality rather than the matter of doctrinal errors: Abelard's opponents ultimately appealed to papal authority in the figure of papal legate Conan of Praeneste and had him ratify the condemnation, based on the fact that Abelard had published his *Theologia* without the Pope's approval.[197]

Although the issues initially raised by William and confirmed by Thomas of Morigny were not the subject of thorough theological analysis in the trial, William's concern for the future of Christian education seemed successfully addressed with Abelard's condemnation. By mid-12th century, Abelard's works ceased to be cited and received by contemporary authors, even in Paris.[198] This does not extend to the success of the scholastic method in the following centuries, which owed an enormous debt to Abe-lard's theological risks and would present the continual struggle with the *quaestiones* he had raised. This development would, of course, take place unbeknownst to William. Returning to this chapter's original question, it remains to ask how William's *Disputatio* can be interpreted in the light of the Council of Sens and its immediate consequences. Reducing William's role to that of an instigator is technically correct regarding the Council's historical proceeding. However, it is important to note a disconnect be-tween William's intention and the motives that contributed to the trial.

Bernard and the other protagonists of the prosecution in Sens were un-doubtedly troubled by Abelard's claims, however less so by his method or his theological errors and more so by their potential political implications. Once the risk seemed averted and the problematic statements condemned, Abelard did not remain the personification of heresy and *superbia* in the minds of his prosecutors. Bernard did not leave his strained relationship with Abelard as such, but at the insistence of Peter the Venerable pursued a successful reconciliation with his former opponent.[199] However, William's emotional engagement in the matter differed significantly from Bernard's reasoning to involve himself in the case. To him, the accusations he raised in the *Disputatio* were a matter of the heart. He was deeply troubled by what he read in the *Theologia*, and Abelard's claims arraigned his most prized possession – his faith. To William, the Abelardian heresy was

---

196   Verbaal, "The Council of Sens," 493.
197   Frassetto, "Precursors to Religious Inquisitions," 61.
198   Knoch, "Der Streit," 304.
199   Knoch, "Der Streit," 304.

much more systemic in nature. It was not sufficiently addressed in legal proceedings but required the broad restitution of monastic ideals, such as intellectual humility.[200]

It seems like the natural consequence of such fundamental concerns that the *Casus Abelardi* was not William's last brush with heresy. Three years after the Council of Sens, William attempted once more to clamp down on theological errors. This time, his target was William of Conches (ca. 1080–1154), whose troubling claims in his work *De Philosophia Mundi* reminded William of the earlier condemned Abelardian teachings. William's main concern, regarding William of Conches work, however, was yet again mainly with his method, his approach to Patristic and traditional authority, or rather with the high significance these authors attributed to human *ratio*.[201] In practice, there were significant parallels in their thought: Both William of Saint-Thierry and William of Conches, were early developers of physiological categories regarding the soul, as well as the notion of an anthropological microcosm that mirrored the macrocosm of the world. These parallels, observed in detail by Marie-Dominique Chenu,[202] reveal that William was, other than Bernard, very much at the pulse of the intellectual revolution taking place around him, and his determination to inhibit specific aspects he considered harmful, indicate that he was highly aware of its brisance.

When he listed and discussed his concerns with William of Conches' work in a letter to Bernard (his *Epistola de erroribus Guilelmi de Conchis*) in hopes of replicating the condemnation of Abelard in Sens, his warnings were not heeded. To our knowledge, however, Bernard did not reply,[203] demonstrating even more now, that he shared neither William's zeal regarding doctrinal purity, nor his ability to understand the nuances of the theological discourse taking place.

---

200   Both Bernard and William agreed in their assessment that Abelard lacked this sort of humility. While William has mainly discussed Abelard's intellectual ambitions as evidence of his pride, Bernard also commented on Abelard's character as it was revealed in more personal writings, such as the *Historia calamitatum*, in which self-pity blended into his prideful behavior (Pranger, *Bernard of Clairvaux*, 29).

201   Heyder, *Auctoritas scripturae*, 313–14. For a study of William of Conches' conception of ratio and William's critique thereof: Klaus Riesenhuber, "Der Streit Um Die 'ratio' in Der Frühscholastik." In *Was Ist Philosophie Im Mittelalter? Qu'est–Ce Que La Philosophie Au Moyen Âge? What Is Philosophy in the Middle Ages? Akten Des X. Internationalen Kongresses Für Mittelalterliche Philosophie Der Société Internationale Pour l'Etude de La Philosophie Médiévale, 25. Bis 30. August 1997 in Erfurt*, Miscellanea Mediaevalia 26, ed. Jan A. Aertsen and Andreas Speer, 460–467. Berlin: De Gruyter, 1998.

202   Marie-Dominique Chenu, *Nature, Man, and Society in the Twelfth Century*, 30f. and 233.

203   McGuire, "A Chronology," 30.

Conclusion to Part 1

This first part of this volume aimed to identify the principles that underlie William's conception of readership and authorship as it arose from his exegetical work and his disagreement with other contemporary approaches. As I have shown, William's epistemological deliberations are central in this regard: as he defines the potential of human knowledge of God, he also defines the limitations of anyone attempting to learn more about the nature of God. Understanding what William believes to be possible and legitimate insight allows conclusions about what kind of scholarship he considers appropriate and admissible. In my discussion of the self-conception arising from the *Expositio* on Romans, I have distinguished between 'natural' and 'humble' knowledge, a distinction I believe to be foundational.

Natural knowledge can be acquired on account of human reason and to the degree to which the human mind is created for rational reflection. It is a kind of knowledge accessible to anyone – Christians and non–Christians alike. William has discussed this form of insight in correlation with the ideas brought forth by the 'philosophers of the world', the secular thinkers who believe their understanding to be self-generated. Notably, William does attribute certain theological discoveries to natural knowledge: the omniscience and omnipotence of the creator, for instance, could be extrapolated from the context of creation and using rational analysis. Yet, William identifies a crucial flaw in acquiring knowledge through reason alone: if the source of theological insight is misconceived, the object itself will always be misunderstood. In other words, if the receiver of knowledge is unaware of whose creation and whose grace has enabled them to acquire it, the knowledge itself will also be inherently flawed.

Throughout William's works, the concept of natural knowledge often appears in his discussions of pride – the sin that makes theological insight impossible. He is talking in these instances not simply of an arrogant attitude but of the fundamental belief that the human mind can penetrate things that God has not revealed. Such pride stands in the way of recognizing truth. As we will see in the upcoming chapter, William attributes this to an ontological reason. The proud mind has distanced itself from the *imago*, in which likeness it was created. Reversely, any proper theological knowledge is reserved for the humble mind. Humility is the ethical and epistemological principle that determines William's definition of Christian scholarship.

He sets the idea of humble knowledge in opposition to what he considers natural knowledge. The difference lies not in whether reason is involved but in the particular role that reason plays. Rozanne Elder has operated particularly with the terminology of the 'eye of reason', as a determinative receptor of insight, not because of its nature but its ability to receive knowledge by God's grace.[1] I would argue in light of my previous discussion of the *Expositio* that William distinguishes between reason as a natural faculty of the mind on the one hand and humbled reason on the other. While the former can be utilized by anyone endowed with it, regardless of intentionality, the latter has subjected itself to the authority of the catholic faith. Humility regarding the teachings of Scripture and the Fathers brings forth an application of reason that does not seek to accumulate new knowledge but to have the transmitted knowledge of the church be further illuminated.

The concept of *ratio fidei in* William's work has received some recent scholarly attention. Tyler Sergent has provided a very insightful definition of the concepts: "Through this *ratio fidei* the Church establishes both its language for and understanding of God. William says that even though words like 'Trinity,' 'homoousia', and 'consubstantial' are not found in scripture, still through the reason of faith, these words came to describe what has always been true. The reason of faith is what provides the means – the cooperation between human reason, divine revelation, and pious authority – for establishing these tenets of faith. In other words, the rule of faith – the credal beliefs of Christianity – are established through the reason of faith".[2]

This definition is very much in line with what we have now observed about William's understanding of authorship and his rejection of approaches such as Abelard's. Reason, for William, is not a highly individualized ability that allows the exceptionally talented to penetrate the divine mysteries deeper than others. Instead, reason is always to be applied in cooperation with tradition; it ought not to question and dissect it, but contribute to the harmony of Christian truth as it reveals itself throughout the ages. We can thus understand William's use of Patristic quotations in the *Disputatio* not as the anti-rationalistic fideism, as which Abelard has portrayed most of the criticism against him, but as an exemplification of the way, in which he believed reason ought to influence Christian scholarship: as the ability that allows one to recognize truth in doctrines and

---

1   E. Rozanne Elder, "The Eye of Reason–The Eye of Love: 'Divine Learning and Affective Prayer' in the Thought of William of Saint Thierry," in *Prayer and Thought in Monastic Tradition: Essays in Honour of Benedicta Ward SLG*, ed. Santha Bhattacharji, Dominic Mattos, and Rowan Williams (London: T&T Clark, 2014), 235.

2   Sergent, "Sources and Influences," 50.

derive spiritual insight from them. Rather than limiting the capacity of the intellect, Scriptural and Patristic authority enable the human intellect to fulfill its intended and appropriate purpose.

Returning to the initial question with which we were concerned (William's concepts of Christian reader- and authorship, respectively) it is to be concluded that rational reflection and faith grounded in authority are not mutually exclusive. Ideally, all human faculties ought to operate in service of the catholic faith, offering clarity and a qualitative consolidation of the truth contained in the entirety of Christian tradition. Christian scholarship cannot be simply a science among other sciences, even if it were deemed superior to them. Because of its source and object, theological knowledge differs fundamentally from the knowledge produced by sciences concerned with temporal issues. William is not opposed, as we have seen, to dialectics or any other philosophical method. Still, he points out a categorical mistake in the applications of methods intended to analyze creation to reflect on the Creator.

Throughout both his own work and his critique of the Abelardian methodology, he makes sure to point out that the pursuit of knowledge of God is not only dependent on the abilities but the *habitus* of the one seeking insight. Suppose humility is indeed the epistemological prerequisite for any knowledge of God. In that case, it becomes clear that theological learning cannot be purely intellectual but entails ethical discipline and personal spiritual growth. To understand the authority of the biblical and Patristic authors in a way that aids that process, they, too, have to be acknowledged not exclusively as intellectual authorities but as figures whose faith, morality, and divine inspiration have ensured their alignment with the *ratio fidei*.

Rozanne Elder, among others, has pointed out that it was not just Abelard who, as I have discussed, was impacted by the conflict surrounding his orthodoxy but that William's work was influenced heavily by this dispute. According to Elder, "Abelard's perceived misuse of logic did not dim William's admiration for reason, but led him to new ways of expressing the need to balance reason with love."[3] While this concluded first part of the study has provided some insight regarding the limitations and potential of the human ratio, it will be in the second part that I will discuss the relationship between reason and love and explore what William considers the nature of spiritual insight.

---

3 Elder, "Prayer in the Thought," 236.

PART 2

Mapping William's Exegetical Process: Receptivity and Originality in His Reading of the Song of Songs

∵

Introduction to Part 2

The preceding analysis of William's relationship with Patristic thought has shown the dependence of his work and his intellectual ideal on Patristic authority. While his Commentary on Romans served as an example of his exegetical vision, which he further defended in the *Disputatio*, the texts I will present in the following provide insight into his process and the application of his ideals. The chapter broadly concerns William's interpretation of the Song of Songs and will illustrate different stages in his *lectio* and literary treatment of the text.

While it is a general concern of my study to bring William out of the shadow of Bernardine illustriousness, it is nevertheless important to discuss the friendship between the two monks as a turning point in William's exegetical focus. The time William spent with Bernard at the infirmary of Clairvaux inspired both his Brevis *Commentatio in Canticum Canticorum* – a testament of their conversations concerning the allegorical reading of this biblical text they deemed central – and the *Expositio super Canticum Canticorum*, William's extensive Commentary. A brief discussion of how William related to Bernard, as one example of a contemporary authoritative figure, will serve as an entry point to the study of William's interest in the biblical themes of the Song of Songs.

Since William relies in his conception of orthodoxy on the perimeters defined by the Fathers, his discussion of the *Canticum* too is primarily grounded in Patristic readings of the text. A central question concerns the ways in which William had accessed and systematized his sources. His florilegia of Ambrose of Milan's and Gregory the Great's references and explanations of the Song offer an ideal starting point. First, they provide a representative overview of the kinds of works William consulted and the particular passages that aroused his interest. These two collections allow us to gain a deeper understanding of William's concrete practice of citation. They further exemplify William's handling of diverging opinions or propositions within a single Father's corpus or between two different Patristic approaches.

It will also be important to note that William invested in making his sources accessible to a broader audience. In doing so, he consciously continued the longstanding tradition of florilegia, demonstrating his allegiance to early medieval ideals of authorship. William understood his task not as an individual quest for knowledge but within a context encompassing past and future Christian thought. His collections of Patristic work relate to the

history that preceded him and reveal much about his vision for future generations of exegetes. It is for them that he provides such a comprehensive
tool of study, ensuring that they will continue to follow the Fathers as their
guides.

Yet, a narrative that presents Patristic tradition as William's only source
of inspiration would undoubtedly fail to grasp the reality of William's social
context. His engagement with the Song of Songs, in particular, has to be
viewed as an early instance of bridal mysticism that would become a vital
aspect of Cistercian exegesis. As Suzanne LaVere points out, "the language
of desire became the quintessential vehicle through which monks expressed
their profound longing for God";[1] thus, examining the thought of William
and Bernard and how they have influenced each other will provide further
insight into the roots of Cistercian spirituality and literature.

The *Expositio* deserves special attention, of course, as it is the final product that represents the kind of exegesis William envisioned on the grounds
of his engagement with Patristic and contemporary Cistercian thought. I
will discuss various central theological themes that arise throughout the
work, such as the aforementioned notion of 'image and likeness', William's
understanding of the human soul, and his usage of erotic language. Concerning his hermeneutics, it will further be of interest to relate the *Expositio*
to the Origenist framework of Scriptural senses and the rich Christian tradition of allegorical interpretation.[2] All three of William's different ways to engage with the Song of Songs are lastly of general interest for the study of
12th-century spirituality, given the incomparable importance of this particular biblical book for medieval mysticism.[3]

---

1   Suzanne LaVere, "From Contemplation to Action: The Role of the Active Life in the
    "Glossa Ordinaria" on the Song of Songs," *Speculum* 82, no. 1 (2007): 54.
2   In fact, as Ann Matter points out, Christian exegetical history had not provided any im-
    pactful non-allegorical readings of the Song of Songs (E. Ann. Matter, *The Voice of My
    Beloved: The Song of Songs in Western Medieval Christianity*, (Philadelphia: University of
    Pennsylvania Press, 1990), 4), suggesting that the history of Christian commentaries on
    the Song is itself a large part of the history of Christian allegory.
3   F.B.A. Asiedu, "The Song of Songs and the Ascent of the Soul: Ambrose, Augustine, and
    the Language of Mysticism," *Vigiliae Christianae* 55, no. 3 (2001): 299.

CHAPTER 3

Bernard, William's Guide through the Song

1   Emerging from His Shadow: The Problem with Bernard

One cannot discuss any medieval reading of the Song of Songs without inevitably addressing the 'Father' of bridal mysticism: Bernard of Clairvaux. Famously called the 'chimera of his age',[1] Bernard's influence and network are hardly matched by any other 12th-century abbot. Just as Bernard was involved in various enterprises and political matters in his time, he played multiple roles in the life of William. His part in the condemnation of Abelard has already been discussed at large. In the following, I will turn my attention to Bernard's contribution to the Cistercian exegesis of the Song, his introduction of bridal love language into medieval exegesis, and the influence these themes had on William.

Bernard's overwhelming renown in this field, along with his close friendship and collaboration with William, has for a long time determined the historiography of William's life and work; his originality and exegetical genius has long gone unrecognized in the light of his friend's fame. Historians have tended to paint William as an uncritical admirer of Bernard, who benefitted from the relationship he established with the renowned abbot. This understanding was certainly exacerbated by the fact that William was Bernard's first biographer, and throughout the *Vita prima*, he abases himself to uplift Bernard and his virtuousness.[2] However, the perception of William as a mere imitator of Bernard has increasingly been challenged by scholars since the 20th century.[3] More recent studies on William's works and biography, especially as it was intertwined with Bernard's, reveal a different picture: one that acknowledges that Bernard relied on William's scholarly expertise and theological input and one of a relationship that

---

1 See for instance: E. Rozanne Elder and John R. Sommerfeldt, eds., *The Chimaera of His Age: Studies on Bernard of Clairvaux,* Cistercian Studies 63 (Kalamazoo, MI: Cistercian Publications, 1980).

2 I will introduce and discuss parts of the *Vita prima* in more detail in the chapter "7.2. The Monastic Life as Christian Ideal" and "Horizontal Authority and Loving Obedience".

3 Brian P. McGuire, "Bernard of Clairvaux and the Cistercian Mystical Tradition," in The Wiley–Blackwell Companion to Christian Mysticism, ed. Julia A. Lamm (Hoboken, NJ: John Wiley & Sons, Ltd, 2012), 242.

was at times complicated and left room for disagreement and critique. The studies of Adriaan Bredero, for instance, had introduced the notion that William might have been deliberately introduced to Bernard by William of Champeaux as a theological advisor or tutor.[4]

While an initial concern for modern scholarship was the clarification of authorship regarding misattributed works, a secondary yet important question pertains to the pair's mutual inspiration and influence. Although the friendship yielded common fruit and helped establish a shared vocabulary for early Cistercian literature,[5] the two approaches remained distinct in many ways. As Rozanne Elder points out, recent research found "appreciation of William as a theologian far more speculative and nuanced than Bernard".[6]

The apparent differences between their theological views and literary styles can partly be explained by their different educational backgrounds, which I have already mentioned regarding William's school education in the preceding chapter. While Bernard's spirituality is expressed throughout his works in such a way that it could ultimately be described as a theological system of sorts, it is evident that William's thought is much more systematic in nature.[7] In the case of their readings of the Song of Songs, this becomes very apparent in their respective choice of genre. Bernard famously treated the biblical book in a series of impactful sermons, using his rhetorical talents and pastoral purview.[8] The diversity of liturgical settings and the somewhat immediate nature of the homiletic arts allowed him to explore the text from various perspectives and apply the Song's language to his discussion of a host of theological themes. William's exegesis is a lot more restricted, as he admits:[9] The purpose of his structured tractate – his

---

4 Elder, "Bernard and William," 123

5 "In a monastic order that emphasized the value of human relationships, they made use of friendship in formulating a language of divine presence" (McGuire, "Bernard and the Cistercian Mystical Tradition," 245).

6 Elder, "Bernard and William," 109.

7 Kurt Ruh, *Geschichte Der Abendländischen Mystik. Bd. 1. Die Grundlegung Durch Die Kirchenväter Und Die Mönchstheologie Des 12. Jahrhunderts* (München: C.H. Beck, 1990), 268.

8 As Ruh explains, the usage of sermons as a means of transmitting exegetical knowledge marks a significant shift in the history of the Song's interpretation, as it bridged biblical scholarship and spiritual direction in a new way (Ruh, *Geschichte der Abendländischen Mystik*, 250). In fact, it allowed him to discuss socio-political issues within a theological and spiritual framework (McGuire, "Bernard and the Cistercian Mystical Tradition," 237).

9 Expositio super Cantica Canticorum, CCCM 87, cap. 1, linea 65: *Non autem profundiora illa mysteria, quae in eo continentur, adtentamus, de Christo et ecclesia; sed cohibentes nos intra nos, et in nobismetipsis nosmetipsos metientes, de sponso ac sponsa, de Christo et*

Expositio – was to expound one particular 'mystical' meaning of the Song in depth. The value of his reading lies in its explicit focus and prioritization. The relationship between the Christ and the soul stands at the center of his spirituality and literary efforts. Thus, while one could assume that the homiletic genre would provide more opportunity for the audience to experience the Song's profoundness in an immediate, even embodied way, William managed to convey the erotic dimension of the text even more intuitively. William's style, as much as it expresses highly structured intellectual reflection, conveys a burning desire for God that exceeds Bernard's in its explicitness and intensity.[10] Ruh attributes these differences in character of the two oeuvres to their authors' distinct processes of composition: "Offensichtlich sind beide Erklärungen völlig unabhängig voneinander ausgearbeitet worden, mit anderen Worten: Es fand kein gegenseitiger Austausch von einzelnen Kommentarteilen statt, kein Einblick in des andern Werkstatt."[11]

Although this might have been the case for their literary productivity, one cannot ignore the prominent role Bernard played in initiating William's interest in the Song and introducing him to its mysteries. William's early work is much more systematic. It displays less personal and spiritual reflection than the works he had written after his encounter with Bernard and his growing interest in Cistercian self-reflection.[12] By the time William started moving from doctrinal treatises to allegorical and experiential exegesis, Bernard had already centered his spirituality on the Song and its imagery. Bernard's emphasis on the erotic language expressed in the Song, both in his pastoral work and spiritual life, was a significant factor in advancing the exegetical shift that began in the 11th century[13] and strongly influenced Western mysticism for centuries to come. The Song of Songs became the ultimate expression of divine love in the monastic context. This is because it not only represents a particular strand of theological thought but because it facilitates experience. The experiential momentum of the Song lies at the core of Cistercian exegesis, as Bernard himself

---

christiana anima, sensum tantummodo moralem aliquem, in quo omnibus audere licet, pro sensus nostri paupertate perstringimus, laboris nostri non alium requirentes fructum, quam similem materiae, id est amorem ipsum.

10   McGuire, "Bernard and the Cistercian Mystical Tradition," 242.

11   Ruh, *Geschichte der Abendländischen Mystik*, 295.

12   Elder, "Bernard and William," 124.

13   This shift can be linked to the Gregorian reform movements and a subsequent return to Origenist principles of exegesis (E. Ann. Matter, "Anselm and the Tradition of the 'Song of Songs'," *Rivista Di Storia Della Filosofia* 48 (1993): 551–52).

pointed out in his third Sermon on the text: *Hodie legimus in libro experientiae*.[14] Read as a love song between God and the individual soul, the Song expresses the monastic understanding of faith as an empirical rather than a theoretical kind of knowledge. As Bernard McGinn puts it: "The emphasis on personal appropriation of the divine mystery is central to the spiritual theology of the White Monks."[15]

The exegetical focus on the Song resulted in a theological emphasis on divine love and its redeeming effect on the human soul. The role that both God's love and, in turn, human desire for God played for Bernard exegetically elucidates the description of Bernardine thought as 'affective mysticism'. The notion that love not only aids but is what fundamentally enables spiritual ascent is an essential thought within this framework.[16] For Bernard and the early Cistercians, the experience of love is transformative, particularly in relation to monastic discipline. Divine-human intimacy should not be misunderstood as fleeting and tied exclusively to rare moments of ecstasy. Rather, the monks should pursue a consistent life of 'brideship'.[17] The identification with the bride and especially the emotional and sensual expressions for which such imagery allows also feature prominently in William's work.

The transformative power of divine love, the monastic life as one that hopes to intensify the experience of spiritual intimacy, and the unabashed usage of erotic language to express theological thought are distinctive elements of early Cistercian writings. The fact that these themes thus dominate in both the works of William and Bernard does, however, not explain the extent or direction of their direct influence on one another. Against the backdrops of the historiographic parameters I have just discussed and the most prominent common ideas that were just noted, I would like to turn next to a discussion of their relationship. In particular, I hope to

---

14   Bernardus Claraevallensis, Sermones super Cantica Canticorum, Library of Latin Texts A. Turnhout: Brepols, 2010, sermo 3, par. 1, vol. 1, pag. 14, linea 7.

15   Bernard McGinn, "The Spiritual Teaching of the Early Cistercians," in *The Cambridge Companion to the Cistercian Order*, ed. Mette Birkedal Bruun, Cambridge Companions to Religion. (Cambridge: Cambridge University Press, 2012), 220.

16   McGinn, "The Spiritual Teaching," p. 228. For Bernard, the love of the bride has the potential to convert the human will toward God – one of the significant steps in the process of ascent (McGuire, "Bernard and the Cistercian Mystical Tradition," 239).

17   Ann W. Astell and Catherine Rose Cavadini, "The Song of Songs," in The Wiley–Blackwell Companion to Christian Mysticism, ed. Julia A. Lamm (Hoboken, NJ: John Wiley & Sons, Ltd, 2012), 30.

illustrate how their shared proclivity for affectivity and spiritual experience was not only expressed in their writing but also exemplified in their actual friendship.

2 Living the Song. Spiritual Friendship as a Foundation of Cistercian Exegesis

Behold, me and you and – I hope – Christ, as a third between us.[18]

In other words: you, me, and Jesus. What might as well be the lyrics to a modern worship song is, in fact, a poetic and theologically valuable reflection on the theory of monastic friendship. It's a literary image conceived by the Cistercian 'master of friendship',[19] Aelred of Rievaulx. It is perhaps fitting that the words best suited to describe the close and peculiar friendship between William and Bernard were written by one of their contemporary brothers.[20] Aelred had devoted an entire treatise, his *De spirituali amicitia*, to spiritual friendship; a notion that blends seamlessly into the Cistercian framework of love and affectivity.[21] However, spiritual friendship and love are not simply synonymous.[22] While love is commanded for all, friendship

---

18   Aelred of Rievaulx. *De Spiritali Amicitia*. Centre Traditio Litterarum Occidentalium, CETEDOC., and Brepols (Firm). 2000. Library of Latin texts. Series A. Series A. [Turnhout, Belgium]: Brepols. http://clt.brepolis.net/LLTA/pages/TextSearch.aspx? key=MAERICM01E (accessed January 10, 2025), Lib. 1, linea 4: *Ecce ego et tu, et spero quod tertius inter nos christus sit.*

19   This is a title, however, he does not officially hold, especially because Aelred, unlike some of his Cistercian brothers, had never enjoyed a scholastic education and hence, was not a *magister* of any kind. A primary resource on studies regarding Aelred of Rievaulx is Marsha Dutton, ed., *A Companion to Aelred of Rievaulx (1110–1167)* (Leiden: Brill, 2017).

20   Bernard and Aelred shared a vigorous correspondence, which was chiefly responsible for Aelred's decision to pursue the work for his *Speculum Caritatis* (Pierre–André Burton, "Aelred of Rievaulx: An Illiterate, or a True Master of Spiritual Teaching?", in *A Companion to Aelred of Rievaulx (1110–1167)*, ed. Marsha Dutton (Leiden: Brill, 2017), 197–98).

21   Bernard McGinn even considers the emphasis on friendship to be the most important Cistercian contribution to 12th-century spirituality (Janet Burton and Julie Kerr, *The Cistercians in the Middle Ages* (Woodbridge, Suffolk: Boydell&Brewer Ltd., 2011), 142).

22   Domenico Pezzini, "Aelred's Doctrine of Charity and Friendship," in *A Companion to Aelred of Rievaulx (1110–1167)*, ed. Marsha Dutton (Leiden: Brill, 2017), 240.

is reserved for the exceptional and deserving. It is "a very particular form of love".[23]

Aelred's focus, as he admits, goes beyond exegetical observations or doctrinal tradition.[24] He even goes so far as to elevate *amicitia* to the status of virtue,[25] an addition to the classic catalog of virtues that is, if not unique, extremely rare. His pronounced appreciation of friendship is groundbreaking, mainly because it is so concrete and tangible in contrast to many theological deliberations on love. As Bernard McGinn points out, in the context of male monastic communities, friendship is "not only a model (as in Bernard's view of the marriage of man and woman) but also a real instrument for learning how to love God."[26] Theoretically, the concept bridges theology and anthropology like few others do since Aelred defines friendship as both human and divine.[27] Practically speaking, it is one of the means of devotion most readily available to medieval monks or, arguably, anyone.

It was clear to Aelred that he could not possibly illustrate such a fundamentally relatable subject in a purely theoretical manner. The fourth book of *De spirituali amicitia* thus consists of stories of his own friendships.[28] Their reality, even as it entails quarrels, envy, or disappointment, is instructive and inspiring. Much more so, one could argue, than an abstract ideal. William and Bernard's friendship might similarly serve as a lived example of the Aelredian concept.

I will discuss their relationship, not merely regarding mutual intellectual contributions but also with the highly experiential, emotional, and personal content of their exegetical conversations in mind. Reading the Song of Songs together was the foundation of their spiritual friendship, and it is hardly surprising that their reflections on their shared time are clothed in the language of the Song. Their intense engagement with the *Canticum* had given them a vocabulary of passion that exceeded that of other monastic authors. It is comprehensible that they would bring it to bear when discussing their emotional life. The inherent liaison between the Song, as the

---

23   Pezzini, "Aelred's Doctrine," 240.

24   McGuire, "Bernard and the Cistercian Mystical Tradition," 248.

25   De Spiritali Amicitia, Lib. 1, linea 121: *Amicitia igitur ipsa uirtus est qua talis dilectionis ac dulcedinis foedere ipsi animi copulantur, et efficiuntur unum de pluribus.*

26   McGinn, "The Spiritual Teaching," 229.

27   He does so in explicit reference to Tullius: *Nonne satis tibi est hinc quod ait tullius: amicitia est rerum humanorum et divinarum cum benevolentia et aritate consensio?* (De Spiritali Amicitia, Lib. 1, linea 79).

28   Pezzini, "Aelred's Doctrine," 243.

ultimate biblical utterance of affection, and monastic friendship already appears in Aelred's conception, albeit incidental. For instance, he applies the metaphor of the kiss to his understanding of friendship, stating that "in a kiss, two spirits meet, blend, and unite."[29] In Bernard's and William's correspondence, however, this imagery is displayed in a much more overt way.

For modern readers, potentially homoerotic aspects within medieval testaments to male friendship do not seem far-fetched. In more recent scholarship, the sexual orientation of Aelred of Rievaulx has become an object of intense study.[30] Such deliberations are, however, highly speculative and assume a transgression from the spiritually allegorical realm to the physical, which, at least regarding William's and Bernard's friendship, cannot be textually evidenced. Although it is certainly fascinating to see that these two men did not only discuss theology but their personal lives using erotic language, it is vital to keep in mind that both eroticism and personal intimacy were not matters of individualist expression. Within the monastic context, the relationships among monks and the particularities of their spiritual imagination were always of concern for the larger community they called their home. As much as the private correspondence between these two friends is thus a reflection of their feelings, it should not be underestimated that as abbots, their self-reflection ultimately sustained their sensitivity to others' spiritual struggles.

Interestingly, William's theoretical reflection on personal devotion hardly entails consideration of friendship. Other than Aelred, and even Bernard himself, he advocated for a more solitary approach to the Cistercian life.[31] Biographically, this becomes clear from his long-standing desire to retire and lead a rather reclusive life as a simple monk.[32] His desire to be Bernard's friend was thus exceptional. One of the tragic ironies of William's life was that the man he selected to be his only close friend was not an enthusiast of intimate friendships. As many interests as the two shared intellectually, it would be a misunderstanding to consider them truly kindred spirits. Rozanne Elder offers a striking observation about their relationship: "As

---

29   Pezzini, "Aelred's Doctrine," 239.

30   see for instance: Frederick S. Roden, "Aelred of Rievaulx, Same–Sex Desire and the Victorian Monastery," in *Masculinity and Spirituality in Victorian Culture*, ed. Andrew Bradstock, Sean Gill, Anne Hogan, and Sue Morgan (London: Palgrave Macmillan UK, 2000) or Brian P. McGuire, "Sexual Awareness and Identity in Aelred of Rievaulx (1110–67)," *The American Benedictine Review* 45 (1994).

31   McGuire, "Bernard and the Cistercian Mystical Tradition," 243.

32   I discussed this aspect of his life in the Introduction.

William felt within himself an ever-growing need for solitude, Bernard increasingly moved in the company of popes and princes."[33] Indeed, Bernard's growing responsibility beyond the walls of Clairvaux and his generally extroverted character stood in stark contrast to William's distaste for public affairs. And although opposites might attract, we can detect a potential for conflict from their correspondence.

This is illustrated in a particularly relatable and human way in Epistle 87 of Bernard's collection of letters.[34] In it, Bernard tries to defend himself against a – sadly undocumented – but scathing allegation William had leveled against him.[35] William had been hoping for a kind of attention Bernard had failed to provide. He felt neglected by the man for whom he held so much affection and accused his friend of not reciprocating his feelings. Rather than referring to his many other obligations and a shortage of time, Bernard used William's fit of jealousy as an opportunity to offer spiritual guidance and provided a beautiful reflection on love amidst human circumstances. His first observation is fascinating because it points to the mysterious nature of the human heart and concedes that even friends who share an advanced spiritual stage will never be able to grasp each other's inner workings fully:

> No one knows what is in man save the spirit of a man that is in him; man sees only on the surface and God alone can search the heart; yet you have been able to weigh and mutually to compare our affection for each other, so as to deliver a verdict not only on the state of your own heart, but even on that of another. I wonder how or on what grounds you have been able to do this, and I cannot wonder enough. It is an error to which the human mind is ever prone not only to consider good to be evil, what is true to be false, and what is false to be true, but also to be doubtful about what is certain, and certain about what is doubtful. You may be right when you say that my affection for

---

33   Elder, "Bernard and William," 118.
34   James ed. and trans., "The Letters of St. Bernard,", Letter 87, 124–127.
35   Julian Haseldine points out, in regards to this letter specifically, that "such complaints about the failures of friends to write or visit recur again and again in letter collections of this period and were part of a language of joking and banter which was far more common than expressions of emotional intensity." (Julian P. Haseldine, "Monastic Friendship in Theory and in Action in the Twelfth Century," in *Friendship in the Middle Ages and Early Modern Age*, ed. Albrecht Classen and Marilyn Sandidge (Berlin, Bostoné: De Gruyter, 2011).

you is less than yours for me, but I am certainly certain that you cannot be certain. How can you know for certain what you cannot be certain about?[36]

One could interpret this lengthy theological statement on the deceptiveness of the mind as a deflection from his shortcomings as a friend or as a defensive reaction.[37] We find an implicit and partial acknowledgment of the accusation's validity later in the letter when he assumes that William had been hurt by Bernard's failure to answer his friend's many letters.[38] This lacking reciprocity points to a more general issue in assessing Bernard's ability to form a close friendship. As Elder rightly points out, the affectionate tone in many of Bernard's correspondences does not allow conclusions on the sincerity of his fondness or commitment to his acquaintances. Much of his language was formed by his cultural context[39] and possibly by his strategic interest in these relationships.[40]

Yet, William's accusation seemed to have offended Bernard deeply,[41] suggesting a more personal dimension of the friendship.[42] Although he attests a potential degree of truth to the reproach that 'his affection for William is less than William's for him', he intentionally leaves room for uncertainty: affection is challenging to assess, and love impossible to measure. Not only does Bernard point out William's inability to comprehend his most intimate feelings, but he also reveals his own emotional uncertainties. In his letter, he includes a passage of prayer, addressing God as the only one who knows both these men's hearts intimately, admitting that he has doubts about

---

36   James ed. and trans., "The Letters of St. Bernard,", Letter 87, 125.

37   Or, as Julian Haseldine does, as "a series of legal metaphors" and "clever conceits" (Haseldine, "Monastic Friendship," 360).

38   James ed. and trans., "The Letters of St. Bernard,", Letter 87, 126.

39   Elder, "Bernard and William," 118.

40   Brian P. McGuire, *Friendship & Community: The Monastic Experience, 350–1250*, Cistercian Studies 95 (Kalamazoo, MI: Cistercian Publications, 1988), 290.

41   Bernard seems particularly defensive, as he reminds his friend, that even the disciples and David admitted their uncertainty and ignorance, "but wonderful to say, you have been able to assert, with I know not what grounds for your confidence: 'My affection for you is greater than yours for me'." (James ed. and trans., "The Letters of St. Bernard,", Letter 87, 125).

42   In his *Vita Prima* of Bernard, William distinguishes between different kinds of relationships from acquaintances to closer friendships, the latter of which William believed to be the case in his own relationship with Bernard. (Elder, "Bernard and William," 117).

their relationship.[43] Whereas he seems unable to offer reassurance to his friend, he asks God to do so. Unsure of the degree of love he holds for William, he prays for an examination of his heart and the ability to love and be loved appropriately:

> O Lord, who dost enlighten the lamp by which I see and hate my own darkness enlighten, I pray thee, my very darkness that I may behold within myself and be glad, an ordered charity which knows and loves only what is worthy of love and in the measure that it is worthy of love and for the reasons that it is worthy of love, and be myself unwilling to be loved save in thee and in the measure that I deserve.[44]

In an Augustinian sense, the legitimacy of love is dependent on its motivation: love and self-centered desire are mutually exclusive. The love of God is the cogent foundation for any interpersonal relationship. Thus, Bernard predicates the love between two friends on the condition of their spiritual worthiness. The love he receives from William and the love he can return depend on their respective ability to love God. Although it is possible that Bernard pursues an underlying rhetorical strategy, it seems here as though he extols William's worthiness to question whether he deserves this amount of affection. The friends' different spiritual journeys lead to a concrete dilemma in their relationship:

> Woe is me, if (as I greatly fear) I am either loved by this man more than I deserve or love him less than he deserves. If the better a man is the more he should be loved, but they are the better who love the more, what else can I say than that I must love him more than myself, because I have no doubt that he is better than myself, but less than I should, because I am capable of less?[45]

Bernard acknowledges here what William laments: whatever feelings the latter harbors, the former does not respond in kind. Each can only love to the best of his ability. In this sense, the intimate salutation that had marked

---

43   "Thou knowest and I feel that by thy gift I love this man for the sake of his goodness. But how much I love him, that I cannot tell, thou knowest. It is thou, Lord, who givest the power to love, it is thou who knowest how much thou hast given him to love me and me to love him." (James ed. and trans., "The Letters of St. Bernard,", Letter 87, 126.)

44   James ed. and trans., "The Letters of St. Bernard,", Letter 87, 126.

45   James ed. and trans., "The Letters of St. Bernard,", Letter 87, 126.

their correspondence – *suus ille quod suus*[46] – takes on a more profound significance. "To his friend all that a friend could wish"[47] points to the limitations of their love. Both Bernard and William loved as deeply as they could, knowing that their distinct levels of affection would cause disappointment for the one and overwhelm the other. It becomes clear from their correspondence that the concrete human dimensions of their friendship fell short of the ideal of perfect charity.

What seems more significant to the spiritual aspect of their relationship, however, is their willingness to hold on to what is imperfect so that it may grow in time. Bernard uses the language of the Song to express the different stages of his development and the need to grow in charity. Assuming the role of the bride, he asks his divine lover to draw him in more closely and reveal to him the source of his ability to love.[48] Growing in his intimacy with Christ would allow him to extend that love more expressively and appropriately to his friends.

Conversely, he asks William to remember God as the true object of his love, even as it is directed toward Bernard. If it is not Christ, whom he loves within his friend, he fails to recognize his friend's true nature. The distance between the two, especially the one William perceives, is a consequence of their spiritual difficulties:

> Why do you try to reach me and complain that you are not able? You could reach me if you but considered what I am; and you can reach me still whenever you wish, if you are content to find me as I am and not as you wish me to be. I cannot think what else you see in me besides what I am, what it is you are chasing which is not me. You do not overtake it, because it is not me, because I am not able to be what you would like me to be and, to use your own words, I do not fail you, it is God in me who fails you.[49]

Of course, Bernard does not intend to suspect God of failing them. His emphasis on God's presence in him allows him to appease his friend; if

---

46   William had initiated this form of address in an early letter and Bernard replied to it
       with the formula *suo illi quod suo* (Elder, "Bernard and William," 117).

47   As translated in Letters of St. Bernard, James ed. and trans., "The Letters of St. Bernard,", Letter 87, 127.

48   Draw me after you that I may reach you and with you receive more fully whence
       comes the power to love (James ed. and trans., "The Letters of St. Bernard,", Letter 87,
       127):

49   James ed. and trans., "The Letters of St. Bernard,", Letter 87, 127.

William's intentions were adequately ordered, he would be able to experience the intimacy for which he so longs. The distance William perceives, he claims, is deceptive and demonstrative of a lack of spiritual trust. Sometimes implicit and sometimes overt, Bernard identifies both himself and his friend with the Song's figure of the bride, who is searching for her lover only to find he was with her all along.

Another letter of Bernard's, letter 89,[50] contains a particularly curious passage in this regard. In it, Bernard seems to break the traditional allegorical reading of the Song in a new and intimately human way:

> I do not ask for my friend back, because I am confident that I hold him; I do not receive him back, because I have never lost him. I cling to him, and there is no one who can take him from me. I embrace again as of old my friend because true friendship never wears thin, else it were not true friendship. I shall hold on to him and 'I shall not suffer him to go until I bring him into my mother's house and into the chamber of her that bore me'.[51]

In this passage, Bernard casts William in the role of the bridegroom. Quoting from SoS 3,4 he describes his perspective on their friendship akin to the emotions of the figurative bride of the Song. Trusting in her bridegroom's devotion and the depth of their relationship, she does not need to fear his loss. While the Song is the biblical expression of love, its essential characteristics apply to Bernard's understanding of 'true friendship' as well; friendship is persistent and endures the test of time.[52] A traditional Christian exegesis of the Song interprets the figure of the bridegroom as an allegory for the person of Christ. Both William and Bernard were explicit proponents of this reading. It is thus interesting that Bernard uses the same language he employs to describe his everlasting relationship with Christ to reassure William of the reliability of their friendship. Such a

---

50   The identification of William as a recipient of this letter (Letter 89, Letters of St. Bernard, p. 128) is not undoubted, but widely suggested, for instance in (*Opere Di San Bernardo*. Edited by Ferruccio Gastaldelli. Vol. VI/2. Milano, 1987, 668, fn.1).

51   James ed. and trans., "The Letters of St. Bernard,", Letter 89, 128.

52   "The concept of true friendship as an eternal, unchanging bond goes back to ancient theory, where it was seen as an aspect of natural virtue, a phenomenon external to the individual and understood in terms of the natural forces of universal harmony, and which at the human level united the virtuous to the public good." (Haseldine, "Monastic Friendship," 358).

passage raises the question of how far mystical language, used to approximate the inexpressible nature of divine love, can directly be applied to human affairs. In this particular instance, Bernard seems to allow for such usage.

This should not suggest any blasphemous intentions or depreciation of Christ's exceptionality in his role. Instead, it signals that spiritual friendship, for Bernard, is essentially divine and not human. The passages in which he emphasizes God's work in and through him reveal his understanding of individuality. Interpersonal love is a divine rather than a human affect. What Bernard claims to love about William – and what he conversely asks William to love about him – is not a particular personality trait, but the presence of God in their hearts. The essential mark of spiritual friendship, vis-à-vis 'sinful' kinds of friendship, is divine grace.[53] Within this framework, the Song's different roles become somewhat interchangeable. While the traditional identification of the monastic reader is with the role of the bride, which is usually read as an allegory for the human soul, the emphasis on divine activity in loving human relationships allowed them to equally identify with the traditionally divine figure of the bridegroom.

Bernard's and William's correspondence reveals thus that their friendship and the way they spiritually interpreted it was deeply steeped in the language of the Song. The way in which William's and Bernard's collaborative exegesis of the Song has directly shaped the way they related to each other on a personal and emotional level is a particularly interesting example of how the reading of Scripture, in general, informed every aspect of the monastic life. Yet, the Song's importance for their friendship is not merely linguistic but also manifested in their shared biographical paths. The initial phase of their friendship can be traced back to William's extended stay at the infirmary of Clairvaux. This encounter tangibly exemplifies one of Aelred's poetic characterizations of friendship: *optimum ergo uitae medicamentum amicus.*[54]

In 1128 Bernard had invited William to Clairvaux for recovery, as both had been suffering from acute illness. According to William's account in the *Vita Prima*, this was when Bernard began to initiate him into the secrets of the Song, or more specifically, the 'moral sense' of the text.[55] Regardless of

53   Haseldine, "Monastic Friendship," 358.
54   De Spiritali Amicitia, Lib. 2, linea 90.
55   Vita Prima Sancti Bernardi, CCCM 89B, Lib. 1, par. 59, pag. 74, linea 1491–1500: *Infirmi ergo ambo tota die de spirituali physica animae conferebamus, de medicamentis*

how William continued his study of the text in creative and autonomous ways, later on, the importance William attributes to this encounter reveals that Bernard was certainly a driving force when it came to William's curiosity about the Song. This is not to say that William had not worked with the text of the Song before – his firm reliance on Bernard's knowledge has to be, at least to a certain extent, a hagiographic exaggeration.

William had already brought extensive knowledge of Origen and his hermeneutics into the relationship with Bernard. What he admired in his friend was not necessarily more engagement with Patristic sources and their doctrinal treatment of the text but insight into the spiritual secrets of the text, meaning its application to the soul's journey of ascent and moral depth. What Bernard may have lacked in systematic education, he made up for in spiritual experience and the extraordinary skill to impart experiential knowledge to others.[56] This kind of charisma and lived spirituality aroused William's curiosity and initiated his fascination with Bernard as a teacher in his own right.[57] One could also conclude that William, in turn, was looking in his relationship with Bernard for something he had been missing. William claims that he lacked a dimension of love that is unveiled only through personal experience.[58]

William's first stay at Clairvaux would not remain the last. Both men endured further episodes of severe illness, which they spent with each other as visitors or patients. William remembered these sojourns fondly, as periods that were marked, despite their physical frailty, by inspiring and stimulating conversation. The infirmary of Clairvaux, in particular, provided a sanctuary,

---

   uirtutum contra languores uitiorum. Itaque tunc disseruit mihi de Cantico canticorum, quantum tempus illud infirmitatis meae permisit, moraliter tantum, intermissis altioribus mysteriis Scripturae illius, quia sic uolebam et sic petieram ab eo. Singulis que diebus quaecumque super hoc audiebam, ne mihi effugerent, scripto alligabam, in quantum mihi Deus donabat et memoria me iuuabat.

56 Verdeyen, "Introduction," in *Exposé sur l'Épître aux Romains*, 10.

57 Elder describes their first meeting as follows: "As he stepped into the dingy hut and met the ailing Bernard, he straightway recognized in the modest surroundings and in the charismatic young abbot the monastic spirit of the ancient desert fathers, ideals familiar to all Latin monks through the ubiquitous Conferences and Institutes of Cassian and the Lives of the Fathers." (Elder, "Bernard and William," 110). I will further discuss the role of Bernard as an 'authority' for William in the chapter "7.3. Horizontal Authority and Loving Obedience".

58 William himself expressed feeling inexperienced and in need of spiritual guidance (*Vita* Prima Sancti Bernardi, CCCM 89B, Lib. 1, par. 59, pag. 74, linea 1500), although this statement could be read as an intentional self-depreciation in the context of the Bernardine Vita.

transcending to a certain degree the rules and hierarchies of the monastic world that allowed them to pursue exegetical and spiritual endeavors at length and in a less formalized way.[59]

As William attests, he recorded their conversations in writing (*scripto alligabam*).[60] It is, however, unclear in which form his records survived and whether they were private or served as the basis for his published *Brevis Commentatio*. Although the contents of this short and somewhat synoptic text are not a part of my analysis per se, its relation to William's reading of the Song and his friendship with Bernard warrant a few words.

3   The *Brevis Commentatio*

The most important problem the *Brevis Commentatio* poses is the question of its authorship and, relating to it, the question of its intended purpose. The discussion of these questions is undoubtedly indebted to the elaborate scholarship of Stanislaus Ceglar,[61] and it is upon his conclusions that I will base my exposition of this work. The text remained undiscovered until 1665, when Charles de Visch, the Prior of the Cistercian abbey of Dunes, first mentioned what he considered an ancient Bernardine codex.[62] The manuscript available to de Visch contained four further works by William of Saint Thierry,[63] the first of which was preceded by an inscription (*Incipiunt soliloquia beati Bernardi abbatis clarevallensis*) that led him to believe that only Bernard could have been the codex's original author.[64]

In his transcript of the manuscript, which he sent to Jean Mabillon, he included further inscriptions pointing to Bernard's authorship of the four works, now attributed to William. Mabillon, in his edition of Bernard's works, first concluded that the *Brevis Commentatio* had to be a "record of Bernard's explanation of the Canticles as narrated by William in his Life of

---

59   Elder, "Bernard and William," 113.

60   Vita Prima Sancti Bernardi, cccm 89B, Lib. 1, par. 59, pag. 74, linea 1500.

61   Ceglar, "The Chronology of his Life," 318–320, and Stanislaus Ceglar, "Introduction," in *Guillelmi a Sancto Theodorico Opera Omnia, Ii: Brevis Commentatio.*, ed. Paul Verdeyen and Stanislaus Ceglar, cccm 87 (Turnhout: Brepols, 1997).

62   Ceglar, "Introduction," in *Brevis Commentatio*, 137.

63   The manuscript in question is ms lat. 128, folios 50–140, preserved in the City Library of Brugge. (Ceglar, "Introduction," in *Brevis Commentatio*, 137).

64   Ceglar, "Introduction," in *Brevis Commentatio*, 137.

St. Bernard".[65] In the second edition, published in 1690, Mabillon came to a different inference. Here he characterized the work as a condensed version of the first 51 of Bernard's sermons on the Song, collected by "some learned and pious man".[66] However, he noted the treatise's distinct style and similarities to William's other works.

The observation that led these early readers of the text to their respective arguments continued to influence the discussion as it continued in the 20th century. Scholars had to consider the remarkable congruence between the *Brevis Commentatio* and Bernardine thought, particularly his sermons, and the style of writing that conspicuously resembled William's. The question of how these two aspects could be compatible and concur in a plausible theory of authorship evoked many theses. Jean Leclerq, for instance, assumed the work to have been written by a secretary.[67] In contrast, Fr. Louis Bouyer proposed that it offered a direct rendering of the conversations Bernard and William had had over time.[68] The latter hypothesis was then further solidified by the study of Dom. J. Hourlier,[69] so that with Ceglar, we can state that the "quest for the real author of BC [...] has been successfully brought to a meaningful conclusion [...]".[70]

That is not to say that the questions, to which degree Bernard and William respectively had shaped their conversation and the final text, are exhausted. Future research on the *Brevis Commentatio* will likely have to continue sorting through the themes, motives, and styles of writing to identify the distinct points of view. Of course, large parts of the text consist of classically Cistercian themes, which are difficult, if not impossible, to assign to a particular author. In the following, I will attempt to present a few themes and images that could indicate William's more active role in the commentary's composition.

The first and most striking observation is that it begins with an introduction to three stages of humanity, according to Augustine: the animal (or sensual), the rational, and the spiritual (or intellectual) stage.[71] This distinction

---

65   as cited in Ceglar, "Introduction," in *Brevis Commentatio*, 138.
66   as cited in Ceglar, "Introduction," in *Brevis Commentatio*, 138.
67   as cited in Ceglar, "Introduction," in *Brevis Commentatio*, 139.
68   as cited in Ceglar, "Introduction," in *Brevis Commentatio*, 140.
69   Jacques Hourlier, "Guillaume de Saint–Thierry et La 'Brevis Commentatio in Cantica'," *Analecta Cisterciensia* 12 (1965).
70   Ceglar, "Introduction," in *Brevis Commentatio*, 140.
71   This threefold distinction of anthropological stages is not to be confused with the earlier mentioned fourfold distinction of salvific states (*ante legem, sub lege, sub gratia* and *in pace plena atque perfecta*).

is central to several of William's works, particularly his Commentary on Romans and his Golden Epistle. On the one hand, the trisection usually serves as a literary structure. On the other hand, they are psychological explanations of human piety, which play a role in the theoretical description of spiritual ascent and the pedagogical guidance of monks. The usage of the Augustinian scheme is by no means exclusive to William, yet the way it is used in the commentary points to his influence rather than Bernard's. In the first chapter alone, the author presents three different interpretations for each stage respectively and introduces them systematically.

The animal stage, he explains, is 'written into the heart, a part of the weak human flesh', stating that it is the most fundamental stage accessible to all people by the humanity of Christ. In a further step, he explains that the purpose of the first stage is the contemplation of Christ's humanity; a lower yet valuable experience that will eventually be transformed, just as the disciples' days with the risen Christ ended, so that they could be filled with the presence of the Holy Spirit.[72] In a third step, he reinforces this point by explaining that the first and possibly the second stage are exemplified by the feeling of Peter, who rebuked Christ when he predicted his death and resurrection, clinging to the memories of Jesus's life, his works, and his words.[73] The third stage is similarly described in different terms: first, as the moment in which one is grasped by God. Then, as the stage in which the mind loses all knowledge of Christ according to the flesh and transcends the memory of his bodily experiences. And lastly, as the stage that allows the soul to abide in divinity, focused entirely on God's nature and rid of all its attachments to humanity.[74]

This first introductory chapter reveals several aspects suggesting William's direct contribution. On the level of content, there is a strong focus on transcendence, including the transcendence of devotion and biblical

---

72   Brevis Commentatio, CCCM 87, cap. 1, linea 13: *Primus adeo delectatur in contemplatione et dulcedine humanitatis Christi, ut merito eis dicat Christus: Expedit uobis ut ego uadam.*

73   Brevis Commentatio, CCCM 87, cap. 1, linea 19: *Quod enim apostoli in corporali domini praesentia passi sunt, hoc isti patiuntur in quadam pia mentis suae phantasia; de humanitatis Christi dulcissima memoria, | et conuersationis et operum eius, et passionis et resurrectionis et ascensionis eius, et bonorum nobis per haec collatorum, eum amoris affectum induentes quo Petrus, tenere et sicut homo hominem Deum amans, suggerebat ei passionis suae seriem praedicenti: Absit a te, domine; propitius esto tibi; non fiet istud.*

74   Brevis Commentatio, CCCM 87, cap. 1, linea 27: *Tertius autem gradus, totus extra hominem supra hominem, totus in Deo, Deum propter Deum, iustum diligit propter iustum, et bonum propter bonum; non quia bonum nobis, sed quia bonum in se.*

imagery. The christological emphasis in Bernard's sermons on the song is attributed rather to the first and the second stage than to the ultimate and aspirational third stage. Although William's core concepts of the *unitas spiritus* or the *fruitio* are not explicitly mentioned in these first passages,[75] it is clear that the author is concerned principally with the soul's transformation in a pneumatological sense.

On a hermeneutical level, the distinction of spiritual stages and their explanations according to theoretical, ethical, and exegetical facets reveal an extraordinary sensibility to the multidimensionality of Scripture and doctrine. The same kind of careful differentiation is applied to various themes throughout the Commentary. While William claims that his conversations with Bernard involved exclusively the 'moral sense' of the Song, the Commentary tackles various passages according to different hermeneutical levels. As Ann Matter points out, this is exemplified clearly in the exegesis of SoS 1,2, "your name is poured out like oil".[76] The Commentary's author lays out different exegetical possibilities. The words could either be spoken by the bridegroom himself, by the bride in regards to the bridegroom, or a statement about the love of God being 'poured out' to all people.

Eventually, the author turns to the moral sense, interpreting it as a word of caution against the careless and 'disorderly' diffusion of oil, differentiating even further between the oil that is rightfully one's own and the oil that belongs to another. According to this particular moral sense, oil stands for "that without which we would not be saved": faith, hope, and charity. Similarly, the act of pouring out is interpreted equivocally as the divine effusing of the spiritual gifts for humanity's sake and the appropriate usage of these gifts by humanity. This allows for a broader and more complex reading of the verse, elaborating on the effects of faith, hope, and charity on the individual soul and its relationship with God. Ann Matter assesses that Bernard had never pursued this kind of systematic exegesis in his own works.[77]

Apart from the clearly structured character of the work, some highly sophisticated theological statements in the Commentary could also point to

---

75   In chapter 3 of the *Brevis Commentatio* the concept of *fruitio* is however mentioned in the context of yet another systematic exploration of the threefold ascent. Here, the author offers a more pastoral take on the scheme: *In primo remissio peccatorum et emundatio uitiorum; in secundo exercitium uirtutum; in tertio uirtutum perfectio et summi boni adhaesio uel fruitio.* (Brevis Commentatio, CCCM 87, cap. 3, linea 4).

76   Matter, *The voice of my beloved*, 131, referencing Brevis Commentatio, CCCM 87, cap. 13.

77   Matter, *The voice of my beloved*, 131–32.

William's active role in its authorship. Interpreting the bridegroom's kiss (SoS 1,2) in a Trinitarian context, the author of the Commentary offers a complex discussion of the three persons of God.[78] The carefulness with which the text treats the divine names, asserting their true substance and conceptual legitimacy, is notable. We find in these passages a particular concern for an orthodox differentiation between the threefold nature and simultaneous oneness of God and even two explicit references to the Greek terminology of hypostasis,[79] which seem slightly out of place in the context of an allegorical exegesis of the Song. As Nathaniel Peters notes, this Trinitarian interpretation of the kiss, defining the Holy Spirit as the kiss between the Son and the Father, can also be found in several other works of William's.[80]

Such a doctrinally cautious and highly systematic interpretation is not typical of Bernard. The bridal kiss, in particular, appears in Bernard's interpretations as the pinnacle of experiential depth rather than theoretical knowledge. After all, this is what William himself claims to have hoped to learn from Bernard. Yet the exegesis in the *Brevis commentatio* is marked by its theoretical complexity. Throughout a long passage, its author differentiates between the active act of kissing and the passive experience of being kissed, allowing him to make profound observations on the nature of revelation and the limitations of the human intellect.[81] The tension between the function of the ratio and the kind of knowledge that transcends all rational potential is a core theme in most of William's works. The creative way in which it is discussed in this commentary makes his direct involvement very likely.

It remains challenging to distinguish Bernard's from William's voice, mainly if one is concerned with avoiding potentially limiting stereotypes. Since they shared a common cultural and spiritual vocabulary, attributing particular motives to one or the other is deserving of an extensive linguistic

---

78   Brevis Commentatio, cccm 87, cap. 6.
79   Brevis Commentatio, cccm 87, cap. 6, linea 6: *Nec fulcitur alter ab altero, ut subsistat, uel sit quod est per alterutrum, sed sunt, sicut diximus, uel secundum Graecos plenae per se subsistentes hypostases, uel secundum Latinos personae, id est per se sonantes, licet una sit et perfecta homousion Trinitas Deus.*
80   Peters, "The Eucharistic Theology," 190.
81   Brevis Commentatio, cccm 87, cap. 6, linea 40–44: *Non os tangimus, id est mutuum illum intellectum. Non os tangimus, quia, ut dictum est: Nemo nouit Filium nisi Pater, et nemo nouit Patrem nisi Filius; sed osculo tangimur, id est, cui uoluerit Filius reuelare. Non os tangimus, quia nec oculus uidit, nec auris audiuit. Osculo tangimur, quia nobis reuelauit Deus per Spiritum sanctum.*

and comparative study. Although I do not intend to present a theory on the Commentary's authorship in the study at hand, I believe it to be plausible that the Commentary is indeed a record of two monks' vivid conversations. Given the repeated highly schematic patterns of the Commentary and the usage of the threefold human stages to order particular themes, it seems possible that William wrote the *Brevis commentatio* in the systematic approach, which he already knew. The experiential language and imagery Bernard had imparted to him during their conversations would have been embedded and incorporated into the exegetical structure he had conceptualized.

Whether or not this was indeed the process of the Commentary's composition, I believe Jean Leclerq's assertion that Bernard found himself challenged by his inquisitive and sometimes even demanding friend to be central.[82] William's explicit desire to learn from Bernard and to have him elucidate his moral interpretation of the Song in a pedagogical way must have influenced Bernard's own thinking. Regardless of any contributions of content William would have made, his inquiry as such introduced the necessity of systematization into their allegorical reading of the Song; an element that would eventually prove to be vital for the future of bridal mysticism.

---

82   "Guillaume de Saint–Thierry est pour Bernard un ami exigeant" (Jean Leclercq, *Recueil d'études sur saint Bernard et ses écrits,* vol. 3 (Rome: Edizioni di Storia e Letteratura, 1969), 20).

CHAPTER 4

William's Florilegia of Ambrose and Gregory

1 The Early Medieval Tradition of Anthologies

There is something nostalgic, even poetic, about the idea of florilegia; this metaphorical 'plucking of flowers' seems to express both the beauty of its objects and the passion of its collector. Yet, historically, these anthologies have served a crucial pragmatic purpose, providing for many medieval authors the only possible access to Patristic thought. This twofold dimension of assembling anthologies is beautifully expressed in the *Liber comitis* by its author, Smaragdus of Saint–Mihiel (†830):

> Seeing that many in the Church wisely seek to investigate the mystical sense of the divine scriptures and pluck from them the figurative fruit, I have made an effort to gather one book from many, filled with the flowers of allegory, acting both as an abbreviator and deriver of the tractates and teachings of the great fathers, namely of Hilary, Jerome, Ambrose, Augustine, Cyprian, Cyril, Gregory, Victor, Fulgentius, John Chrysostom, Cassiodorus, Eucharis, Tychonius, Isidore, Figulus, Bede, Primasius, and also of those who must be approached cautiously, such as Pelagius and Origen, as if reducing powerful rivers and whirling eddies of the sea into moderate currents.[1]

Smaragdus understands florilegia as a practical contribution to Christian exegesis. Reading Scripture, to him, is not an individual project but the church's communal effort to incorporate divine truth into her vision of a faithful life. Since this is not a simple task by any means, exegetes at any

---

[1] *Cernens in Ecclesia plurimos divinarum Scripturarum mysticos sagaciter perquirere sensus, earumque typicos mavelle decerpere fructus, hunc ex multis unum, allegoriarum floribus plenum curavi colligere librum, et de magnorum tractatibus prolatisque sermonibus Patrum, id est Hilarii, Hieronymi, Ambrosii, Augustini, Cypriani, Cyrilli, Gregorii, Victoris, Fulgentii, Joannis Chrysostomi, Cassiodori, Eucherii, Tychonii, Isidori, Figuli, Bedae, Primasii et de caute legendis, Pelagii et Origenis, quasi de magnis fluminibus pelagique gurgitibus in modicos rivulos, pariter derivator, pariterque exstiti breviator* (Liber comitis, PL 102:13C) as translated in Matthew Ponesse, "Standing Distant from the Fathers: Smaragdus of Saint–Mihiel and the Reception of Early Medieval Learning," *Traditio* 67, no. 1 (2012): 71.

stage of Christian history do well to rely on the insights of the great minds of the past. Therefore, the systematic compilation of their works is to be considered an essential piece in an exegete's toolkit. Florilegia, as Smaragdus envisions them, are not simply making Patristic texts available as raw data but could be considered roadmaps of sorts.[2] They guide their readers through treacherous terrain on the safe paths of orthodoxy. Further, the cited Patristic passages appear abbreviated, edited, and ordered in such a way that they can easily be used to facilitate focused exegetical work. Smaragdus' most well-known work, the Liber Comitis, exemplifies this, as it is an original composition rather than a mere compilation.[3]

Smaragdus is not an individual case. The importance of florilegia in the Carolingian age has often evoked the notion of the epoch as primarily receptive and lacking any innovative drive. Such characterization fails to do justice to great Carolingian thinkers and tends to misjudge the value of anthologies for centuries of Christian education. Yet, the nature of florilegia raises the complex question of intellectual ownership. More recent scholarship has pursued the justified cause of rediscovering the intellectual and innovative efforts of Carolingian thinkers,[4] also reevaluating the definition and role florilegia played in the narrative of the 'Carolingian renaissance'.[5] This kind of scholarship is thus quick to identify a sense of originality, not only in early medieval commentaries but also in the florilegia themselves. Within such a framework, originality has to be redefined.

---

2   The fundamentally pedagogical purpose of these works shines through Smaragdus' own work, as Rutger Kramer points out: "The wish to educate is visible throughout Smaragdus' entire oeuvre" (Rutger Kramer, "Monks on the Via Regia: The World of Smaragdus of Saint–Mihiel," in *Rethinking Authority in the Carolingian Empire* (Amsterdam: Amsterdam University Press, 2019), 131).

3   Kramer, "Monks on the Via Regia," 150.

4   "While acknowledging the limitations to the period's intellectual and cultural activity, current scholarship demonstrates greater appreciation for its intensity and innovativeness [...]. In place of older theories about the uncritical reception of ancient culture, historians are now more likely to stress the active engagement of eight– and ninth–century scholars and artists with their sources, their efforts to select and rework them in ways attuned to contemporary social, political, and intellectual contexts, and the diversity of responses to that heritage, ranging from ardent admiration to outright rejection of some features" (Cecilia Chazelle and Burton Van Name Edwards, "Introduction," in *The Study of the Bible in the Carolingian Era*, Medieval Church Studies 3 (Turnhout: Brepols, 2003), 9).

5   I use this term with caution, as I do with the concept of the '12th-century renaissance'. Yet, the fact that the idea itself receives more and more scholarly interest points to the development I am describing: a growing interest in the rediscovery of Carolingian spirit of discovery.

A modern reader would rightfully point out the lack of an academically honest practice of citation,[6] making it inherently difficult to differentiate between appropriated Patristic thought and so-called 'original' ideas. Ann Matter believes such an approach to be misguided: "Originality in medieval biblical commentary should not be judged by what 'new' interpretations remain when all of the sources have been bracketed; indeed, the resulting texts would sometimes be limited to conjunctions and prepositions! Rather, originality is here *the process* of borrowing, re-working, using old material in new ways to show the imagination and talents of a given author."[7]

Matter's observation is important insofar that it allows us to detect different kinds of intellectual effort that would have gone unnoticed in an all too narrow focus on new material and original thought. Yet, it is questionable whether we can apply this redefinition to the composers of florilegia and call them original in their own right; after all, many of them would have rejected the label themselves. Originality was not the academic virtue as which it is heralded today. The degradation of early medieval scholarship's reliance on past authority, as it was promoted to contrast and elevate later scholastic thought, has perhaps led to a defensiveness that fails to appreciate the value that pre-scholastic medieval authorship has attributed to traditionalism. A modern reader, consciously or unconsciously, tends to embed the notion of intellectual property into their narrative of early medieval scholarship. Yet, this concept is not applicable as such and does not fit the self-conception of these authors.

Theological knowledge, as the earlier quoted Smaragdus revealed, did not belong to the individual mind that produced it but to the church as a whole. The compilation of Patristic thought could thus not have been understood as the theft of intellectual property but as a profound appreciation of the intellectual treasure to which all Christian thinkers were already privy. The purpose of literary contributions to the Christian tradition was not to introduce new, revolutionary findings into communal discourse but to proceed along the well-established path of tradition. Within such a framework, Christian knowledge is, per definition, continuous:[8] Truth is scripturally anchored and cannot be 'added to' in a quantitative sense; it can, however, be culturally translated, made available, and meditated. This is the kind of intellectual labor the composers of florilegia set out to do. The

---

6 Evans, *The Language and Logic of the Bible*, 80.
7 Matter, *The voice of my Beloved*, 6.
8 Evans, *The Language and Logic of the Bible*, 80.

fact that past and contemporary thought was blurred in their efforts was not due to methodical negligence but due to their sense of duty.

Moreover, the congruence between one's own thought and that of the Fathers was a testimony to one's orthodox faith.[9] Carolingian authors were anxious that what they thought and taught was affirmed by the Fathers of the Church,[10] especially considering the most notable concern of Carolingian education: the proper reading of Scripture. The desire to understand the complexity of Scripture stood at the center of Carolingian intellectual life,[11] as is evidenced by a large number of manuscripts of exegetical nature.[12] The intensity of Patristic reception in this period was part of establishing an exegetical science.[13] However, the Biblical text and the works of the Fathers needed to be organized and made available to medieval readers before they could become the object of systematic study.[14]

The pedagogical value of the works that present exegetical insight, doctrinal guidance, and historical access is also evidenced by the oeuvre of possibly the most prolific Carolingian author, the venerable Bede, who is often treated as a Church Father in his own right by later medieval writers. His influence reveals the different dimensions of Patristic reception: the Fathers

---

9   As Willemien Otten puts it: "The past to which the Carolingian renaissance refers can be seen as the age of the Fathers: the early Christian period in which the Latin Fathers Ambrose, Jerome and Augustine, and their Greek counterparts Athanasius and Gregory of Nyssa lived" (Willemien Otten, "The Texture of Tradition. The Role of the Church Fathers in Carolingian Theology," in *The Reception of the Church Fathers in the West. From the Carolingians to the Maurists*, ed. Irena Dorota Backus (Leiden: Brill, 1997).

10   John J. Contreni, *Learning and Culture in Carolingian Europe: Letters, Numbers, Exegesis, and Manuscripts*. Variorum Collected Studies Series (London: Routledge, 2011), 120.

11   It is, however, important to note, that the return to Patristic commentaries the reading of Scripture was accompanied in the Carolingian age by a rediscovery of ancient dialectic art. Even during the lifetime of Charlemagne, Biblical scholars commented on Scripture in the form of *quaestiones*, as evidenced by the writings of Bede or Peter the Archdeacon's *Questiones in Danielem Prophetam* (Riché and Lobrichon, *Le Moyen Âge et la Bible*, 158–59).

12   Chazelle, "Introduction," in *The Study of the Bible in the Carolingian Era*, 5.

13   "Peu à peu en cours des viiie et Ixe siècles les méthodes et les instruments de travail des lettres qui veulent pénétrer les secrets de la divina pagina se mettent en place en s'appuyant sur l'expérience de l'exégèse patristique et en définissant les buts et les moyens d'une véritable science exégétique" (Riché and Lobrichon, *Le Moyen Âge et la Bible*, 146).

14   The production of florilegia was one aspect of a broader establishment of "research tools", such as glossaries, concordances, *postillae* and *distinctiones*, "meant to help scholars and preachers alike to use biblical texts more efficiently" (Schildgen and Hawkins, "Introduction," in *Medieval Readings of Romans*, 2).

were not only authoritative in matters of doctrine, but practical and moral role models as well. For Bede, in particular, the Church Fathers were revered as such because they did not only receive enlightenment for themselves but understood it as their purpose to pass on their insight to future generations of Christians.[15] Following the Fathers meant thus to accept their calling as one's own and pursue truth for pastoral and pedagogical purposes.[16] Bede had access to what was, at the time, a substantial amount of books from over a hundred authors, most of whom are influential figures of Christian history.[17] While reading these texts certainly influenced his theological stances, it most importantly compelled Bede to make them accessible to a larger audience.

The significant achievement of Carolingian authors lay in the ways they assembled, structured, and preserved the texts they were working with. It allowed these authors to frame Patristic notions according to their theological priorities and to determine the future reception of Patristic authors in a way that fit their purposes.[18] Carolingian collections of Patristic thought varied in their concrete approach. All of them share a distinct desire to systematize the knowledge they present.[19] Some tended to a structure resembling the notion of *sententiae*, organizing the citations according to doctrinal questions. Others, including most florilegia, assembled their citations according to particular Biblical books.[20] This latter approach is also followed by William in his florilegia of Ambrose and Gregory, as I will discuss, given that he does not consult them to answer particular dogmatic questions but hopes to present the Fathers' observations regarding the Song of Songs.

For instance, specific omissions, abbreviations, or the establishment of otherwise not apparent connections between certain passages were conscious literary decisions that affected not only the form but the content of such referential works. J.J. Contreni asserts that "the compilatory mode

---

15 Evans, *The Language and Logic of the Bible*, 57.

16 Hannah W. Matis, "Early–Medieval Exegesis of the Song of Songs and the Maternal Language of Clerical Authority," *Speculum* 89, no. 2 (2014): 364.

17 "He received many such books through Benedict Biscop and Ceolfrid, who collected them in Gaul and Rome, but he not only had books, he followed the advice of Augustine of Hippo and read them. He had access at Wearmouth and Jarrow to over a hundred authors, including Basil (On the Hexameon (sic!), trans by Eustathios), Cassian, Cassiodorus, Chrysostom, Cyprian, Eusebius, Gregory Nazienzen, Hilary, Isaidore, Origen (On Genesis), Prudentius, Rufinus, Sedulius, and especially Augustine, Jerome, Gregory, and Ambrose." (Evans, *The Language and Logic of the Bible*, 60).

18 Matis, "Early Medieval Exegesis," 358.

19 Grabmann, *Geschichte der Scholastischen Methode*, vol. 1, 183–84.

20 Riché and Lobrichon, *Le Moyen Âge et la Bible*, 154.

encouraged deep thought and originality."[21] In light of the reservations I had just voiced regarding the description of these works as 'original', I would like to nuance that understanding in stating that florilegia always reflect the particular intellectual intention pursued by their collectors. Arranging and editing passages under a collective theme or regarding specific doctrinal questions has to be classified as an extraordinary intellectual service both to themselves and to the readers and users of their compilations.

The fact that the usage of Patristic quotations and authority is always reflective of a distinct objective is especially noteworthy in light of the historical context from which the genre arose. The golden age of the florilegia was that of the Carolingian reform, a complex political and social endeavor. An important aspect of this reform movement was the development of church law. Creating an ecclesiastical system of ordinances and regulations required a clear definition of authority. The focus on canonicity as a concept and the importance of authoritative common ground led to a revived appreciation of the Church Fathers.[22] In turn, the respect for Patristic thought and a shared tradition was deployed to create a sense of belonging and unity, strengthening Carolingian authority. The dissemination of knowledge and the creation of a functional system of education were of utmost social importance.[23]

The ecclesio-political usage of Patristic citations is exemplified in the life and work of Theodulf of Orléans (ca. 760–821). In his function as Charlemagne's advisor, Theodulf substantiated his theological convictions with Patristic authority in a calculated way and to further his cause. He did so, particularly in the context of the iconoclastic controversy with the Eastern Church, and likely composed the infamous *Libri Carolini*.[24] His enthusiastic reception of the works of Gregory the Great had the implicit goal of

---

21   Contreni, *Learning and Culture*, 120–21.
22   The concept of canonicity further affected florilegia literature indirectly, given that these collections traditionally referred back to the canonical *Decretum Gelasianum de libris recipiendis et non recipiendis* in their selection of cited works (Grabmann, *Geschichte der Scholastischen Methode*, vol. *1*, 182). The decree could be used politically in the Carolingian age, as evidenced by Charlemagne's advisor Theodulf of Orléans, who referenced the decree, in order to disparage certain authorities claimed by the Eastern Church.
23   Contreni, *Learning and Culture*, 89.
24   The complex relationship between orthodoxy and authority in the Libri Carolini is discussed in a nuanced and thorough way by Ann Freeman, in her study on Theodulf's role in their composition, "Theodulf of Orleans and the Libri Carolini." *Speculum* 32, no. 4 (1957).

bypassing the authority of pope Hadrian, consulting Gregory's formidable authority to support his position in the conflict (namely tolerating images in the church but not their worship).[25] To disparage the Patristic authorities claimed by Greek theologians, Theodulf also made specific use of pope Gelasius' decree *De libris recipiendis et non recipiendis*.[26] The same decree would later influence the tradition of florilegia over centuries, as most authors relied on the Gelasian canon to select cited works,[27] revealing the genre's inherent potential for subjective framing.

Whether it was for explicitly political or less calculating reasons, Carolingian authors did not simply reiterate Patristic thought but deliberately introduced the Fathers' works into their contemporary discourse.[28] One of the prominent authors of the age, Hrabanus Maurus (ca. 780–856), is a suitable representative of this approach. He employed Patristic passages to support his position in controversies surrounding orthodoxy or the church reform movement and even to answer matters of pastoral practice. Patristic knowledge, especially the works of Augustine and Gregory the Great, informed his perception of contemporary social and clerical issues, and he developed a creative way to make that knowledge fruitful for his time.[29]

For Hrabanus and other authors who followed in his footsteps, the main object of Patristic reception was to gain a deeper understanding of Scripture. The return to the Fathers guaranteed a faithful exegesis and, what is more, a church life grounded in biblical principles. Scripture itself, as well as the discoveries of its interpreters, were thought to belong to one continuous and harmonious tradition; the fount out of which Christian thinkers ought to draw inspiration and insight. Authors like Hrabanus hoped to provide their readers with an encyclopedic orientation of this common Christian tradition.[30] His approach has been described as "almost an exegesis of

---

25   Evans, *The Language and Logic of the Bible*, 71.

26   Evans, *The Language and Logic of the Bible*, 72.

27   Grabmann, *Geschichte der Scholastischen Methode, vol. 1*, 182.

28   Owen M. Phelan, *The Formation of Christian Europe: The Carolingians, Baptism, and the Imperium Christianum* (Oxford: Oxford University Press, 2014), 71.

29   Phelan, *The Formation of Christian Europe*, 72.

30   "Rhabanus Maurus war ein Polyhistor, eine enzyklopädische Natur" (Grabmann, *Geschichte der Scholastischen Methode, vol. 1*, 196). Heil takes not of Hrabanus' reputation and the value of his works for his audience, quoting Notker Balbulus, who had written in a letter to Salomon III of Constance: "[F]or explanations (glossulas) on the whole of holy scripture, it will be enough if you have Hrabanus" (Johannes Heil, "Labourers in the Lord's Quarry: Carolingian Exegetes, Patristic Authority, and Theological Innovation, a Case Study in the Representation of Jews in Commentaries on Paul," in *The*

exegesis, seeking to illuminate both the Bible and the Fathers at the same time".[31]

The central *locus* of the intellectual life of the time was the monastery. Exegetical literature was, thus, in the Carolingian age, primarily monastic literature.[32] While these monasteries played a prominent political role and were the focal point of the aforementioned reform efforts,[33] the spiritual dimension of early medieval exegesis should not be overlooked. Carolingian monasteries mainly followed the Benedictine ideals, both intellectual and moral. Therefore, their intense interest in the writings of the Fathers has one of its roots in the Benedictine Rule itself. For Benedict, as for the Christian tradition as a whole, the first source of wisdom and spiritual growth was Scripture. However, as Benedict advised his followers, reading Patristic works and exemplary Christian literature (such as the *vitae* of Saints) was expected for those pursuing perfection.[34] From Benedict onward, a monk's task included engagement with Christian tradition beyond the Biblical text. This tendency to introduce further resources into one's private *lectio* grew throughout the Middle Ages, necessitating the dissemination of texts at a larger scale. Over time, monasteries became near-exclusive locations for producing and preserving books. Monastic libraries continued to be invaluable for Christian thought, even as Cathedral schools superseded them as educational institutions.[35]

12th-century theology owes an outstanding debt to the Carolingian monks who had established libraries and ensured the possibility of relying on a continuous tradition of Christian authorship. The Carolingians had understood the task of preserving the past as such a vital part of their mission that 12th-century authors often found it challenging to assess the extent of early medieval contributions. The tradition of producing florilegia and

---

   Study of the Bible in the Carolingian Era, Medieval Church Studies 3 (Turnhout: Brepols, 2003), 76–77).

31   Matthew Gabriele, "The Last Carolingian Exegete: Pope Urban II, the Weight of Tradition, and Christian Reconquest," *Church History* 81, no. 4 (2012): 808. Gabriele's observation extends to Hrabanus' contemporary, Haimo of Auxerre as well.

32   Lohr, "Peter Abälard," 96–97.

33   Phelan importantly points out "the centrality of monasteries in cultivating a context within which intellectuals nurtured innovative approaches to reform and from which they disseminated concrete programs of renewal" (Phelan, *The Formation of Christian Europe*, 89).

34   Contreni, *Learning and Culture*, 94.

35   see my discussion of the development in the earlier chapter "1.2. Scripture in the 12th century".

infusing even one's own Biblical commentary with Patristic quotations made the early medieval period both 'virtually invisible' and yet indispensable for the centuries that followed.[36] In the 11th or 12th century, students of the *sacra pagina* relied primarily on florilegia in their study of Scripture and the Fathers, notably Augustine.[37]

While the developments of the 12th and 13th centuries might make it seem like the earlier medieval tradition offered mere preliminary work and acted as a stepping stone for theology to develop into something different and much more innovative, it is important to note that some monastic authors hoped to continue their exegetical work in the early medieval spirit. Both the Gregorian and the Cistercian reforms emphasized the importance of doctrinal and ecclesial authority.[38] Exegesis and Patristic reception stood at the center of the monastic ideal these movements were propagating and were considered the cornerstones of spiritual progress.[39]

The exponents of such monastic reform efforts shared a common interest with early medieval authors they followed: the delimitation and promotion of orthodox thought in all areas of the Christian life, according to the Fathers' interpretations of the Biblical message. While this goal was pursued in the Carolingian age with the production of various and heterogeneous collections of citations, one of the responses of 12th-century scholarship to this problem was the coordinated effort of creating the *glossa ordinaria,* the 'ordinary gloss'.[40] Although the gloss could be considered one of the turning points of theological scholarship, transforming the history of exegetical literature and education,[41] its development did not mark a fundamental caesura

---

36   Evans, *The Language and Logic of the Bible*, 66. It is, however, important to note, that some Carolingian authors were considered authorities in their own right (such as Haimo of Auxerre or Hrabanus Maurus) and their works were received widely in later the Cluniac monasteries (Gabriele, "The Last Carolingian Exegete," 804).

37   Contreni makes mention of the *Liber de divinis Scripturis* and Eugippius's *Exceprta ex operibus sancti augustini*, as common sources, akin to textbooks (Contreni, *Learning and Culture*, 95).

38   Given that the centers of Cistercian reform were located in medieval France, it is comprehensible that "in all essential respects the French learning of the eleventh century seems to root directly in the soil of the Carolingian tradition" (Haskins, *The Renaissance of the Twelfth Century*, 17).

39   Riché and Lobrichon, *Le Moyen Âge et la Bible*, 143.

40   Jinty Nelson and Damien Kempf, "Introduction," in *Reading the Bible in the Middle Ages,* ed. Jinty Nelson and Damien Kempf, Studies in Early Medieval History (London: Bloomsbury, 2017), 2.

41   LaVere, "From Contemplation to Action," 55.

of intention. The purpose of the gloss was to provide access to a continuous and orthodox tradition and facilitate theological reflection; the florilegia of the early medieval period could be considered its literary ancestors.

William was a contemporary and possibly even a conscious witness of the gloss's early formation.[42] The school of Laon is today considered the likely point of origin for the *glossa ordinaria*.[43] Although it is unknown whether William knew of the project of the gloss, he was undoubtedly familiar with the methods of exegesis and the intellectual values taught at the school. Although not directly contributing to the gloss, his work concerning the interpretation of the Song of Songs still reveals a strikingly similar concern. The primary cause of the *glossa ordinaria* was the harmonization and insurance of clerical education.[44]

William's cause, as we will see, is similarly pedagogical, mainly focusing on the intellectual and spiritual formation of monks. Set into relation with such efforts as the *glossa ordinaria*, William cannot be denounced as a singular proponent of a long-outdated intellectual ideal. The cultural shift, taking place on the verge of the scholastic age should not lead us to qualify William and his adherents as dinosaurs, choosing to be oriented towards the past exclusively. A concern for the future of Christian thought guided William's interest in Patristic exegesis. With his florilegia, he pursued a goal he shared with the pre-scholastic and scholastic composers of the *glossa ordinaria*. As Beryl Smalley had noted already in regards to such extraordinary Carolingian authors as Paschasius Radbertus (785–865) and John Scotus Eriugena (ca. 800–877), "the labour of compilation led in itself to more independent work."[45] The critical engagement with Patristic statements on which scholastic thinkers prided themselves is simply unthinkable without the faithful compositions and expositions with which the composers of florilegia provided them.

2   William's Florilegia and Their Role in His Literary Corpus

In the last chapter, I had already identified the crux at the heart of florilegia research as the tension between the originality we would like to attribute to

---

42   The Gloss of the Song was likely compiled in the 1120s (Mary Dove, "Sex, Allegory and Censorship: a Reconsideration of Medieval Commentaries on the Song of Songs," *Literature and Theology* 10, no. 4 (1996), 321).

43   Riché and Lobrichon, *Le Moyen Âge et la Bible*, 177.

44   Schildgen and Hawkins, "Introduction," in *Medieval Readings of Romans*, 3, and Smalley, *The Study of the Bible*, 53.

45   Smalley, *The Study of the Bible*, 38.

their composers out of admiration for their work and their self-conception that more often than not rejected the thought of originality in their contribution. A similar problem arises from the study of William's florilegia. The purpose of their composition has been a subject of much debate, and several theories about William's intention in their compilation have been developed. One very intriguing line of interpretation, supported namely by Hermann Kutter and André Wilmart, attempted to place the florilegia into the context of William's accusations against Abelard.[46] It is so tempting because William's conflict with Abelard is the most prominent case in which William had to defend and introduce his own orthodoxy into a particular theological discourse. However, the idea that he would do so by simply collecting a host of citations from indisputable authorities has more to do with Abelard's belittling portrayal of his adversaries than with William's much more complex approach. If the florilegia have, however, as Verdeyen asserts, been composed during 1124 and 1125,[47] this theory does not hold up; more so, the Song of Songs only very indirectly touches on points of contention between William and Abelard, and would have been a poor choice of Scripture, had the display of his superior orthodoxy indeed been his motivation.

The second line of interpretation, defended mainly by André Adam, is significantly more plausible. He believes the florilegia to be preparatory work for his *Expositio* on the Song.[48] This notion deserves some exploration. Against the backdrop of the previous discussion on early medieval florilegia and their purpose, the idea is hardly far-fetched: florilegia had been used as reference works and provided especially novice Bible scholars with guiding exegetical ideas. As Beryl Smalley points out, "by the end of the ninth century, a beginner could read almost anyone of the biblical books with the help of a commentary pieced together from one or more of the Fathers."[49] The compilation and the consumption of florilegia could be described as 'academic priming'. Depending on the theory of chronology applied, the florilegia could have been composed after his stay at Clairvaux and before his work on the *Expositio*. If that were the case, their compilation could be viewed as a central part of his literary process.[50] After learning directly from Bernard, William would have inserted a period of research into his long

---

46 Wilmart, "La serie et la date," 165.

47 Verdeyen, "La chronologie des oeuvres," 199.

48 André Adam. *Guillaume de Saint-Thierry. Sa vie et ses oeuvres* (Bourg: Impr. du Journal de l'Ain, 1924), 51–52.

49 Smalley, *The Study of the Bible,* 38.

50 This is also the explanation that Rozanne Elder seems to believe in, on the basis of Antony Van Burink Paul Verdeyen's position that the florilegia were actually composed in the abbey of St. Thierry (Elder, "William and the Renewal of the Whole Man," 109).

phase of engagement with the Song of Songs, during which he focused on gathering Patristic observations. Kutter and Wilmart's basic idea of contextualizing the florilegia with William's concern for orthodoxy could, in fact, be introduced in such a narrative as well, assuming that William wanted to compare the contemporary interpretation developed in Clairvaux with traditional readings of the Song.

Interpreting the compilation of Patristic passages as an important step in William's exegetical process is plausible. Still, it does not explain why he composed these florilegia as literary works – not only available to himself but produced for future readers as well. Such a 'byproduct' had not come from any of his other exegetical or doctrinal works, even though it is apparent that he had also extensively studied the Fathers for all of his other treatises. Further, the theory is on particularly shaky grounds, given that William's Commentary exhibits very few Gregorian excerpts and not one Ambrosian citation.[51] Had the florilegia indeed been preparatory work for himself, the laboriously assembled passages would have made their way into the Expositio more straightforwardly.

In his Golden Epistle, William explains that he had set out to continue the unfinished pursuit of the Venerable Bede (672–673):

> I excerpted from the books of Saint Ambrose, in which he examined the Song of Songs – a great and prestigious work. I did it similarly with excerpts from the Blessed Gregory, but more extensive than Bede did.[52]

We find here a clear expression of William's admiration for Bede's efforts to systematize Patristic works and make them available for future generations of Biblical scholars. Bede's historiographic concern also resonates in William's endeavor. With his florilegia, he presents the works of two orthodox representatives of allegorical exegesis, thus historically contextualizing the Cistercian fascination with the Song. William's statement in this passage and the fact that he had made so little explicit use of the excerpts in his own work make Jean–Marie Déchanet's interpretation the most likely. He had understood the florilegia as an intellectual gimmick of sorts, an intense

---

51   Verdeyen, "Introduction," in *Exposé Sur l'Épitre aux Romains*, 23.

52   Epistula ad fratres de monte dei, CCCM 88, Prol., par. 11, pag. 226, linea 69: *Excerpsi enim ex libris sancti Ambrosii quicquid in eis disseruit super Cantica canticorum, opus grande et inclytum. Similiter etiam ex beati Gregorii, sed diffusius quam Beda fecerit.*

engagement with Patristic material that reflected little original thought and was composed to satisfy his particular interest and the few who shared it.

In recent years, however, the exceptional research of Mark Del Cogliano has allowed (in his own words) 'a fresh look' at William's florilegia.[53] In the following, I would like to devote a few words to his observations and his nuanced interpretation of William's compilatory efforts. First, Del Cogliano's approach stands out because he differentiates between the two florilegia, attributing different roles to both of them respectively. As he convincingly shows, based on an in-depth analysis of the quotations and William's adaptations, the two florilegia are structured in fundamentally different ways. A first and important indication of that distinction is the fact that the Ambrosian anthology is introduced with a prologue, in which William interweaves his own notes with selected Ambrosian citations. More so than the compilation of passages, the prologue offers insight into William's reasoning for particular editorial choices and shows which themes and motives in the Ambrosian corpus he is most interested in. It is thus reasonable to devote some deliberations to the *Excerpta ex libris beati Ambrosii* and William's motivation for their compilation.

2.1   *Reading between the Lines: Ambrose as a Moral Authority*
On a surface level, the *Excerpta de libris beati Ambrosii* are just that: excerpts from various Ambrosian works. Yet, as Del Cogliano points out, the work is less transparent than its title, and the superimposed literary structure initially suggests. The florilegium is organized into 145 chapters, each containing one or more citations.[54] The work is not thematically structured but instead follows the Biblical text closely. Although this is typical of early medieval florilegia and commentaries, it is nevertheless noteworthy given the approaches that emerged from the 12th century onward. The florilegia (the *Excerpta ex libris beati Gregorii* are also structured according to the Biblical text) are thus more suitable for authors who were looking to provide their Biblical commentaries with Patristic citations or research interpretations of a particular passage of the Songs than they would become for

---

53   I am referencing here Mark Del Cogliano, "A Fresh Look at William of Saint–Thierry's Excerpts from the Book of Blessed Ambrose on the Song of Songs," in *Unity of Spirit: Studies on William of Saint–Thierry in Honor of E. Rozanne Elder*, ed. F. Tyler Sergent, Aage Rydstrøm–Poulsen, and Marsha L. Dutton, Cistercian Studies 268 (Collegeville, MN: Cistercian Publications, 2015).

54   Del Cogliano, "A Fresh Look," 87.

scholastic thinkers who would structure his treatises according to theological themes.

However, what makes William's Ambrosian florilegium challenging to use – at least for a modern reader concerned with the accuracy of the citations – is that he does not always refer to the actual titles of the Ambrosian works from which he draws his passages. Instead, he subsumes different works under groups: *De sacramentis* and *De mysteriis* are both categorized as *De sacramentis*; *Isaac vel anima*, *De Iacob* and *De patriarchis* are gathered together as *De patriarchis*, and *De virginitate* and *De virginibus* are both referenced as *Ad sororem*.[55] William could not have intended the confusion this would cause, but his motivation for renaming these works remains unclear. It is possible that the versions of the texts available to him had already been grouped in such a way that William had believed several works to be one instead. In other instances, it is possible that William might have developed the titles according to the information he had to go on or the significance he attributed to them.

This seems to be the case with his citations from *Super beati immaculati*, which he reads as *Expositio psalmi cxviii*.[56] Whether the editor in question was William himself or a composer of florilegia, with which William had worked, it is clear that someone established a connection between the Ambrosian title and the Scriptural passage it refers to (Ps 118) and redefined the work as a Biblical Commentary on the Psalm. Suppose William himself had been the author of these revised titles. That would indicate, to a certain degree, how he weighed and understood the Ambrosian works. Did he, for instance, believe that Ambrose had composed an allegorical interpretation of the Patriarchal stories in Genesis, thus re-contextualizing a series of doctrinal, exegetical, and pastoral works as a single and exhaustive Biblical commentary? While it would be intriguing to read these titles as reflections of William's notion of the figure of Ambrose and his role, there is not enough information to go on without running the danger of wild speculation.

This is, at their core, the problem that the *Excerpta de libris beati Ambrosii* pose. To gather valuable information on William's intention and the way he wanted it to be received, it is necessary to read between the lines. Unlike the prologue to the Commentary on Romans, which had been relatively clear about the work's purpose, the prologue to the Ambrosian florilegium

---

55   Del Cogliano, "A Fresh Look," 88.
56   Del Cogliano, "A Fresh Look," 88.

is much more reserved. The clues it provides must be searched between the lines and derived from the implicit information the selection of passages and the few alterations of the original text provide. Reading the prologue of the *Excerpta de libris beati Ambrosii* is thus akin to walking a tightrope, careful not to miss any of its valuable clues and yet cautious not to over-interpret.

The prologue is structured into five introductory chapters that consist of direct citations, which are each changed to various, though usually minor, degrees. The first chapter starts with a citation containing rather significant terminological alterations. Del Cogliano was the first to identify the citation in question as drawn originally from *De apologia David* 8,43.[57] The alterations themselves are pretty exciting and point by and large to William's particular interest in the nature and the significance of the spirit.[58] However, I would like to focus on something more telling, namely the Ambrosian argument reflected in this chapter. The text reads as follows:

> Osculetur me osculo oris sui. Non hic foeditatis incentiua sed castitatis celebrantur mysteria, ubi spiritualiter agitur et affectuali quadam contemplatione de nuptiis et coniunctione Christi et ecclesiae, increati spiritus et creati, carnis ac spiritus.[59]

In this passage, the erotic language of the Song is contextualized, and the reader is provided with a 'proper' way to approach the text. William sets the citation into the context of SoS 1,1, yet the citation he chose does not discuss that first verse at all in its Ambrosian context. William's choice is deliberate and thematic. Instead of presenting his readers with an Ambrosian interpretation of the Scripture he quotes, he chooses to contrast the intimacy of the Biblical text with a word of caution: the 'carnal imagery' of the Song is not be understood as such. This is, of course, a preliminary hermeneutical observation that represents William's sensibility regarding Scriptural senses.[60] In light of William's exploration of erotic language in his own interpretation, however, this warning takes on a greater significance.

---

57   Del Cogliano, "A Fresh Look," 88.
58   Del Cogliano, "A Fresh Look," 95.
59   Excerpta de libris beati Ambrosii, CCCM 87, par. 1, linea 3. These texts are not translated, as the other citations in this book are, given that their Latin wording is essential to the analysis.
60   I will discuss this in more detail in the upcoming chapter "5.2. The Different Senses of Scripture".

The Ambrosian words defend not only the purity of the Biblical text but also the purity of the controversial bridal imagery employed by such authors as William and Bernard. In this instance, William doesn't appropriate Ambrose's words to give doctrinal validity to his claims, as he does in the *Disputatio* against Abelard,[61] but instead to provide his project with moral legitimacy. Ambrose is an excellent choice of author to achieve that. As Karl Shuve has shown in his study on the Song of Songs in early Christianity, one of Ambrose's main contributions to the reception of the text was the way in which he connected it to themes of virginity and social virginhood. Placing Ambrose's interpretation of the text into the historical context of the "culture wars of the late fourth century",[62] Shuve explains that the Song was used, somewhat counterintuitively, by defenders of asceticism.

We have already seen in William's usage of Patristic and Biblical authors, namely the figure of Paul, that William is highly aware of the historical context and the domains of the authorities he employs. He must have known Ambrose not only as a campaigner against heretics but also as a defender of virgins and the moral conscience of the early church. At the same time, he is highly skilled at contextualizing these Patristic voices for the 12th-century Cistercian context in which he lived.

This initial Ambrosian citation offers an authoritative response to the tension in William's work: the asceticism and discipline he fights for as a monastic reformer, on the one hand, and the sensual language and the intensity of experience that speaks from his works on the other. Although the Song of Songs was read both in monasteries and in schools and not considered problematic by itself, the explicit nature of the bridal interpretation put forth by the early Cistercians was not uncontroversial, with William sometimes considered even more daring than Bernard.[63] The in-depth discussion of Jesus's body, the human body, and the contribution of the human *affectus* to the spiritual ascent, leads to an expressive sensuality that requires a transparent hermeneutical system. The fact that he provides one at the outset of the florilegium might offer some indication of its larger purpose.

---

61   see the chapter "Orthodoxy and Autority in William's Disputatio".
62   Karl Shuve, *The Song of Songs and the Fashioning of Identity in Early Latin Christianity*, Oxford Early Christian Studies (Oxford: Oxford University Press, 2016), 26.
63   I will discuss this aspect of William's interpretation of the Song in the chapter "5.5. The Breasts of God: William's sensual spirituality".

The second chapter of the prologue serves a similar purpose. Yet, the passage he cites from *Super beati immaculati* does not discuss the Song but is an interpretation of Psalm 118,89 and the meaning of the 'circumcision of the heart'.[64] It provides moral and pastoral guidance on the divine path. Faithful Christians ought not to attach themselves to bodily things and, more importantly, not interfuse earthly with heavenly concerns. In the context of William's *prologus*, this passage takes on the meaning of a hermeneutical caveat. The pure words of Scripture ought to be meditated by a pure spirit to yield the depth of its mysteries. William adds to this passage an excerpt that Del Cogliano identifies as drawn from *De paenitentia*[65] but significantly altered. Here again, the Ambrosian original does not discuss the Song, but instead the dancing of David. Ambrose argues here that David's dancing before the ark was not one of the 'reprehensible acts' he rejects because it was done out of true spiritual sentiment and for the sake of honest worship. William's alteration is thrilling for several reasons. First, he re-contextualizes Ambrose's statement by omitting his general dismissal of frivolity, making the citation appear like a defense of expressiveness and enjoyment within the religious context.

This is all the more astounding because William adds the example of kissing to the citation, stating thus that "everything, whether it is kisses or similar things, is appropriate when it is applied to religion".[66] On a literary level, the introduction of the theme of the kiss allows him to adopt the Ambrosian sentiment to the reading of the Song. Yet, this bold addition does not only condone the usage of the Song's erotic motives in a religious context but the act of kissing as a spiritual practice. It is this kind of audacious language that reveals the necessity of the prologue's first two citations and their rejection of a carnal interpretation. With his adaptation, William does not intend to declare the physical act of kissing another person as an act of worship, but to legitimize the intimate kiss of Christ as a fitting image for spiritual experience. In essence, he appropriates the authoritative voice of Ambrose to justify the starting point of his own exegesis.

The third chapter of the prologue is significantly longer. It contains two different citations from *De virginibus*, which both discuss the order and significance of the stages of spiritual ascent. These are the first citations in the

---

64   Del Cogliano, "A Fresh Look," 97.
65   Del Cogliano, "A Fresh Look," 98.
66   Excerpta de libris beati Ambrosii, CCCM 87, par. 2, linea 1: *Siue enim de osculis siue de talibus totum decet quicquid defertur religioni* [...].

prologue that are drawn from an Ambrosian discussion of the Song. While the first two chapters presented more general hermeneutical guidelines for interpreting the text, the third chapter is also the first that concerns the exegetical content. Suppose the prologue is indeed to be understood, as several of these citations suggest, as a methodological introduction to the reading of the Song. In that case, this third chapter states clearly that the Song's central meaning is the dynamic development of the bride's relationship with her beloved.

The first citation discusses the bride's progress, from the lightheartedness of the first kisses, through the arduous labors of virtue to the ultimate achievement, the constitution of the towers of holiness. The bed chamber that first tasted sweet and aroused anticipation in the bride 'changes its scent' throughout the process. After the initial infatuation, active effort is required to attain a stage in which the relationship is solidified and protected. Del Cogliano observes that William seems to operate here on the basis of a manuscript that already contains an alteration from the original text, prompting him to cite *atque illa impatiens duri laboris exercitataeque virtutis,* instead of *atque illa tam patiens duri laboris exercitataeque virtutis.*[67] He argues that the version William uses makes less sense than the Ambrosian original, believing the representation of the bride as patient in her spiritual growth to be more doctrinally sound.[68]

However, if the original version had indeed been the more obvious choice, we could expect some confusion from such a doctrinally careful reader like William. Instead, he not only accepts the phrasing he finds in the Ambrosian manuscript but chooses this particular passage with its allegedly cumbersome statement for the prologue of his florilegium. More than simply being undeterred, William would have been intrigued by this alternate phrasing. The theme of impatience and eagerness can also be found in other works of his, prominently so in several passages of William's own Commentary on the Song itself. The bride appears as the impatient lover, crying out after the bridegroom who had left her unexpectedly and asking him eagerly to kiss her;[69] after her time in the cellar, she impatiently asks him, 'where he is going and where he lies down at noon;[70] yes, love itself is to be sought impatiently.[71]

---

67   Del Cogliano, "A Fresh Look," 102–103.
68   Del Cogliano, "A Fresh Look," 103.
69   Expositio super Canticum Canticorum, CCCM 87, cap. 4, linea 157.
70   Expositio super Canticum Canticorum, CCCM 87, cap. 41, linea 77.
71   Expositio super Canticum Canticorum, CCCM 87, cap. 24, linea 3.

While impatience can also be viewed as a vice stemming from a lack of trust or humility, in the context of William's spirituality, it is an earnest expression of the soul's desire. The theme of impatience and longing is thus also a recurring motif in William's prayers (the *Meditativae orationes*), where he describes his heart's desire for God as impatient (*impatiens est ad te cor meum*).[72] Throughout the prayers, William does not shy away from discussing his frustration, both with himself and with the long phases of distance from God. Against the backdrop of this sincere and experiential approach to the ever-transforming human relationship with God, the Ambrosian citation in question takes on a new and more vital meaning. The frustration he experiences as an inherent part of the spiritual journey is embedded in a narrative of a gradually solidified and intensifying relationship.

In the fourth chapter of the prologue, there is further clarification of the spiritual ascent as a journey structured into particular stages. The short Ambrosian admonition, drawn from *Super beati immaculati*, points to an element of William's thought that plays a lesser role in his exegetical and theological works but appears prominently in his Golden Epistle: his pastoral concern for the individual monk. Stating with Ambrose that "knowing what to do, but not knowing in what order to do it, is not perfect understanding", William invokes his readers to be humble and disciplined in their progress and not to overestimate themselves.[73] The passage also implicitly frames the Origenist idea of self-knowledge as perfect knowledge, which is, as we will see, central to William: examining the self includes an awareness of one's own stage (*gradus*) and the appropriate tasks.

Like the prologue's fourth chapter, the fifth and last one seems to be addressed to the readers of the florilegium. Here, William excerpts a passage from *De virginibus*, in which Ambrose speaks directly to his audience. In it, Ambrose reflects on the value of his exegetical and theological statements and explains how those who hear them ought to put them to use. William's choice of citation to conclude the prologue is proof of his literary skills, as it is the essential element that makes this collection of citations feel like a traditional prologue. Just as he did in the prologues to his commentaries, William includes here 'a reader's manual' that does not lack the obligatory confirmation of humility. While opinions may vary, the readers shall ponder what seems elucidating and spiritually encouraging to them. He thus allows Ambrose to endorse the following collection of his words

---

72   Meditativae Orationes, cccm 89, meditatio 3, par. 3, pag. 14: and 6, par. 25, pag. 40.

73   I will further discuss this string of ideas in the chapter "7.4. Concepts applied: The monk's image-likeness".

and simultaneously explains to the users of his florilegium what he considers its primary purpose: just like his own commentaries, the collection of Ambrosian passages, too, should serve the purpose of spiritual formation.

This would also mean that the florilegium did not necessarily fulfill the purpose of providing theological and exegetical insight or providing motives and imagery for William's Commentary, which, as mentioned earlier, does not contain any explicit citations. Even more so, Ambrose can hardly be viewed as a direct predecessor of the Cistercian line of interpretation. Ambrose's reading of the Song was marked mainly by identifying the bride with virginal souls and bodies, on the one hand, and by the so-called ecclesial strand of the Song's allegorical tradition. The latter was one of the two main interpretations that emerged from the originally Origenist framework that allowed for a reading of the Song's central relationship as one between God and the church or between Christ and the individual soul.[74] These two strands of reading have influenced the history of Christian exegesis to different extents.

While the ecclesial interpretation has been critical throughout the early Middle Ages and has long served to solidify the Christian social identity, the emphasis on the individual soul has been determinative of later medieval mysticism and was primarily influenced by Cistercian writings. Of course, the two traditions are in no way mutually exclusive and are often intertwined. This is especially the case in the Ambrosian works that William cites most in his florilegium, namely *De Virginitate, Super beati immaculati,* and *De Isaac vel anima.*[75] Exegetically, these works exemplify how Ambrose "moves seamlessly from speaking about the Church as the bride of Christ to considerations of the individual soul as the beloved".[76] If one were to seek a systematic differentiation between the two interpretations, one would hardly find them in Ambrose's commentaries.[77] Instead, the

---

74   Although both of these readings are distinctly christological, it was deeply steeped in the traditionally Jewish model of interpretation (Matter, *The Voice of my Beloved,* 30–31).

75   Sporadically William also quotes from *De Virginibus, De Sacramentis,* the *Expositio Euangelii secundum Lucam,* the *Libri de Sancto Spiritu, De Officiis Ministrorum, De Patriarchis, De Mysteriis, De Nabuthae, De Bono Mortis* and several of Ambrose's letters.

76   Asiedu, "The Song of Songs," 303, referencing here solely *De Isaac vel anima.* However, as we will see from William's citations, this is also applies to the other two works.

77   Ernst Dassmann, *Die Frömmigkeit Des Kirchenvaters Ambrosius von Mailand: Quellen Und Entfaltung,* vol. 29, *Münsterische Beiträge Zur Theologie* (Münster: Aschendorff Verlag, 1965), 150.

Ambrosian exegesis is contextual and dynamic, allowing for combinations of the two main motives that are well represented in William's florilegium.

However, the general style and emphasis of the Ambrosian usage of the Song, which is mainly rooted in his ecclesio-political and pastoral concerns,[78] differ distinctly enough from the individualistic and mystical interpretation presented by William and other Cistercian authors that an influence in terms of exegetical content can be ruled out. While some motives appear in both Ambrose's and William's readings, these are usually images and terms that trace back to common Origenist ideas. I would even go so far as to say that while Ambrose's reading mainly intended to elevate the status of the church, William is more critical of the *ecclesia*.

Other than Ambrose, for instance, he identifies the church with the city (*civitas*); a cesspool of vice at her worst and at her best, a place for the soul to experience the grace of God.[79] These, at times, negative references to the church are related to William's reform efforts and his belief that the monasteries of his time lacked monastic discipline and devotion.[80] As we contextualize Ambrose's and William's interpretations, it becomes clear that they identify the 'true bride of Christ' to be the church or the individual soul, respectively, not excluding the other reading per se but revealing fundamentally different concerns.

The hypothesis arising from this brief discussion is that William uses Ambrose here as an authority not primarily in a doctrinal sense, as he does in the *Disputatio*, but in a moral and pastoral sense. The florilegium, then, would have been composed neither for the sake of a few academically inclined exegetes nor for the sake of demonstrating William's orthodoxy against Abelard but as a work of spiritual guidance. However, this understanding further intensifies the need for differentiation between William's Ambrosian and the Gregorian florilegium.

2.2   *Restoring Gregory's Voice*

I return again to the theory proposed by Mark Del Cogliano, who is, as I have mentioned, the first to provide two distinct interpretations for William's florilegia. His argument is mainly based on the apparent differences in the composition of the two works. Unlike the *Excerpta de libris beati*

---

78   Dassmann, *Die Frömmigkeit des Kirchenvaters*, 142.
79   Expositio super Canticum Canticorum, CCCM 87, cap. 30, linea 36.
80   I will discuss William's efforts in this regard in the chapter "7.1. Innovation, Restoration or Renewal".

Ambrosii, the Gregorian florilegium does not have a prologue and is significantly shorter. Overall, William's editorial interference with the original texts is much less noticeable. That does not mean that William was any less careful and strategic in its compilation – on the contrary. The *Excerpta ex libris beati Gregorii,* as Del Cogliano presents them, attempt to create one coherent Gregorian commentary on the Song of Songs. This is indeed not the sense one gets from the Ambrosian florilegium. There, William excerpted from various works and sometimes even used passages, as I've mentioned regarding the prologue, that did not refer to the Song in their original context.

Although William structured his Ambrosian florilegium according to the Biblical text, the collection does not read as a continuous interpretation but sometimes offers different readings on one particular verse and is concerned with a variety of themes, sometimes making the chapters appear disconnected from one another. On the other hand, the Gregorian collection is drawn to a large extent from the *Moralia in Job,* a beloved staple of medieval monastic libraries,[81] as well as from the *Regula pastoralis,* the *Homiliae in evangelia,* and the *Homiliae in Hezechihelem.*[82]

While it is unclear, which reference works William has used for the *Excerpta de libris beati Ambrosii,* he claims that he employed Bede's collection of Gregorian statements for his *Excerpta ex libris beati Gregorii* and significantly expanded on it. Indeed, he used all but one of Bede's references and added many more, likely from his own research.[83] Del Cogliano attempts to show that William applied a "unique method of excerption" to the text, characterized by a careful rearrangement of passages.[84] He supports this theory with an analysis of selected alterations William made. The examples he provides reveal that William did not re-contextualize passages and add content that significantly alters their intended meaning as he did with the

---

81   "No ambitious library was considered complete without the six volumes of his Moralia in Job, that great 'reservoir in the history of literature,' his Homilies on Ezekiel, the stories and marvels of his Dialogues, and the exposition of a Bishop's duties in his Pastoral Care." (Haskins, *The Renaissance of the Twelfth Century,* 80) In fact, we know of Gregorian manuscripts at the library of Saint–Thierry, offering a glimpse into the possible literary environment of William and his brothers (Matter, "Anselm and the Tradition of the Song," 560).

82   as referenced in Verdeyen ed., *Excerpta ex libris beati Gregorii,* CCCM 87.

83   Mark Del Cogliano, "The Composition of William of St. Thierry's Excerpts from the Books of Blessed Gregory on the Song of Songs." *Cîteaux: Commentarii Cistercienses* (2007), 64.

84   Del Cogliano, "The Composition," 61.

Ambrosian citations. Instead, his alterations of the Gregorian text can largely be attributed to a desire to restore and stay true to the Gregorian intention.

One of the ways in which he achieves that is by interweaving originally distinct passages from different sources that refer to or interpret the same verse into one coherent interpretation. The chapters of the Ambrosian florilegium are introduced by the name of the Ambrosian source from which they are drawn. The Gregorian collection, however, is structured as a verse–by–verse commentary and contains no indication of the works employed. Some chapters consist simply of one long citation, but most are curated composites. If this is the case, I support Del Cogliano's general argument, for instance, in chapter 1,7, which discusses SoS 1,8. William's version reads as follows:

> Sollerter electi quique a quo et ad quid sint creati conspiciunt, et, recta consideratione acceptae imaginis, sequi uulgi multitudinem dedignantur. Vnde sponsus sponsam suam alloquitur dicens: Nisi cognoueris te, o pulchra inter mulieres.[85]

> Id est nisi honorem tuum, quo ad similitudinem Dei es condita, bene uiuendo cognoueris, a conspectu meae contemplationis egredere, et imperitorum uitam imitare populorum. Nam gregum nomine imperiti populi designantur.[86]

> Semetipsam namque ea quae est inter mulieres pulchra cognoscit, quando electa quaeque anima, etiam inter peccantes posita, quia ad

---

85 The Gregorian original reads as follows: *Sollerter quippe a quo et ad quid sunt creati conspiciunt, et recta consideratione acceptae imaginis sequi uulgi multitudinem dedignantur. Vnde et sponsi uoce sponsae in canticis canticorum dicitur: nisi cognoueris te, o pulchra inter mulieres, egredere et abi post uestigia gregum et pasce haedos tuos* (Gregory the Great. *Moralia in Iob.* Centre Traditio Litterarum Occidentalium, CETEDOC., and Brepols (Firm). 2000. Library of Latin texts. Series A. Series A. [Turnhout, Belgium]: Brepols. http://clt.brepolis.net/LLTA/pages/TextSearch.aspx?key=QGREG1708_ (accessed January 10, 2025), Lib. 30, par. 17, linea 7–9).

86 The Gregorian original reads as follows: *Nam quod gregum nomine imperiti populi designantur, sponsi uerba testantur, qui sponsam suam alloquitur dicens: nisi cognoueris te, o pulchra inter mulieres, egredere et abi post uestigia gregum; id est nisi honorem tuum, quo ad similitudinem dei es condita, bene uiuendo cognoueris, a conspectu meae contemplationis egredere, et imperitorum uitam imitare populorum* (Moralia in Iob, Lib. 16, par. 44, linea 9).

auctoris sui imaginem ac similitudinem sit condita meminit, et iuxta
perceptae similitudinis ordinem incedit.[87]

MOR. 30, 17,13–22

In this chapter, William's diligence becomes especially apparent. He has
slightly altered the terminology of the first citation, adding, for instance,
the term *electi*.[88] This, however, does not change the passage's meaning. Instead, it clarifies the passage's original context, as Gregory discusses the
spiritual particularity of the 'chosen' (*electi*) in the preceding paragraphs.
He also abbreviates the reference to the Song, which does not take away
from the citation because the complete reference can be found in the chapter's title.

The first significant alteration is the insertion of a citation from Mor. 16.
The excerpts' original context is different, as Gregory discusses here the
authoritative nature of the Fathers' doctrines and the danger of false teachings.[89] William, however, omits this discussion and seems exclusively
interested in an elucidating clarification Gregory had added here to his reference of SoS 1,8. William must have felt it necessary for a proper understanding of Gregory's interpretation of this central verse to include this
explanatory passage from Mor. 16 because it expresses Gregory's pastoral interest in self-knowledge as something that ought to be put into practice
through contemplation and active pursuit of virtue. This more practical application of the verse is not present in Mor. 30 but would have belonged, for
William, to a comprehensive presentation of Gregory's thoughts on the
verse.

The chapter ends again with a citation from Mor. 30, revealing that William used the passage as a conceptual framework, which he could supplement with the information he held to be valuable. While chapter 1,7 is by
no means the only example of this methodology,[90] I chose to discuss this

---

87   The Gregorian original reads as follows: *Semetipsam namque ea quae est inter mulieres*
      pulchra cognoscit, quando electa quaeque anima etiam inter peccantes posita quia ad
      auctoris sui imaginem ac similitudinem sit condita meminit, et iuxta perceptae similitu-
      dinis ordinem incedit (Moralia in Iob, Lib. 30, par. 17, linea 12).

88   Del Cogliano notes this alteration too (Del Cogliano, "The Composition," 61) but does
      not, as I would, read it as an attempt to recover the original Gregorian meaning.

89   Moralia in Iob, Lib. 16, par. 44, linea 9.

90   We can find it for instance in cap. 3 of the *Excerpta ex libris beati Gregorii,* where Wil-
      liam integrates an altered excerpt from *Homiliae in Hiezechielem* into a longer citation
      from *Homiliae in evangelia.* See Verdeyen ed., *Excerpta ex libris beati Gregorii,* CCCM
      47, 411.

case because it reveals William's handling of specific core ideas in Gregory's thought. The concept of self-knowledge is also central in William's Commentary, and the way he edits the Gregorian passages shows that William might have been significantly more interested in the layers and dimensions of Gregory's thought than in his exact wording. As Del Cogliano attests to with his more detailed study of William's alterations and additions to the text, William is not shy to adapt his original source; yet, even the most significant alterations do not change Gregory's thought.[91] Most of his alterations have an elucidating concern and serve to make Gregory's intended meaning understood, even outside their original context. Using this creative method, he can make Gregorian concepts more generally applicable and valuable to readers with particularly exegetical but also broader theological interests. He is essentially restoring Gregory's voice and allowing him posthumously to present an extensive reading of the Song and its motives.

These observations might also be vital to understanding the role of the florilegium within William's corpus. On a surface level, the *Excerpta ex libris beati Gregorii* present a similar problem to the *Excerpta de libris beati Ambrosii*, namely that these carefully researched citations did not make their way into William's own Commentary. Yet, the situation is notably different from his reception of Gregorian thought. While there are indeed conspicuously few direct quotations from Gregory, the *Expositio* is still enriched with Gregorian ideas. While, as I've explained, Ambrose's reading of the Song is not to be placed in the same allegorical tradition in which William participates, Gregory has been directly influential for the mystical interpretation put forth by such authors as William and Bernard.

Gregory was, of course, especially valued by 12th-century Cistercians as the Godfather of monastic reform[92] and as the embodiment of the delicate interplay between the vita activa and the vita contemplativa,[93] pursued by many Cistercians. He was also a proponent of the 'mystical sense' of Scripture, which emphasizes the soul's journey into the arms of God and culminates in the experience of intimacy,[94] which is central to the Cistercian reading of the Song. Gregory's approach is often heralded as the royal road of medieval exegesis.[95] The number of direct citations cannot measure

---

91   Del Cogliano, "The Composition," 71.
92   Grabmann, *Geschichte der Scholastischen Methode, vol. 1*, 144.
93   Ruh, *Geschichte der Abendländischen Mystik*, 157.
94   Matter, "Anselm and the Tradition of the Song," 552.
95   Riché and Lobrichon, *Le Moyen Âge et la Bible*, 142.

his influence on William. In the upcoming chapter, I will discuss two Gregorian themes that feature prominently in William's interpretation of the Song and his spirituality as a whole. The already mentioned concept of self-knowledge on the one hand, and the Gregorian declaration *amor ipse notitia est*, on the other. Reworded as *amor ipse intellectus est*, the latter can even be considered the central theme of William's *Expositio*.

Del Cogliano had defined the Gregorian florilegium as "a stand-alone work produced by William's meticulous attention to detail and editorial genius, perhaps to fulfill his desire to hold in his hands a genuine Gregorian commentary devoted to the Song of Songs."[96] I believe this interpretation to be very plausible. However, as he suggests, it is not as incompatible with some of the heretofore presented theories. While I agree that the usage of the Gregorian collection cannot be reduced to that of a mere reference–work, compiled to aid the composition of the Expositio directly, I do believe that the time of the florilegia's alleged production still places them within the broader timeline of William's exegesis of the Song. His intense engagement with Gregory's thought has allowed him to systematize it, contemplate it, and get a broader sense of the theological themes embedded in the Song's text. 'Preparatory' might not be the proper term to describe the role of the *Excerpta ex libris beati Gregorii*, but it can still be deemed highly educative in light of William's immersion into the world of allegory.

This is the case to a different extent with the Ambrosian collection as well, the role of which I have described as instructional for William's hermeneutical considerations. I believe it to be a telling aspect of William's larger exegetical process that he took time to get involved in-depth with the thought of two very different authorities and was able to implement their thought according to what he considered their respective intellectual strengths. These two florilegia and their distinct styles are evidence of William's dynamic relationship with Patristic authority, which allows for different degrees of appreciation and different forms of reception. In the following chapter, I will focus on the extent of originality and the practical application of Patristic thought in the *Expositio* itself.

---

96   Del Cogliano, "The Composition," 76.

CHAPTER 5

William's Own *Expositio* and Its Original Contributions

1 Origen as an (Il)legitimate Source

In light of William's conflicts with Abelard and William of Conches, his concept of orthodoxy (and, in turn, his treatment of any heterodox deviations) deserves special attention. William's appreciation of Patristic theology, in particular, exemplifies what he considers proper doctrine and exegesis. The authority of the Fathers outweighs, for him, the logical abilities of the mind. However, the case becomes a lot more complicated when the authority in question is himself a "figure of doubtful orthodoxy".[1] William's reception of Origen, who was both an inevitable source in matters of Christian allegory and a controversial author, influenced by Neoplatonic thought, reveals thus tangibly the tension inherent to his writing.[2]

On the one hand, William hopes to emphasize the importance of authority in defining the limitations of theological thinking. Yet, at times, his sense for the mystical and focus on the experiential dimension of Christian spirituality seems to burst these parameters wide open. This is not to say that William's interest in the purity of doctrine and the depth of mystical union is paradoxical per se. Many medieval authors have found themselves in a similar place, as they interwove the well-grounded systems of theology with the threads of monastic faith. One could even say that this tension constitutes the creative soul of medieval exegesis. It indeed accounts for William's distinguished character as an author. His acknowledgment of the value of spiritual and, to a certain degree individual experience counters the image of a rigid denunciator in a battle against innovation. And in turn, his accountability towards Patristic and Biblical authority makes his mysticism an expression of humble reverence to tradition rather than freethinking

---

1 Matter, *The Voice of my Beloved*, 12.
2 Carmen Angela Cvetković is right to note, in the context of medieval Origen reception, the famous Jeromian statement: *laudavi interpretem, non dogmatisten* (Hieronymus, Clavis Patrum Latinorum 0620, epist. 84, vol. 55, par. 2, cited in Cvetković, "Conflict and Authority," 532).

© DELPHINE CONZELMANN, 2025 | DOI:10.1163/9789004730878_010

impetuosity.[3] The carefully adjusted way he received an author as ambivalent as Origen exemplifies this beautifully.

It is reasonable to assume that William was well aware of Origen's heterodox reputation. Although he does not explicitly mention any caveats for the usage of Origen, as we find them in the work of the already quoted Smaragdus of St.–Mihiel,[4] the complex history of Origenist thought was known to medieval authors.[5] Possibly it contributed to the fact that Origen was rarely cited by name before the 12th century.[6] However, the medieval practice of citation was generally more implicit than nominal. As Ann Matter summarizes: "No medieval author could make many points by citing a heretic. But it is also standard procedure in medieval exegesis to draw on as many references as possible while acknowledging as few as necessary."[7] While the history of Origenist reception in the early Middle Ages is certainly not as rich as the reception of other prominent Church Fathers,[8] his commentaries definitely influenced various medieval exegetes, even if they did not explicitly mention Origen as their source.[9]

One of the reasons for William's particular interest in Origen, especially as it continued to increase throughout his literary lifetime, could be the monastic core of Origen's work. Jean Leclerq points out the correlations between Origen's contemplative approach to Biblical exegesis and his growing influence during the periods of monastic reform, during which the same spirit of reading was shared.[10] This resurgence of Origenist thought, or spiritual, allegorical exegesis, could explain William's availability of Origenist

---

3   Which should certainly not imply that this is the case for other exponents of medieval mysticism, but rather suggest that the dismissal of mystic theology as such is misguided, as the example of William demonstrates.

4   Liber comitis, PL 102:13C.

5   Beryl Smalley point out that "medieval students realized that certain of Origen's views had been condemned as heretical; but this could be abstracted and did not prevent their learning from him" (Smalley, *The Study of the Bible*, 13); something, that is indeed true of William as well.

6   Suzanne LaVere even goes as far, as considering the Gloss the "first work to cite Origen by name" (LaVere, "From Contemplation to Action," 59).

7   Matter, *The Voice of my Beloved*, 36.

8   Most scholars believe Origen's influence on early medieval exegesis to be at most indirect (Matter, *The Voice of my Beloved*, 35)

9   LaVere, "From Contemplation to Action," 59.

10   As cited in Jean–Marie Déchanet, "Introduction," in *Exposé Sur Le Cantique Des Cantiques*, by William of Saint–Thierry, trans. Maurice Dumontier, Série Des Textes Monastiques d'Occident 8, Sources Chrétiennes (Paris: Éditions du Cerf, 1962), 20.

text and his readiness to use them. Indeed, the monastic tradition of copying and transmitting Origen's Biblical commentaries made William's direct reception possible in the first place. Although he might have initially consulted secondary sources, such as John Scot Eriugena, he soon turned to the copies of Origen's exegetical works that were available to him in the library at Signy.[11] Déchanet proposed the convincing theory that William had Origen's Commentary on the Song of Song directly at hand while writing his own.[12]

We can even gather from William's own writings that he not only considered Origen a permissible author but a significant part of the Patristic canon. Without reservation, he lists him among such figures as Augustine, Ambrose, and Gregory.[13] The many implicit references in his work confirm that he strongly appreciated Origen, particularly regarding hermeneutical questions. This is especially interesting, as the overt use of Platonism is one of his main points of critique against Abelard. Yet, he does not seem to take issue with the strong platonist influence in Origenist thought. His admiration of Origen is a characteristic he shares with his biggest adversary; Origen was an important source for both Abelard's and William's Romans Commentary, respectively.[14] William was by no means unique among his contemporaries in allowing himself to use and even openly refer to Origen. Yet, his usage seems less guilt-ridden than that of other 12th-century authors, as he does not hide, understate or justify his use.[15]

---

11   This likely included Origen's sermons on Gensis, Exodus, Leviticus, Numbers, Joshua, Judges, Kings, the Song of Songs and Isaiah, as well as the Rufinus translations of his Commentary on the Song of Songs, and Periarchon (Déchanet, "Introduction," in *Exposé sur le Cantique des Cantiques*, 32).

12   Déchanet, "Introduction" in *Exposé sur le Cantique des Cantiques*, 33–34. Déchanet supports this theory with an observation made by Henri de Lubac, that William only seems to directly reference Origen up to §168 (Déchanet, "Introduction," in *Exposé sur le Cantique des Cantiques*, 350) of his own commentary; corresponding to the exact Biblical passage, at which Rufinus' incomplete translation of Origen's commentary breaks off (Déchanet, "Introduction" in Exposé sur le Cantique des Cantiques, 351).

13   Expositio super Epistolam ad Romanos, cccm 86, Praef., linea 8.

14   Henri de Lubac, *Medieval Exegesis: The Four Senses of* Scripture, vol. 1 (Grand Rapids, MI: Wm. B. Eerdmans Publishing Co., 1998).

15   Henri de Lubac, in his narrative of 'the Latin Origen', names various strategies medieval authors employed, to make their Origenist reception less conspicuous. This included, citing Origen under the name of Jerome (Lubac, "Medieval Exegesis Vol.1," p. 167), harmonizing his thought with that of other authorities Lubac, "Medieval Exegesis Vol.1," 175) or including passages of proactive defense (Lubac, "Medieval Exegesis Vol.1," 222).

This observation is noteworthy, as it relativizes the image of an author who defines orthodoxy solely based on historical ecclesial authority. It speaks to William as a thinker who recognizes Patristic authority out of his sincere faith in their participation in divine inspiration and not out of respect for their social status. Yet, as I have already discussed, the way William uses Origenist material differs from the ingenious way he relies, for instance, on Augustinian thought.[16] This underpins the observations made in the preceding chapter that William attributes different kinds of value to different Patristic authors: his appreciation for Augustine was all-encompassing and structural, while distinctly moral and pastoral concerns fueled his reception of Ambrose. Similarly, in his Commentary on the Song of Songs, we must identify differences between explicit quotations to Origenist works and more indirect references to thoughts and themes that – historically tracing back to Origen – might have been available to William through other sources.

The role of Gregory in William's usage of Origenist material is not to be underestimated. As already mentioned, several central themes of Origenist origin, such as the idea of self-knowledge, appear prominently in Gregorian texts William had employed in his florilegium. Therefore, William's engagement with these ideas is as much evidence of his reception of Origen as it is of his appreciation of Gregory. As we will see, direct quotations of Origen's works are often not reflective of these larger theological themes but contain historical and etymological knowledge, for which Origen was an important source. That is to say that William's usage of Patristic works was highly nuanced and contextualized. Different Fathers played different roles, each according to their strengths and talents[17] – just as is the case with brothers in the communal context of a monastery. In the following, I will further discuss the extent and limitations of Origen's presence in William's *Expositio* and the ways in which he, as an author of original ideas, appears in the work.

---

16   I have done so in the earlier chapter, "1.5. Reading (alongside) the Fathers", where I have referred mainly to the study of Thomas P. Scheck and his response to the theories put forth by such authors as Jean–Marie Déchanet.

17   A similar strategy is employed by Herbert of Bosham, when he differentiated between Origen as a 'faithful interpreter' and as a 'catholic dogmagist'; the latter being a role that he could under no circumstances fulfill (Lubac, "Medieval Exegesis Vol.1," 176). Yet, William does not reverberate this distinction, as Herbert does, applying it rather implicitly.

2   The Different Senses of Scripture

Origen's most significant impact on medieval exegesis is grounded in the fact that he had opened up a whole world of allegorical reading to the Christian study of Scripture and made a later refined distinction of 'senses' possible in the first place. He had pointed to a great diversity of potential meanings of the Biblical text, both comprehensible and hidden, and had even described a graded theory of readership in response. William's exegetical conclusions in his Commentary on the Song certainly differ from Origen's. They strongly relate to his monastic context, yet there seems to be a shared understanding of the text's quality and intention. Literarily, he follows the Origenist framework closely, and thus one could speak of Origen as one of William's guides through the Song. In the following chapter, I will explore the similarities and deviations of William's work from Origen's hermeneutics, focusing on his differentiation of Scriptural senses.

While Origen's concept of the allegorical sense has been groundbreaking, the course of Latin exegesis was founded mainly on the fourfold scheme that John Cassian had further developed.[18] He distinguished between the literal (or historical), the typological (or allegorical), the tropological (or moral), and the anagogic sense of Scripture. Yet, many medieval authors did not adhere to these clear distinctions but used the scheme creatively and fluidly. Especially the terms 'mystical', 'allegorical', 'moral' and 'spiritual' are often used interchangeably or with varying connotations.[19] While this impedes, to a certain extent, a systematic reading of medieval exegesis from a modern perspective, it also reveals that these authors did not feel a need to neatly and transparently categorize their hermeneutics, suggesting an implicit common ground. The Cassian scheme and the basic Origenist differentiation pointed to the significant plurality of meaning in Scripture, which medieval readers sought to explore in its vastness.

This does not mean, however, that allegorical exegesis could mean anything these authors wanted it to mean. It should not be understood as a forced and woolly second layer of interpretation for passages in which the literal meaning alone does not seem exhaustive. The allegorical reading describes an interpretation that focuses on the Christological dimension of the

---

18   Cassian had famously exemplified his model according to the four possible interpretations of the word 'Jerusalem', as either the literal city, the church of Christ, the celestial city, or the human soul in his *Collationes* (Matter, *The Voice of my Beloved*, 54).

19   Matter, *The Voice of my Beloved*, 54–55.

text and its figurative meaning concerning the person of Jesus Christ.[20] In their variety, the Biblical *signa* all point to the *res*, Christ incarnate. In monastic exegesis, the sign and the signified are not as clearly distinguished. Divine reality unfolds within Biblical imagery, and the Biblical narrative becomes a part of the history of salvation.[21] Defined as such, allegory unveils a new spiritual dimension. Hermeneutically, the allegorical sense can incorporate the tropological, the anagogic, and in some cases, as we will see shortly, even the historical sense.[22] Like a prism, allegorical exegesis is both focused and multifaceted.

Bernard speaks of an 'umbrageous and hidden forest of allegory' referring to the Song of Songs in particular.[23] William, too, was well aware of the immensity of the Song's depth and figurative potential. In his introductory words to the Commentary, he thus makes a note of the limitations of his project. Reminiscent of his conversations with Bernard, whom he had asked 'not to touch the mysteries hidden in the Sacred Book, but rather to offer him its moral interpretation only',[24] he explains that he will focus on the moral sense in the *Expositio* as well:

> We are, however, not going to explore the more profound mysteries regarding Christ and the church that are contained in it; furled into ourselves and measuring ourselves according to ourselves and according to our limited means, it is simply one particular moral sense – the sense of bridegroom and bride, of Christ and the Christian

---

20   Rainer, "Überlegungen zum Verhältnis", 75.

21   " [...] the monastic figure is to be seen as a refined version of the figure used to denote the general coherence of Christian history: it indicates a real but provisional fulfilment of history within a broader context of a universal, historical fulfilment which is yet to come" (Pranger, *Bernhard of Clairvaux*, 14–15).

22   In most cases, medieval exegesis reiterates the two-fold Origenist distinction, and believes that Scripture can be read "'historically' and 'with the more sacred mystery'" (Henri de Lubac, *Medieval Exegesis: The Four Senses of* Scripture, vol. 2 (Grand Rapids, MI: Wm. B. Eerdmans Publishing Co., 2000), 25), which if applied to Cassian's scheme, suggests that the historical sense is sectioned off from the three other senses. As I will argue, however, William's understanding of the historical sense is such, that it is compatible with the other senses as well.

23   Déchanet, "Introduction," in *Exposé sur le Cantique des Cantiques*, 14, referencing Bernardus Claraevallensis, Sermones super Canticum Canticorum, sermo 16, par. 1, vol. 1, pag. 89: *Putavi, fateor, unum ad hoc sermonem sufficere, silvam que istam umbrosam latebrosam que allegoriarum pertransire nos cito, et ad planitiem moralium sensuum itinere diei quasi unius pervenire* [...].

24   Déchanet, "Introduction," in *Exposé sur le Cantique des Cantiques*, 10.

soul – which everybody is entitled to venture, that we will touch on. The only fruit of our labor, which we expect in return, is the likeness to its subject: love itself.[25]

It is not the moral sense in its entirety, but just a particular aspect (*sensum morale aliquem*) that William hopes to discuss in his Commentary. He is not precise in his hermeneutical distinctions, and it remains unclear which kinds of interpretation he decides to exclude from his inquiry. It is likely that he did not intend to restrict himself but to acknowledge the existing limitations of individual exegetical projects as such. There are still a host of mysteries future generations of inspired readers will have to explore.[26] However, he is interested in the relationship between Christ and the Christian soul, as the Song's bridegroom and bride. More concretely, it is the intimacy of their encounter that he is interested in exploring.

The *Expositio* begins with a prayer, in which William identifies himself and the reader of the Commentary with the bride, singing the Song of affection for her beloved.[27] His invocation reveals the purpose of his *lectio*: to fully experience the bride's arrival in her lover's arms, to witness her joy and her relief as his own. Literarily speaking, the Commentary is a guide for the faithful soul on her journey toward God. This direct application of the Biblical narrative to the lived spirituality of the reader is what he understands as Scripture's moral meaning. One can even go so far as to say that the ultimate aim of allegorical interpretation is its transformative effect on the exegete's soul.[28] One of the main features William shares with Bernard and

---

25   Expositio super Cantica Canticorum, CCCM 87, cap. 1, linea 65: *Non autem profundiora illa mysteria, quae in eo continentur, adtentamus, de Christo et ecclesia; sed cohibentes nos intra nos, et in nobismetipsis nosmetipsos metientes, de sponso ac sponsa, de Christo et christiana anima, sensum tantummodo moralem aliquem, in quo omnibus audere licet, pro sensus nostri paupertate perstringimus, laboris nostri non alium requirentes fructum, quam similem materiae, id est amorem ipsum.*

26   "Il laisse à plus malins que lui, à plus aventureux, aussi, pleine d'ombre et de mystérieuses cachettes, creusée d'amples vallées profondes aux épais fourrés, la forêt des allégories" (Déchanet, "Introduction," in *Exposé sur le Cantique des Cantiques*, 13–14).

27   Expositio super Cantica Canticorum, CCCM 87, cap. 1, linea 31: [...] *ut caste te amet sponsa tua, anima christiana, dotata sanguine tuo, pignerata Spiritu tuo; ut inter uitae huius aerumnosas pressuras, in taedio peregrinationis suae a te et prolongati incolatus in terra aliena, cantet tibi amatoria sua, et respiret, et leuior ei fiat dolor suus* [...].

28   Not to be forgotten in this context is the frequent correlation between 'mysterium' and 'sacramentum' in the Latin language. Augustine understood the Biblical texts as "books of the divine sacraments" (Lubac, "Medieval Exegesis Vol.2," 20). When William thus speaks of exploring the moral mysteries of Scripture, it is not unreasonable to

Origen is that his reading of the Song begins, as Ann Astell and Catherine Rose Cavadini point out, "in medias res, after the soul who speaks has already advanced toward perfection".[29]

Yet, the allegorical dimension of the text is surprisingly not the first or only one that William introduces his readers to. Following Origen, he understands the Song as a 'nuptial drama' (drama nuptualis), referring to the text's 'historical sense'. Historicity is a rather complex notion in the context of Biblical truth. At first sight, it seems merely to describe the circumstances and intentions of the Biblical author, the text's 'original purpose'. On this surface level, William does not seem to deviate much from the Origenist position. Like most medieval authors, he too agrees with the premise that King Solomon himself had been the author of the Song, and referring to Origen directly, he believes that Solomon had intentionally written it in 'dramatic form and the style of a comedy'.[30] The factual information he provides to illustrate the text's supposed genesis is taken, almost literally from Origen, as he presents the Solomonian biography as the Song's framework. According to both authors, the Song's historical setting was the King's wedding to the Pharaoh's daughter.[31] This, however, is as far as their agreement goes.

Although he adopts Origen's terminology and follows a well-established exegetical tradition as far as the historical specifics go, his understanding of 'historicity' and the significance of historical meaning within a larger hermeneutical context differs significantly from that of his Eastern teacher. Indeed, he refers to the historical sense regularly throughout the Commentary. Literarily, his mentions of the historical context guide the reader through the text and help them find their way back into the Commentary after particularly complex and challenging passages.[32] The historical background functions as the text's basic scaffolding or an instrument of reader

---

assume a sacramental element to his reading, in as far as the process of interpretation itself holds the potential to allow for divine activity to unfold in the reader.

29   Astell and Cavadini, "The Song of Songs," 31.

30   Expositio super Cantica Canticorum, CCCM 87, cap. 2, linea 41: [...] in modum dramatis et stilo comico [...].

31   Expositio super Cantica Canticorum, CCCM 87, cap. 2, linea 58–59: Propositi uero dramatis historialis, fabulae seu parabolae, hoc potest esse argumentum.
       Rex Salomon filiam Pharaonis Aegyptii duxit uxorem.

32   For instance in his introduction to the seventh stanza: Expositio super Cantica Canticorum, CCCM 87, cap. 42, linea 6: Paululum ad superiora redeamus, ut historicum sensum, et ordinem dramatis inspiciamus.

guidance. As such, it is distinguished from the allegorical or moral sense of Scripture, taking on a supportive rather than essential role. How William presents historicity thus mitigates the original Origenist understanding.

Whereas Origen believes the Salomonian context to be factually histori-cal, William presents it as a 'historical drama, a fable, or a parable'.[33] For him, the term 'historical' does not necessarily imply actual historicity. It is historical, only in the sense that it expresses what the author had in mind when he wrote the text, whether that was an invented love story or even a fitting image. As Déchanet puts it: "Peu importe"![34] Does that mean that the *sensus historicus* has no real value within William's framework? By no means. But its significance is not tied to historical accuracy. Even if Solomon did not write the Song in the context of his actual wedding – yes, even if that wedding never actually took place – his intention and the Song's mean-ing are not diminished. As far as they relate to God, history and story can hold truth equally.[35]

Many of these references take on an encyclopedic and educational pur-pose. William often relies on Origen for translations from Hebrew or Ara-maic. This is not an observation that exclusively applies to William's work; various medieval authors, including Bernard, used Origen as a source for et-ymological insight.[36] Biblical names, geographical knowledge, or explana-tions regarding ancient culture are critical elements of Origenist influence in medieval literature. Through the lens of Origen's extensive wealth of knowledge, the images of ancient Israel or Egypt become tangible realities for William's 12th-century audience.

Déchanet, in his introduction to the work, emphasizes its linguistic re-semblances to the Origenist exegesis. Indeed, his expressive and sensual im-agery provides an ideal point of departure for our inquiry. As Déchanet describes, the Commentary is held in a thoroughly Origenist style to such an extent that it allows the reader to 'taste and enjoy' the Origenist

---

33   Expositio super Cantica Canticorum, cccm 87, cap. 2, linea 58: *Propositi uero dramatis historialis, fabulae seu parabolae, hoc potest esse argumentum.*

34   Déchanet, "Introduction," in *Exposé sur le Cantique des Cantiques*, 15.

35   "When William of Saint Thierry, addressing himself to God, said to him: 'the Scripture of thy Truth,' he was thinking of something quite different from the historical iner-rancy of the Bible! It was about the Truth of God, about his Word, 'God from God, Light from Light,' having come to make himself our food" (Lubac, "Medieval Exegesis Vol.2," 82).

36   His interpretation of the names Jesus and Christ, for instance, is so common that it is impossible to trace William's exact point of reference, which could even be a case of oral tradition (Déchanet ed., Exposé sur le Cantique des Cantiques, 126–27).

virtuosity.[37] One could, of course, attribute this affinity to our author's possible personal admiration for Origen's poetic language. Yet the imagery he adopts serves a special purpose. Most of the passages in which he directly uses Origen's figurative language allow him to set the scene. They provide the reader with visual and sensory information that helps them experience the soul's journey through the Song. Even more so, the historical dimension he presents to his readers serves both a pedagogical and anagogical purpose. He rarely offers information without simultaneously explaining its spiritual significance. The content he receives from Origen as historical thus gains new meaning in the context of his pastoral teaching. Even seemingly minor linguistic or geographical information provides William with an opportunity to guide the reader further into the Scriptural mysteries.

An example of such a spiritual reinterpretation is his explanation of the area of Engaddi. Origen provides his reader with the basic information that Engaddi is a 'field located in Judea, that doesn't yield as many vines as it does flowers of balm.'[38] William incorporates this information into a contrasting account about the island of Cyprus, which he apparently gathered from SoS 1,13. The result centers on the observation of the specific types of fertility these areas display:

> Between Cyprus, an island in the sea, and Engaddi, a place in Judea, there are significant differences regarding their geographical location and the generosity of their fertility. The glory of Cyprus is the fertility of its vines, that of Engaddi is the quality of its ointments.[39]

In this instance, the knowledge William provides supports his sacramental theology. Just as the differing local harvests from Cyprus and Engaddi show

---

37   "Combien d'images suggestives que nous n'aurions pas l'idée d'aller chercher dans les pages touffues et même les tableaux grandioses d'Origène, et qu'il nous et possible de goûter, de savourer dans le texte de Guillaume!" (Déchanet, "Introduction," in *Exposé sur le Cantique des Cantiques*, 38).

38   Origen sec. Transl. Rufini. *Commentarium in Canticum canticorum*. Centre Traditio Litterarum Occidentalium, CETEDOC., and Brepols (Firm). 2000. Library of Latin texts. Series A. Series A. [Turnhout, Belgium]: Brepols. http://clt.brepolis.net/LLTA/pages/ TextSearch.aspx?key=PORRUA198_ (accessed January 10, 2025), Lib. 2., pag. 170, linea 24: *'Engaddum' autem ager terrae Iudaeae est non tantum vineis quantum balsamis florens*.

39   Expositio super Cantica Canticorum, CCCM 87, cap. 17, linea 10–12: *Cyprus autem insula maris, et Engaddi locus Iudeae, longe ab inuicem disparantur, tam locorum diuersitate quam generosae fertilitatis dissimilitudine. Cyprum etenim insignem reddit fertilitas uinearum; Engaddi uero balsami nobilitas*.

a variety of natural gifts, they also signify a variety of spiritual gifts, represented in the Christian sacraments. The Cypriot wine symbolizes the joy of the resurrection, counteracting the 'bitterness of the myrrh', which in turn represents the pain of Christ's passion. The balm from Engaddi, on the other hand, symbolizes the Holy Spirit, which infuses the sacramental wine and bestows the salvific power of the resurrection onto those consuming it.

This method of blending the historical and allegorical sense of Biblical imagery is particularly interesting in the cases in which William adds to or changes the information Origen provides to support his spiritual concern. He does so with the etymology of the word Engaddi. The traditional reading of the term, most probably emanating from Origen's works, is that of Engaddi as *fons haedi,* the fount of rams.[40] William acknowledges this reading but adds to it a theologically significant secondary reading. According to William, the name could also be translated as *fons gratiae,* the fount of grace. It is unclear which sources, if any, he has used to support this reading. William combines his etymology with the one he finds in Origen, stating that 'Engaddi is the fount of grace, which the ram enters from the left and leaves at the right, having been turned into a lamb'.[41]

The theme of salvation is a central pastoral concern throughout the *Expositio.* As the case of Engaddi shows, the linguistic information William receives through Origen functions as a literary frame for his kerygmatic intention; a frame which he makes to fit the message by freely altering it. A similar case is William's interpretation of the word Bethel/Bether. Again, he presents different etymologies, which serve to support his theological application of the term. He first cites the two interpretations that Origen offers: Bethel as the *domus Dei* and Bether as the *domus consurgens.*[42] In this case, he does not merely use Origen to offer linguistic insight but also receives his exegetical conclusion: Bethel represents the sons of God in which Godself, the Holy Spirit, while Bether signifies a continuous striving toward higher things.[43]

As he did with the word Engeddi, William offers his own interpretation. His sources again unknown, he translates Bethel as *domus vigilarum,* giving

---

40 This Origenist reading, however, is so widespread that there's also a possibility that William received it through Gregory or Jerome (Déchanet ed., Exposé sur le Cantique des Cantiques, 207).

41 Expositio super Cantica Canticorum, cccm 87, cap. 17, linea 51: *Adhuc etiam Engaddi "fons haedi" interpreta|tur, id est fons gratiae, in quo haedus a sinistra transiens ad dexteram agnus efficitur.*

42 Expositio super Cantica Canticorum, cccm 87, cap. 39, linea 84.

43 Expositio super Cantica Canticorum, cccm 87, cap. 39, linea 92.

the following theological reasoning: [...] *domus vigilarum, in qua jugiter vigi-lant, qui pia ac sollicita expectatione expectant Sponsum Dominum, quando revertatur a nuptiis.* William's concern for the rules and particularities of monastic life has inspired this addition: Bethel represents spiritual disci-pline and the mystical focus on an intimate closeness to God.

However, it is not merely such 'encyclopedic' and linguistic knowledge that undergoes a spiritual transformation in the hands of William. He ap-plies this treatment to the main themes of the Song as well. It becomes clear that the reason why William does not consider the historicity of Ori-gen's *sensus historicus* a necessity is that he ultimately values all possible senses of scriptures according to their allegorical, theological content. This allows him to present particularities of the biographical background Origen offered regarding the alleged author of the Song as spiritual teachings in their own right. He does so, for instance, when discussing the non-Jewish cultural and ethnic background of Solomon's bride.

The bride's 'Egyptian dark skin' (*aegyptia nigredine*) is a central theme in William's work.[44] However, he turns the Biblical discourse on race into a matter of purity – a theological move that is just as representative of Wil-liam's hermeneutical approach as it seems suspicious from a post-colonial perspective.[45] The bride's physical appearance, he explains, reflects the state of the soul's ascent, or in other words, her appearance before God. As the soul literally reflects on her complexion, she is really reflecting on her state of mind. The allegorical darkness of her skin, so William, stems from the 'obscurity of her troubled conscience' (*caliginem turbatae conscientiae*). It is by virtue of her faith, however, that her true beauty remains intact.[46] Again, William seems to recognize the theme of salvation, by divine grace and through human faith, in every line of the Song. None of the Song's poetry is without theological impact on the reader's soul and her journey to-ward God.

This understanding of the text's intention also manifests in William's re-flection on his own hermeneutic priorities. While he reevaluates the

---

44   Expositio super Cantica Canticorum, CCCM 87, cap. 2, linea 60.

45   The negative implications of blackness and the racial history of this particular image have been problematized by several Biblical scholars. The complexity of the question, both linguistically and culturally, cannot be satisfactorily discussed at this point. A syn-optic introduction to the matter is offered for instance in Mark S. M. Scott, "Shades of Grace: Origen and Gregory of Nyssa's Soteriological Exegesis of the 'Black and Beauti-ful' Bride in Song of Songs 1:5." *The Harvard Theological Review* 99, no. 1 (2006).

46   Expositio super Cantica Canticorum, CCCM 87, cap. 8, linea 23: *Confitetur se nigram ob caliginem turbatae conscientiae, licet formosam non diffiteatur per fidei rectitudinem; sciens sicut in cellariis regis enutrita | non humilitatis esse, sed impietatis, fidem negare.*

historical information he receives from Origen as potential fiction, he detects a new kind of historical sense of Scripture. The Song, according to William, is not only literarily set in historical time but becomes history as it affects its reader.[47] The drama unfolding between the characters of the text unfolds in reality, too, as the reader contemplates the Song's message. Just as William emphasizes the importance of faith for the experience of salvation, he notes the significance of faith for the process of reading and interpreting Scripture. The faithful reader gets to participate in the love between the soul and her beloved, as expressed in the text: "[...] and as one walks by faith, rather than by sight, one can apply piety and wisdom tentatively, until what is externally a parable becomes true history in oneself."[48]

History, for William, is not a matter of the past but takes place in the present. Monastic, 'mystic' theology often poses the question of the relationship between Biblical piety and immediate inspiration. William's concept of the *historia veritatis* could offer an answer, at least in regards to his own beliefs. It is by virtue of her faith that the soul receives divine affection, just as the Biblical authors had. Reading their accounts of their souls' special relationship with God bridges the gap between historical and present reality, as the experience God shares with God's creation is timeless: it's the continuous history of salvation. William's understanding of the *sensus historicus* does not differ significantly from Bernard's. For both Cistercians, the 'literal' dimension refers to the actual enactment of the Biblical events within the reader's soul.[49] Exploring the historical sense of Scripture thus means primarily facing one's part in the larger history between Christ and the *anima christiana*. Understood this way, the literal sense is as much part of William's exegetical project as the allegorical. His spiritual interest in experiencing the Song to its fullest allows him to transcend the hermeneutical distinction between the senses. Instead, he synthesizes them into one coherent narrative that has the potential to unfold 'in the reader's hearts as they read it with their eyes'.[50]

---

47 This notion is reminiscent of Bruno of Segni's identification of the historical sense with an "allegory made literal" (Ann W. Astell, *The Song of Songs in the Middle Ages* (Ithaca, NY: Cornell University Press, 2018), 46).

48 Expositio super Cantica Canticorum, CCCM 87, cap. 29, linea 45: *Et quamdiu per fidem ambulat et non per speciem, pie et sapienter suis utatur rudimentis, donec exterior haec parabola dramatis, fiat in eo historia ueritatis.*

49 Ruh, *Geschichte der Abendländischen Mystik*, 260.

50 Expositio super Cantica Canticorum, CCCM 87, cap. 1, linea 50: *Ob hoc epithalamium, canticum | nuptiale, canticum sponsi et sponsae, aggredientes reuoluendum, et inspiciendum opus tuum, sancte Spiritus, te inuocamus, ut amore tuo repleamur, o amor, ad intelligendum canticum amoris; ut et nos colloquii sancti sponsi et sponsae aliquatenus efficiamur participes; ut agatur in nobis quod legitur a nobis.*

3   'Know Thyself'. William's Spiritual Anthropology and His
     Understanding of Image-Likeness

As we have seen, Origen's Biblical exegesis provided a literary framework
for William, which he then transcended to develop an interpretation of the
Song that was meaningful for his monastic context. Both Origen's hermeneutical guidance into the complexity of allegorical writing and his oratori-
cal language lend themselves to the practical, spiritual application William
pursues. Readers of the *Expositio*, while not consuming a consistently Origenist piece of work, will nevertheless encounter many thought-provoking
Origenist impulses woven into the fabric of a thoroughly Cistercian canvas.
This includes not only literary elements but also concretely theological
motives. One of the formative exegetical themes of the Commentary is the
Greek concept of self-recognition: 'Gnosthi Seauton' – Know thyself. Originally an expression of delphic philosophy, the tenet of self-knowledge
found its way through Eastern Neoplatonist theology into the Western tradition of thought. Integrating itself seamlessly into the interplay between
'an omniscient God and humanity, who knows only its ignorance',[51] the notion of self-knowledge lies at the center of Christian mysticism. Discussing
William's reception of this motive will allow us to understand better his
position within a larger context of mystic authorship, particularly his contribution to Cistercian anthropology.[52]

     Such an analysis will offer further insight into the influence of Patristic
thought in his work. This is especially the case since the rather Origenist
notion of self-knowledge is inherently connected to the Augustinian motive
of image-likeness, provoking the question of whether the *Expositio* is ultimately more Origenist or Augustinian in its approach. While it is worth
questioning whether these two great minds can be played off against each
other, given William's appreciation for both and his fundamental belief in
Patristic unanimity, it is nevertheless appropriate to mention the scholarly
debate surrounding this issue. One of the most distinguished authorities on
the matter of William's Patristic sources is Jean–Marie Déchanet. His many

---

51   Alois M. Haas, "Christliche Aspekte Des 'Gnothi Seauton'. Selbsterkenntnis Und Mys-
      tik," *Zeitschrift Für Deutsches Altertum Und Deutsche Literatur* 110 (1981): 71.

52   McGinn identified the 'Delphic maxim' of self-knowledge as the core notion of Cister-
      cian anthropology. He argues, that the *gnosthi seauton* meant, for these early Cister-
      cian authors, "recognising the dignity of human creation and the present misery of
      sinful human existence", providing thus the basis for their moral thought. (McGinn,
      "The Spiritual Teaching," 226).

studies, including "Aux sources de la spiritualité de Guillaume de Saint–Thierry" and "Guillaume de Saint–Thierry, aux source d'une pensées", are indispensable to the study of William's work.[53] Particularly regarding the *Expositio*, Déchanet had famously argued for the importance of William's Greek sources. He believed the Commentary on the Song to be the work in which Origenist theology takes on the shape of William's spirituality and the product of a period during which William had devoted himself to reading Origenist texts.[54]

He pins his argument on various Origenist themes, which he detects in the Commentary. This includes the distinction between the three states of the soul: *animalis, rationalis,* and *spiritualis*. Déchanet interprets this three-fold distinction as an adaptation of the Pauline scheme (*corporalis, animalis,* and *spiritualis*) in an Origenist sense (ψυχή, γνῶσις, and πνεῦμα). For Déchanet, the Alexandrian is William's 'guide and companion' on his adventurous journey through the Song.[55] And since one could also consider Bernard to fulfill that role, Déchanet does not fail to note the Origenist identification of the church as God's bride; a line of interpretation barely appearing in Bernardine exegesis.

However, this theory of a predominant Origenist influence did not remain unchallenged. One of the notable critics of Déchanet's source assessment is David Bell.[56] His studies attempt to counterbalance a

53   Jean–Marie Déchanet, *Guillaume de Saint–Thierry, Aux Sources d'une Pensees* (Paris: Beauchesne, 1978); Jean–Marie Déchanet, *Aux Sources de La Spiritualité de Guillaume de Saint–Thierry. Premiére Série d'études* (Bruges: Charles Beyaert, 1940), originally published as: "Aux Sources de La Doctrine Spirituelle de Guillaume de Saint–Thierry: 1, Saint Grégoire de Nysse." *Collectanea O.C.R.* 5 (1938–39): 187–198, 262–78); and Jean–Marie Déchanet, "Guillaume et Plotin." *Revue de Moyen Age Latin* 2 (1946).

54   Déchanet, "Introduction," in *Exposé sur le Cantique des Cantiques*, 35.

55   "Et voilà que, pour avoir pris comme guide, comme compagnon d'avenure, le grand Docteur d'Alexandrie, il a été amené à nous décrire cette 'âme individuelle à l'intérieur de l'Église', à nous présenter son 'union personnelle avec le Verbe, comme la conséquence de l'union du Christ avec son Église'" (Déchanet, "Introduction," in *Exposé sur le Cantique des Cantiques*, 41–42).

56   F. Tyler Sergent concisely presented the conflict in his discussion of William's sources and influences (Sergent, "Sources and Influences," 36–39). He also discusses the contributions of John D. Anderson, E. Rozanne Elder, and Thomas Michael Tomasic to the question. Alongside Bell, Anderson identifies more likely sources for some of William's core concepts, which include, besides Augustine, such authors as Ambrose, Jerome, Leo the Great, and Isidore of Seville (John D. Anderson, "Introduction." in *William of Saint Thierry: The Enigma of Faith*, Cistercian Fathers 9 (Kalamazoo, MI: Cistercian Publications, 1991), 17–18.

possible overemphasis of Eastern influence in William's thought and redis-
cover Augustine's importance as William's primary source of theological
material. In direct criticism of Déchanet, Bell calls to "declare a morato-
rium on seeking Greek sources for William's ideas",[57] arguing that William
had more likely accessed these ideas through Latin authors.[58] While I disagree with the choice to dismiss the quest for Eastern thought in William's
works entirely, I see value in Bell's assertion that Déchanet's enthusiasm
for Alexandrian thought runs the danger of failing to "appreciate the great
depth and richness of Augustine's doctrine of the image and likeness
of God".[59]

The particular example of image-likeness as a theological motive is well
suited to discuss potential methodological issues with Déchanet's hypothesis. As Rozanne Elder has pointed out with recourse to Pierre Courcelle, to
identify an author's sources, 'doctrinal similarities' are a first and yet an ultimately insufficient indicator.[60] Indeed, William establishes such a strong
connection between the Origenist notion of self-knowledge and the Augustinian theme of image-likeness that detecting Alexandrian terminology
alone does not prove his direct use of Origen as a source. Even if he receives some theological input from an Eastern Father, his implementation
of the thought might ultimately be shaped by his reading of Western authorities. To illustrate this, I will devote the following chapter to the themes
of self-knowledge, image-likeness, and their respective impact on the theological character of the *Expositio*.

Notably, William's introduction of the *gnosthi seauton* into his works was
not unique by the standards of his time. The motive was widely popular
in 12th-century literature and was used by many of the prominent figures
immediately surrounding William. It was, in an adapted form, the title of
one of Abelard's works (*Scito teipsum*) and even Bernard made use of the
theme,[61] as the motive itself appears prominently in the Biblical text of the

---

57   Bell, *The Image and Likeness*, 17.
58   Bell, "The Alleged Greek Sources," 113.
59   Bell, *The Image and Likeness*, 18.
60   As a second part of his methodology, Courcelle suggests the identification of 'textual
      parallels' between an author and their alleged source. Elder acknowledges that both
      Déchanet and Hourlier had made use of this twofold methodology, but that their find-
      ings are no proof of William's direct use of Greek sources (Sergent, "Sources and Influ-
      ences," 41).
61   Haas, "Christliche Aspekte," 80.

Song. In SoS 1,7,[62] as William cites it, the bridegroom admonishes his bride with the following words: *si ignoras te, O pulchra inter mulieres, egredere.*

Besides Origen, several Fathers had understood these words to indicate self-knowledge, most significantly Gregory. William, too, takes this verse as the primary reason to introduce the concept into his Commentary. Self-knowledge is hardly the exclusive main theme in the *Expositio*. But, like the Biblical passage itself, it seems to serve the purpose of evoking further connotations, which coalesce into a web of exegetical and theological ideas. These associations are traceable throughout the Commentary, as William does not attempt to hide the interconnectedness of his favorite motives.

A first very apparent connection of themes seems evoked by the Biblical language itself. As the bridegroom asks his bride to 'follow the tracks of the sheep and graze [her] young goats by the tents of the shepherds'[63] (*egredere, et abi post vestigia gregum; et pasce haedos tuos, juxta tabernacula pastorum*) the reader is presented with images of a rural landscape and the notions of travel and pursuit. There is a spatial, almost geographical aspect to the text: the bride is prompted to leave her current abode and seek out a different place. This notion of translocation evokes for William the idea of different spiritual *loci*, in regard to which he proposes a reading of the text:

> This is to say: what you ask me to teach you, is not unknown to you. Rather, it is yourself, you do not know. If you believe to not know me, it is yourself you do not know. And if you do not know yourself, it is because you have gone out of yourself.[64]

The bride's inability to know her groom is reduced to an inability to know herself. This inability in return stems from the assertion that the bride had 'left herself' (*egressa es a te*). Knowledge of God is tied to an allegorical *locus*, in which God can be found. If one leaves this *locus* in pursuit of something other – something that lies beyond oneself – any further search for God will prove futile. William takes the Biblical *egredere* less so as a request or demand, but rather as an assumption about the bride's spiritual state. The bride's departure is not a consequence of her ignorance, but rather her

---

62   This is according to William's structure. Many modern translation consider this to be the eighth verse of the Song, e.g. the NIV, from which I quote below.

63   SoS 1:8 NIV.

64   Expositio super Cantica Canticorum, CCCM 87, cap. 12, linea 6–8: *Ac si dicat: Quae indicari tibi petis a me, non ignoras, sed scire te ignoras. Idcirco enim uideris tibi ignorare me, quia ignoras te. Ideo ignoras te, quia egressa es a te.*

ignorance necessarily follows her departure. William's interpretation thus transforms the concrete imagery of the Song into an epistemological assertion. He postulates two *loci*: the figurative closeness of the bride to herself and her lover, which facilitates the knowledge of self and God, and a place in which both kinds of knowledge are no longer possible.

This reformulation of the text's geographical language into a spiritual notion of translocation is not original to William. Rather, it is an ideal example of William's web of thematic associations. His 'locus of ignorance' namely corresponds to the Neoplatonist idea of the *regio dissimilitudinis*; the 'region of unlikeness'.[65] This notion was influential for Augustine, as he established his theory of image and likeness. A single Biblical passage becomes a magnifying glass in William's learned mind, under which he then investigates a range of Patristic themes. The *gnosthi seathon* is not the Commentary's Leitmotiv, as Déchanet suggests,[66] but rather one liaison in a thread of related and mutually influential ideas. The way he integrates these themes into the larger fabric of his work makes his exegesis distinctly mystical[67] rather than a particular thought. Similarly, his ability to get different notions into fruitful dialogue with one another marks the character of his Patristic reception. This example reveals that the Commentary, by its very nature, cannot be classified as distinctly Origenist nor Augustinian: William's Origen reminds him of Augustine's thought at every corner.

This becomes even more apparent as we trace the idea of self-knowledge through the *Expositio*. Throughout the Commentary, human self-knowledge and the *imago Dei* are an inseparable literary pair. This is unsurprising, given that they are intimately tied together:[68] The soul, who is the image of

---

65   The term is taken from Plotinus' *Enneades* (see Déchanet, "Guillaume et Plotin", 245–248). I have discussed this concept and its Platonic roots earlier in the chapter "1.7. Humilitas and the Ideal Reader".

66   Alongside the *ordo caritatis*, the *gnothi seaton* represents for Déchanet one of the two core developments of the Expositio (Déchanet, "Introduction," in *Exposé sur le Cantique des Cantiques*, 9).

67   "Hoheslied 1,7, das hier zitiert wird und Wilhelm von Saint Thierry Anlaß gibt, das delphische Orakel nicht Apollo, sondern Christus in den Mund zu legen, ist eine Kernstelle der christlichen Mystik, weil – nach der Interpretation der Mystiker – die Unterlassung der Selbsterkenntnis an die Verbannung in die regio dissimilitudinis, in den Bereich der Selbstentfremdung zum Bräutigam der Seele, zu Christus gebunden ist". Haas, "Christliche Aspekte," 83.

68   Expositio super Cantica Canticorum, CCCM 87, cap. 12, linea 29: *Si, inquit, ignoras te, egredere; hoc est ideo a temetipsa egrederis, quia ignoras te. Sed cognosce te, quia imago mea es, et sic poteris nosse me, cuius imago es, et penes te inuenies me.*

God, can perceive God by contemplating herself. This is a fundamental pre-requisite, not only of William's but of Cistercian anthropology in general.[69] The *Expositio*, however, examines this relatively simple observation from many different angles and employs it for several purposes. Knowledge of the self via the *imago* has various ethical and moral implications, through which William guides his reader with exegetical and linguistic dexterity.

First, William presents self-knowledge as a kind of self-care. Making full use of the Song's colorful language, he compares the soul's ignorance to the bride's failure to maintain her beauty. If we consider the bride's beauty a gift bestowed upon her by her divine lover, her negligence regarding her appearance constitutes a spiritual affront. The bridegroom's response and demand for her to leave is, in consequence, not friendly advice but the reaction of a man frustrated with a partner who fails to please him.[70] With this exegetical context in mind, the Delphic 'Know thyself' is not merely a philosophic suggestion but an instruction for proper worship. Striving to know oneself equates to a spiritual beauty regime. In the context of mo-nastic asceticism, which generally favors self-harm to self-care practices and even exhibits an active depreciation of physical beauty, this is an orig-inal, almost funny reversal of spiritual and worldly values. In a classically mystical twist, pursuing spiritual and worldly goods are mutually exclusive.

William treats the theme of self-knowledge as an aspect of spiritual for-mation. It is not an abstract concept but a concrete stage of ascent, a very practical direction for those pursuing intimacy with God. As such, it is un-surprising that William elaborately connects it to his discussion of morals and virtues. The parameters he had set up for intellectual work, which we had discussed in the context of his Romans Commentary, reappear here in a more spiritual light. Simplicity and humility, on the one hand, and idle curiosity, on the other, are now attributed to the two *loci* of the bride. Knowledge of self and God is found in undemanding contemplation; no in-tellectual flights of fancy are required to sense the goodness of God.[71] 'Know

---

69   McGinn, "The Spiritual Teaching," 226.

70   Expositio super Cantica Canticorum, CCCM 87, cap. 12, linea 26: *Potest etiam uideri pulchritudinis ista commemoratio, neglectae pulchritudinis exprobratio. Sicut cum dicit: Egredere, non est consilium amici, sed quasi emissio irati.*

71   Expositio super Cantica Canticorum, CCCM 87, cap. 12, linea 33: *Quaere ergo Deum in simplicitate; senti de eo in bonitate; satage eum jugiter habere in memoria, et amando intelligere, et intelligendo amare; et in sensu bonitatis ejus percipies sensum aeternitatis ejus, uitae modum, statum mentis bonae.*

thyself' is essentially an invitation for the soul to sit in divine presence. The negative directive to leave, conversely, comes with moral associations of its own:

> Get out and leave. This is to say, leave me and the likeness to me, and go to the place of unlikeness. Leave yourself, and walk on the detours of concupiscence and curiosity. Leave, it is stated, and lead your goats to the pasture, which are assigned to the left; lead your lascivious incli- nations to pasture outside of yourself. Leave and follow the tracks of the disappearing masses. Pasture with those who lead themselves to pasture, who love themselves. Go near the tents of those who have be- queathed their tents to their offspring and who have proclaimed their names unto their own lands but have not – as the Psalmist said – in- scribed them unto the heavens.[72]

The 'region of unlikeness' is a region of vices. It is the absence of the *imago* in the soul, inhibiting the ability, or rather the desire to pursue a virtuous life. The sin of *superbia*, which William had primarily focused on in the *Ex- positio* on Romans, takes on a prominent part here again.[73] Misguided de- sires, curiosity, egotism, and greed are the marks of a life separated from God. Christ's 'egredere' is no punishment. Instead, it presents the bride with an alternative: she can choose him and enjoy the pleasures of true love or go out into the far country of unlikeness, living in sin.[74] William presents the passage as an ethical choice with spiritual consequences.

---

72   Expositio super Cantica Canticorum, cccm 87, cap. 12, linea 40: *Ac si dicat: Abi a me, a similitudine mea in locum dissimilitudinis; a te uero in deuia concupiscentiae uel curiosi- tatis. Abi ergo, ait, et pasce haedos tuos, qui ad sinistram deputantur, lasciuos scilicet motus tuos, in eis quae sunt extra te. Abi post uestigia gregum pereuntis multitudinis, in pascuis semetipsos pascentium, semetipsos amantium, circa tabernacula eorum, quorum tabernacula in progenie et progenie; qui uocauerunt nomina sua, sicut dicit psalmista, in terris suis, nec habent ea scripta in caelis.*

73   In turn, *humilitas* is a central mark of likeness to the divine. This becomes evident, for instance, in the passages regarding SoS 2,1, where Christ proclaims to be the example of humility, which the bride ought to approximate: *Ac si dicat: Si tendis ad plenitudi- nem fruitionis, age, sata\ge, ut habeas similitudinis meae plenitudinem, hoc est in omni perfectione uirtutum perfectae humilitatis, cuius exemplar ego tibi sum, flos campi et lil- ium conuallium* (Expositio super Cantica Canticorum, cccm 87, cap. 22, linea 16). See on this passage also: Ruh, *Geschichte der Abendländischen Mystik*, 303).

74   Expositio super Cantica Canticorum, cccm 87, cap. 12, linea 49: *Sed non sic, o sponsa Christi, non sic: quin potius cognosce temetipsam; praesto tibi esto ad discernendam temetipsam.*

Pursuing self-knowledge means choosing a closeness – a likeness – to God. Pursuing other, worldly kinds of knowledge, however, erases this likeness and any access one might have to divine insight. This line of thought is not unique to William but has accompanied a long tradition of mystic epistemology. As Alois Haas points out in reference to Etienne Gilson: 'The cognitive contemplation of the self and the God interior intimo meo et superior summo meo has to be purchased with an epistemologically critical stance towards knowledge of the world – an anti-physicism of sorts'.[75] William is certainly a proponent of this tradition throughout his oeuvre, as evidenced in his *De Natura corporis et animae*, where he cites SoS 1,7 to discuss his preference of self-knowledge over any knowledge of the world.[76]

Yet, his immersion into the language of the Song in the *Expositio* allows William to avoid here an overtly self-righteous attitude, which usually accompanies such skepticism. Instead, it enables him to tell the story of a loving groom urging his bride not to abandon him. The reader, identifying with the bride, is not judged but encouraged to choose in her best interest. The pleading Christ reassures the soul of her value and beauty, asking her to preserve them alongside him:

> O image of God, recognize your own dignity, so that the image of your creator may shine through you. You believe yourself to be vile, but you are a precious thing. As much as you abandon the one whose image you are, you are infected by foreign images. But if you begin to breathe the one in whom you were made, and if you embrace discipline, you will soon cast off and soon flee the red treacherous images that do not cling enough.[77]

---

75   "[D]ie erkenntnismäßige Einkehr bei sich selbst und beim Deus interior intimo meo et superior summo meo [muß] durch eine erkenntniskritische Haltung gegenüber der Welterkenntnis – durch eine Art Antiphysizismus – erkauft werden" (Haas, "Christliche Aspekte," 75).

76   Alois M. Haas, "Et Descendit de Caelo Γνῶθι Σεαυτόν (Juvenal, Satir. XI, 27). Dauer Und Wandel Eines Mystologischen Motivs," *Zeitschrift Für Deutsches Altertum Und Deutsche Literatur* 108, no. 2 (1979): 78.

77   Expositio super Cantica Canticorum, CCCM 87, cap. 12, linea 62–65: *O imago Dei, recognosce dignitatem tuam; refulgeat in te auctoris effigies. Tu tibi uilis es, sed pretiosa res es. Quantum ab eo defecisti cuius imago es, tantum alienis imaginibus infecta es. Sed cum in id quod creata es, respirare ceperis, si fortiter apprehenderis disciplinam, superductos adulterarum imaginum fucos, nec satis inhaerentes, cito excuties, cito effugies.*

In this passage, William does not only explain the concrete process of self-knowledge (and its loss) but expresses the essence of his anthropology and hamartiology. It is to the extent that the soul leaves her image that she is compromised by 'foreign images' (*alienis imaginibus*). As soon as these images are rejected by the application of religious discipline, however, the divine likeness will be restored. William touches here on a notion that will become the foundation of Eckhartian mysticism and his concept of detachment. In the Eckhartian iteration of this idea, God enters the soul only to the extent that the soul lets go of the world and, ultimately, herself. For him, as for William, images are of great spiritual significance: "In letting go of possessiveness toward images and knowledge, one becomes 'free and maidenly' as Jesus himself was".[78] In William's words, the bride gets closer both in spirit and in nature to her beloved. Christ, the true *imago Dei*, in whose likeness creation was made (making her the *imago facta*),[79] is also whom the soul grows to resemble once she returns to her original state.

It is a cornerstone of Cistercian anthropology to believe that the divine *imago* can never be entirely destroyed. A 'residual likeness' remains, even as the soul is distanced from the image and cannot be lost.[80] Cistercian authors owe this insight to the Augustinian understanding of humanity and its different states, which is, in turn, a Christian reformulation of Neoplatonist anthropology. The idea of an ontological ground in the human soul that retains its divinity and forms the foundation for authentic identity echoes in the Augustinian concept of human likeness to God. Similarly, human 'fallenness' from its original state is conceptualized as a gradual loss – a distancing[81] – from the original image in both the Neoplatonist and the Augustinian framework. Adapting the narrative of the *regio dissimilitudinis*, Augustine conceptualized evil not as a substance in itself but as 'dissimilitude' from the one true divine substance.[82] The soul who lives in sin wanders in unlikeness.[83]

---

78   Amy Hollywood, *The Soul as Virgin Wife: Mechthild of Magdeburg, Marguerite Porete, and Meister Eckhart* (Southbend, IN: University of Notre Dame Press, 1995), 146.

79   Elder, "The Christology of William," 87.

80   Elder, "The Christology of William," 87.

81   Although not conceptualized as a 'spatial distance', but as a defect (Groves, "Image–Likeness," 107).

82   Margaret W. Ferguson, "Saint Augustine's Region of Unlikeness: The Crossing of Exile and Language," *The Georgia Review* 29, no. 4 (1975): 851.

83   Thomas Michael Tomasic, "The Three Theological virtues," *Recherches de Théologie Ancienne et Médiévale* 38 (1971): 89.

Augustine's teaching is, however, not merely Neoplatonist philosophy in a Christian cloak. His introduction of the notion of divine grace is not a superficial addition but a fundamental reversal of the original concept. In fact, Augustine rejects the pagan groundwork precisely on the grounds that it lacks the necessity of divine intervention. The idea that the human soul could remedy her lost state on her own is folly to Augustine.[84] William, following his teacher, describes the philosophers' incomplete insights as results of their *superbia*, failing to give reverence to divine grace as the one source of knowledge, as I have already noted in my discussion of his Romans Commentary.[85]

The juxtaposition of likeness and unlikeness might provide a fitting framework for the 'Doctor of Grace', but his doctrine became influential for the future of Christian mysticism because it centered not on human potential but on the significance of Christ's incarnation. Christ's descent into the 'far country' can restore within the human will the desire for likeness; the desire to return to its original state.[86] While, thus, William makes use, as Augustine does, of some Neoplatonist terminology, it is the particularly Augustinian twist that influenced him the most. Cistercian anthropology is oriented not toward humanity's grappling with its fallen state but toward the divine sacrifice that allows the soul to return to herself.

Surely these two ideas could be understood as two sides of the same coin. Yet, such matters of emphasis should never go unnoticed, as they are often what distinguishes particular theological approaches from others. William's focus on grace and its effect on the human soul constitutes the literary tone of the *Expositio*. This is not a work that aims at scolding its readers for their lack of discipline. It is a piece of pastoral care, reassuring its readers of the divine assistance they receive in pursuing their spiritual progress.[87] 'Know thyself' is an ethical demand, but it is one which the soul is encouraged and supported to fulfill not by herself but by the transformative power of her divine lover. According to William's interpretation, the bridegroom of the Song does not corner his bride with an impossible ultimatum but instead liberates her to choose her own beatitude. This characterization is

---

84 Ferguson, "Saint Augustine's Region of Unlikeness," 851.

85 see the chapter "1.7. Humilitas and the Ideal Reader".

86 "It is precisely because Christ is consubstantial with God that His Word provides a redemptive escape from the 'regio dissimilitudinis'" (Ferguson, "Saint Augustine's Region of Unlikeness," 861).

87 This dimension of the theme in William's thought will be discussed in more detail in the upcoming chapter "7.4. Concepts applied: The monk's image-likeness".

essential in the monastic context, in which Christ acts as a concrete presence in the lives of the religious. It is by Christ's love that the soul is free to
return the affection:

> It is love, which, if it is free, likens us to you, to the extent to which
> the sense of life binds us to you; the sense through which the one who
> lives in the spirit of life senses you. The one who, as the Apostle says,
> contemplates your glory unveiled, is transformed into its image, from
> glory to glory, as if through the Spirit of the Lord.[88]

This passage is situated at the beginning of the *Expositio*. It determines the
work's intention and core message. Free love is what constitutes likeness to
the divine. It is what constitutes human nature, as it was originally intended. Despite his abbatial role and concern for monastic reform, William
conceptualized spiritual progress not in a legalistic and disciplinarian way
but with a strong focus on free will – or, rather, a will freed by Christ. While
residual likeness remains an aspect of the soul despite its fallen state,
and full likeness is perfected entirely by God, the human will plays a significant role in pursuing a 'transitional potential likeness', as Elder calls it.[89]
Whether the soul accepts the offer of restoration is a choice. The language
of the Song explains the necessity of this freedom unlike any other: a loving
relationship is not based on coercion or guilt but on genuine mutual desire.
William's exegesis gives voice to a Christ that desires nothing more than to
be desired by his Beloved. They resemble each other in their shared and
freely given love for one another.[90]

Of course, William upholds a distinction between divine and human love.
Amor is the term he designates to the natural human affinity for God, while

---

88   Expositio super Cantica Canticorum, cccm 87, cap. 1, linea 11: *Amor enim est, qui cum
      liber est, similes nos tibi efficit in tantum, in quantum nos tibi afficit sensus uitae, quo te
      sentit quicumque uiuit de spiritu uitae; qui, sicut dicit apostolus, reuelata facie, speculans
      gloriam tuam, in eandem imaginem transformatur, a claritate in claritatem, sicut a
      domini Spiritu.*
89   Elder, "The Christology," 89.
90   The closeness of erotic language and the theme of image-likeness in William's work is
      especially apparent in this passage: *Ecce, hoc est in hoc affectu pietatis, in hac forma
      confessionis, in hac specie perfectionis, in imagine Dei. In hoc etenim homo ad imaginem
      Dei conditus est, ut pie Dei reminiscens, hoc est ad intelligendum humiliter intelligens,
      hoc est ad amandum ardenter ac sapienter amans, usque ad fruendi affectum animal
      rationale exsisteret; hoc est enim Deum timere et mandata eius obser|uare, quod est
      omnis homo* (Expositio super Cantica Canticorum, cccm 87, cap. 18, linea 4–5).

caritas is God's love working in the soul through the Spirit. The soul experiences a process of ascent, a "progressive upward spiralling development [...] from unlikeness to likeness to God",[91] marked by a gradual evolution of the operative kinds of love. The initiating force is the human choice and the soul's decision to pursue a relationship with God. Through the process of ascent, this natural desire is transformed and assumed by divine charity.[92] Sin, in turn, is not an ontological state of the soul but the human will, lacking the desire for unity with the divine. Both in terms of sin and spiritual devotion, William characterizes the human soul as an active participant in a dynamic conversation with God. As Tomasic describes his particular reception of the Patristic theme: "The pivotal point of William's theocentric language, arising from the cultural milieu of Neo-Platonism, rests on the acceptance of the fact that man is made to the image and likeness of God, that this existential image is not merely a finished byproduct, but an ongoing, creative process [...]".[93] The Song of Songs is an ideal expression of Cistercian spirituality because of its dramatic character. It doesn't describe a set situation but an evolving relationship.

In a broader sense, William's introduction of the theme of image-likeness into his exegesis also reveals his literary intention. Theological insight is never self-serving but instead builds the foundation of spiritual growth. William is concerned, first and foremost, with the concrete application of his theology. In the notion of the *imago Dei,* doctrinal content leads the way for practiced spirituality. In the words of Bernard McGinn: "The dense web of themes of early Cistercian theology found in sermons, commentaries, treatises and letters treated God, Christology, and ecclesiology not as topics for abstract perusal, but as the foundation for a way of life, based on the proper grasp of what it meant to be created in the image and likeness of God [...]."[94] The *imago*, as an image of the Trinity (*imago trinitatis*),[95] facilitates human knowledge of the triune God. Yet, this knowledge is not theoretical but experiential – both in its acquisition and its purpose – as the following passage illustrates:

---

91   Elder, "Bernard and William," 128.
92   "In his late Golden Epistle, he continued this distinction, defining amor as a strong will for God; dilectio as cleaving to or being conjoined with, God, and caritas as fruition, enjoyment" (Elder, "Bernard and William," 128).
93   Tomasic, "The Three Theological Virutes," 102.
94   McGinn, "The Spiritual Teaching," 225.
95   McGinn, "The Spiritual Teaching," 225.

Every soul who, for its own benefit, receives some grace from the gen-
erosity of God, receives from this gift also some knowledge of the
Giver. This is to keep man (*homo*) from being ungrateful to God and to
turn him towards his benefactor. The person who burns with humble
love is inclined towards God and is conformed to the One, towards
whom they are inclined, through the power of the One, towards whom
they are inclined.[96]

The grace God offers freely lets the receiving soul turn towards God in gratitude. Gratitude, then, as an expression of genuine love, leads the soul to
conformity and likeness with the divine nature, or more accurately, with the
image that is Christ himself. Knowledge of self and God is thus not simply a
matter of theological insight but inner transformation. The consequences of
theological stipulation are of a real, ontological nature as far as they determine the possibility of human participation in divine substance. His teachings on the Holy Spirit, for instance, do not present detached pneumatology
but reveal a Trinitarian God who communicates to the human soul her origin and destiny.[97]

In light of this observation, William's doctrinal disagreements with Abelard take on a new quality. Their quarrel is not about theoretical doctrines
but about the salvation of souls. Abelard's assertions about the names of
God and his relativization of Christ as the second person of the Trinity have
practical implications within William's framework. If Christ was not
the second person of the Trinity and thus both fully God and fully man, inextricably connected, then the basis for the soul made *ad imaginem Dei* to
be returned to her divine substance would be missing.[98] More so, if the
human spirit is not indeed made 'to the image' of the Trinity, the line of

---

96   Expositio super Cantica Canticorum, cccm 87, cap. 1, linea 36–39: *Quaecumque enim
      anima ad utilitatem suam, aliquam donante Deo accipit gratiam, cum dono ipso, donan-
      tis etiam accipit intelligentiam, ut non sit homo Deo ingratus, sed ad donantem semper
      sit conuersio eius. Cui cum ardentius intendit humilis amor, ipsi cui intendit conforma-
      tur; quia intendendo in hoc ipsum ab ipso efficitur.*

97   "William's insistence on the importance of the three persons as subsistent relations
      and his emphasis on the Father as the source and origin of the whole divinity under-
      line the constitutive role of each of the three persons in our growing likeness (*simili-
      tudo*) to God. His mystical theology is Spirit-centred, both in an innertrinitarian sense,
      because the Spirit is the one who makes the three persons one, and in an extratrinitar-
      ian way, since the Spirit is sent to bring us to where we were always destined to be."
      (McGinn, "The Spiritual Teaching," 222).

98   Explained by Elder in positive terms (Elder, "The Christology," 90).

reasoning that leads the soul through self-knowledge to conformity is broken at a pivotal point.[99] While it is certainly possible that William's reading of Abelard's theological statement is less than favorable and contains certain misunderstandings, it becomes clear from his exegesis why he pursued Abelard's condemnation with such spiritual fervor. Considerations on anthropology and theology, for William, should primarily serve the purpose of leading the soul to God. As such, they leave little room for philosophical speculation. This will become even clearer in the following, as I will discuss a theme adjacent to those of self-knowledge and image-likeness, namely the role of love in theological understanding.

4   Love. An Intellectual Principle

As I have already observed, William tends to assemble different Patristic motives into a spiritual mosaic, endowing his theological framework with beautiful imagery and poignant dogmatic observations adopted from his favorite Fathers. Some of those motives heavily influence the overall tone of his work and help his readers find their way through its complexity. One of these central motives is Gregory the Great's *amor ipse intellectus est* – love itself is intellect.[100] As the preceding paragraphs have shown us, William's core interest in the *Expositio* is to visualize human understanding of God, by employing the erotic language of the Song of Songs. Our look at themes of likeness and self-knowledge thus prepared us to understand his more fundamental premise, namely the idea that love and knowledge coalesce in their one true divine object.

In its original Gregorian form, William's Leitmotiv is *amor ipse notitia est*.[101] William's amendment likely does not intend to offer a critique of

---

99   It is thus hardly coincidental that the conflict with Abelard was followed with an intensified emphasis on will and reason in William's teaching on the human mind (Elder, "The Christology," 86).

100   William was not the only Cistercian author, who returned to this Gregorian notion to inform his own mystical thought (McGinn, "The Spiritual Teaching," 228).

101   "Amor ipse intellectus est. Le fameux leit-motiv de tout l'Exposé inspiré de l'amor ipse notitia est de S. Grégoire, Hom. in Evang., XXVII; PL 76, 1207, et inséré ici–même dans un contexte qui en souligne la portée: en tant qu'Époux, Dieu connaît l'âme en se communiquant à elle; pareillement, c'est en se donnant, en se prêtant, pour tout dire, aux effusions de son Dieu, que l'âme mérite de le connaître, car alors elle le possède; 'elle se repaît de lui' – on va nous le dire – dans un complexe où l'Époux est tour é tour possédant et possédé" (Déchanet ed., in Exposé sur le Cantique des Catiques, 152).

Gregory but allows him to adapt the notion to his context and needs. While *notitia* translates to the content of understanding or informative knowledge, *intellectus* is the faculty of understanding itself.[102] The shift seems only slight but is representative of William's dynamic spirituality. Love is the conclusion and the cognitive process as a whole. Both William's image of God and his anthropology are revealed in this slight change of terminology. God, for humanity, is not merely the distanced object of insight – a notion he criticizes in the emerging dialectical approach to theology[103] – but a concrete interlocutor, one that does not only communicate but communicates his very self.

The word *intellectus* describes as much a human faculty and ability as it does divine activity in the human soul. As we will see in the following, William's concept of intellect is closely intertwined with his Trinitarian theology, particularly his pneumatological emphasis, and his ethical reflection on the Christian thinker's ideal attitude. It is, in other words, a core piece of his thought that reconciles his theoretical and practical concerns. *Amor ipse intellectus est* is both a theological assertion about the nature of God's love and an exhortation of his readers that intellectual gratification cannot be sought in separation from God.

A first and significant distinction lies in William's versatile usage of such words as *intellectus* or *scientia*. In his exegesis, he often focuses more on spiritual knowledge (or humble knowledge); something he differentiates from natural knowledge. This distinction already appeared in his Commentary on Romans, there in the context of his critique of philosophy.[104] In the Commentary on the Song of Songs, William is less polemic[105] and seems more interested in the process of thought as such. Throughout his work, William uses his terminology rather flexibly, which can complicate attempts

---

102   Ruh translates *notitia* to the German 'Erkenntnis', and *intellectus* to "das höchste Erkenntnisvermögen" (Ruh, *Geschichte der Abendländischen Mystik*, 299).

103   Tomasic makes a similar observation on the nature of William's project when he states: "Without the intersubjective nexus as the very foundation of living, William's understanding of faith, hope and love would remain sterile, academic curiosities" (Tomasic, "The Three Theological Virtues," 104). Although he does not draw a clear parallel between these 'academic curiosities' and scholastic theology is very reminiscent of William's accusations against the philosophers of this world.

104   see the chapter "1.7. Humilitas and the Ideal Reader".

105   However, we still find subtle reminders of his conflict, particularly with Abelard in the *Expositio*. In one of these passages, he operates with an Origenist image, describing wordy eloquence as silver (*argentum*) and loving wisdom as gold (*aurum*) (Déchanet ed., in Exposé sur le Cantique des Cantiques, 180, n. 3).

to systematize his concept. Yet, it is clear that the process of acquiring spiritual insight differs from cognitive processes taking place in the world and regarding physical objects.[106] While the mind can understand physical objects or worldly phenomena through its rational abilities, the 'divine object' – if at all an object, in the actual sense of the word – cannot be grasped in the same manner:

> The mind discerns the object which it grasps with the natural intellect through reason; but what the mind cannot entirely perceive, it cannot discern. The Holy Spirit breathes where it wants, when it wants, in the manner it wants, and as much as it wants.[107]

In this passage, William clarifies who is in charge, and it is certainly not the human mind. Natural intellect describes the ability to discern the elements of a perceivable object; it allows the mind to understand and take hold of those objects. Yet, this rational operation cannot be applied to objects that evade perception: the Spirit of God. From William's witty writing, one could almost get a sense of the Spirit as defiant in nature, attempting to elude human understanding. The Spirit flows whenever, wherever and in whichever way it desires, thus remaining indiscernible for the *ratio*.[108]

This is where William's concept of spiritual intelligence becomes important. While he maintains the doctrinally crucial concealment of the divine

---

106   Eph. 3,19 is an important passage for William, because it allows him to value charity over rational knowledge, as he does in this passage: *Ex continuae eius praesentiae illuminante gratia, fixam in Deum, et stabiliter affectam uult habere memoriam; illuminatum de ipso intellectum; supereminentem in eum scientiae caritatem [...]* (Expositio super Cantica Canticorum, CCCM 87, cap. 20, linea 117).

107   Expositio super Cantica Canticorum, CCCM 87, cap. 16, linea 18–20: *Quod enim naturaliter intelligendo capit, rationaliter discernit; quod uero non sufficit percernere, non praeualet discer|nere. Sanctus etenim Spiritus sicut ubi uult spirat, sic quando uult et quomodo uult et quantum uult [...]*.

108   It is, despite all criticism of worldly philosophy important to note that William does not attribute any sinfulness to rationality. In fact, ratio is what liberates the mind from the bondage of physical desires. If put at the service of love, rationality might even be an asset to love, as he explains here: *Sic que alterum alteri cooperatur in bonum, dum amor rationem confortat ad adtrahendum, ratio amorem ad amplectendum; amor ratione munitur, ratio uero ab amore illuminatur* (Expositio super Cantica Canticorum, CCCM 87, cap. 27, linea 91). Ratio is thus not bad in and of itself, but it needs to be set aside, in order to be ultimately surpassed by something more perfect: *cum retroacta ratione amor pius ipse efficietur intellectus suus* (Expositio super Cantica Canticorum, CCCM 87, cap. 29, linea 48).

mystery by reminding his readers of their rational limitations, a spiritually fruitful theology ought to allow for some accessibility as well. For an Augustinian such as William, there needs to be a possibility for the human mind to enjoy and experience God. It is thus unsurprising that his definition of spiritual knowledge is fundamentally experiential. This is laid out, in a slightly more systematic way, in his later work, The Mirror of Faith (*Speculum Fidei*), which is as Déchanet observes 'the best introduction to the *Expositio*'.[109] Although he does not speak here of natural and spiritual intelligence as much as of science (*scientia*) and wisdom (*sapientia*),[110] the latter distinction provides a helpful conceptual definition since these two categories are already set up in the Expositio. Our focus ought to lie mainly on his notion of *sapientia*, as it constitutes the kind of knowledge brought about by an intellect of love. He describes it in the following:

> This is the wisdom of God, whereby God savors the wise; the one living of the Spirit of life to the point of sensing his love; the one loving to the point of imitating God's resemblance, the one sensing in the temporal things the same as Christ, our Lord, has sensed in him; the one having in regard to eternal things and God the kind of sense, about which the sage says: 'Knowing you is all-consuming sense (*sensus*)'.[111]

One does not attain wisdom but instead savors it, tastes it, and feels it. William's definition emphasizes the word's etymology: *sapere*, in his interpretation, takes on its full sensual potential. To know God does not mean to

---

109   "Il n'est pas de meilleure introduction à l'Exposé de Guillaume sur le Cantique des Cantiques, que le Miroir de la foi du même auteur." (Déchanet, "Introduction," in *Exposé sur le Cantique des Cantiques*, 17).

110   In the *Expositio*, however, *sapientia* and *scientia* are often taken together, in order to describe the human striving for closeness to God on multiple levels (Expositio super Cantica Canticorum, CCCM 87, cap. 4, linea 24). As the opposing notions, as which they are presented, they might relate more to William's distinction of *ratio* and *amor*, thus presenting a version of neoplatonist distinction of eyes – one that perceives time, and the other perceives eternity. (Ruh, *Geschichte der Abendländischen Mystik*, 294). The image of the eye appears explicitly in the *Expositio*, e.g. when William says: *Oculum que spiritualis intellectus lumini gratiae aperiens* [...] (Expositio super Cantica Canticorum, CCCM 87, cap. 16, linea 6).

111   Speculum fidei, CCCM 89A, par. 75, pag. 110, linea 949: *Haec est enim sapientia Dei, qua sapit Deus sapienti; uiuenti de Spiritu uitae eius usque ad sensum amoris eius; amanti usque ad imitationem similitudinis eius; in temporalibus sentienti in seipso quod et in Christo Iesu Domino nostro; in aeternis uero et ad Deum, eum habenti sensum de quo dicit quidam sapiens: Scire enim te, sensus est consummatus.*

acquire factual knowledge about God but to feel for God the same love that Godself feels (*ad sensum amoris eius*). Within this framework, God becomes the primary agent. It is the experience of God – as Jesus Christ has lived it himself – and not the human experience that determines the kind of knowledge in question and the methodology of its pursuit. Rather than initiating the search for enlightenment, the human soul participates in divine knowledge by virtue of the love it passively receives.

Both William and Gregory emphasize the event of incarnation as the ultimate act of divine love. In the incarnation, God 'bows down' to humanity and establishes the relationship that allows the soul to enter the realm of divine perception.[112] The sacrificial love of Christ imparts this 'sapiential' knowledge to the faithful, who are willing to accept it. Thus, Christ takes on, in his role as *redemptor mundi*, a secondary role as a teacher: *Diligens enim hominem quodammodo usque ad contemptum sui, docuit hominem Deum diligere usque ad contemptum sui;* [...].[113] This conception seems to omit Jesus' parabolic teaching and his rabbinic office or at least classify them as secondary. It is not merely by theoretical reflection that Christ imparts his knowledge on his pupils, but by demonstrating divine nature. William shares this pedagogical understanding of the Christ event with Gregory. The motif occurs especially in Gregory's Homilies on Ezechiel, one of the primary sources of William's Gregorian reception. Interpreting Paul, Gregory emphasizes the knowledge Christ's followers have received in him (*in illo*) rather than from him.[114]

This strong accentuation of Christ's life and sacrifice as the source of wisdom is also reflected in William's concept of learning. While Biblical and Ecclesial teachings play a significant role in theological education, especially in safeguarding doctrine, as we have seen in the *Disputatio*, the *Expositio* presents spiritual formation as something that primarily takes place in the lived relationship of the human mind and God. If intellect is love, the element of receptivity and human dependence on God becomes central. To

---

112   Excerpta ex libris beati Gregorii, CCCM 87, cap. 2, linea 264: *Sed quia et diuina fecit et humana pertulit, quasi per fenestras uel per cancellos ad homines prospexit, ut Deus et appareret ex miraculis, et lateret ex passionibus, et homo cerneretur ex passionibus, sed tamen esse ultra hominem ex miraculis agnosceretur,* quoting verbatim from Gregory's *Homiliae in Hiezechihelem prophetam* (CPL 1710; CCSL 142) Lib. 2, hom. 1.

113   Speculum fidei, CCCM 89A, par. 74, pag. 110, linea 941.

114   Homiliae in Hiezechihelem prophetam (CPL 1710; CCSL 142) Lib. 2, hom. 6, linea 31: *His diuitiis abundare discipulos idem magister gentium uiderat, cum dicebat: diuites facti estis in illo, in omni uerbo et in omni scientia.*

William, the interplay between passive reception and active inspiration is not a violent dynamic but an intimate dance expressed in the erotic imagery of the Song.

Knowing becomes intersubjective[115] as the bridegroom and the bride reveal themselves to one another. Although the bride takes on the receptive role, one cannot be 'spouse' without the other; thus, their identity is constructed on the basis of their mutual relationship. The activity of God is not one that aggressively overpowers the soul but instead draws her closer in an attractive manner. For the soul, to get a hold of her groom means to let herself be held. Applied to the nature of intellectual processes, this interaction takes place as follows:

> As the Holy Spirit begins to illuminate the Spiritual intellect through abundant grace, it [the spirtual intellect] operates in the human soul in a way that differs the more from the human intellect, as the nature of the soul differs more profoundly from the nature of the boundless light. What the soul perceives through natural intellect, it does not grasp as much as it is grasped by what it cannot perceive through the intellect.[116]

While the soul is able to grasp (*capere*) an object with her natural intellect, her spiritual intellect confronts her not with a perceivable object but with another subject. Rather than being able to catch it, she thus becomes caught herself in the process of spiritual understanding. According to William, this process fundamentally differs from any other 'operation' of the human intellect. This is because the intellect at work is no longer simply human in nature.

Illuminated by the Holy Spirit, the soul operates by grace rather than her human capacity. Inspired, it grows in likeness to the divine Spirit and is no longer limited to human potential. This definition of the inspired intellect is especially significant regarding William's understanding of authority. He draws the ultimate conclusion: *non enim Paulus, sed gratia Dei secum.*[117]

---

115   Tomasic, "The Three Theological virtues," 101.
116   Exposito super Cantica Canticorum, CCCM 87, cap. 16, linea 13–16: *Intellectus etenim spiritualis, cum illuminari ceperit abundantiore gratia | Spiritus Sancti, tanto differentius operatur in anima humana ab intellectu humano, quanto sublimius a natura ipsius animae differt natura luminis incircumscripti. Quod enim naturali intellectu intelligit anima, capit; illo autem intellectu non tam capit quam capitur.*
117   Exposito super Cantica Canticorum, CCCM 87, cap. 20, linea 106.

Paul's achievements as a Biblical author, an apostle, and a teacher of the church were not his own. It is thus not his own, but the authority of divine grace in him, that would become constitutional for the development of Christian thought.

The Spirit, for William, is the primary force of spiritual life. As Kurt Ruh remarks, William's texts convey the impression that 'their author speaks from deep experience: there are things one cannot invent or cast into language'.[118] This is especially true when he speaks of the Spirit and the various effects of inspiration on the mind. The Spirit does not reveal itself to the soul in one particular form but as a complex and multifaceted persona:

> In the same way, the purity of love and the divine affect operate: they touch more gently, attract more forcefully and bind more sweetly the one who is affected. Entirely spirit and act, they transfuse the faithful lover in God by comforting, conforming, and stimulating them towards enjoyment.[119]

Here, it becomes clear that the Spirit displays various characteristics. Touching the soul sweetly and gently one minute, attracting her forcefully the other, the Spirit is both the soul's consoler, in line with the Biblical tradition of the Paraclete, and her lover, in a tangible enactment of the Song's drama. William expresses here not simply a pneumatological concept but his own experiences, which alternate in pace, character, and intensity in the course of monastic life.

While the divine–human relationship is thus always experienced in new and different ways, there is one type of relationship that exceeds all others in intimacy: union. The *unitas spiritus* is one of William's core concepts throughout his work. Recent scholarship has paid particular attention to this idea,[120] and I will further expand on it when discussing his Golden

---

118 "Immer wieder steht man unter dem Eindruck, dass ihr Verfasser aus tiefer Erfahrung heraus spricht: Es gibt Dinge, die man nicht 'erfinden' und schon gar nicht in Sprache fassen kann." (Ruh, *Geschichte der Abendländischen Mystik*, 310).

119 Expositio super Cantica Canticorum, CCCM 87, cap. 19, linea 66: [...] *idem agit puritas amoris ac diuinus affectus, suauius afficiens, fortius que attrahens, et dulcius continens sentientem, totum que et mente et actu in Deum transfundens fideliter amantem, et confortans et conformans, et uiuificans ad fruendum.*

120 The emphasis is reflected for instance in the collection of essays for Rozanne Elder with the title 'Unity of Spirit'.

Epistle, where the concept features prominently. For now, I would like to present how it appears in the *Expositio*.

His daring pneumatology is one of the ways in which William's thought stands out from Bernard's. It is also one of the notions in which William displays the most controversial potential. It has been a question of much scholarly interest to which degree the concept of *unitas spiritus* suggests a deification of the soul and whether William runs into the danger of disintegrating the human identity of the soul. I would argue that, as far as the account of the notion in the *Expositio* is concerned, this is not the case. The *unitas* is, first and foremost, the fullness of spiritual experience. As such, it naturally surpasses all other kinds of insight and modes of understanding. William describes a sensibility that overtakes the mind and leads it beyond physical perception, rational ability, and human intelligence:

> And grace abounds to the point of experiencing something certain and real of God. Suddenly, however, the illuminated sense of love (*sensus amoris*) becomes sensible, in an entirely new way, to the things that no corporeal sense can dream of, and no rationality can grasp, and no intellect can understand, apart from the intellect illuminated by love.[121]

William describes a sudden renewal (*modo quodam novo*) of the intellect and the introduction of a fundamentally new intellectual process. It is a process that no longer operates with rational abilities, such as the use of language.[122] McGinn describes this kind of renewed intellect as "a form of connatural knowing – both a *sensus amoris* and the kind of *intelligentia amoris* enshrined in the saying amor ipse intelligentia est".[123] Epistemologically, this mode of knowing rests on William's concept of image-likeness. The soul is drawn into likeness with her creator and receives a sensibility akin to the divine:

> This is where, for the man (sic) of God, sensing something of God through the good experience of the affect means to become likened to

---

121 Expositio super Cantica Canticorum, CCCM 87, cap. 19, linea 47: *Nam et cum nonnunquam superabundat gratia usque ad certam de Deo et manifestam experientiam rei, fit repente sensui illuminati amoris modo quodam nouo sensibile, quod nulli sensui corporis sperabile, nulli rationi cogitabile, nulli intellectui extra intellectum | illuminati amoris fit capabile.*

122 Sergent, "Sources and Influences," 62.

123 McGinn, "The Spiritual Teaching," 228.

God according to the nature of the thing that is sensed and love of the one sensing.[124]

It is important to note that William speaks here of *similitudo*; the soul does not become divine, but she receives similarity to the *imago*. It is not the soul in its entirety that is deified, particularly because it is only 'something of God' (*aliud de Deo*) that is accessible to her through this new sensibility. Although the *intellectus*, William describes here is indeed divine in nature, illuminated entirely by divine grace, this form of intellect remains distinct from the human intellectual faculty.[125] The fact that William, in a typically Cistercian manner, uses relational language to describe the illumination of the intellect with divine love shows that a certain distance between God and the soul remains necessary. The bride and bridegroom encounter and love each other, but do not become each other, for that would make experiencing each other impossible.

The final end of the *intelligentia amoris* is thus not the completeness of theological knowledge, but the enjoyment of love (*fruitio*) and the dwelling in grace. The soul, in experiencing the *unitas* does not lose her own identity in the divine but instead restores her authentic self. Made in the likeness of the *imago*, the love that illuminates her intellect is her intended nature. As Aage Rydstrøm–Poulsen points out "the soul, and therefore the human can only become what it actually is and is meant to be in unity with its Creator. Anything else is simply a mistake and leads to destruction".[126]

In this sense, William's original notion of the *unitas spiritus* can be considered a natural continuation of the Augustinian way in which he discusses likeness through grace and unlikeness as sin. The *intellectus spiritualis* as a gift of grace, an aspect William emphasizes thoroughly, is thus not an indication of a possible pan(en)theist tendency in William's thought.[127] Rather, it is an expression of human participation in divine love, made possible through the soul's communion with the Holy Spirit.

---

124 Expositio super Cantica Canticorum, CCCM 87, cap. 19, linea 51: *Vbi homini illi Dei non est aliud de Deo sentire, quam per bonae experientiae affectum similitudinem eius contrahere secundum qualitatem et sensae speciei et sentientis amoris.*

125 Ruh, *Geschichte der Abendländischen Mystik*, 294.

126 Aage Rydstrøm–Poulsen, "William of Saint–Thierry on the Soul," in *A Companion to William of Saint–Thierry* (Brill, 2019), 102.

127 Glenn E. Myers, "William of Saint–Thierry's Legacy: Progress toward Trinitarian Participation in the Unio Mystica in Johannes Tauler's Sermons," in *A Companion to William of Saint–Thierry* (Brill, 2019).

William's concept, however, does not only make him suspect of pan(en)theism but also raises questions regarding the workings of the Spirit. Some of the passages quoted above, speaking of the waywardness of the Spirit, or the suddenness, with which the soul is seized, could convey the impression of a Spirit that erratically overpowers the will. There is a certain degree of validity to this understanding since the human will, once conformed to likeness, is indeed subjugated to the divine will and no longer free in the actual sense of the term.[128] However, William's mysticism differs significantly from later forms of visionary literature, and his understanding of *unitas* should not be interpreted as a sort of spontaneous ecstasy. Instead, the unity he speaks of is the fruit of a virtuous life.

In this sense, leading up to the ultimate experience of unity, the human will and its freedom play a significant role. As we have seen in the preceding chapter, Christ's sacrifice allows the soul to turn toward God freely and in gratitude. This essential feature of Cistercian anthropology remains important for William as he discusses the ways in which the soul prepares herself for unity. Using the language of the Song, William emphasizes the soul's desire as a means through which she is drawn to her divine lover. The Spirit can affect the soul in such a forceful and impactful manner because it is desirable to her.[129] Desire, as he conceptualizes it, is simply the human will turned toward God. Within this framework, the will is therefore not overpowered or coerced but freely delivers itself to the one it wholeheartedly desires:

> Yet a good will is already the beginning of love. Vehement will, almost as though pointed to something absent, is desire, but pointed at something that is present, it is love, so that what is loved is close to its lover in the intellect.[130]

---

128   Rydstrøm–Poulsen, "William and the Soul," 102–103.

129   In another passage William explains that the Spirit 'having become wisdom to the soul, accomplishes in and through her what it wants' (*factus ei sapientia; quodcumque uult facit in ea, uel per eam* (Expositio super Cantica Canticorum, CCCM 87, cap. 28, linea 61)). While the latter part of this sentence seems to diminish the role of the soul and presents her as essentially will-less, the first part of the sentence is crucial. The soul has accepted the Spirit as wisdom, and thus trusts the Spirit to guide her steps. This insight changes the tone of the assertion and lets the soul appear as an active and willing participator in her fate.

130   Expositio super Cantica Canticorum, CCCM 87, cap. 15, linea 47: *Sed bona uoluntas iam initium amoris est. Vehemens autem uoluntas, uel quasi ad absentem desiderium est, uel affecta circa praesentem amor est; cum amanti id quod amat in intellectu praesto est.*

William, continuously describing the soul's ascent and the development of the intellect in terms of a dynamic relationship between lovers, allows him to hold divine grace and human will together in tension; something which few theologians succeeded in, usually overemphasizing one or the other. In the 'good will' (*bona voluntas*) divine love can take hold. It is, in this sense, indeed a necessity and a foundation that makes the ultimate experience of unity possible.

William's appreciation for the will also reveals the ethical agenda of his exegetical project. As much as it is a gift of grace, spiritual ascent necessitates the active participation of the soul and her virtuous intentions. He explains the inherent correlation between the soul's morality and her spiritual experience regarding gratitude. A soul who turns her memory in gratitude toward all the blessings she has received from God deserves the *intellectus spiritualis*, and the experiences of love that come with it.[131] Here William's concept is slightly reminiscent of the Neoplatonist notion that the intellect is "derived from the virtues as a recollection of one's scatteredness and lostness in the world back to the ontological integrity of the self".[132] In William's case, however, it is not the memory of a likeness lost but the memory of a likeness accessible through gifts of grace that leads to the 'joy of spiritual intellect' (*spiritualis intellectus gaudium*).[133] A life lived in gratitude is a key to intellectual and spiritual fruition.

William's treatment of the Gregorian principle, *amor ipse intellectus est,* clearly stands in the context of his concern for his readers' spiritual progress. Growing to know and growing to love God, ultimately revealed as the same process, are the foundation of mystical ascent. With his exegesis, William does not only hope to develop a coherent concept of spiritual intellect but instead wants to help his readers reenact the journey of the soul, narrated in the Song. When he speaks of her desire, he hopes to kindle the flames of desire in his reader's heart; when he emphasizes the importance of a grateful will, he instructs his brothers – as an Abbott does – in obedient spirituality. One passage, in particular, illustrates this literary and pedagogical intention as beautifully as few others do:

---

131 Expositio super Cantica Canticorum, CCCM 87, cap. 16, linea 9: *Beneficiis etenim Dei non ingrata memoria cito spiritualis intellectus gaudium meretur; qui etiam continuo in suaues quasdam amoris experientias delectabiliter potius quam scienter resoluitur.*

132 Tomasic, "The Three Theological Virtues," 108.

133 Expositio super Cantica Canticorum, CCCM 87, cap. 16, linea 9.

> [The bride] begins to recognize now, as she had first been known her-
> self. And as much as she knows, she loves, as she has first been loved.
> The first recognition between the bridegroom and the bride has been a
> gift of divine wisdom; the first love has been infused freely by the Holy
> Spirit; the recognition between bride and bridegroom is love itself and
> to that extent, love itself is intellect.[134]

Here, the bride, having received the first affections from her beloved, becomes more courageous in her display of love. Reassured by the *sensus amoris* she received as a token of affection, she begins to experiment more
freely and becomes more daring.[135] Such a realistic description of a young
heart that, after hesitantly starting to trust, falls intensely in love cannot be
inspired by anything but William's experience. Understanding the Song as
something he has experienced as a monk, William seems to encourage his
brothers to follow him on this path, as if saying: "Give in to this inexplicable
feeling!" The soul's journey with its impediments and successes is not as
much something to be understood but something to be emulated.

5   The Breasts of God: William's Sensual Spirituality

William unfolds his concept of the *unitas spiritus* as his work progresses so
that his readers experience the gradual intensification of the soul's relationship with God through their *lectio*. It is, therefore, worth discussing William's language at the beginning of the *Expositio*, when the soul is in
anticipation and unity is longed for rather than experienced. While William
expresses unity and fruition in explicitly erotic terms, describing the lovers'
kiss or even their withdrawal to the conjugal chamber, the Commentary
commences with imagery marked by different sensual aspects. As we have
seen, William does not only describe but creates the spiritual experience.

---

134   Expositio super Cantica Canticorum, CCCM 87, cap. 10, linea 71–73: *Iam enim inci-
      pit cognoscere, sicut prior cognita est; et in quantum cognoscit, diligere sicut prior
      dilecta est. Prior enim sponsi ad sponsam cognitio diuinae fuit sapientiae donatio;
      prior dilectio sancti Spiritus gratuita infusio; cognitio uero sponsae ad sponsum et
      amor | idem est, quoniam in hac re amor ipse intellectus est.*
135   Expositio super Cantica Canticorum, CCCM 87, cap. 10, linea 67: *Hinc dilectionis dili-
      gentis se sponsi amicas suauitates per illuminati sensum amoris largius ac dulcius
      sponsa incipit experiri* […].

This experience is not unilateral but the soul's journey itself, marked by different phases. Experiencing the divine on varying levels of spiritual progress means experiencing many different faces of God on different levels of sensuality.[136] Not all of them are erotic per se, although, as I will discuss, the erotic sphere can hardly be escaped or strictly separated from the sensual world of the Song.[137] The following passages aim at presenting the variety of sensual imagery, which William uses to describe experiences of the divine, and his virtuous use of poetic language.

A first (at least theoretically) non-erotic image of God is the parental one. It is engrained primarily in the Trinitarian doctrine, and images of fatherhood have impacted the Christian tradition over centuries. Yet, medieval mysticism, in particular, has also turned to God as the mother, particularly in their feminization of the Christ figure.[138] The works of Caroline Walker Bynum have been tremendously influential in their discussion of this literary tradition, both in the works of medieval women mystics and the Cistercian authors of the 12th century.[139] Especially in feminist and

---

136   In his tractate *De natura et diginitate amoris* William makes use of a motive common to the 12th century: the senses of the Church, represented by the senses of the physical Christ as head of the church (see *De Natura et Dignitate Amoris*, CCCM 88, par. 29, pag. 199: *In huius corporis capite, id est prima et antiquiori uel superiori parte, quae est primitiua Ecclesia, quatuor sunt sensus: uisus, auditus, odoratus et tactus*). This motive is shared by such as Hugh of Saint Victor (and Hildebert of Lavardin (1055–1133). In this image, as Boyd Taylor Coolman points out, "[...] the traditional phrase sentire cum ecclesiae might be invoked, in its more literal denotation of sensing or perceiving, to capture this scholastic approach to the spiritual senses" (Boyd Taylor Coolman, "Alexander of Hales," in *The Spiritual Senses: Perceiving God in Western Christianity*, ed. Paul L. Gavrilyuk and Sarah Coakley (Cambridge: Cambridge University Press, 2011), 126).

137   I am acknowledging here a criticism raised by Karma Lochrie, that the erotic sphere is often separated from other expressions of sensual experience, in an attempt to maintain a heteronormative conventionality in the interpretation of mystic texts (Karma Lochrie, "Mystical Acts, Queer Tendencies," in *Constructing Medieval Sexuality*, ed. Karma Lochrie, Peggy Mccracken, and James A. Schultz (Minneapolis: University of Minnesota Press, 1997).

138   "This feminization is regarded as part of a cluster of shifts in devotional belief and practice emphasizing Christ's humanity, physical access to the sacred, and the deployment of social roles to define Christ's relationship to the mystic as mother, husband, lover, and child." (Lochrie, "Mystical Acts, Queer Tendencies," 187).

139   Caroline Walker Bynum, *Fragmentation and Redemption: Essays on Gender and the Human Body in Medieval Religion* (New York, NY: Zone Books, 2002); Caroline Walker Bynum, *Holy Feast and Holy Fast: The Religious Significance of Food to Medieval Women*, The New Historicism (Berkeley, CA: University of California Press, 2000); Caroline Walker Bynum, *Jesus as Mother*, vol. 16, Publications of the Center for

queer studies of the Middle Ages, the motive of the 'gendered' God has become important in recent decades. As Walker Bynum has pointed out, to categorize this kind of imagery simply as a part of late affective mysticism displayed mainly by women authors would "not only [ignore] the Patristic roots of the image and of the general 12th-century interest in the human Christ but also fails to note the particular characteristics of the 12th-century theme, which puts much less emphasis than the later medieval image on suffering and birth–as–separation much more emphasis on breasts and nurturing, the womb, conception, and union as incorporation."[140]

This is especially true for the works of William, whose spirituality rests on the reception of divine inspiration. His language expresses this focus in the imagery of loving union and spiritual caretaking. He is interested primarily in the possibility of real experience. Not only Christ but the Spirit as well are described in terms that touch upon the readers' senses. As Rozanne Elder poignantly states: "There can be no sense in the human body without the soul, nor can there be a soul without the senses".[141] God is felt, smelled, and savored. It is within this context of broad sensuality, which transcends an all too narrow focus on sexuality that I would like to discuss a few of the images William employs. The first one is named by Walker Bynum as central: the breasts of God. In his use of this motif, William was undoubtedly influenced by the texts of Bernard in as far as he transforms the erotic implications of the female breasts in the Song into an image of maternal nurturing.

Bernard used the notion of breastfeeding to describe the divine gifts of grace and discuss the duties and responsibilities that come with an abbacy.[142] This is accompanied by Bernard's famous conceptualization of the abbot as a mother-figure. Although William shares his concern for ecclesial roles of authority with Bernard, rooted in his biographical disinclination to fulfill the role of the abbot, his usage of the breast motive does not primarily stand in this ecclesial context. This is also reflected in the fact that his discussion of the breasts does not prompt him to speak of God as a

---

Medieval and Renaissance Studies (Berkeley, CA: University of California Press, 1982); and Caroline Walker Bynum, "Jesus as Mother and Abbot as Mother: Some Themes in Twelfth–Century Cistercian Writing," *The Harvard Theological Review* 70, no. 3/4 (1977).

140   Walker Bynum, "Jesus as Mother, Abbot as Mother," 258.

141   E. Rozanne Elder, *Formation for Wisdom, Not Education for Knowledge. Religious Education in Pre–Modern Europe* (Leiden: Brill, 2012), 192.

142   Walker Bynum, "Jesus as Mother, Abbot as Mother," 264.

mother.[143] Instead, the breasts remain male insofar as they are explicitly the *ubera sponsi*. Their nurturing function is overtly feminine, yet that does not make their holder female. The feminine breasts do not seem to curtail the desirability of the male groom but are part of it:

> As if she was interrogated on the origin of such a quick presumption; such a confident claim on a kiss, she says: "from these breasts, Lord, flows your comfort", because your breasts taste better than wine; sweeter to suckle; more effective to bring joy; more likely to intoxicate. Because they have fed me, I desire the kiss. I am inebriated to the point of presumption.[144]

This passage conjures an image of intimacy that blurs the line between erotic and maternal experience. The act of breastfeeding is presented here not only as nurturing but as enticing. It is because the bride was privileged to suck on her lover's breasts that she now desires to kiss him. The offering of the breast is a sign of affection, as mentioned above, that encourages her hope and lets her become more daring in her advances. It becomes clear from this kind of language why William does not draw the same conclusion as Bernard. The bride does not become a child in her affections but is consumed by her desire. A desire that is directed not at a mother but a lover.

William's allegorical exegesis, in this instance, therefore, only purportedly de-sexualizes the image of the Song. Indeed, the Biblical theme is adapted significantly insofar as he does not acknowledge the breasts as the bride's features, as which the Scriptural passage explicitly presents them. Yet, he does not seem to do so to remove the erotic connotations of the female breast from the text, as it so clearly remains present in his interpretation. What, therefore, might be his intention? It is important first to acknowledge that, apart from their erotic effect, the bridegroom's breasts serve a variety of theological functions for William, some of which are original and others that are adaptations of Patristic notions.

A central role of the breast, or rather of their lactation, is to heal the soul. A soul that has been regularly breastfed will recover more easily if she is

---

143   Walker Bynum, "Jesus as Mother, Abbot as Mother," 264.

144   Expositio super Cantica Canticorum, cccm 87, cap. 5, linea 6–10: *Quasi enim interrogata unde tam festina praesumptio, tam fidens osculi exactio: Ab uberibus, inquit, domine, consolationis | tuae. Quia meliora sunt ubera tua uino, dulciora ad sugendum, potentiora ad laetificandum, faciliora ad inebriandum. His enutrita sum ad osculum desiderandum, inebriata ad praesumendum.*

poisoned.[145] Although a modern reader might draw here an analogy to the supposed benefits of breastmilk for the human immune system, biological correlations are not what William has in mind. Instead, he uses an Origenist image, namely the *venenata dogmata*, poisonous heretic beliefs which require the antidote of orthodox doctrine.[146] For William, the milk from the divine breasts will purify the soul who was poisoned in such a manner, particularly if she had already received it several times before (*aliquando suxerunt*). Here, again, William shows that experiences with God are not abrupt and singular but a relationship that requires growth, patience, and fidelity.

As truth and authority, for William, are always closely intertwined with inspiration, milk also is not simply associated with right doctrine but with the works of the Spirit. For him, the odor of the breasts is representative of the seven spiritual gifts.[147] I will later discuss William's olfactory imagery in more detail, but it is important to note here that he combines two Patristic notions. Origen had considered the milk of the breasts to signify pure doctrine and the odor of the groom to represent the Spirit as such. William merges these two interpretations, as he describes the milk not only as something to be tasted but to be scented, emphasizing the Spirit's role in maintaining doctrinal accuracy. He establishes a parallel connection in a third explanation of the breasts:

> Where there are two testaments, there are two breasts of the bridegroom (*sponsi ubera*), from which the milk of all sacraments, accomplished in time for our eternal salvation, is suckled, in order to attain the meal, which is the Word of God, God before God.[148]

Here, the two breasts represent the two Biblical testaments. This passage is particularly important because it explicitly discusses the meaning and the operating principles of Scripture. The Bible pours out the milk 'of all

---

145   Expositio super Cantica Canticorum, cccm 87, cap. 5, linea 25: *Nam et si uirulentum aliquid aliquando aliunde suxerint, necesse est sanari ea ac mundari ad contactum sacrorum uberum horum, et uirtutem et odorem salubrium unguentorum tuorum.*

146   Déchanet ed., in Exposé sur le Cantique des Cantiques, 123, n. 3.

147   Expositio super Cantica Canticorum, cccm 87, cap. 5, linea 33: [...] *fragrantia unguentis optimis.*

148   Expositio super Cantica Canticorum, cccm 87, cap. 7, linea 39: *Vbi duo Testamenta duo ei sunt sponsi ubera, ex quibus lac sugitur omnium sacramentorum pro salute nostra | aeterna temporaliter gestorum, ut perueniatur ad cibum, quod est Verbum Dei, Deus apud Deum.*

accomplished mysteries' that prepares us for the true aliment: the word of God. In the idea of the study of Scripture as spiritually preparatory, William presents a continuation of an Origenist theme, as he uses the analogy of milk preparing the soul for solid food (*cibum*).

Origen had considered certain books of the Bible to be suited for different levels of spiritual maturity – the Song of Songs remaining reserved for those who have already experienced growth through the study of all other books. The milk, representing the kinds of books that displayed a mainly literal meaning, prepared the soul for the books that could only properly be understood allegorically.[149] William takes this imagery even further, as he considers the Biblical nourishment as a whole to be preparatory. The kind of solid food that strengthens the spiritual body is Christ himself. The sacramental undertones of this kind of language are not by any means coincidental.

The Eucharist was, for William, of great theological importance, having been the first Cistercian to present a systematic theology of the Eucharist (in his *De Sacramento altaris*).[150] As Nathaniel Peter points out, William uses the imagery of the Song's kiss not only to describe the *unitas spiritus* but also the union achieved in the Eucharist.[151] The language he employs in the *Expositio* is very fitting to describe the sacramental mystery throughout. The God that William encounters in the Song is a thoroughly sensual one. What better way to express the divine experience than the Eucharist, which is truly the culmination of physical and spiritual experience? What God is more sensually appreciable than the one that can be eaten and tasted? This kind of real fulfillment is what William expresses when he speaks of God's breasts, 'feeding' the sacraments (*lac sugitur omnium sacramentorum*) to the hungry soul.

To a certain degree, the sacramental meaning is already implied in the Biblical statement: your breasts taste better than wine. As an element of the eucharist, the wine is no longer a symbol of worldly pleasure and intoxication but rather the blood of Christ shed for the salvation of humanity. In the texts of other Cistercian authors, such as Aelred, the milk is associated with the wound on Christ's side. The blood that flows from it turns to the wine of wisdom, the water into the milk of consolation.[152] For Aelred these two

---

149 An interesting study on the motive and its reception can be found in Nadean Bishop, "Denial of the Flesh in Origen and Subsequent Implications," *Mystics Quarterly* 14, no. 2 (1988).

150 Sergent, "Introduction," in *A Companion to William of Saint-Thierry*, 6.

151 Peters, "The Eucharistic Theology," 162.

152 Walker Bynum, "Jesus as Mother, Abbot as Mother," 267.

substances were representative of an elitist distinction within the church. The blood (similar to the *cibum* in Origen's explanation) reveals knowledge of God to the few that are able to receive it, while the milk nurtures "the soul of the ordinary believer".[153]

William's conception differs from Aelred's in a few significant points. First, the notion that higher experience is meant for a selected few does not speak from William's works. Rather his strong pneumatological emphasis conveys the impression that all souls have the potential to be drawn toward God and go through the process of ascent. Milk represents thus not the food for the ordinary believer, but for the soul who is still at the beginning of her spiritual progress. Second, William does not describe this path of spiritual growth as one that leads from milk to blood but from the breasts to the mouth of God:

> The bride is deprived of this continual and blessed connection and this eternal kiss on account of the weakness of the human condition. She thus attaches herself to [your breasts], incapable to reach your mouth. She lowers her mouth to your breasts and on them she rests, saying: your breasts taste better than wine.[154]

This passage describes the interaction between the soul and Christ as loving intimacy. Because the soul is not yet ready to receive the kiss of fruition, she lowers her mouth to his breast. The idea that the bride who is longing for a kiss considers the breast an alternative to the lips of her lover reveals the erotic dimension of the theme.[155] Breasts are, for William, not primarily maternal but a source of spiritual satisfaction within the generally erotic framework of the Song. Although the breasts are often described as a source of consolation or calming reassurance (*in eis requiescit*), the comforting presence is not associated in a gendered way with the role of the mother but is presented as a loving gesture of the bridegroom.

Undoubtedly, the breasts are not simply erotic symbols for William. While the bride seems inclined to kiss the divine breasts in a show of affection, the context of spiritual progress makes it clear that they do not

---

153   Walker Bynum, "Jesus as Mother, Abbot as Mother," 267.

154   Expositio super Cantica Canticorum, CCCM 87, cap. 5, linea 28: *Cum ergo a perenni illa ac beata coniunctione et aeternitatis osculo pro infirmitatis humanae conditione sponsa deficit, circa haec se afficit, et ad os illud tuum non pertingens, os suum reflectit ad ubera tua, et in eis requiescit dicens: Quia meliora sunt ubera tua uino.*

155   As it does, very similarly in this passage: *Ac si dicat: Etsi interim non mereor gaudium uultus tui, uel osculi oris tui, saltem odorem mihi ne subtrahas unguentorum tuorum* (Expositio super Cantica Canticorum, CCCM 87, cap. 6, linea 31).

lose the connotation of nurturing either. Instead, the two aspects are interwoven. Milk is recognized as the 'first nourishment of grace',[156] and in
opposition to the carnal pleasures of the world, a source of spiritual pleasure.[157] The soul experiences the breast both as a child, in terms of her spiritual progression, and as a lover, regarding her desire. This intentional
ambiguity raises the question of whether William considers the divine
breasts, particularly their ability to lactate, a female feature. The textual evidence suggests that he does not. Rather, it seems they are symbols that
allow him to illustrate the allegorical body of the bridegroom as attractive,
fertile, and able to fulfill all the bride's needs and desires.

In her response to Walker Bynum's scholarship, Karma Lochrie has particularly criticized the notion that Cistercians had to either feminize God or
cast themselves in a female role to derive effective meaning from erotic language; a widespread scholarly interpretation, which she characterizes as follows: "The ever-vigilant Cistercian, on his guard against the heterosexual
crisis, makes the necessary adjustment by assuming the role of child to par-
ent and eliminating sexuality altogether from his affective relationship with
Christ."[158] Countering this interpretation, she argues for a "conjunction of
the erotic with the maternal, and of mystical pleasure with nurturing".[159] I
would argue that few others represent this precise conjunction as William
does in his exegesis.

Indeed, he does not seem concerned with the boundaries or consistency
of gendered language. This could allow two different kinds of conclusions:
either that the 'heterosexual crisis' of Cistercian authorship never existed in
the first place or that William himself was not as affected by it. As I do not
intend here to comment on the Cistercian tradition as a whole, I have to
state, for now, the latter: William did not make an effort to maintain hetero-
normativity in his language.

That does, however, not necessarily imply that he was consciously trying
to disrupt it. William's literary aim was, as I have pointed out before, to create a spiritual experience by allowing his readers to enter the narrative of
the Song. In the *Expositio*, the bride is a foil of projection, both for his readers' souls and for his own. A sincere and wholehearted *lectio* of the Song
does not result in a theoretical understanding of the soul's journey but

---

156   Expositio super Cantica Canticorum, cccm 87, cap. 5, linea 40: *Mox, inquit, ut ueni ad
      te, nudasti mihi ubera dulcedinis tuae* [...].
157   Expositio super Cantica Canticorum, cccm 87, cap. 5, linea 40: [...] *ex dulcedine suaui-
      tatis tuae et conscientiae bonae meliora super omne uinum sapientiae saecularis, uel lae-
      titiam carnalis uoluptatis* [...].
158   Lochrie, "Mystical Acts, Queer Tendencies," 187
159   Lochrie, "Mystical Acts, Queer Tendencies," 187

encourages the reader to embark on it. Both the Biblical and William's exegetical language work to set the appropriate scene. Whether Christ appears
here in a male, female or trans body is not paramount. What matters are
the sensual experiences of the soul with the divine body, and these are as
manifold as the images William employs.

Maternal and erotic are by far not the only spheres from which he draws
his imagery. To express sensuality, for William, truly means to touch upon
all human senses. Olfactory language, for instance, plays a significant role.
As we have seen before, the bridegroom's lactating breasts might exude a
natural odor. But even more prominent to the soul are the perfumes and
ointments of her Beloved. Christ appears as the 'anointed' in a very perceivable way. His scent entices the bride and signals to her that he is near,
even if she cannot see him. William interprets this notion with his teachings
on virtue:

> The odor of the perfume emitted to the young women is, in regard to
> the bridegroom, the reputation of his virtues: the attractive provoca-
> tion of charity. The unction itself remains, instructing the bride in all
> things.[160]

The bridegroom's virtues attract the 'young women' of the song, inviting
them to follow his example and convincing them to pursue the virtue of
charity. In this passage, sensual attraction is described as the occasion of
spiritual conversion. The will, transformed into desire, is the driving force
of the soul's journey. In another passage, William connects his description
of passionate attraction with the return to image-likeness. The scent of her
bridegroom reminds the soul of all the affection she has already received
from him. Desire transformed into sincere gratitude causes her to pursue him:

> She pursues the fugitive through confession and the memory of her
> blessings – the breasts and the perfume, the odor and the oil that was
> effused, which is the best and most rational mode of prayer, pleasing
> God. It is an efficient way to obtain future blessings to not be ungrate-
> ful in regard to the memories of past ones.[161]

---

160   Expositio super Cantica Canticorum, CCCM 87, cap. 6, linea 12: *Odor unguentorum ad*
       proficientes adolescentulas est fragrans in sponso uirtutum opinio; tractus, caritatis
       prouocatio. Vnctio uero docens de omnibus sponsam manet.

161   Expositio super Cantica Canticorum, CCCM 87, cap. 6, linea 21: *Prosequitur que fugien-*
       tem confessione et commemoratione beneficiorum suorum, uberum scilicet et

At the memory of the milk she received to drink and the odoriferous essen-
ces she was privileged to smell, the soul runs after her Beloved. For William,
this kind of grateful pursuit of God is equivalent to a wise prayer, as the
gratitude for blessings received guarantees more to come. The motive of the
pious *memoria*, which leads the soul toward likeness, reappears several
times in conjunction with sensual language.[162] This is characteristic of William: although he is interested in the theoretical dimension of such concepts as self-knowledge and the return to the *imago*, he is conscious of
different levels of spiritual maturity. Some, like himself, might be able to
contemplate abstract notions in a meaningful way, yet others – particularly
novices – need more relatable imagery, a visual or otherwise sensual guide,
to experience the divine. Thus, at times, the *Expositio* seems to take on the
character of guided meditation. In his use of language, William reveals himself to be interested primarily in the concrete effect of his words on the
faith of his readers.

This practical concern becomes evident in the passages in which William
addresses physical rather than 'simply' allegorical sensuality. Emerged in the
realities of the monastic life, William is well aware that spiritual experiences
are not just projected onto a Biblical narrative or sublimated into *lectio* but
that the actual corporeality of a monk contributes to his religious life. What
a monk sensually perceives within a cloister's walls can intensify his relationship with God. Particularly the daily monastic routine, its practices, and
rituals created such opportunities for embodied spirituality. William discusses, for instance, the experience of hearing the names of Christ, very
likely in the context of audible prayer or the signing of hymns:

> Hearing your name, whether it is "Lord", "Jesus", "Christ", brings joy
> and happiness to my ears. As soon as the name reaches my ear, the
> mystery of the name shines in the heart, love in affect, revealing to the
> Lord devoted servitude; to the Savior – called "Jesus" – piety and love;
> and to Christ the King obedience and reverence.[163]

---

unguentorum, odoris et olei effusi, quia optimum et rationabile est orandi genus, gratum
que Deo, et efficax ad obtinenda futura beneficia non ingrata recor|datio praeteritorum.

162   For instance in this passage: [...] *et redeundum ei est ad memoriam cellariorum et ube-*
      rum [...] (Expositio super Cantica Canticorum, CCCM 87, cap. 7, linea 33).

163   Expositio super Cantica Canticorum, CCCM 87, cap. 5, linea 56: *Audito enim nomine*
      tuo, siue "domini", siue "Iesu", siue "Christi", continuo auditui meo datum est gaudium et
      laetitia, quia mox ut nomen sonuerit in auditu, mysterium etiam nominis effulget in
      corde, amor in affectu; suggerens | ad dominum deuotam seruitutem; ad saluatorem,
      quod sonat Iesus, pietatem et amorem; ad Christum regem, obedientiam ac timorem.

In this passage, William illustrates the substantial effects that terms of reverence – Lord, Jesus, and Christ – exert on those who hear it. The very moment in which the divine name 'hits the ears', the divine mystery rings true in the heart. Thus, through the senses, the faithful soul is animated to turn toward God. This not only presents the senses, which in Christian mysticism are often considered hindrances, as potentially positive factors in the process of ascent, but it also points to the theological importance of nominal designations. Although William does not expressly address his conflict with Abelard in this context, it is impossible to read this passage without recollecting his insistence on the importance of the Trinitarian titles. They are not just names but contain themselves the creating, redeeming, and inspiring power of the One that carries them.

What William describes, though, is not simply onomatopoetical magic. A name has the potential to invoke a mental visualization, such as a concrete idea or distinct memory. William explains the spiritual effect of hearing the divine names, as a process that primarily involves human *memoria*. The soul, enticed by the sound of the name, is reminded instantly of its beholder and the kinds of blessings she had received from him:

> It is rightful, Lord Jesus, that all bow their knee at the sound of your name, in the heavens, on earth, and in hell. There is not one name that has no relation to us, and not one relation that does not reveal to us one of your goodness; Lord, you reign through your blessings; "Jesus", you save; "Christ", that is the "anointed" king and priest, you reign and you intercede.[164]

There is, William believes, no possible designation for God that magically invokes an image of the soul's relationship with her divine lover. Thus, whatever the soul audibly perceives of God, sets her into a particular relationship with God. Not only is she reminded of the divine acts, but of herself as the one who is blessed, saved and subject. In other words, the sensual experience contributes here to restore the soul's true and authentic self, her intended status, and her likeness.

---

164   Expositio super Cantica Canticorum, CCCM 87, cap. 5, linea 61: *Merito enim, domine Iesu, in omni nomine tuo omne genu flectitur caelestium, terrestrium et infernorum, quia nullo nomine nominaris, nisi aliqua ad nos relatione; nec ulla est alicuius nominis tui relatio, quae non sit aliqua alicuius boni tui ad nos delatio; quia "dominus" dominaris benefaciendo; "Iesus" saluas; "Christus", id est unctus rex uel sacerdos, regis uel propitiaris.*

This shows, as many of the examples mentioned that William's language is not just poetic but is directly reflective of his theological concepts. The sensuality of his mystic spirituality is not just a literary choice. On the one hand, it is the product of an author who is so personally affected by the works of the Spirit that his description of his spiritual journey naturally results in a tangible portrait of the human–divine relationship. On the other hand, it is part of William's pedagogical program to address not only his readers' minds but also their hearts and senses. His understanding of spiritual guidance considers the human experience in its entirety to be an active part of the soul's journey. His spiritual instruction, therefore, demands a multisensual approach.

F. Tyler Sergent has pointed out that it is unclear whether the *fruitio*, the culmination of spiritual experience, is something William believes to be possible in the current life or in the life to come. He attributes this to "William's own uncertainty and the vicissitudes of contemplative life".[165] While this might be true for the particular notion of the ultimate *unitas* of the soul with God, I would argue that William does not hold an all too narrow focus on the kiss as the climax of spiritual experience.

Rather, his work is brimming with the potential of sensuality; although the intensity and type of relationship the soul experiences change throughout the Song, she is never untouched. Even in her longing moments, seemingly separated from her bridegroom, she remains consumed by her desire, which is itself an expression of divine love.[166] Whether this erotic dance can come to fruition remains reserved for the afterlife or not is thus a secondary question for William. What he is confident in, and that is what defines his exegesis, is that the soul is enveloped in the sweetness, the bitterness, the gentleness, and the beauty of God here and now.

---

165   Sergent, "Sources and Influences," 63.

166   The theme of the longing soul in the context of spiritual frustration is a central theme in William's meditations, as is beautifully illustrated in the following passage: *Ignosce, Domine, ignosce improbitati et importunitati meae. Adhuc audemus, quia ardemus. Ignis tuus urget nos, quem uenisti in terram mittere, et uoluisti uehementer accendi. Obsecro te per omnipotentissimam bonitatem tuam et per mansuetissimam semper in nos patientiam tuam, patere adhuc me aliquid quaerentem, et dic animae meae quid est quod desiderat, cum faciem tuam desiderat* (Meditativae Orationes, CCCM 89, Med. 3, par. 7).

Conclusion to Part 2

Jean–Marie Déchanet has described the *Expositio* as an expression of William's eclecticism: in his work, he seamlessly combines the theories of the Fathers, the ecclesial tradition, and his original ideas.[1] About his Commentary on Romans, William himself had raised the question to what extent the work is really his own, or not rather an edited collection of different Patristic voices. Is it appropriate to ask this same question about his exegesis of the Song of Songs? Discussing William's exegetical process more broadly – not merely based on his Commentary but on his various intellectual and personal encounters with the Song's text – enables us to view his relationship with authority as developing and changing rather than rigid. We have identified different forms of receptivity and originality throughout the various highlighted aspects of his engagement with the Song, and I would like to iterate some of the most prominent.

I have hesitated to discuss Bernard as a figure of authority influencing William's work, as the supposed dependence on Bernard has long kept scholarship from viewing William as an autonomous author. Yet it is undeniable, given William's account of their relationship, that he had considered his friend an inspirational teacher. Bernard's personal spirituality had made him privy to the kind of mystical insight for which William was striving. In the *Expositio* on Romans, William noted that the authorities on whose works his own depended were both the Fathers of the past and the contemporaries whose claims did not transgress the boundaries the Fathers had set. Bernard is one of the few concrete examples of such influential contemporaries. While I would not go as far as to give equal status to Bernard and the Church Fathers, that have heavily influenced the systematic and doctrinal aspects of William's work, the "mechanism" of authority seems to be the same in both cases. An author's authority depends on their spiritual growth, a factor comprised of both discipline and morality, as well as divine grace.

In the upcoming chapters, I will discuss, among other texts, the *Vita Prima Sancti Bernardi* – the hagiography William composed of his friend – and will be able to go into more detail regarding the esteem William had for Bernard not merely on an intellectual, but a spiritual level. Yet, to conclude the recent chapters, I would like to emphasize what William's inclusion of

---

1 Déchanet, "Introduction" in Exposé sur le Cantique des Cantiques, 51.

© DELPHINE CONZELMANN, 2025 | DOI:10.1163/9789004730878_011

contemporary thought into the chorus of authoritative voices means for his work and self-conception. The awarding of an authoritative status is not limited to the authors of the early church. William's understanding of authority heavily depends on his anthropology, his conception of image-likeness in particular. It is the return of the soul to its intended likeness to the Creator that allows for any kind of theological knowledge. Consequently, authority is not a matter of a person's ecclesial standing per se but of their spiritual development. Hence, the ranks of the church Fathers are not closed but open to those who lead exemplary and enlightened lives.

William's Commentary on the Song differs from his Commentary on Romans, particularly regarding its stated intention. Whereas in the latter, he claimed to lay out the opinions of the Fathers, in the former, he presents his approach as much more experiential. Yet, as Déchanet points out, "even though he wants to rely only on the experience of love – his love – the author cannot but stay true to the [...] Fathers of the Church".[2] His own experience of God is, even if only in parts, the same experience as the one that has provided insight for the Fathers. Any knowledge revealed from the same divine source participates in the same kind of truth. According to his representation of the work, William believes his interpretation of the Song to be orthodox and in line with traditional thought because it was written in the same Spirit, in which the Patristic readings of the text were also composed.

However, this kind of inspired knowledge, accessible through likeness, is not to be mistaken with the idea of a literal, verbal inspiration. On the contrary: it provides a broad path of acceptable truth, within which there is much room for personal expression and emphasis. William carefully differentiates between each of the Fathers' respective claims to authority. This has become especially apparent in my discussion of his florilegia. William clearly distinguished between the works of Ambrose and Gregory, both because of their historical priorities and specialties and his admiration for each of them. Ambrose was very useful to William (both regarding the Song and his conflict with Abelard) by virtue of his uncontroversial defense of the purity of the catholic faith. His florilegium of Ambrose, thus, has the character of a compilation of different noteworthy citations, much like a reference book. On the other hand, William's great appreciation for Gregory

---

2   "Si personnel que soit l'Éxposé, l'auteur, bien que 'replié sur lui–même' et ne voulant faire appel qu'à l'expérience de l'amour, de son propre amour, pour tout dire, l'auteur ne peut que rester fidèle [aux] Pères de l'Église" (Déchanet, "Introduction," in *Exposé sur le Cantique des Cantiques*, 51).

encompasses matters of personal and communal ethics, exegetical virtuosity, and mythical insight. His florilegium thus reads much less disjointed than the one he compiled of Ambrosian content and much more like a carefully composed commentary in its own right.

A similar distinction between particular Fathers is observable in the Patristic reception William displayed in his Commentary on the Song. As I have shown, his usage of Origen differs fundamentally from his usage of Augustine, both in kind and extent. While Augustine, the Doctor of Grace, provides the larger theological framework of William's thought, especially regarding doctrinal questions. William's Cistercian thought is thoroughly Augustinian in its structure; Augustinian ideas permeate the *Expositio*, despite Augustine's lack of particular interest in the Song and thus very few direct citations. Origen, on the other hand, despite being quoted and referred to much more explicitly in the Commentary, has significantly less impact on its theological nature. The Origenist references in question can be considered exegetical complements: They primarily provide etymological information, historical context, and linguistic embellishments. Although some of the central themes of his work are indeed originally Origenist, they are either transmitted to him through the works of other Fathers, such as Gregory (as is the case in his reception of the theme of self-knowledge), or they are presented in conjunction with Augustinian ideas, giving them the character of literary motives, rather than defining concepts.

While it seems as though William creates a hierarchy of Fathers, I would like to point out that he always does so regarding specific questions. In his conversations with Bernard and in his Expositio, it was his explicit goal to discuss 'one particular moral sense', acknowledging that there are many more interpretations to expound. Within this acknowledgment, there is an openness towards depths of meaning in exegetical approaches that differ from his own and an appreciation for various readings. While there certainly are Church Fathers he was more eager to receive, and whose content he more readily incorporated in his thought than others, he does not do so because he attributes more knowledge or insight to them, but simply more value for his projects.

Throughout his works, William desires to present tradition as a harmonious choir, focusing not on the possible dissonances between the Fathers but on how their voices work together to produce a single tune. In the preface to his *Expositio*, he boldly excluded the 'bothersome' questions, which might lead to doubt regarding the doctrinal homogeneity among the Fathers. While Abelard's assumption of disagreement within the Patristic corpus essentially led him to understand his task as a philosophical 'referee' of sorts, discussing conflicting positions from a logical distance, William was working with a different basic supposition: his fundamental belief in divine inspiration as the foundation of all valid theological reflection required him to defend the idea of Patristic unanimity – not only as a result of his inquiry but as its starting point. Within this framework, William could not present his exegetical contributions as innovations or necessary amendments but as yet another voice in the choir of catholic tradition, adding intensity and depth.

PART 3

William's Vision for Life in the Monastic Community

∵

Introduction to Part 3

In this last part of this book, I turn my attention to an aspect of William's life that underlines most of his spiritual and doctrinal works: his concern for the Cistercian reform movement. Even beyond his years serving as the abbot of Saint–Thierry, his care for the monastic communities he served has informed his literary efforts. On account of the source selection, this part is the shortest of the three parts of this volume; this, however, should not lead to conclusions regarding its significance. It is through William's efforts for the Cistercian movement that his defense of orthodox faith and his exegetical work have to be revisited. The purpose of the following chapter is thus to embed William's understanding of authority in the context of 12th- century monasticism, its documents, and its most prominent figures.

The primary source that will provide insight into this question is the *Epistula ad Fratres de Monte Dei* – The Golden Epistle. William had written it for the Carthusian community of Mont Dieu. It is a text primarily discussing the spiritual formation of the new members of their community. In it, William reflects on the ideals of early monasticism, which were – both for the Carthusian and the Cistercian movement – the central point of reference in their reform efforts. The text allows conclusions regarding the importance William ascribed to monastic reform as such, as well as the aspects he highlighted. While the text is more practical in nature, discussing the concrete elements of a monk's everyday life, it also reveals how William made his complex doctrinal ideas fruitful for his readers' personal spiritual growth. It enables us, thus, to understand more clearly what William considered the appropriate application and interpretation of his thought.

In the first upcoming chapter, I will contextualize the Golden Epistle and its role in these times of change for Christian monasticism, specifically the Carthusian context for which it was written, and William's own Cistercian background. This also entails touching upon the relationship between the Carthusian and the Cistercian stream and the consequential possibility of a Cistercian monk and former Benedictine abbot providing a formational document for a community that was not his own. This will provide insight into the text's significance during this period, and frame William as an author who contributed considerably to the reform of monastic practice in the 12th century and beyond.

Since the purpose of this volume is the study of authoritative ideals arising from William's works, they merit specific attention in the second

© DELPHINE CONZELMANN, 2025 | DOI:10.1163/9789004730878_012

chapter of this part. While the Golden Epistle will certainly serve as the main source, other texts, particularly the *Vita Prima Sancti Bernardi* provide helpful illustrations. In the *Vita prima*, a hagiographic account of Bernard's life, William's understanding of the ideal hierarchical structure of monastic communities and his appreciation for the Bernardine brand of authority becomes especially apparent. More narrative in kind, the *Vita prima* enriches the structured and pedagogical tone of the Epistle. Together, these two texts paint a lively image of William's vision for future monasticism.

It is important to note that these deliberations do not directly translate into a well-balanced portrayal of the reality of reform monasticism. William's perspective, both on the virtues he believed Bernard to personify and on the ideals he attributed to the Cistercian community, are somewhat skewed by his well-attested preference for a more eremitic interpretation of the otherwise cenobitic and community-focused Cistercian movement. The way this chapter understands the term of reform, then, is subject to some limitations: The concrete changes pursued by many Cistercian figures, for instance in the field of liturgical structure and music, are not my primary focus, but rather provide the background of my study on William's usage of ideals when discussing conceptions and applications of authority in monastic reform.

Reform always entails rethinking certain aspects of tradition and introducing what some might consider new or innovative. Given what we have already learned of William's general stance towards (primarily doctrinal) innovation, it will be important to define what he believes 'reform' to be and what it is not. As Karl Morrison has pointed out, innovation was only ever successful and possible within the medieval framework in the form of mimetic reform. Reformers claimed not to introduce entirely novel ideas but to recover what they considered foundational and longstanding Christian ideals.[1] In this light, we will have to analyze William's beliefs regarding authority, tradition, and the necessity of renewal.

Yet authority also plays a significant role for the development of communal life and practice. Based on the Epistle and William's appreciation of Bernard's leadership in the *Vita Prima,* I will take a closer look at how he believes authority should be exerted within the context of spiritual brotherhood. It will become clear from this discussion that the concepts which I have presented in the context of William's exegetical work, such as the ideas of self-knowledge, and image-likeness, are indeed not theoretical or intellectual gimmicks but are intended to shape and influence everyday monastic life concretely.

---

1   see Morrison, *The Mimetic Tradition of Reform in the West,* 172–177.

CHAPTER 6

The Golden Epistle in the Context of Reform

1   A History of Misattribution

Before I discuss the historical background of monastic reform in the 12th century, it is necessary to discuss briefly the history of the Golden Epistle's attribution to William. The text's reception history played a significant role in the century-long disappearance of William from the gaze of Christian scholarship. The first interesting aspect of the text's reception is that it was transmitted primarily by the Cistercian order, despite having been originally addressed to the Carthusian community of Mont–Dieu. As Jean–Marie Déchanet pointed out, two families of manuscript versions exist, the larger of which is the Cistercian family.[1] Most of the early manuscripts were copied under the name of William. However, as the circle of distribution widened over time, the Epistle was attributed to other, more famous authors. Some manuscripts witness the authorship of Anselm of Canterbury or Guigo I.[2] By the 14th century, the Epistle was associated exclusively with Bernard's name.[3] The most plausible explanation for this history of misattribution is the communities' admiration of Bernard's exceptional authoritative status throughout the Middle Ages and beyond. A monastic library was more interested in possessing a work of Bernard, who was considered the Father of affective mysticism and whose influence was, rightfully, believed to be indispensable to the flowering of the Cistercian order. It might be one of the ironies of William's life that his profound advancement of Bernardine veneration contributed to the obscurity of his own corpus.[4]

Notably, many of the Epistle's later manuscripts only contain excerpts of the Epistle. Rather than standalone works, they were part of collections.

---

1   Jean–Marie Déchanet, "Les manuscrits de la Lettre aux Frères du Mont–Dieu de Guillaume de Saint–Thierry et le problème de la «préface» dans Charleville 114," *Scriptorium* 8, no. 2 (1954): 237.

2   Elder, "The Eye of Reason – The Eye of Love," 230.

3   Myers, "William's Legacy," 197.

4   Bernard McGinn, *The Growth of Mysticism: Gregory the Great Through the 12 Century,* vol. 2, The Presence of God. A History of Western Christian Mysticism (New York, NY: Crossroad, 1996), 226.

Some of these collections concerned Carthusian theology and canon law,[5] while others were anthologies of Bernardine and pseudo-Bernardine works.[6] However, even as early as the 14th century, the authorship of Bernard did not go entirely uncontested. Famously, Jean Gerson had already raised questions concerning the theological and stylistic compatibility of the Epistle with other Bernardine works.[7] His doubts, however, did not incite a larger controversy. It was not until 1924 that William's authorship was finally held to be proven by the scholarship of André Wilmart.[8]

Based on autobiographical passages in the preface of the Epistle, the discovery of William as an author of the Epistle also led to the correct attribution of some of his other works.[9] Ever since these groundbreaking findings were made public, William has moved in the focus of Cistercian research, and scholars have successfully worked at liberating him from Bernard's shadow.[10] Given the context of the Epistle's original composition and the fact that the community of Mont–Dieu requested William's works because of his authoritative role in 12th-century monasticism, the rediscovery of his authorship could be viewed as a restoration of the status he had enjoyed in his time.

Since the aspect of authority is central to the reception history of the Epistle, I would like to briefly mention one of the earlier print versions of

---

5   A suitable example is a manuscript collection from 1466, currently preserved at the University of Basel. It was written by a scribe of the Carthusian monastery in Basel and contains other texts from Bernard, Petrus de Alliaco, Jean Gerson, Marsilius Carthusiensis, and other authors. The texts are both theological, concerning for instance the nature of Christ, and very practical, concerning such matters as the consumption of meat in Carthusian practice (*Theologica und Juridica mit Bezug auf die Karthäuser*, manuscript collection, *A VI 14, 1466*, currently preserved at the University of Basel, https://www.e-codices.unifr.ch/en/description/ubb/A-VI-0014/HAN (accessed January 10, 2025)).

6   An example would be the late 15th-century codex *S. Bernardus Claraevallensis, Opuscula Selecta*, manuscript, *zbs S 231, 15th century*, currently preserved at the Benediktinerkloster Mariastein, https://www.e-codices.unifr.ch/de/list/one/bkm/S-0231 (accessed January 10, 2025).

7   As Aage Rydstrøm–Poulsen retraces, Gerson's criticism was received in the early 20th century by the French scholar Pierre Pourrat, who noted heterodox tendencies in the work (see Rydstrøm–Poulsen, "William and the Soul," 125).

8   Wilmart, "La série et la date," 157–167.

9   Rydstrøm–Poulsen, "William and the Soul," 125.

10   As Elder has put it, "the subsequent trickle of researchers delving into his thought and the events of his life has become a rising tide." (Elder, "The Eye of Reason – The Eye of Love," 230).

the text, which reveals possible motifs and benefits that communities and individual authors could have generated from the misattribution to Bernard. As an English print from the 16th century shows, the Epistle could be attached to later visionary and mystic literature as a preface of sorts. The early modern edition in question was printed in 1535 by Thomas Godfray under the following title: "An epistle of sai[n]t Bernarde, called the golden epistle, whiche he se[n]t to a yo[n]g religyous man whom he moche loued. And after the sayd epistle, foloweth four reuelations of Saint Birget".[11] Although the version is not representative per se, it allows several interesting observations regarding the creative repurposing of the original text for later communities.

First, the Epistle was significantly shortened. The text was reduced to its more general moral message. It thus lacks most of the contextual information that could have allowed for the correct identification of its author. For instance, the biographical references to William's other works are entirely missing. Even more so, the Epistle does not name its original addressees, the community of Mont Dieu. Instead, the text is introduced as "An epystell of saīt Bernard / whiche he sente to a yonge relygyous man whom he moch loued / that is called the golden Epystell." The version asserts that the Epistle was a personal letter, rather than an instructional text, written for a particular monastic community. The Latin plural is translated consistently as singular and the text contains no references to Mont Dieu nor the Carthusian order.

The most exciting aspect of the version is that it was published alongside the visions of Saint Bridget of Sweden. It was thus considered a well-suited preface for other works that shared some of its core themes. The prepended excerpt of the Epistle essentially introduces the concept of a good life, as exemplified by Bridget. The selected passages of the Epistle concern particularly the importance of leaving the secular world behind and finding joy in the suffering that comes with such a grave decision. These passages provide a well-suited backdrop for the biography of Bridget. Her wealthy, pagan past is contrasted with her conscious conversion and devotion to Christ; a life lived in self-imposed poverty that resembles William's idealization of the

---

11   Godfray, Thomas. *An epistle of sai[n]t Bernarde, called the golden epistle, whiche he se[n]t to a yo[n]g religyous man whom he moche loued. And after the sayd epistle, foloweth four reuelations of Saint Birget*, book, A–C (C8 blank), *1535*, currently preserved at the British Library, https://www.proquest.com/docview/2240870350/citation/9DEA5E3DD6E64DEDPQ/1 (accessed January 10, 2025).

Carthusian life pretty closely. Although the Council of Basel had confirmed the orthodoxy of her teachings in 1436, her texts were rather daring. Around the time the version in question was printed (1535), harsh criticism of Bridget's visions was voiced, especially from reformers, such as Martin Luther, who had called her 'crazy Bridget' (tolle Brigitte).[12] Eamon Duffy had characterized her texts and doctrinal statements as "clearly immensely attractive to lay people," but not "easy to accommodate within even the wide bounds of fifteenth-century orthodoxy".[13] The fact that her visions were printed during this particular time, not as a standalone work but attached to a widely received text, presumably written by one of the most illustrious figures of the Middle Ages, certainly enhanced the authority of Bridget's texts.

Brian McGuire has argued that the early misattribution of the Golden Epistle to such authorities as Bernard "only served to make works such as the Golden Epistle better known and more available".[14] The usage of the letter as an introduction or confirmation of legitimacy for other works supports this notion. To a certain extent, it is paradoxical that a work that has, as I have mentioned above, furthered the obscurity of William's works for a long time has also allowed his thought to become much more widespread and miscellaneously used than it would probably have under his own name. Once William's authorship was confirmed, the relevancy the Epistle had gained throughout the ages warranted the increasing scholarly attention he subsequently received.

Research on the reception of the Golden Epistle has significantly benefitted from Volker Honemann's studies of medieval manuscripts.[15] Special attention has been given to the usage of the text in later mystical authorship

---

12   Luther, Martin. *An Kurfürsten zu Sachsen und Landgrafen zu Hessen von dem gefangenen Herzog zu Braunschweig. 1545.* Edited by Otto Clemen. *Band 4 Schriften von 1529–1545.* De Gruyter, 2016, 407.

13   Duffy, Eamon. *The Stripping of the Altars: Traditional Religion in England; c.1400–c. 1580* (New Haven: Yale University Press, 2005), 255.

14   McGuire, "Bernard of Clairvaux," 245.

15   see Volker Honemann, *Die "Epistola Ad Fratres de Monte Dei" Des Wilhelm von Saint–Thierry: Lateinische Überlieferung Und Mittelalterliche Übersetzungen,* vol. 61. Münchener Texte Und Untersuchungen Zur Deutschen Literatur Des Mittelalters (München, 1978); "Eine Neue Handschrift Der Deutschen Epistola Ad Fratres de Monte Dei," in *Überlieferungsgeschichtliche Editionen Und Studien Zur Deutschen Literatur Des Mittelalters. Kurt Ruh Zum 75. Geburtstag,* ed. Konrad Kunze, Johannes Gottfried Mayer, and Bernhard Schnell, 1989; and "The Reception of William of Saint–Thierry's Epistola Ad Fratres de Monte Dei during the Middle Ages," in *Cistercians in the Late*

and the ways in which such concepts as the *unitas spiritus* have possibly shaped the intensity of 13th- and 14th-century mysticism. Glenn E. Myers, for instance, has discussed the Epistle's influence on Johannes Tauler (1300–1361) and his concept of the *unio mystica*.[16] Another interesting study has been brought forth by John Arblaster and Paul Verdeyen, focusing on how the theology of the Hadewijch of Brabant (1200–1260) is similar to and was possibly influenced by the anthropology and Trinitarian conception of William.[17] Given these initial observations, I believe the field to be promising because of the text's long history of misattribution. While Bernard's influence on Martin Luther has been documented,[18] medieval and Reformation authors, who have as yet been identified to have been influenced by Bernard, might, in light of the Epistle's re-attribution to William, be found to have relied upon his thought instead.[19]

2 Two Perspectives on Reform

I will now turn my attention to the immediate historical context of the Epistle's composition. William addressed his Epistle to the Carthusian community of Mont–Dieu in the French Ardennes. By that time – the composition of the Epistle was dated to 1144/45[20] – William had already retired to the Cistercian community of Signy. This begs the question, of course, to what extent the Cistercian and the Carthusian communities were in dialogue with each other and influenced by each other's key authors. Indeed, the

---

      Middle Ages, ed. E. Rozanne Elder, Cistercian Studies 64 (Kalamazoo, MI: Cistercian Publications, 1981).

16   Myers, "William's Legacy," 67–92.

17   John Arblaster and Paul Verdeyen, "The Reciprocity of Spiritual Love in William of Saint–Thierry and Hadewijch," *International Journal of Philosophy and Theology* 78, no. 1/2 (2017): 39. Paul Verdeyen has proposed such a connection already in an earlier study, in which he discussed not only Hadewijch's, but also Jan van Ruusbroec's possible reception of William: Paul Verdeyen, "De Invloed van William van Saint–Thierry Op Hadewijch En Ruusbroec," *Ons Geestelijk Erf* 51 (1977): 3–19.

18   see Franz Posset, *Pater Bernardus: Martin Luther and Bernard of Clairvaux* (Kalamazoo, MI: Cistercian Publications, 1999).

19   Bernard McGinn has observed for instance that the Golden Epistle had significant impact on the work of 13th-century German mystic David of Augsburg, who had attributed the Epistle to Bernard (Bernard, McGinn, *The Flowering of Mysticism: Men and Women in the New Mysticism (1200–1350)* (New York, NY: Crossroad, 1998), 115–16).

20   Verdeyen, "La chronologie des oeuvres," 194, as cited in McGuire, "A Chronology," 15.

similarities between the two communities – particularly during their respective founding phases – are striking. To understand why William would address a community that was not his own, we must explore the direction of monastic reform during this time and the central elements these two exponents shared with one another.

The 11th and 12th centuries were times of immense creativity regarding different forms of monastic living. In his comprehensive study on Medieval Monasticism, Gert Melville presents many of the then-arising movements and communities under the heading "Return to the Desert".[21] These movements, Melville argues, are usually founded by a charismatic leader with the intention to retreat from the world, and particularly the worldliness that had, in their eyes, tainted existing monastic communities as well, to live a more austere life. He names, in particular, the Grandmonites (founded by Stephen of Thiers) and the Carthusians (founded by Bruno of Cologne),[22] yet the Premonstratensians (founded by Norbert of Xanten) and the Cistercians (founded by Robert of Molesme) would fall under the same category. In a time of great financial, cultural, and intellectual prosperity, these communities shared a rejection of wealth, political entanglements, and intellectual grandeur and desired a life of poverty instead.[23] Melville identifies three steps in developing these 11th- and 12th-century communities: the renunciation of worldly attachments, the proclamation of a religious movement by a charismatic figure, and the institutionalization of the movement into a community with shared rules.[24]

However, this process unfolded in a different manner for all of these communities. Differences occurred particularly in the extent to which they were able to implement their theoretical ideals of secludedness, and in their respective perspectives on the role of community. The fulfilment of their ideals of solitude, inwardness and personal spiritual growth could be viewed on a spectrum: While the Carthusians, for instance, emphasized eremitic elements within a cenobitic structure, communal life was much more active and encouraged within a Cistercian framework.

Their respective processes of institutionalization further complicates a contrasting study of the various reform movements of the 12th century. In

---

21   Gert Melville, *The World of Medieval Monasticism: Its History and Forms of Life* (Collegeville, MI: Liturgical Press, 2016).

22   Melville, *The World of Medieval Monasticism*, 106.

23   Burton and Kerr, *The Cistercians in the Middle Ages*, 1.

24   Melville, *The World of Medieval Monasticism*, 121–22.

the case of the Cistercians, Constance Hoffman Berman argues that until the community was transformed into an order, the term Cistercian described "a way of life and not a group to which one belongs".[25] This is important to note, given the similarities between some of these communities and the active contact between their respective founding figures. It is perhaps not helpful to view these communities as competitors in a field of religious options;[26] rather, they could be viewed as partners in the larger project of spiritual reform, on which they had distinct perspectives. This notion is exemplified, for instance, by the fact that Bernard had considered the Premonstratensians and the Cistercians to be cousins or close relatives.[27]

Therefore, the extraordinary success of the Cistercians cannot be understood as a singular phenomenon but only in the context of the general climate of spiritual yearning in which it was founded. Louis Lekai expresses this when he speaks of the "loud and spontaneous echo Cîteaux's spirituality evoked among the congenial members of the devout generation".[28] Without the simultaneous and shared impact of other groups pursuing similar ideals, Cîteaux might have just been an isolated case of intensified, and liturgically simplified monastic life.[29] None of the communities of this time could have in and of themselves become a 'reform movement' if the desire for fundamental and structural reform had not been more widely shared.

What they had in common, justifying their claim to reform, was their rejection of what has largely become known as the Cluniac tradition.[30] One of

---

25   Constance Hofmann Berman, *The Cistercian Evolution: The Invention of a Religious Order in Twelfth-Century Europe* (Philadelphia: University of Pennsylvania Press, 2010), 222–23.

26   This is not to say, however, that there was no room for criticism among each other (see Ian P.Wei, *Intellectual Culture in Medieval Paris: Theologians and the University, c.1100–1330* (Cambridge: Cambridge University Press, 2012), 52).

27   see Brian McGuire, "Monastic and Religious Orders, c. 1100–c.1350," in *The Cambridge History of Christianity: Volume 4: Christianity in Western Europe, c.1100–c.1500*, ed. Miri Rubin and Walter Simons, 4: 54–72. Cambridge History of Christianity. Cambridge: Cambridge University Press, 2009, 63.

28   Louis J. Lekai, *The Cistercians: Ideals and Reality* (OH: Kent State University Press, 1989), 50–51.

29   As it was, however, Cîteaux could be considered "but one experiment – a highly successful one – in a series of attempts to find the most perfect form of monastic life and observance" (Burton and Kerr, *The Cistercians in the Middle Ages*, 1).

30   Thomson and Winterbottom point out that this rejection is what made the Carthusians and Cistercians similarly prone to criticism "singling out hypocrisy and a false sense of superiority as vices peculiar to the new Orders" (Winterbottom and Thomson, "Introduction" in For and Against Abelard, xxi).

the primary concerns was the limitation of the liturgical practice, which had become a central and, in some cases, even exclusive monastic task for the Cluniac Benedictines.[31] The Cistercian effort to simplify the daily liturgy should, however, not imply that they rejected the great importance of the liturgy for a monastic community – even though it was perceived as such by some Cluniac critics, such as Matthew of Albano, as William himself points out.[32] Julie Kerr summarizes the Cistercian perspective on the matter as an effort "to impose a liturgy that was simple and faithful to the Rule of St Benedict, and stripped away appendages that had steadily accumulated over the centuries".[33] The concrete changes were a reduction of the daily liturgy to the eight canonical hours and a daily conventional mass, and a recitation of the psalmody within a week, rather than, as was Cluniac custom, within a single day.[34] With these changes, the Cistercians sought to return the liturgy to the role the earliest Benedictine communities had assigned for it.

For many Cistercians, this meant to pay great attention to liturgical details, and to put great effort into its preservation. Diane Reilly explains the contribution of Early Cistercian monks to the history of liturgical documents beautifully, as she points out: "The manuscripts they copied, confined to 'the Bible and the patristic tradition' identified by Leclercq as the core of liturgical learning, are replete with images that both echo the lections and chants they had heard communally, and affirm the importance of hearing, speaking, and ingesting the Word".[35]

The simplification of liturgical life also extended to what was perceived as Cluniac excess, though various Cistercian authors emphasized different aspects in their criticism. While Bernard famously criticized the splendor and extravagant decor of Cluniac churches in his *Apologia ad Guillelmum*

---

31   Wim Verbaal, "Cistercians in Dialogue: Bringing the World into the Monastery," in *The Cambridge Companion to the Cistercian Order*, ed. Mette Birkedal Bruun, 233–44, Cambridge Companions to Religion (Cambridge: Cambridge University Press, 2012), 235.

32   *Dicitis: "Silentium imposuistis, psalmodiam abiecistis et opera manuum nequaquam facitis". Dicitis: "Silentium imponere, psalmodiam decurtare, ad opera <manuum> non exire, quae est ista noua lex? Quae est ista noua doctrina? Vnde noua ista doctrina? Vnde noua ista praesumptio et inaudita?" Et post aliquanta: "Dilectissimi, redite ad cor, et nolite ambulare in magnis neque in mirabilibus super uos* (Responsio Abbatum, cccm 89, linea 172–176).

33   Julie Kerr, "An Essay on Cistercian Liturgy," for *Cistercians in Yorkshire* (University of Sheffield, 2004), 3.

34   Kerr, "An Essay on Cistercian Liturgy," 3.

35   Reilly, *The Cistercian Reform*, 16.

Abbatem, written to William in 1125,[36] and warned against an overexcitement of the visual senses, Aelred of Rievaulx focused on the auditory senses, arguing heavily against "musical embellishments," as Julie Kerr points out.[37]

The Cistercian criticism of 'excessive liturgy' ought to be framed, however, in the context of their desire to revive the Benedictine rule, specifically its balance between *ora* and *labora*. The simplification and reduction of liturgical times allowed for a reintroduction of, or rather a renewed emphasis on labor as a part of the monks' daily lives. The significance attributed to labor was a feature of many monastic reform movements.[38] To facilitate the tasks required within a particular community, and to allow them to live in a largely self-sustaining way, while remaining committed to their spiritual ideals, both the Cistercians and the Carthusians, as well as other groups, relied on the practice of including so-called *conversi* – adult converts – into their communities.[39] These *conversi* would sometimes consist of local hermits and small, unaffiliated ascetic groups looking for a rule to adopt or leadership to which they could subject themselves.[40]

A second important purpose of the liturgical simplification, beside the revival of labor as monastic requirement, was a special attentiveness to times of personal and devotion. For the Cistercians, individual prayer, notions of spiritual friendship and communal love became central. The Carthusians, on the other hand, while certainly not neglecting the importance of prayer, had a stricter approach to silence and individual reclusion, which intensified the focus on written culture in these communities. During their founding period, the Carthusians were known and revered for their diligent transcriptions and well-equipped libraries.[41]

Both the Cistercians and Carthusians referred in their ideals to the lives of the early Desert Fathers and Eastern tradition, transgressing and expanding on the Benedictine Rule to different degrees. The roots of Christian monasticism, they believed, were defined by a commitment to poverty, strict

---

36   see on this text for instance: Conrad Rudolph, "Bernard of Clairvaux's Apologia as a Description of Cluny, and the Controversy over Monastic Art," *Gesta* 27, no. 1/2 (1988).
37   Kerr, "An Essay on Cistercian Liturgy," 3f.
38   Hoffman Berman, "The Cistercian Evolution," xiv.
39   Melville, *The World of Medieval Monasticism*, 105.
40   Constanze Hoffman Berman illustrates on the basis of the Silvanès chronicle that such communities had to decide whether to join the Cistercian or the Carthusian *ordo* (Hoffman Berman, "The Cistercian Evolution," 112).
41   Bennett Gilbert, "Early Carthusian Script and Silence," *Cistercian Studies Quarterly* 49 (1 September 2014): 371.

discipline, and reclusion. While the Cistercians, however, understood the ideal of solitude to be directed at the community as a whole, deriving from it the necessity to build their monasteries in remote territories,[42] the Carthusians emphasized solitude in regard to the individual monk.[43] While eremitic tendencies can certainly also be identified in the Cistercian perspective, Carthusian introduced the eremitic ideal as much as it was possible for them, without losing the necessity for communal organization.

The seriousness with which the Carthusians pursued their vocation and turned away from their worldly attachment thus appeared attractive to some but dissuasive to others. The tension between the active pursuit of an ecclesial career and the passive 'retreat to the wilderness' is exemplified beautifully in a letter that Bruno of Cologne, the founder of the Carthusian order, wrote to an old friend of his, Raoul the Green. In it, he sings praises of the simple life he leads with his brothers in Calabria:

> How can I speak adequately about this solitude, its agreeable location, its healthful and temperate climate? It is in a wide, pleasant plain between the mountains, with verdant meadows and pasturelands adorned with flowers [...]. Only those who have experienced the solitude and silence of the wilderness can know what benefit and divine joy they bring to those who love them. There, strong men can be recollected as often as they wish, abide within themselves, carefully cultivate the seeds of virtue, and be nourished happily by the fruits of paradise. There, one can try to come to clear vision of the divine Spouse who has been wounded by love, to a pure vision that permits them to see God. There they can dedicate themselves to leisure that is occupied and activity that is tranquil. There, for their labor in the contest, God gives his athletes the reward they desire: a peace that the world does not know and joy in the Holy Spirit.[44]

---

42   However, Janet Burton and Julie Kerr point out, that the Cistercian ideal of the desert was "more metaphoric than real" (Burton and Kerr, *The Cistercians in the Middle Ages,* 189).

43   see for instance Guigo I. *The Consuetudines of Guigo I, 5th Prior of the Carthusian Order. Translated from Latin.* Translated by Ugo–Maria Ginex. St. Mary's Hermitage Nr. Canterbury, 2018, 66 (chapter 80, "Eulogy of the solitary life"). Here, Guigo I. discusses solitude as an epistemological necessity for revelatory insight. He uses several Biblical examples (Isaac, Jacob, and Jeremiah, among others) to show that God often imparted knowledge to the patriarchs and prophets in moments of seclusion.

44   Bruno of Cologne. "Brief an Radulf Den Grünen." In *Quellen Geistlichen Lebens. Das Mittelalter,* ed. Gisbert Greshake and Josef Weismayer, 2: 20–28. Ostfildern: Matthias Grünewald Verlag, 2008, 21.

Bruno does not make the monastic seclusion sound so tempting without a cause. He intends to remind Raoul of a vow the two friends had made years ago to surrender their lives to monastic discipline.[45] Whereas Bruno followed through and devoted his life to Carthusian monasticism, Raoul stayed in Reims, pursued his clerical career, and eventually became provost of the cathedral chapter. To Bruno, that decision was problematic in a twofold way: first, Raoul had broken a vow he had made before God and thus lived in sin. Second, he had pursued worldly fame rather than the virtue that comes with withdrawal and monastic simplicity.

Bruno makes it clear that he believes the monastic life to be superior to any life led within the 'world', whereby he considered all non-monastic but clerical duties to be worldly as well. Bruno associated the world outside the monastic community with sinful desires, anxiety, agitation, and misery, to which only seclusion would provide rest and tranquility.[46] Even by other contemporary groups, the Carthusian way of life was considered the pinnacle of asceticism and monastic perfection.[47]

The reform movements often acknowledged each other's strengths and specialties. This becomes most apparent in the friendship between exponents of different communities. A fascinating example of the close interaction between different groups is the contact between Bruno of Cologne and Robert of Molesme, one of the founders of the Cistercian order: Bruno and his followers had sought refuge in 1081 in the abbey of Molesme, which subsequently offered them shelter in another abbey nearby.[48] Yet the story is not only proof of the interaction between the two but also of their fundamental differences. Bruno was concerned that living so close to Molesme, which had become somewhat of a monastic hot spot at the time, was not conducive to his vision of secluded life and, soon after arriving, already moved his small community to a more remote place.[49] This anecdote about their respective founding fathers also exemplifies the difference between the Carthusian and the Cistercian realization of their shared ideals. While the Cistercians believed strongly in the significance of solitude for one's personal spirituality, many of their leading figures nevertheless remained politically active – Bernard being the most prominent example. The Carthusians,

---

45 Bruno of Cologne, "Brief an Radulf Den Grünen," 22–28.
46 Bruno of Cologne, "Brief an Radulf Den Grünen," 22–28.
47 Mathilde van Dijk, José van Aelst, and Tom Gaens, "Introduction," in *Faithful to the Cross in a Moving World: Late Medieval Carthusians as Devotional Reformers*, Church History and Religious Culture 96 (Leiden: Brill, 2016), 2.
48 Melville, *The World of Medieval Monasticism*, 104.
49 Melville, *The World of Medieval Monasticism*, 104.

on the other hand, applied their zeal for the reclusive and solitary life in a much more rigorous way.

This short introduction to the Cistercian and Carthusian perspectives on the monastic reform of the 12th century leads up to the question of why William, as a Cistercian author, had addressed such an instructive and foundational work as the Golden Epistle to the Carthusian brothers of Mont Dieu.

3   William as an Author for the Carthusian Movement

William's biography, in many ways, reflects the desire for seclusion in the face of ecclesial responsibilities that was a driving force for reform. He had often expressed to Bernard the desire to leave his abbatial duties behind and become a simple monk; a wish that was eventually fulfilled when he was able to retreat to Signy in 1135.[50] In the prologue of the Golden Epistle, it becomes apparent that his personal yearning for solitude also led to a great appreciation of the Carthusian way of life. In the community of Mont Dieu, and their application of the reform ideals, he believed to find the ideals of early monasticism exemplified in their purest form:

> Why not feast in the Lord and rejoice? The most precious part of the Christian religion that seemed to almost touch the heavens was dead and resurrected; disappeared and was recovered. We heard it with our own ears and could not believe it. We read it in books and were astonished at the ancient glory of the solitary life and the great grace of God in it. And suddenly we discovered it in the meadows of the forest, in Mont Dieu, the fertile mountain, where the beauty of the desert brings fruit and the hills surround themselves with exaltation. There this life offers itself to all through you. In you it reveals itself, having been unknown it becomes known. In a few simple ones, the One himself reveals it to us, who had through a few simple ones subjected to himself the whole world, to the world's astonishment.[51]

It is clear that William had, despite his commitment to the Cistercians, tremendous admiration for the eremitic rigor of Carthusian communities and

---

50   I discussed this concepts, its limitations and the relevant literature in the Introduction.

51   Epistula ad fratres de Monte Dei, CCCM 88, Lib. 1, par. 2, pag. 228, linea 9.

viewed them as inspirational. He seems specifically impressed by the effect the community had on the outside-world: Their spiritual discipline, he believed, was meant to "astonish" the world, and, I would argue, convert others to their way of life on account of their sincerity.

The Golden Epistle seems to be an expression of the period, during which the distinct reform movements could still very much be considered adjacent expressions on a spectrum of spiritual longing. In general, William offers little reflection on the differences between the orders in question throughout the entire Epistle. He addresses the community of Mont Dieu as brothers in Christ, indicating merely their common monastic vocation. This reveals that he did not perceive Carthusian communities as competitors or opponents but as companions in a shared struggle to live according to ancient monastic ideals. According to a theory brought forth by John Green and Krijn Pansters, William could have even considered joining the community at Mont Dieu, which was founded around 1135 and thus around the time he finally made the decision to retire to Signy.[52] There is no source that corroborates this theory, either from the perspective of William or the community of Mont Dieu. Yet, it becomes clear from the Epistle itself that William must have been very familiar with the community and its members.

As Jean–Marie Déchanet explains, the Epistle was sent to Haymo, the prior of Mont Dieu, and an unidentified elder, along with several of his own manuscripts.[53] It is clear that William willingly and gladly shared his corpus with the Carthusian monks at Mont Dieu, and hoped to contribute to the intellectual and spiritual life of the community there. He asks his Carthusian brothers very explicitly to read his works, suggesting that through their shared understanding, his thought is of interest to them. Regarding the concrete audience of the Epistle, William differentiates between the elders and the novices of the community. Addressing Haymo and the unidentified "H." in the prologue, he makes clear that it is not them, but the younger monks, that require the council of his words:

> Thus, from the time I have left you until now, I have been determined to dedicate my daily labors not to you, who do not need it, but to

---

52   Krijn Pansters and John Green, "The Golden Epistle and the Ladder of Monks: Aspects of Twelfth–Century Carthusian Spirituality," in *The Carthusians in the Low Countries. Studies in Monastic History and Heritage*, Miscellanea Neerlandica 43 (Leiden: Brill, 2016), 194.

53   Déchanet, "Les Manuscrits, " 238.

brother Stephen and his other young brothers and the novices who come to you, that they may have them and read them so that they might find in them something that is useful to comfort them in their solitude, and incites holy endeavors.[54]

Two important things are implied in this passage. First, it shows that William knew these monks and likely considered them his personal friends. William wrote the Epistle after his stay at Mont Dieu[55] and was thus not only knowledgeable on the Carthusian phenomenon but also the local circumstances of the community of Mont Dieu in particular. Second, William considered these Carthusian priors his equals and himself capable and partly responsible for the Carthusian formation of their novices. This is plausible because the Cistercians and the Carthusians share a core stance regarding new entries to their communities. They both underscored the significance of spiritual maturity as a prerequisite to becoming a monk, abolished in their order the practice of child oblation and consequentially also the need for monastic schools.[56] When William thus speaks about pedagogical content for the novices, he is not talking about basic education but spiritual formation on an already sophisticated level.

In terms of doctrinal content, he must have believed his works to be compatible with Carthusian thought. Despite his commitment to the Cistercian community of Signy, and his staunch defense of Cistercian reform in his *Responsio Abbatum*, he clearly had a great affinity for the ideals that were particularly important to the Carthusian communities. Indeed, many of the themes he discusses in the Golden Epistle also featured prominently in early Carthusian documents. This becomes clear, for instance, in the parallels between William's Golden Epistle and the instructional works of two central Carthusian authors: Guigo I. (1083–1136), the author of the *Consuetudines* (written earlier than William's Epistle) and Guigo II. (1114–1193), the author of the *Ladder of Monks*, written after.[57] The purpose of this chapter

---

54   Epistula ad fratres de Monte Dei, CCCM 88, Prol., par. 2, pag. 225, linea 9: *Ideo ex quo recessi a uobis usque nunc, qualemcumque laborem meum cotidianum statui dedicare, non uobis qui non indigetis, sed fratri Stephano et sociis eius fratribus iunioribus, et nouitiis uenientibus ad uos, quorum doctor solus Deus est, ut habeant et legant, si forte aliquid ibi inuenerint utile sibi, ad solatium solitudinis suae et sancti propositi incitamentum.*

55   Déchanet, *L'homme et son oeuvre*, 96.

56   Joseph H. Lynch, *The Medieval Church: A Brief History* (London, New York: Longman, 1992), 248. More about this topic can also be found in Joseph Howard Lynch, "The Cistercians and Underage Novices," *Citeaux* 24 (1973).

57   Pansters and Green, "The Golden Epistle and the Ladder of Monks," 194. William was by far not the only Cistercian writer, influenced by Carthusian writings – the

is not to argue that William was influenced or, in turn, influenced any of these texts but to use them as a representation of the distinctly Carthusian thought of the time.

The *Consuetudines* are, in short, an anthology of Carthusian customs and rules. Like William, Guigo I. sings the praises of the solitary life, retracing its holiness to the life of the early Fathers. As William does in the Epistle, he refers to several examples, mainly from the Old Testament, to illustrate the eremitic life he envisions. The ideal of the hermit had not been a part of the Benedictine Rule,[58] to which the Cistercians remained largely faithful. But regarding the possibility of a more anchoritic influence, William seems to favor the Carthusian conception, as expressed in the works of Guigo I., over the Cistercian ideal and practice of a community shaped according to Benedictine principles. Both William and Guigo I. hold and defend contemplation and personal (rather than merely territorial) seclusion as essential, indispensable parts of the pious life. They are proponents of a genre that emerged at the end of the 11th century and is concerned with the formation of the monks' spirituality.[59]

The structure of the Golden Epistle, however, does not align directly with that of Guigo I.'s work but has its own particular emphasis. He focuses primarily on the theme that Guigo I. expounds on in Book I of the *Consuetudines*: the cell and the cell monks' novitiate. It is the concept of the cell in both its literal and spiritual sense to which he devotes most of his attention. As Guigo I. does,[60] he sees the cell monks, living in solitude, as true successors of early monasticism.[61] Both authors defend contemplation and seclusion as essential parts of the pious life. They are proponents of a genre that emerged at the end of the 11th century, concerned with the formation of monks, especially regarding their inner spirituality.[62] Themes such as the passionate longing for divine love, ceaseless prayer, and the formation of

---

Consuetudines in particular. Aelred, for instance was heavily influenced by Carthusian practice and thought (Alexandra Barrat, "The 'De Institutione Inclusarium' of Aelred of Rievaulx," *The Journal of Theological Studies* 28.2 (1977): 531).

58 Barrat, "The 'De Institutione Inclusarium'," 528–29.

59 Cédric Giraud, "Ut Fiat Aequalitas: Spiritual Training of the Inner Man in the Twelfth–Century Cloister." In *Horizontal Learning in the High Middle Ages*, ed. Micol Long, Tjamke Snijders, and Steven Vanderputten, Peer–to–Peer Knowledge Transfer in Religious Communities (Amsterdam: Amsterdam University Press, 2019), 67.

60 see for instance Guigo I. *The Consuetudines of Guigo I, 5th Prior of the Carthusian Order. Translated from Latin.* Translated by Ugo–Maria Ginex. St. Mary's Hermitage Nr. Canterbury, 2018, 66 (chapter 80, "Eulogy of the solitary life").

61 see in more detail in the upcoming chapter "7.1. Innovation, Restoration and Renewal."

62 Giraud, "Ut Fiat Aequalitas," 67.

the soul through devotional reading appear prominently in the works of both authors.

William also recognizes many of the dangers and difficulties of the secluded life in the cell, which Guigo I. had already pointed out. Regarding the admission of novices, William especially shares Guigo I.'s caution and expresses similar warnings.[63] Both authors are acutely aware of the harshness of a life lived according to a more eremitic ideal and emphasize that candidates must be examined according to their spirit, discipline, and suitability. The refusal to accept children as new entries into their communities, as mentioned above, stems from their awareness of the impossible challenge the cell presents for anyone who does not wholeheartedly desire such a life.[64] Earnest love for the solitary and contemplative life is imperative for both Guigo I. and William.[65]

In their comparative study on the Golden Epistle and Guigo II.'s *Ladder of Monks*, John Green and Krijn Pansters further explore the thematic similarities and differentiating nuances between William's texts and contemporary Carthusian thought. William is, for one part, far more concerned with the speculative theology that informs the concrete practice, whereas Guigo II. focuses on spiritual insight achieved through practice. As Green and Pansters put it: "The Golden Epistle's starting point, by contrast, is the view from the foot of the mountain, perhaps that of the novice, and outlines the strenuous nature of the climb to the summit. The Ladder, rather, develops a 'transfiguration' experience."[66] As Guigo I. was in his Consuetudines, Guigo II. seems to have been, in his *Ladder of Monks*, concerned with how

---

63   William is especially concerned about novices whose prideful attitudes make their persistence in the solitary cell an impossibility: *Sic et animalem discretum, novitium prudentem, incipientem sapientem: in cella posse diu consistere, in congregatione durare, impossibile est. Stultus fiat, ut sit sapiens* (Epistula ad fratres de Monte Dei, cccm 88, Lib. 1, par. 55).

64   This is stated in explicit terms, when Guigo says: "Thus, to the novice who asks for mercy are presented with the harsh and bitter observances which are placed before his eyes – as far as possible – all the little consideration and harshness of life he wishes to take upon himself. If after that he remains undaunted and steadfast and if, in accordance with what blessed Job says, his soul chooses to separate himself from the love of temporal things and his bones choose death" (Ginex trans., The Consuetudines of Guigo I, 34, chapter 22,1).

65   As I will discuss in the following analysis of the Epistle, William did not only have the spiritual safety of the individual in mind, but also the cohesion of the community as a whole.

66   Pansters and Green, "The Golden Epistle and the Ladder of Monks," 196.

the monk's daily routine, as well as the order's liturgy, can guide them on their path toward God.

For William, both liturgy and structure are external expressions of a primarily interior and spiritual process. It is notable, however, that in his entire work, liturgical considerations occupy a marginal role, in favor of an in-depth theory of personal spiritual growth. The absence of a major discussion of Cistercian liturgy in his workds is perhaps yet another feature that makes William a less-than-typical proponent of the Cistercian position.[67]

As he did in his exegesis of Romans, William structures his Epistle according to the three anthropological states: The animal (*animalis*), the rational (*rationalis*), and the spiritual (*spiritualis*) state.[68] The letter thus reflects the progression of the human mind and its gradual transformation toward perfection, a structure that is aligned with the letter's general purpose: To support the spiritual formation of novices. Although William is well aware of the importance of the communal aspect for any order, it is clear that his focus lies on the individual and their relationship with God. He carefully interlaces the practical life at Mont Dieu with thoughts on the inner workings of the soul and its ideal state. In doing so, he is able to relate his more general conception of the soul's ideal state to a more specific context, exemplifying that contemplative perfection looks the same for monks of all monastic affiliations. Thus, the Golden Epistle, unlike the *Consuetudines*, should not be read as a monastic rulebook for a particular order or community.

Instead, it is William's ode to solitude and private devotion, which are significant aspects of the monastic life. It is a work that exemplifies what Andrew Jotischky described as the "communicative repertoire" that

---

67   This absolutely should not imply that William disregards the need for liturgical practice, but rather, that it is not the focus of his works. There are two significant exceptions to this rule The Responsio Abbatum, in which he defends the Cistercian reform efforts, and his Eucharistic theology, developed for instance in De Sacramento altaris and his polemic against Rupert of Deutz. However, even in these two contexts, he treats the monastic liturgical practice only as an aside.

68   Thomas X. Davis emphasizes, rightfully, that "these aspects are not three levels or steps of ascent, as if one could definitively leave one level and move onto the next or because of some failure one returns to the previously [sic] level" (Thomas X. Davis, "The Trinity's Glorifying Embrace: *Conscientia* in William of Saint–Thierry," in *A Companion to William of Saint–Thierry*, ed. F. Tyler Sergent (Brill, 2019), 143). In the Epistle they do function as literary categories for William to differentiate spiritual challenges and dimensions of ascent, but they do should indeed not be interpreted as successive steps.

facilitated reform monasticism "through the composition and dissemination of texts from one monastic community to another".[69] William's particular care for the community of Mont Dieu does not, therefore, signify his preference for Carthusian theology as such but rather for the intensity and candor with which these monks follow their vocation; a vocation he believes should lie at the center of the Cistercian order as well.

---

69   Andrew Jotischky, "Monastic Reform and the Geography of Christendom: Experience, Observation and Influence," *Transactions of the Royal Historical Society, 6th Series* 22 (2012): 73.

CHAPTER 7

William's Monastic Ideal

1   Innovation, Restoration, or Renewal?

William's active contribution to the Cistercian reform has already been mentioned several times. Yet, his enthusiasm for these new reform movements seems to stand in contrast to the spirited defense of tradition he displayed against novel teachings. In the following, I will discuss William's understanding of reform and innovation and how he contrasts these two notions. The historiographic concept of a 12th-century 'renaissance'[1] highlights the theme at the core of William's ambivalent relationship with novelty: the monastic currents emerging during this period believed themselves to revive the ideals of the early church. However, it becomes clear from William's texts that this renewal – much like the innovations he criticized – was not devoid of controversy. The Epistle, as much as it is an exhortation and instruction of the community of Mont Dieu, is also a defense of his reform efforts. This is made explicit when he addresses the kind of criticism the Carthusians – and likely also the Cistercians – faced:

> I say 'novelty' because of the evil tongues of impious people, from whose contradictions God may hide you in the concealment of God's face. Because they cannot darken the manifest light of truth, they get upset over the mere use of the word 'novelty'. They are the old ones, and in their old-fashioned minds, they do not know how to reflect upon new things. They are old skins that cannot contain new wine. If they were filled, they would burst.[2]

Readers, who are primarily familiar with William's attacks on Abelard and William of Conches, might easily be surprised by the caricature of conservatives he presents in this passage. Although he does not explicitly name any particular adversaries, he is most likely talking about a similar brand of Benedictines which Bernard had addressed in his *Apologia ad Guillelmum*. A

---

1   see my brief discussion of notable literature regarding this terminology and concept in the Introduction.
2   Epistula ad fratres de Monte Dei, CCCM 88, Lib. 1, par. 20.

poignant expression William uses in his Commentary on the Song of Songs, that of the 'perfumed cells' (*aromaticae cellae*),[3] could be an indicator that William accuses his opponents of decadence and a lack of discipline. As Gillian R. Knight has pointed out, the allusions he makes to their wealth, luxury, and extravagant architecture are very reminiscent of Bernard's critiques in the *Apologia*.[4] Bernard had written the text at the behest of William; therefore, they likely shared not only political concerns but also critics. Yet Bernard was as reluctant as William to name his addressees.

He does refer to the 'Cluniacs' twice in the *Apologia*, but it has been argued that the word Cluniac could also have been used as an umbrella term for all traditional Benedictines.[5] It is also important to note that neither Bernard's nor William's critique ought to be understood as a condemnation of the Cluniac order, but instead of the particular figures and practices they considered abusive within the order.[6] Nevertheless, both the *Apologia* and William's Epistle confirm that the reform orders had come under fire and that some viewed their demands as too unconventional.[7] Abbot Geoffrey of Saint Mary of York (ca. 1152–1212), for instance, is said to have expressed horror at the Cistercian practices he had to witness, using the term novelty in a distinctly accusatory way.[8] William's rival in other matters, Peter Abelard, addressed the issues he took with the Cistercian attitudes and practices in his sermon *Adtentite a falsis prophetis*, accusing them of acting as though they were the only ones "resuscitating" the religious order.[9]

---

3   William uses this term in the Expositio super Cantica Canticorum, CCCM 87, cap. 41, linea 31. In a slightly different form (*cellas non tam eremiticas quam aromaticas*) it also appears in the Golden Epistle itself (Epistula ad fratres de Monte Dei, CCCM 88, Lib. 1, par. 148).

4   Gillian R. Knight, "The Language of Retreat and the Eremitic Ideal in Some Letters of Peter the Venerable," *Archives d'histoire Doctrinale et Littéraire Du Moyen Âge* 63 (1996): 35. Rozanne Elder fittingly calls Bernard's criticism a 'satirical tirade' (Elder, *Formation for Wisdom*, 200–201).

5   Conrad Rudolph, "Bernard of Clairvaux's Apologia as a Description of Cluny, and the Controversy over Monastic Art," *Gesta* 27, no. 1/2 (1988): 125.

6   Burton and Kerr, *The Cistercians in the Middle Ages*, 35.

7   For a study of Bernard's argumentative response to the criticism raised against the Cistercians, see Marvin Döbler, "Bernhard von Clairvaux und seine Apologia an Abt Wilhelm zwischen innerchristlichem Pluralismus und Religionskritik," *Zeitschrift für Religionswissenschaft* 15, no. 1 (1 September 2007).

8   Burton and Kerr, *The Cistercians in the Middle Ages*, 4.

9   *Tales uereor nonnullos esse qui in nostro, id est monachili, proposito nouiter exorti ordinem huius religionis quasi iam penitus extinctum se solos suscitasse* profitentur (Peter Abelard, CCCM 286, sermo 35 (contra Cistellenses)). See on this text: Chrysogonus Waddell, "'Adtendite a falsis prophetis': Abaelard's earliest known anti-Cistercian diatribe," *Cistercian studies quarterly* 39 (2004).

Most notable among these critical voices is, however, that of Cardinal Matthew of Albano, which William addressed directly in his *Responsio Abbatum*.[10] In Matthew's letter to the Chapter of Benedictine Abbots of the province of Reims in 1131,[11] he used the term novelty explicitly and polemically against the Cistercian reformers:

What is this new doctrine? Whence comes this new doctrine come? Whence comes this new rule? Whence comes, if I dare say, does this new and unheard-of presumption?[12]

Even though the Golden Epistle was not written in the context of William's defense against such accusation, I suggest the above-quoted passage be read in light of Matthew's words. Given William's own distaste for the term novelty, for instance in his *Disputatio*,[13] it is interesting that he attacks the *veteri* who, like Matthew and other Cluniac critics of the Cistercian reform seem to object to whatever they perceived as new. Yet, in his Golden Epistle and other works, William makes sure to differentiate between positive and negative kinds of novelty and tradition respectively.

---

10 William had written the *Responsio abbatum* in response to Cardinal Matthew of Albano, defending his introduction of a General Chapter of Benedictine Abbots, an innovation inspired by Cistercian practice (Sergent, "Introduction," in *A Companion to William of Saint–Thierry*, 2).

11 On the Chapter of Benedictine Abbots in 1131, that provided the context and background of the conflict in question, I suggest: Steven Vanderputten, "The First 'General Chapter' of Benedictine Abbots (1131) Reconsidered," *Journal of Ecclesiastical History* 66 (October 2015), and the earlier: Stanislaus Ceglar, "William of Saint Thierry and His Leading Role at the First Chapters of the Benedictine Abbots (Reims 1131, Soissons 1132)," in *William, Abbot of St. Thierry: A Colloquium at the Abbey of St. Thierry*, trans. Jerry Carfantan, Cistercian Studies 94, (Kalamazoo, MI: Cistercian Publications, 1987).

12 *Quae est ista noua doctrina? Vnde ista noua doctrina? Vnde ista noua regula? Vnde ista, si auderem dicere, noua praesumptio et inaudita?* (Matthew of Albano, Epistula ad abbates OSB Remensis prouinciae de primo capitulo prouinciali Remis a.d. 1131 habito, CCCM 89, pag. 100).

13 I discussed William's issues with the term at length in chapter "2.3. Orthodoxy and Authority in the Disputatio". His distaste is especially palpable in the following quote in which he criticizes Abelard's project and its effect: *Petrus enim Abaelardus iterum noua docet, noua scribit, et libri eius transeunt maria, transsiliunt Alpes, et nouae eius sententiae de fide, et noua dogmata per prouincias et regna deferuntur, celebriter praedicantur et libere defenduntur, in tantum ut in curia etiam Romana dicantur habere auctoritatem* (Disputatio adversus Petrum Abaelardum, CCCM 89A, par. 1, pag. 13, linea 14).

In his *Responsio Abbatum*, where William names and addresses the criticisms raised against the Cistercians, mainly by Cardinal Matthew of Albano, he mentions that this distinction was not necessarily well received. Claiming to change older and newer customs on the basis of the Benedictine rule's own authority, the Cistercians were called "authors of prevarications" (*praevaricationum auctores*).[14] Yet, his main argument is reiterated throughout the *Responsio*: They are not bound by the customs of the Cluniacs, but by the Benedictine rule itself, and by virtue of their freedom in Christ, the Cistercians should therefore be allowed to adapt customs, in order to be able to follow the rule more closely.[15] The distinction between mutable customs (*consuetudines*) and the immutable rule (*regula; regula sancti Benedicti*) is central to William's understanding of reform. While improvements, changes, and thus innovations of some sort are permissible in regard to customs, the rule and its authority remain untouched.[16]

So, William's embracing of the changes the reform orders introduced should not suggest that his stance on novelty for the sake of novelty, something of which he had accused Abelard and William of Conches, had changed. In the Golden Epistle William reiterates his moral objection to what he calls 'idle curiosity', and the desire for novelty that results thereof:

> A miserable and evil division takes place in the lamentable soul. Spirit and reason attempt to preserve for themselves the good will, the intention of the heart, and the eager obedience of the body, but the animal wickedness claims the affect and the intellect for itself, and the mind often remains fruitless. Thus, the sin of curiosity spouts from the weaker souls, in whom the desire of the flesh and the world has not yet perished. Therefore, they search for their solitude and silence,

---

14   *Nos uero de multiplicitate mandatorum arguimur, tamquam praeuaricationum auctores, si de multiplicitate mandatorum antiquorum uel <nouorum> unum aliquod, regulae auctoritate propter utilitatem, necessitatem, uel sui apud nos utilitatem, mutare praesumpserimus* (Responsio Abbatum, CCCM 89, linea 12).

15   *Profitemur quia non sumus ancillae filii sed liberae, qua libertate Christus nos liberauit, qui de seruitute peccati in libertatem spiritus nos uocauit. Profitemur nos non in consuetudines Cluniacenses iurasse, sed in legem et regulam sancti Benedicti* (Responsio Abbatum, CCCM 89, linea 33).

16   With this distinction William is entirely in line with the Cistercian position, who were praised, even by their critics for their reverence and observance of the Benedictine rule (James France, "The Cistercian community," in *The Cambridge Companion to the Cistercian Order*, ed. Mette Birkedal Bruun, Cambridge Companions to Religion (Cambridge: Cambridge University Press, 2012), 80.

disorderly comforts that are inappropriate for their profession; covert deviations of the will from the regal path of common institutions; hence, the taste for novelty and the weariness of the familiar. These attempts seem to alleviate the diseased soul's itch and disgust for a short moment through the rubbing but warm and enflame it instead, causing an even worse sensation of burning and itching.[17]

In this passage, William identifies the lust for novelty as a coping mechanism for weak souls who seek to distract themselves from the difficulties of their vocation. Not yet detached from the sensual world, they are easily bored by the monotone routine of the monastic life. They thus search for diversion and excitement, which, as William warns, will not fulfill their desire for long. He compares the need for novelty to a medicine that is soon replaced by another because it fails to heal the disease at its root. This unsustainable kind of curiosity can find many different expressions. Embedding his admonition into the concrete Carthusian context, William addresses particularly new kinds of occupation and labor and new readings (lectiones).[18] He makes abundantly clear that the monastic reform he envisions should not be driven by disdain for the customary or a craving for novelty.

William's most important clarification regarding this question is that the reform efforts are about renewal (renovatio) rather than innovation (innovatio).[19] Although Carthusian communities are pursuing their vocation with a newfound sense of purpose and enthusiasm for the monastic life, their tenets are, in fact, not new at all.[20] William believes monasticism in its truest form to be rooted in the Eastern traditions of the early church, something he points out at the very beginning of the Epistle:

---

17   Epistula ad fratres de Monte Dei, CCCM 88, Lib. 1, par. 65.

18   Epistula ad fratres de Monte Dei, CCCM 88, Lib. 1, par. 67, pag. 241, linea 476: Hinc enim quotidie fiunt nouae occupationes, nouae actionum uel laborum adinuentiones, lectiones diuersae, non ad aedificandum animum, sed ad fallendum tardantis diei taedium; ut cum damnauerit solitarius omnia uetera, omnia solita, et defecerint noua, non restet nisi odium cellae et fuga matura.

19   Renovatio was a central term terms that were often used within the context of the reform movement were recalescere and recuperari (Jotischky, "Monastic Reform," 58).

20   William's claim that the reform movements he is defending are not in fact innovative but restorative, is not a mere idealization on his part. Indeed many reform texts proposed new rules on the basis of a thorough engagement with existing traditions (Lutter, Christina. Vita Communis in Central European Monastic Landscapes. Meanings of Community across Medieval Eurasia. Brill, 2016, 369).

To the brethren of Mont Dieu, who brought the light from the East
and the ancient religious zeal from Egypt into the darkness of the west
and the Gallic coldness through the exemplary life of solitude and
heavenly behavior. To them and with them, my soul ought to run in
the joy of the Holy Spirit and the smile of the heart; with the fervor of
love and the full devotion of the obedient will.[21]

Although William does not name any monastic fathers or mothers, in particular, he shows acute historical awareness in this passage,[22] as the earliest
anchorite traditions can indeed be traced back to Egypt and Syria. Later in
the Epistle, William names the example of Makarios the Egyptian, Anthony
the Great, and Arsenius the Great.[23] It is important to note that he does not
identify Benedict as the source of monastic living in the West, as Robert of
Molesme did when he considered Benedict the intermediary between Eastern and Western monasticism.[24]

While William invokes Benedict as authority in his *Responsio Abbatum*,
in order to justify the Cistercian adaptations of Cluniac liturgy and customs,
and in his *Vita prima sacnti Bernardi*, in order to illustrate Bernard's faithfulness to the Benedictine rule as a Cistercian extraordinaire, in his Golden
Epistle references to Benedict cannot be found. I would argue that his
choice of monastic authorities differs depending on whether he addresses
Cistercians (and their critics), or Carthusians. While he insists on the importance of the Benedictine rule with its liturgical and communal directives
whenever he discusses the Cistercian communities specifically, in his
Golden Epistle he seems more concerned with conjuring up an image of the
eremitic roots of monasticism in the deserts of the past.

However, when he speaks of the 'desert's beauty' (*speciosa deserti*),[25] it
should also be noted that his understanding of the desert indicates solitude
and withdrawal from the world that can be practiced within the confines of
monastic communities as well, reflecting the distinctly Carthusian blend of
eremitic and cenobitic life. The ideal of the desert in his writings, more so
than acting as a practical guide, reflects the Eastern Fathers' willingness to

---

21   Epistula ad fratres de Monte Dei, CCCM 88, Lib. 1, par. 1.
22   As Jotischky rightfully points out, this awareness of historical circumstances does not
     indicate a great knowledge of early monastic texts, and speaks rather of a 'myth of
     Egypt' (Jotischky, "Monastic Reform," 59).
23   Epistula ad fratres de Monte Dei, CCCM 88, Lib. 1, par. 13.
24   Jotischky, "Monastic Reform," 60.
25   Epistula ad fratres de Monte Dei, CCCM 88, Lib. 1, par. 13.

devote themselves to God entirely. Therefore, both anchoritic and cenobitic communities could live according to the Spirit of the desert fathers.[26]

This principle seems to apply, for William, both regarding Carthusian and Cistercian efforts of renewal, as is evidenced by his framing of the foundation of Clairvaux in the *Vita Prima Bernardi*:

> Indeed, first of all, he dedicated his youthful enthusiasms to reviving the fervor of the ancient religion in the monastic order. To this end, he devoted all his effort, by his example and his words, among the brothers in the community within the boundaries of the monastery.[27]

The Cistercian movement, for William, is primarily about reigniting the passion for an ascetic life, even though the historical authority he invokes here, the 'ancient religion' (*antiqua religio*) is rather vague. Although he supported concrete changes on an institutional level as well, as evidenced by the *Responsio abbatum*, the core of his engagement is spiritual renewal. What he witnesses in personalities like Bernard's and in communities like that of Mont Dieu is an inner renovation, which then results in apt changes. This understanding is very much in line with the emphases of Carthusian reformers who prioritized the interior process of renewal.[28]

I would argue, though, that interior spiritual renewal and concrete, external reform are, in the context of 12th-century monastic reform necessarily dependent on one another. In the case of Cistercian reform, as mentioned earlier, the reintroduction of (manual labor) into the daily life of monks, for instance, was crucial, and considered a necessity for both the individual's spiritual growth and the community's stability.[29] The same goes for the Cistercian changes regarding periods of fasting, and their diets. These rules are thought of, at least in William's case, as an extension and facilitation of a process which needs to take place interiorly in the first place.

William's Epistle exemplifies this idea, when he instructs the novices on the danger of idleness. Discussing at length the 'animal' state – the lowest

---

26   Knight, "The language of retreat," 8.

27   *Et primum quidem circa resuscitandum in monastico ordine antiquae religionis feruorem, primitias iuuentutis suae dedicauit, exemplo et uerbo in conuentu fratrum intra saepta monasterii ad hoc omni studio uacans.*Vita Prima Sancti Bernardi, CCCM 89B, Lib. I, par. 42.

28   Van Dijk, Van Aelst and Gaens, "Introduction," in *Faithful to the Cross in a Moving World*, 5.

29   Jotischky, "Monastic Reform," 64.

stage of spiritual progress, during which the conquest of sensual ties is of utmost importance – William emphasizes the need for obedience. In line with the Cistercian and the Carthusian underlining of spiritual maturity and gratuitousness of the will, he believes the novices to require strict provisions.[30] For William, the call for discipline that is typical of reform movements takes on the role of spiritual nurture. Through obedience to rigorous rules, the monks' will is continuously formed according to God's will. No rule, however, is to be obeyed for its own sake:

> Pursuing idle occupations in order to avoid idleness is ridiculous. Idle is what has no use or does not pursue a useful goal. One should, however, not act simply in order to spend a day with more delight or without the boredom of idleness but in order to gain something from the accomplished chores for the sake of the soul's progress in the conscience, adding something to the heart's treasure daily; thus, one should believe not to have lived on a day, on which one cannot remember doing one of the things, for which one lives in the cell.[31]

William reveals in this passage that he is seeking reform of monastic institutions as a means of the reform of souls. He contrasts the mindlessness of following a community's daily routines with the vision of mindful and reflective progress. It is not the purpose of monastic asceticism to torture the recluse but to transform them and remind them of their love of a life devoted to God. While the Cluniac communities had prioritized the liturgy of the offices at the expense of many other aspects of monastic life, outlined in the Benedictine rule, both the Carthusians and the Cistercians introduced tasks into the liturgical rhythm of their monks' lives that would require their mental presence. That could be labor – manual labor and the copying of texts – or intensive prayer.[32] At the core of these efforts was a revitalization of conscious and active religious life.

---

30   Epistula ad fratres de Monte Dei, CCCM 88, Lib. 1, par. 68: *Propter quod pia simplicitas, et in professione religionis et solitudinis nouus homo, qui non habet uel rationem ducentem, uel affectum trahentem, uel discretionem moderantem, sed ui quadam utitur in semetipsum, tamquam a figulo figmentum, lege quadam mandatorum, quasi manibus alienis faciendus est, et formandus in omni patientia, et in rota uolubilis obedientiae et in igne probationis suae, plasmatoris et formatoris sui uoluntati et arbitrio est subdendus.*

31   Epistula ad fratres de Monte Dei, CCCM 88, Lib. 2, par. 82.

32   Nicolas Bell, "Liturgy," in *The Cambridge Companion to the Cistercian Order*, ed. Mette Birkedal Bruun, Cambridge Companions to Religion (Cambridge: Cambridge University Press, 2012), 258.

This new emphasis was accompanied by radical changes in the way the function of monasteries was perceived. The liturgical focus in Cluniac practice served important social purposes. As Verbaal pointed out, "monks had the task of praying for the entire society, just as nobility had the duty to defend it and farmers to feed it. Monastic life had a social obligation, liturgy, to which individual life was subjected."[33] Families sent their children to monasteries as a form of sacrifice, in exchange for which the monasteries' liturgical life would guarantee these families' salvation.[34] The Cistercian perspective reversed this notion: personal spiritual progress was the main objective of the monastic life, including its liturgical practice, while their relationship with the world outside the monastery was mostly based on pragmatic necessity.

William addresses this new social purpose several times in the Epistle. The monastic world, precisely if it secludes itself from the secular world, as William proposes, offers an example by contrast. The virtuousness of the monks ideally has an impelling effect on the public:

> Your simplicity has already provoked many to imitate it; your contentment and extraordinary poverty put the greed of many to shame; your seclusion causes in many people the fear of things that seem to cause turmoil.[35]

What William has in mind is not inspiring motivation, but rather transformative humiliation. The extraordinary obedience of communities like Mont Dieu ought to fluster those who follow the sinful path of greed and essentially shame them into submission. This is, William claims, what 'holy novelty' consists of: the restoration of a religious vigor that causes embarrassment to those less virtuous.[36] In his *Vita Prima* he offers an illustrative depiction of the community in Clairvaux as the exemplification of the grueling asceticism – they allegedly spent their days "in hunger and thirst, in cold and exposure, in constant vigils", consuming only "gruel made out of

---

33   Verbaal, "Cistercians in dialogue," 235.

34   Verbaal, "Cistercians in dialogue," 235.

35   Epistula ad fratres de Monte Dei, CCCM 88, Lib. 1, par. 9: *Vestra enim simplicitas iam multos prouocat ad aemulationem; uestra sufficientia et altissima paupertas iam multorum confundit cupiditatem; uestrum secretum iam earum rerum quae tumultum facere uidentur, pluribus incutit horrorem.*

36   William explicitly uses the term 'holy novelty' (*hoc sanctae nouitatis instauretur ornamentum*) in Epistula ad fratres de Monte Dei, CCCM 88, Lib. 1, par. 9.

beech leaves"[37] – that had both an alarming and fascinating effect on those who encountered it.[38]

This desire to pursue a 'true piety', inspiring repentance within and beyond monastic communities, was a shared element of the reform orders that developed from the 12th century onward. The *imitatio Christi* was a central element of the monastic self-conception, leading, for instance, to a renewed emphasis on suffering and poverty. A perspicuous expression of this conceptual development was the emergence and success of mendicant orders, or, in the late Middle Ages, the *Devotio Moderna*. The way in which the Cistercians and Carthusians defended the ideals of voluntary suffering and poverty certainly makes them precursors of these later phenomena in this regard.

In what I would call one of the more explosive passages of the Epistle, William presents the Carthusians with the future their order will enjoy if they continue on their path:

> The future of this holy order in this region will depend on you, on your example, and on your authority. You will be called fathers and founders by your successors with the reverence that is appropriate for followers. Whatever you state and what has become a common habit through your practice and observation, your successors will have to obey without revocation, and nobody will be allowed to change it. You will be for your successors what the immutable laws of the highest and eternal truth are for us; everybody should explore and know them, but nobody should be allowed to contradict them.[39]

---

37   Vita Prima Sancti Bernardi, cccm 89B, Lib. i, par. 25: *Vbi simpliciter aliquanto tempore Deo seruierunt in paupertate spiritus, in fame et siti, in frigore et nuditate, in uigiliis et angustiis multis. Pulmentaria saepius ex foliis fagi conficiebant.*

38   The place was remote and hardly ever visited, because, as he claims "the way of life there was too austere and poor. For a person truly seeking God, however, it held no terrors [...]" ([...] *ob nimiam uitae ipsius et paupertatis austeritatem. Quae tamen cum animum uere Deum quaerentem minime terrerent* [...]; Vita Prima Sancti Bernardi, cccm 89B, Lib. i, par. 8, as translated in William of Saint–Thierry, Arnold of Bonneval, and Geoffrey of Auxerre. *The First Life of Bernard of Clairvaux*. Edited by Hilary Costello. Collegeville, MN: Cistercian Publications, 2015, 11).

39   Epistula ad fratres de Monte Dei, cccm 88, Lib. i, par. 21: *Ex uobis enim, ex uestro exemplo, ex auctoritate uestra, in regione hac pendere habet omnis posteritas ordinis huius sancti. Vos in eo patres, uos in eo institutores, cum debita imitationis reuerentia, appellabimini a successoribus uestris. Quicquid a uobis statutum, quicquid uobis*

The passage's provocative nature lies in the idea that one of the privileges these simple monks will receive on account of their piousness is authority. More specifically: An authority of customs (*consuetudines*) should not be questioned by their successors. This is an especially puzzling passage given his defense of the Cistercian reform, in the context of which he provided a distinction between the rule itself, and the customs to which one ought not be bound.[40] Not only does William present the Carthusians as followers of the early Fathers, but as future Fathers themselves.[41] Their renewal is, therefore, not simply a renewal of ideals and practices but a regeneration of the extraordinary authority of the early church. The monks, William claims, will be revered by their successors in the way that Christians revere the divine truth itself.

Although William's concession is extraordinary and provocative, if not ecclesiastically and socially dangerous, the passage should not be read disregarding William's general statements concerning orthodoxy. First, the rhetoric of this passage cannot be discounted. William's statement has to be viewed as hyperbolic praise and encouragement, at least to a certain extent, as it would otherwise contradict his own statements regarding the possibility of monastic reforms. Second, William speaks exclusively about the monks' routines and habits, categorically excluding any changes of doctrine. He is addressing particularly the practical adjustments the community's local and climatic context demands, aware that the living conditions in the mountain region of the Ardennes differ significantly from those in the desert. For William, reform aims to enable communities to realize the monastic ideals of the early church in the face of particular challenges. While the main intention of reform movements should be renewal rather than innovation, introducing new practices is possible per se; yet, William emphasizes, never to overthrow tradition, but only to restore its underlining principles.

---

  tenentibus et seruantibus in consuetudinem fuerit missum, absque omni retractatione a posteris uestris tenendum erit, et seruandum, nec fas erit ab aliquo immutari.

40 as cited above from: Responsio Abbatum, CCCM 89, linea 33.

41 This expresses a similar notion to what Ralf Stammberger considers the 'dual role' (*Doppelrolle*) of authoritative Christian thinkers: "Zum einen steht sie auf den Schultern der Väter, zum andern werden sie ihrerseits von nachfolgenden Generationen in der Rolle von Vätern und Kirchenlehrern gesehen. In erster Linie aufgrund der von ihnen vertretenen Lehre, dann aber auch aufgrund der Integrität ihres Lebenswandels" (Ralf M. W. Stammberger, "Einleitung," in *Väter der Kirche: ekklesiales Denken von den Anfängen bis in die Neuzeit; Festgabe für Hermann Josef Sieben SJ zum 70. Geburtstag*, ed. Johannes Arnold, Rainer Berndt, and Ralf M. W. Stammberger (Paderborn: Verlag Ferdinand Schöningh, 2004), 550–51).

This is exemplified convincingly as William explains to the monks how they should relate to the extravagant architecture of their cells. The elegant buildings should not be torn down but rather used in a way that best serves the community's needs – William recommends converting the infrastructure into a much-needed infirmary.[42] The existence of the cells should be accepted but detested and serve as a monument to the spiritual rejection and hatred of worldly wealth.[43] William's evaluation of the Cluniac remnants expresses the careful strategic diplomacy required to defend and enforce the reform efforts. The kind of reform, he claims, that the Cistercians and the Carthusians are pursuing revives rather than destroys tradition.

William's general understanding of reform is, therefore, highly contextual. While the spiritual practices and devotion of the earliest monastic communities serve as a prototype to which their 12th-century successors hope to conform,[44] contextual differences and particularities are not disregarded. William displays, as he did in his exegetical text, historical awareness and compassion for differences in needs and abilities, according to the monks' spiritual progress. Reform, as mentioned before, is not as much is both institutional and spiritual renewal, and thus bound to commitments of faith as well as practicality. In this light, the Epistle functions as a guide that hopes to reawaken the enthusiasm for God, private devotion and asceticism in each of its readers and presents to them at the same time a monastic rule that best supports and reflects their spiritual needs.

2   The Monastic Life as Christian Ideal

Discussing medieval monasteries, the question of how they interacted with the secular public – how they 'brought the monastery into the world', so to

---

42   Epistula ad fratres de Monte Dei, CCCM 88, Lib. 1, par. 155: *Obsecro ergo ut maneant cellae illae delicatiores sicut factae sunt, sed non crescat numerus earum; sint que in ualetudinaria fratribus | animalibus et infirmioribus, donec conualescant, hoc est incipiant desiderare non ualetudinaria infirmorum, sed tabernacula militantium in castris Domini.*

43   This is an ideal he also expresses in the *Vita prima*, when he describes Clairvaux as a place "that spoke to them of the simplicity and humility in the buildings, mirroring the simplicity and humility of those living there" ([...] *cum in simplicitate et humilitate aedificiorum simplicitatem et humilitatem inhabitantium pauperum Christi uallis muta loqueretur*; Vita prima Sancti Bernardi, CCCM 89B, Lib. I, par. 35, as translated in ed. Costello, "The First Life of Bernard," 40).

44   Jotischky, "Monastic Reform," 58.

speak – is often of special interest. But whereas the orders of the early Middle Ages were primarily concerned with facilitating social penitence through liturgy, the reform orders displayed a renewed interest in personal transformation. For William and many Cistercians, this desire for individual spiritual progress was not necessarily restricted to their own members but extended beyond the walls of their communities.[45] As Brian McGuire notes, the Cistercians "are perhaps the first and last monastic group in medieval Europe who sought to convert the entire world by bringing as many as possible into the monastery".[46]

An episode that illustrates this desire to essentially transform the world into a monastic community is the story of Bernard's sister, which William tells in the *Vita prima*. The narrative begins with a visit from Humbeline to her brothers at Clairvaux. Humbeline is portrayed initially as a 'finely dressed' woman, married to a wealthy man and strongly attached to worldly pleasures. Her desire to meet her brothers is met at first with a series of slurs uttered by Bernard and her brother Andrew, who, according to the Vita, called her 'wrapped dung' (*stercus inuolutum*), unseemly pointing out the contrast between her beautiful appearance and her 'ugly' heart.[47] Humbeline, barely inferior to her brother in the field of arguments, gave an emphatic plea in response. The very sin for which her brother had shunned her required his attention and guidance. Promising that she would obey what Bernard commanded, he finally agreed to meet her and sent her home a changed woman. Although she did not immediately leave her marriage, she committed to a life of humble poverty, and after her husband's death, she joined the monastery of Jully.[48] This story is just one of many interactions with the outside world that William recounts, and it reflects that conversion lies at the heart of the Cistercian self-conception. The Cistercian monastery was considered an island of virtue, a refuge of simplicity, inspiring others to

---

45   For a detailed study of the ways in which the Cistercian order interacted with the secular world, particularly in the form of economic exchange, see Constance Brittain Bouchard, *Holy Entrepreneurs: Cistercians, Knights, and Economic Exchange in Twelfth–Century Burgundy* (Ithaca, NY: Cornell University Press, 1991).

46   McGuire, "Monastic and religious orders," 59.

47   Vita Prima Sancti Bernardi, CCCM 89B, Lib. I, par. 30.

48   William recounts the entire story in the Vita Prima Sancti Bernardi, CCCM 89B, Lib. I, par. 30. Humbeline would go on to become second head of the house at the nunnery of Jully, and Bernard's sister–in–law Elizapeth was the community's first prioress. However, as Janet Burton and Julie Kerr point out, the land was originally offered to Molesme, and only later handed over to Bernard for the sake of the nunnery's foundation (Burton and Kerr, *The Cistercians in the Middle Ages*, 27).

imitate the life its inhabitants led and welcoming those who desired to follow their example.

Although William addressed his Epistle to an explicitly religious and not
a secular community, the text is in many ways representative of the Cistercian mission to attract new members and introduce monastic principles to
the broader public. In it, he does not only treat the community of Mont
Dieu as an ideal model of monasticism but the recluse as an ideal expression of Christian faith. Thus, according to William, there are fundamental
differences between monks and secular Christians and how they relate to
divine truth.

The secluded life, he explains, is the holy life in its most perfect form.[49]
He retraces the initial inspiration to lead a monastic life to the 'heat' in the
hearts of Jesus' disciples shortly after His death and resurrection.[50] William's
regular use of terms such as enthusiasm (*fervor*) or longing (*desiderium*)
throughout the *Vita prima* makes it clear that he considers those willing to
leave the world to pursue their faith to experience the most intense and
intimate form of divine love. A critical element that distinguishes monks
from secular Christians, for instance, is their capacity to find enjoyment in
their relationship with God:

> Others ought to serve God, but you should adhere to God. Others
> ought to believe in God, know and love and worship God, but you
> ought to savor, understand, recognize and enjoy God.[51]

This passage is reminiscent of the sensual themes in William's exegetical
works and his meditations. The savoring of God, that is to say, the sensual
experience of God was central to the Cistercian experience, as Diane Reilly
points out, explaining that early Cistercian "texts and imagery reveal
such a focus on the importance of experiencing Scripture through the

---

49   With this assertion, William is not alone. Guigo I and Hugh of Grenoble too, consid-
     ered seclusion to be imperative for true piety (Van Dijk, Van Aelst, Gaens, "Introduc-
     tion," in *Faithful to the Cross in a Moving World*, 5).

50   *Epistula ad fratres de Monte Dei*, CCCM 88, Lib. 1, par. 13: *Post passionem uero Domini,
     calente adhuc in cordibus fidelium effusi eius sanguinis recenti memoria, solitariam
     hanc uitam profitentibus, paupertatem spiritus sectantibus, et in spiritualibus exercitiis,
     et contemplatione Dei pingue otium altero in alterum zelantibus, deserta repleta sunt.*

51   *Epistula ad fratres de Monte Dei*, CCCM 88, Lib. 1, par. 16: *Aliorum est enim Deo seruire,
     uestrum est adhaerere. Aliorum est Deum credere, scire, amare, et reuereri; uestrum est
     sapere, intelligere, cognoscere, frui.*

senses."[52] Indeed, this sensual aspect is a distinct feature of William's writing as well. Here, in the confines of a determined Cistercian community, he seems to argue, the environment is especially conducive to an intensive experience of divine love and intimate knowledge of God.

His idea of the *vita contemplativa* is that of an intense loving relationship that prioritizes the pursuit of mystic knowledge. While Christians are called to relate to God as obedient servants, monks are called to be lovers of God, thus fundamentally changing their position in the cosmic hierarchy. William even goes so far as to align the monastic life with the angelic life[53], expressing his awe of the monastic Fathers by calling them "either heavenly people, or earthly angels".[54]

It is notable, however, that William is careful not to let his high praise incite a prideful attitude in the novices of Mont Dieu. A stern warning against any complacency directly follows his accolade of the monastic life. His words address both the monks' self-perception and the way they judge the secular world. While their vocation endows them with angelic status, they are to view themselves as wild animals; the cell, he says, is perceived as a cage for those who could not be tamed in any other way.[55] He exalts those who can turn to external tasks and requirements without abandoning their inner devotion.[56] True faith, he implies, is found in those who do not lose sight of their purpose amidst the tasks of the *vita activa*.

---

52   Reilly, *The Cistercian Reform*, 16.

53   Epistula ad fratres de Monte Dei, cccm 88, Lib. 1, par. 15: *Altissima est enim professio uestra, caelos transit, par angelis est, angelicae similis puritati.*

54   Epistula ad fratres de Monte Dei, cccm 88, Lib. 1, par. 158: *Ipsi quos quo nomine dignius appellem nescio, homines caelestes an angelos terrestres, degentes in terris sed conuersationem habentes in caelis, laborabant manibus suis et de labore suo pauperes pascebant, esurientes ipsi; et de uastitate heremi urbium carceres alebant, et infirmos et in quibuslibet necessitatibus positos sustentabant, uiuentes pariter de labore manuum suarum et habitantes in labore manuum suarum.*

55   Epistula ad fratres de Monte Dei, cccm 88, Lib. 1, par. 18: *Feras uos potius indomitas et incaveatas, et bestias quae aliter et communi hominum more domari non poterant, aestimate et appellate.*

56   Epistula ad fratres de Monte Dei, cccm 88, Lib. 1, par. 18: *Longe supra uos uirtutem eorum suspicientes, et gloriam admirantes, qui ambidextri fortissimi, sicut Aoth ille iudex Israël, qui utraque manu utebatur pro dextera, quamdiu licet deuotissime intus uacare amant caritati contemplandae ueritatis, et cum necessitas uocat, uel officium trahit, promptissime se foras mutuant pro ueritate adimplendae caritatis* (transl.: Far above you, contemplate the courage, admire the glory of certain brave ambidextrous who, like Aoth, that judge of Israel who used either hand as the right, love to devoutly contemplate the truth of charity as long as they may, but when necessity calls for it, or

This emphasis on occupation, be it study or manual labor, is, despite him not mentioning Benedict, a clear expression of William's faithfulness to the Benedictine rule as well as its Cistercian interpretation. However, it also stands in the context of the significance he attributes to humility throughout his work. Reminding the monks that spirituality can also be pursued outside the monastic walls, and apart from reclusive devotion is meant to humble the monks and deter them from any judgmental and haughty feelings towards the world, which would jeopardize their virtue. This becomes clear in the following passage:

> Do not believe that the sun that shines for all shines in your cell only; that is sunny just for you and that God's grace operates in your heart alone. Is God only God for the hermits? God is God for everybody. God has compassion for all and does not hate anything that God has created. You should rather think that it is sunny everywhere but for you and that God thinks less of you than of everybody else.[57]

While the monks are thus to renounce the world and its pleasures, they are not to condemn it. God's grace is not exclusive to the monastic standing and, more importantly, not tied to human activity but rather to divine sovereignty. The solitary life, therefore, is no guarantee for salvation but reflects a humble and receptive attitude. William makes this very explicit when he advises the community of Mont Dieu not to accommodate any novices or monks who display the slightest sign of pride.[58] A false sense of superiority,

---

duty compels them, readily lend themselves outward to fulfill the truth of love). Nowhere in William's work do we find an explicit defense of the Crusades. Yet, this particular passage raises the question of whether William was in any way involved in the discourse, as Bernard had been. The example of Aoth, who defends truth and follows his calling, by courageously going to war, is certainly reminiscent of the theological exaltation of Crusaders, that was prevalent at the time.

57 Epistula ad fratres de Monte Dei, CCCM 88, Lib. 1, par. 20: *Nolo ergo ut nusquam arbitreris lucere solem communem diei nisi in cella tua; nusquam esse serenum nisi penes te; nusquam operari gratiam Dei nisi in conscientia tua. An solitariorum Deus tantum? Immo et omnium communium. Miseretur enim omnium Deus, et nichil odit eorum quae fecit. Malo te cogitare ubique esse serenum nisi apud te, et peius te de te quam de alio aliquo aestimare.*

58 Epistula ad fratres de Monte Dei, CCCM 88, Lib. 1, par. 144: *Bona tamen uoluntas, etsi multum sit bruta, non est deserenda; sed salutari consilio ad laboriosam et actuosam uitam transmittenda; superba autem, quamtumuis prudens sibi uideatur, dimittenda sibi est, et abigenda. Si enim admittitur superbus, prima die qua ingreditur habitare, incipit leges dare; nimium uero stultus discere non potest quas inuenit.*

he believes, is damaging both to the individual and the community – a warning that was possibly informed by some of the criticisms raised against the Cistercians, particularly by Peter Abelard, who took issue with the Cistercians' contempt of more urban monasteries.[59]

Despite these admonitions, it is undeniable that William views the monks of Mont Dieu as privileged, especially regarding the spiritual knowledge they can receive. Monks, he believes, are privy to a kind of insight into the divine will that allows them to hear and fulfill it.[60] William finds the Biblical imagery best suited for this kind of intimate knowledge in Gen 32,30. Drawing on the story of Jacob, the iconic father of contemplation, William defines the monastic calling as the pursuit of a 'face-to-face' encounter with God.[61] He does not seem to have in mind a form of mystic ecstasy that allows for a sudden visionary ecstasy but rather a diligent and life-long quest for divine unity.

The Epistle's instructional passages could be viewed as a guide for the novices to navigate the struggles of this quest. A glance at William's *Meditativae Orationes* reveals the spiritual difficulties he experienced within the monastic routine.[62] The boredom to which he alerts the novices of Mont Dieu, is only one of these. The pain he expresses in many of his prayers is one of unfulfilled longing. The monk – whose purpose is, as he defines it in the Epistle, to enjoy and experience God intimately – is confronted with the reality of weeks and months during which he feels distanced from God. In his second meditation, he narrates beautifully what such long periods of waiting can do to a monk's soul:

> She [the *anima*] loves you as her faith shows you to her, but it does not suffice for the mind to see. Therefore, she burns with desire to see you and to sacrifice her piety and justice to you, but the more it is postponed, the more she is confused. And because your faithfulness, in which she trusts, does not penetrate her faith with light as

---

59   *qui in solitudinibus monasteria sua erigentes quoscumque huius propositi in ciuitatibus uel castellis habitare uiderint seculares monachos uocant, quasi locus potius quam deuotio iustificet* (Peter Abelard, CCCM 286, sermo 35 (contra Cistellenses).

60   Epistula ad fratres de Monte Dei, CCCM 88, Lib. 1, par. 51.

61   Epistula ad fratres de Monte Dei, CCCM 88, Lib. 1, par. 25: *Nam et ipsum Montis Dei nomen bonae spei praefert omen; scilicet quod sicut psalmus dicit de monte Dei, habitatura sit in eo generatio quaerentium Dominum, quaerentium faciem Dei Iacob, innocens manibus et mundo corde et quae non accepit in uano animam suam.*

62   The *Meditativae Orationes* will serve as the basis for this book's concluding chapter.

quickly as she desires, she is so confused at times that she can hardly believe that she believes in you. Then she hates herself because she believes that she does not love you.[63]

This passage highlights several negative emotions that arise from unfulfilled expectations. Unanswered prayers, or seasons of spiritual loneliness, might lead to self-doubts, confusion, impatience, and anxiety. While William considers the monastic rank privileged among Christians, he does not romanticize it in any way: although it is a monk's purpose and calling to enjoy God, a monk should never anticipate his reward with a sense of security or even hubris. The journey of faith, he emphasizes, is not only shaped by the hopes the individual monk attaches to it but primarily by the will of God.

Neither in his prayers nor in the Epistle does William offer clear-cut instruction or advice on how to cope with the pain of longing, the unattainability of God. Yet, it is informative that he addresses the problem most explicitly in his prayers. Calling upon God is a monk's primary resource. William's understanding of monastic reform is represented in the way he treats the practice of prayer. While the Cluniac tradition tended to eclipse personal prayer with the Divine Office, William reflects on prayer's conversational, confessional and spiritual nature – whether as a part of private devotion or communal liturgy. In doing so, he reflects what Wim Verbaal described as a cornerstone of Cistercian spirituality: "Liturgical activities, praying and singing of psalms, were imbued in all aspects of monastic life. Each task had to be ventured upon as an opportunity for personal prayer and meditation".[64] The external setting, which monastic routine places on the practice, such as structure and frequency, are meant to invoke spiritual yearning in the individual. So, while the Cistercian simplification of the daily liturgy has to be kept in mind, William's perspective does not necessarily express its devaluation, but a rediscovery of its spiritual value.

Prayer, therefore, should be a habit toward which a monk intuitively turns, regardless of his circumstances. The Epistle names a great variety of prayers: short and highly focused ones for particular requests; long and winding theoretical ones, not unlike William's meditations; enthusiastic

---

63   Meditativae Orationes, cccm 89, Med. 2, par. 14: *Amat te qualem te sibi fides describit, sed mens uidere non sufficit. Ardens que faciei tuae desiderio cui sacrificium pietatis et iustitiae suae offerat, oblationes et holocausta, cum differtur, magis turbatur. Et cum non tam cito fidei tuae cui se credidit impetrat illuminationem, in tantum nonnumquam stupescit, ut credere se in te uix sibi credat et ut oderit se quia, ut sibi uidetur, non amat te.*

64   Verbaal, "Cistercians in dialogue," 238.

ones (*alacres*);[65] prayers of thanksgiving and supplication;[66] and lastly, joyous and intimate conversations with God.[67] In his fifth meditation, William identifies the inner attachment of the heart as the unifying element of true prayer. Like any other practice of devotion, prayer is a means to express and receive divine love, making the heart and its desires the primary focus in most of William's instructions.[68] Solitary prayer, for instance, requires the intercession of the Spirit, for it depends on the heart's active turn toward God.[69] Similarly, communal prayers are possible in an inspired state of exultation but can also pose difficulties for the human mind.[70] The spiritual life in the monastery is often presented, in William's works, as a challenge.

Whatever has the ability to facilitate devotion also holds the potential to obstruct it. William illustrates this impressively when he explains that even the contemplation of the crucifixion may hinder spiritual prayer if the mind focuses overtly on Jesus' physical form.[71] Similarly, novices are not to be burdened with the reading of complex theological texts, despite their relevance to the intellectual life of the monastery, because the novice mind is not yet used to them and is easily tired out.[72] When William speaks of the necessity of spiritual practice for the monastic life, he does not envision a rigid schedule – a 'one size fits all' religious ritual – but instead a dynamic habitualness that considers individual and communal needs and hardships.

Returning to the specific context of the Golden Epistle, it follows that the Carthusian tenet of solitude is never an end in and of itself but needs to be cautiously applied to support the monks in their spiritual progress. This becomes especially apparent in William's discussion of the cell as the central

---

65   Epistula ad fratres de Monte Dei, CCCM 88, Lib. 1, par. 176.

66   Epistula ad fratres de Monte Dei, CCCM 88, Lib. 1, par. 177: *Et ipsae sunt quas Apostolus alio ordine dinumerat, obsecrationes, orationes, postulationes, gratiarum actiones.*

67   Epistula ad fratres de Monte Dei, CCCM 88, Lib. 1, par. 179.

68   Sergent, "Sources and Influences," 62.

69   Meditativae Orationes, CCCM 89, Med. 5, par. 2: [...] *sed nisi tu me praeuenias in benedictionibus dulcedinis tuae, locum quidem facile inuenio, sed non tam facile cor solitarium.*

70   Meditativae Orationes, CCCM 89, Med. 5, par. 3: *Orare in turba tuum fuit, cui nihil defuit, quod tamen cum sic exigeres, nec nos refugimus.*

71   Bell, David N. "The Mystical Theology and Theological Mysticism of William of Saint–Thierry," in *A Companion to William of Saint–Thierry*, ed. F. Tyler Sergent (Brill, 2019), 71, citing: Oratio Domni Willelmi, CCCM 88, pag. 170.

72   Epistula ad fratres de Monte Dei, CCCM 88, Lib. 1, par. 172: *Difficilium etiam lectio scripturarum fatigat, non reficit teneriorem animum, frangit intentionem, hebetat sensum uel ingenium.*

part of the monks' life at Mont Dieu. The stability of location and seclusion are primarily matters of inner transformation: the restriction of the monk's body to life within the cell is meant to teach him contentment with his own company.[73] Physical obedience is thus not the monastic objective, but only a means to increase inner obedience. William does not conceptualize the cell-bound life as an ideal status but rather as a temporary inevitability necessary to achieve a spiritual state that would be sustainable outside the cell.

To exemplify this, he uses the image of the infirmary, with which he would have associated positive memories of collaboration, friendship, and recovery, rather than suffering. He compares the cell to a medical ward,[74] isolating patients from the sources of their sickness and providing the right circumstances to look after themselves.[75] Like a medication that unfolds its true efficacy only if it is applied steadily over a certain amount of time and is not frequently switched, the cell's remedies of solitude and quietness are not to be suspended and interrupted with distractions of any kind. They will heal the soul of its insubordination and equip it with obedience, a resource it ought to employ long after its convalescence.[76]

Despite the apparent importance of solitude, William stages the scene in a dramatic way: the patient is, in fact, not on his own but is aided in his recovery by a physician and four vigils. Although the first association of 'physician' in a spiritual context is usually Christ, I believe it more likely that William considers the physician to be the cell itself. In several passages, he treats the cell as a personality in its own right, which feeds, embraces, and cares for its occupant[77] and even decides – like a sentient being – with whom it will pursue a relationship and whom it will reject.[78] The cell is thus both physician and infirmary. It is the setting within which the monk's

---

73   Epistula ad fratres de Monte Dei, CCCM 88, Lib. 1, par. 94: *Doceat illud posse consistere in loco, cellam pati, se cum que morari, quod in proficiente bonae compositionis initium est, et certum bonae spei argumentum.*

74   As I have noted, he advises the community to transform the more extravagant cells into actual infirmaries (Epistula ad Fratres de Monte Dei, CCCM 88, Lib. 1, par. 155).

75   Epistula ad fratres de Monte Dei, CCCM 88, Lib. 1, par. 96: *Incumbat ergo immobiliter ualetudinario suo; sic enim appellare solent medici ualetudinum curandarum officinam, et remedii suscepti prosequatur usum usque ad sanitatis experimentum.*

76   Epistula ad fratres de Monte Dei, CCCM 88, Lib. 1, par. 97.

77   Epistula ad fratres de Monte Dei, CCCM 88, Lib. 1, par. 34.

78   William uses the crass imagery of abortion (*a se proicit quasi abortiuum*) in order to exemplify the cell's violent rejection of anyone unworthy (Epistula ad fratres de Monte Dei, CCCM 88, Lib. 1, par. 37).

spiritual progress occurs. The concrete formation, however, seems to be shaped by the so-called vigils.

Initially, William speaks only of three vigils that attend to the monk's needs, particularly when he is overwhelmed by the loneliness of his confinement. Additionally, they are ensuring the monk's 'safety', meaning the inviolability of his virtue. The first vigil is God, whose role William, rather surprisingly, does not spend much time expounding, likely because it does not need any clarification for the novice, who already consciously devoted his life to God. The second vigil requires more explanation, as it is the monk's conscience. It takes on a critical role in the monks' 'recuperation', as it demands honesty and candor regarding his ailments. In a rather pictographic passage, William explains the importance of a guilty and, therefore, accurate conscience:

> If you want to convalesce soon, do not dare to do anything by yourself, as marginal as it may seem, without consulting the physician. If you expect the help of a physician from him, it is necessary for you to always show your ulcer to him without embarrassment. Be ashamed of it, but reveal everything and hide nothing. At confession, some recount the tale of their sins like a fable. They name the diseases of their soul without shame, almost without remorse, and without feeling pain. The one who is in pain quickly bursts into tears and opens up in sighs. But when a hopeless insensitivity accompanies an evil disease because the patient feels no pain, then he is removed from health the closer he seems to be to it.[79]

The role of the conscience is here essentially diagnostic: it unforgivingly reveals even the ugliest symptoms of the monk's affliction and is essential to their treatment. The pain of remorse, William explains, is what makes

---

79   Epistula ad fratres de Monte Dei, CCCM 88, Lib. 1, par. 98–99: *Si ergo ad sanitatem festinas, uide ut nil uel modicum de temetipso agere praesumas, medico inconsulto; a quo, si operam medicantis exspectas, necesse est ut ulcus semper tuum detegere ei non erubescas. Erubesce, sed tamen reuela totum, nec abscondas. Sunt enim qui confitendo sicut fabulam enarrant peccatorum suorum historiam, et aegritudines animae suae sine confusione dinumerant, et pene sine paenitentia, et sine affectu doloris. Cito enim lacrimas inuenit et resoluitur in gemitum, qui habet sensum doloris. Si uero malae aegritudini desperabilior stupor accesserit, hic in eo quod non dolet, quanto sanitati uidetur propinquior, tanto ab ea fit remotior.*

healing possible. The presence of the second vigil in the cell, therefore, ensures the monk's sense of shame and repentance, keeping him from actively
sinning again.

Despite the second vigil's crucial role, it is clear to William that this mon-
umental task could not be entrusted to the fallible human conscience alone.
The necessity of the third vigil – the 'spiritual father' – is thus consequential.
While the conscience allows for an inward confession, the presence of an
abbot or confessor is vital to secure the regularity and truthfulness of these
confessions. More so, William instructs the novices to "run to [their spiritual
father] with all their issues",[80] revealing the value he attaches to communal
relationships. Without supervision or pastoral care, the novices would lack
an essential part of their spiritual recovery.

Although William names only three vigils at first, he recommends – according to his judgment, as he claims – a fourth figure, towards which the
novices ought to turn on their journey. This last addition reveals the limitations William sets for the eremitic life, particularly regarding the novitiate
and his awareness of the harshness of solitude:

> Choose for yourself, at my advice, a person whose exemplary life lives
> in your heart and whom you revere so much that every time you think
> of them, you rise in awe of them, sort yourself out and collect yourself.
> As if they were present, the thought of them ought to improve every-
> thing that needs improvement in you, in the affection of mutual love
> but without causing harm to the remoteness of your solitude. They
> might be with you and stand by you whenever you want and encoun-
> ter you, even when you do not want it.[81]

It is challenging to read William's praise of spiritual friendship without addressing once again the impact his time in Clairvaux had on both his physical and his spiritual convalescence. His advice to seek out a person one
admires fondly and who holds great authority reads like a description of his

---

80   Epistula ad fratres de Monte Dei, CCCM 88, Lib. 1, par. 101: [...] *patri spirituali obedien-
     tiam caritatis, ad quem de omnibus recurras.*

81   Epistula ad fratres de Monte Dei, CCCM 88, Lib. 1, par. 103: *Elige tibi tu ipse consilio
     meo hominem cuius uitae exemplar sic cordi tuo insederit, reuerentia inhaeserit, ut quo-
     tiens eius recordatus fueris, ad reuerentiam cogitati assurgas, et temetipsum ordines et
     componas. Qui cogitatus, ac si praesens sit, in affectu mutuae caritatis emendet in te
     omnia emendanda, et tamen nullum patiatur damnum secreti sui solitudo tua. Hic prae-
     sens tibi adsit quandocumque uolueris; occurrat saepe et cum nolueris.*

relationship with Bernard.[82] William's conception of the cell as an infirmary is, in many ways, the sharing of his experience as one that has artfully blended periods of solitude and isolation with the joys of community. Human nature is not destined for absolute solitude, even as it is called to monastic life. Throughout the Epistle, William sympathizes with the novices' need for company.

Of course, this passage is not an authorization of actual interpersonal contact; yet it acknowledges the individual desire for relationships. William reveals that the presence of a guiding figure is vital to spiritual growth. One especially poetic passage in the Epistle explains how these relationships function without relying on conventional interactions: "while both remain silent, they talk to one another. They are separated from one another but delight in one another. They progress with each other's help, and while they do not see each other, one sees in the other what is to imitate, while he sees in himself only what is to mourn".[83]

The vision of the monastic life that William presents to the novices of Mont Dieu is thus reflective of the Carthusian conception that considers the ideals of both eremitic and cenobitic monasticism complementary rather than mutually exclusive.[84] Although his admiration of the Carthusian way of living stems in part from a personal longing for seclusion and solitude, he maintains that communal support is a central aspect for any monk's development. Yet, the monastic reform shows that community can be 'done' differently.[85] Collective endeavors receded into the background,[86] though more so for the Carthusians than the Cistercians, whereas mutual enthusiasm for the individual journey and a common subjection to the same set of

---

82   see the chapter "3.2. Living the Song. Spiritual Friendship as a Foundation of Cistercian Exegesis".

83   Epistula ad fratres de Monte Dei, CCCM 88, Lib. 1, par. 193: [...] *mutuo in silentio sibi colloqui, et in absentia ab inuicem se ad inuicem magis frui, proficere de inuicem, et cum se non uident ad inuicem, in alio uidere quod imitandum est, in seipso nonnisi quod flendum est.*

84   This position was also supported by Cluniac authors, such as Peter the Venerable (Knight, "The language of retreat," 43).

85   As Lutter rightfully points out, "community is not only imagined, but also 'done'", explaining that shared practice and spiritual training are contributing intensely to the establishment of 'community' in a broader sense (Lutter, "Vita communis," 363).

86   William even goes so far, as to encourage the monks to celebrate the Eucharist 'spiritually' and by themselves in their cell – certainly not exclusively, but in addition to the communal reception of the sacrament (Epistula ad fratres de Monte Dei, CCCM 88, Lib. 1, par. 119).

rules were emphasized. The community William envisions in his Golden Epistle centers on a shared vision and ideal, which all individuals pursue, although at different paces and to different degrees, through the same means of spiritual discipline. Considering oneself part of such a community enhances the experience and increases the rigor, as William exemplifies using the model of the early Fathers.

These religious men, he explains, established the practice of monastic life by attempting to surpass each other in their contemplative efforts.[87] The monk's life, he makes clear, ought to inspire others to follow along the same path. This is true particularly in the Cistercian case, both within the community itself and beyond its walls. It is, at the same time, William's contribution to overcoming the frequently observed disparity between the monastic desire to turn away from worldly things and at the same time, to bring salvation into the world.[88] By leading exemplary lives, he believes, the monastery will be able to honor both of its commitments, either encouraging each other in the journey they had already begun or putting to shame those still pursuing a life of sin and supporting them in their 'recovery'.

3   Horizontal Authority and Loving Obedience

William's strong focus on the individual's own spiritual journey begs the question which role hierarchical relationships and communal experience play in the face of a possibly over-interiorized conception of monastic life. The monastic life presents a tension between required submission to social rules and their simultaneous transcendence. In this light, William's understanding of ecclesial (rather than literary or intellectual) authority needs to be examined in more detail. As a central element of the rule of Saint Benedict, and Benedictine life as such, obedience to – primarily abbatial[89] – authority is necessarily reflected in William's writings as well.

First, it is important to note that the significance William attaches to authority differs according to the various stages of monastic education. Authoritative figures are required mainly in the first phase of a monk's profession. Since William addresses most of his Epistle to novices, it is an optimal source to comprehend the way a monk's relationship with his

---

87   Epistula ad fratres de Monte Dei, CCCM 88, Lib. 1, par. 13.
88   Lutter, "Vita communis," 366.
89   France, "The Cistercian community," 81.

superiors changes throughout his formation. William reveals that authoritative statements and imposed discipline are not permanent ideals of monasticism but rather temporary necessities; they can provide what a person is still lacking in spiritual knowledge, with the objective of contributing to their self-sustaining wisdom. He states this most explicitly in the following passage:

> Whoever reigns and orders themselves in their conscience can be trusted and left to their own devices in their cell without hesitation. But that is for the perfect or for those advancing towards perfection. We have thus presented it to the beginners and novices, so that they may know what they lack and to what they ought to extend the intention of their zeal.[90]

The enlightened monk becomes his own guardian – his own *paterfamilias*[91] – over time. The novice, however, is not yet equipped to keep his passions and his senses under control. Yet again, the human conscience is decisive for William. External castigation and discipline teach the conscience to discern what furthers and what hinders a monk's spiritual growth, continuously transforming it into an authoritative force in and of itself. More so, those who have achieved spiritual perfection are not bound to any kind of human authority. Not only is this a theoretical or conceptual truth for William, but it directly affects how he instructs the community of Mont Dieu to treat its members. The advanced may live even more isolated from their brothers and their spiritual fathers, creating space for eremitic autonomy within the communal setting. This was also true for the structure of daily life in Cistercian communities.[92] It was especially reflected in Bernard of Clairvaux's attitude towards the monks' regimen, insisting that no one ought to overexert themselves or look down on others.[93]

The novices, William claims, have little alternative but to follow authoritative teachings and instructions blindly, as neither their *ratio* nor their inner desire naturally lean towards righteousness yet. They are, as William

---

90   Epistula ad fratres de Monte Dei, cccm 88, Lib. 1, par. 139: *Qui sic semetipsum regit et ordinat in conscientia sua, optime sibi credendus et committendus est in cella sua. Sed hoc perfectorum est, uel perfecte iam proficientium. Quod ideo proponimus incipientibus et nouitiis, ut sciant quid desit sibi, et quo extendere habeant intentionem studii sui.*

91   Epistula ad fratres de Monte Dei, cccm 88, Lib. 1, par. 138.

92   Burton and Kerr, *The Cistercians in the Middle Ages*, 103.

93   Burton and Kerr, *The Cistercians in the Middle Ages*, 115.

ascertains, still tied to their human senses – they are rooted in the animal stage (*animales*). Their relationship towards authority is, therefore, one of imitation rather than comprehension.[94] Although 'following authority blindly' might sound like potentially dangerous behavior, especially to modern readers, it reveals the value of cenobitic monasticism, William wanted to highlight: real human connection allows for an intuitive kind of learning. The novices are thus able to grow by performing actions and emulating attitudes they see modeled in their brothers and their spiritual ancestors. The authority of contemporary confreres is comparable to the authority of monastic founders, Church Fathers, or even Biblical authors; more than doctrinal, it is practical in nature, as it teaches the novices how, rather than simply what to believe.

Therefore, the most significant aspect of the novices' education is not their perceptive faculty or their understanding, but their obedience. That does not mean William despises or rejects the idea of individual aptitudes in general. Instead, he makes careful distinctions, demonstrating that an obedient and humble spirit is indispensable regardless of individual gifts:

> Even if one is talented, thrives in art, and excels on account of their intellect, those are instruments both of sin and of virtue. One should not shy away from being instructed on how to use the same for good and for evil. That is the special deed of virtue. Talent ought to adapt the body, artistry ought to inform nature,[95] and reason ought to make the spirit docile rather than proud. Talent, artistry, reason, and the like we possess freely, but not virtue. Virtue ought to be taught in humility, sought through effort, and possessed through love. Because virtue is worthy of all of these things, it cannot be taught, sought, and possessed in any other way.[96]

---

94 Epistula ad fratres de Monte Dei, CCCM 88, Lib. 1, par. 43: *Sunt etenim animales, qui per se nec ratione aguntur, nec trahuntur affectu; et tamen uel auctoritate permoti, uel doctrina commoniti, uel exemplo prouocati, approbant bonum ubi inueniunt, et quasi caeci, sed ad manum tracti sequuntur, | hoc est imitantur.*

95 The Latin text says here *ars naturam informet*, which could well be a transformation of the classical *ars imitatur naturam*. Much has been written about the latter concept, notably about its role in the scholastic theology of the later Middle Ages (see, for instance, Arne Moritz, ed., *Ars imitatur naturam. Transformationen eines Paradigmas menschlicher Kreativität im Übergang vom Mittelalter zur Neuzeit* (Münster: Aschendorff, 2010).

96 Epistula ad fratres de Monte Dei, CCCM 88, Lib. 1, par. 69: *Nam etsi callet ingenio, si uiget arte, si praeeminet intellectu, instrumenta sunt haec tam uitiorum quam uirtutum.*

Creativity or knowledge could be used both for good and evil. Their presence in a monk's soul might well increase his value for the community but is in no way determinative of his virtuousness. All kinds of talents need to be ordered towards virtue by humility. Unlike any intellectual or artistic talents, humility is not a God-given gift but requires steady practice and effort and the willingness to subject oneself to the rules of the monastery. With persistent obedience, William explains, will-less habituation is slowly transformed into a joyful desire.[97]

This process is facilitated by concrete effort and exercise. Within such a framework, it becomes clear that William's understanding of authority within the communal context is not one that simply teaches doctrine but models behavior – a truly Benedictine concept, pursued diligently by the Early Cistercians.[98] The authorities of the monastery are not written statements but lived lives. This relativizes a characterization of William as a conservative thinker lacking intellectual innovation. Authorities, both Biblical and Patristic, are not to be quoted verbatim but rather imitated through practice and routine. In the Epistle, more so than in any of William's exegetical works, the apostle Paul acts as a spiritual guide passing on concrete practices,[99] such as fasting and abstinence, rather than merely teaching theological ideas.

William conceptualizes authority within the community itself in a similar way. Although he hardly addresses the hierarchal structure of the order in the Epistle, the *Vita prima* clearly represents how he envisions the social and authoritative relationships among the monks and their superiors. The fact that the Life of Bernard is, in tendency, a more hagiographical than biographical piece of work, should not deter us from taking it into account

---

> *Non ergo refugiat doceri uti eo in bono, quo et in malo uti potest, quod proprium uirtutis opus est. Ingenium corpus adaptet, ars naturam informet, intellectus non elatum faciat animum sed docibilem. Ingenium quippe, ars uel intellectus, et alia huiusmodi gratuito habentur, aliter uirtus. Doceri uult cum humilitate, quaeri cum labore, haberi cum amore. Cum omnibus his digna sit, nec aliter uel doceri uel quaeri uel haberi possit.*

97 William likens that transformation to clay that is formed by a potter's hands, perfected by the "potter's wheel of obedience" (Epistula ad fratres de Monte Dei, CCCM 88, Lib. 1, par. 68). The monk ought to constrain himself, in order to escape the constraints of sin and exercise new behaviors, in order to let go of old habits. Through this process, the old desire of sin will be superseded by a desire for God, allowing him to derive just as much pleasure from renouncing worldly pleasure than he used to derive from indulging in them (Epistula ad fratres de Monte Dei, CCCM 88, Lib. 1, par. 92).

98 France, "The Cistercian community," 81.

99 Epistula ad fratres de Monte Dei, CCCM 88, Lib. 2, par. 215.

when discussing William's understanding of authority: Especially because he presents in it an idealized image of Bernard, it allows us to see more clearly the underlying ideals he introduces, sometimes explicitly but often implicitly, in his works.

In the *Vita Prima*, he describes Bernard not only as a spiritual example for the individual monk but as the ideal abbot, shaping the community's life through leading by example. Despite his physical deficits and weakness, Bernard serves here as the model of the diligent monk, carrying out whatever his constitution allowed him to.[100] William explains that Bernard's diligence and readiness to fulfill any task required or asked of him stemmed from extraordinary obedience. Set against the backdrop of the Epistle's instructions, it becomes clear that obedience is not simply to be practiced by the novices for the sake of their progression but is the cornerstone of monastic living as such. Only those willing to subject themselves to the will of God in total humility can expect obedience in return. Bernard's great authority among his brothers is grounded in his willingness to serve them and to apply an even harsher discipline to himself than he demands from them. This depiction of Bernard as an ideal authoritative figure is reflective of the shift between the Cluniac and Cistercian conception of authority; as Wim Verbaal frames it, "the shift is light but significant: instead of the authorities to which one submitted, it was now the person who submitted who took center stage."[101] This notion, William claims, also differentiates the ideal monastic authority he envisions from secular and even clerical authority.[102]

He ascribes this to the inherently human nature of relationships. From his own and very ambivalent experience as an abbot, William knows that authoritative figures can easily incite jealousy and envy in their subjects. It is a negative impact of which he is highly aware, as he continuously stresses the effect of abbatial behavior on the monks' virtues. Authorities, he believes, should foster their virtuousness and certainly not add to their sin by creating an environment of resentment. While it is a cornerstone of the

---

100 Vita Prima Sancti Bernardi, CCCM 89B, Lib. I, par. 38: *Semper enim priora sua nulla reputans, maiora moliebatur ad non parcendum corpori, ad studiis spiritualibus robur addendum, corpus suum uariis infirmitatibus per se attenuatum, ieiuniis insuper et uigiliis sine intermissione atterendo.*

101 Verbaal, "Cistercians in Dialogue," 235.

102 Vita Prima Sancti Bernardi, CCCM 89B, Lib. I, par. 70: *Et hac fultus auctoritate, ubicumque necessarium est in ecclesia Dei, cum oboedientiae uel caritatis urget necessitas, nullam refugit incommoditatem laboris sui. Cuius enim uoluntati tantum detulit, cuius consilio sic se humiliauit omnis tam saecularis quam ecclesiasticae dignitatis altitudo.*

Cistercian concept that the monks should strive for perfection and encourage and inspire each other, William warns heavily against an atmosphere of fear and envy (*invidia*).[103] Bernard, he claims, knew how to display humility and "promote charity" (*prouocatione caritatis*) in his words.[104] In doing so, he exemplified the ideal Cistercian abbot, who leads through love rather than power. One could call it a horizontal model of authority, for it does not insist on a hierarchical superiority but bases its claim to authority on spiritual insight. The monks subject themselves to Bernard's authority by "submitting their thoughts and understanding to his thoughts and understanding".[105] Such a relationship of authority is necessarily grounded in trust, admiration, and charity.

The Cistercian order was, in a way, founded on the principle of charity. At least in name: As the prologue of the *Carta Caritatis* states, the Cistercian constitution's sole concern is "love and the care of souls in divine and human matters".[106] The early Cistercian authors, in particular, displayed a great appreciation of interpersonal relationships, defined by charity.[107] Aelred of Rievaulx's theology, which considered spiritual friendship foundational for spiritual progress, is an expression of the Cistercian focus on relationality.[108] Although William does not emphasize the concept of *amicitia*

---

103 Vita Prima Sancti Bernardi, CCCM 89B, Lib. I, par. 71: *Sed et ipse omnem inuidiam aut mortificat exemplo humilitatis, aut mutat in melius prouocatione caritatis, aut si nequior aut durior est, obruitur pondere auctoritatis.*

104 Vita Prima Sancti Bernardi, CCCM 89B, Lib. I, par. 71. The twofold task of an abbot, as Janet Burton and Julie Kerr describe it, "[...] to show compassion and inspire love yet also command authority and preserve order [...]" (Burton and Kerr, *The Cistercians in the Middle Ages*, 84) is in William's conception really only one task: the abbot exerts authority precisely by humbling himself and 'provoking charity'.

105 Vita Prima Sancti Bernardi, CCCM 89B, Lib. I, par. 70: [...] *sic hodie ubique terrarum spirituales quique loquente eo seu tractante stant cedendo praecedenti et sensibus eius uel intelligentiis submittunt sensus suos omnes et intelligentias suas.*

106 *Hoc etiam decretum cartam caritatis uocari censebant, quia eius statum omnis exactionis grauamen propulsans, solam caritatem et animarum utilitatem in diuinis et humanis exequitur* (as quoted from: Monika R. Dihsmaier, *Carta Caritatis – Verfassung der Zisterzienser*, Schriften zur Rechtsgeschichte 149 (Berlin: Duncker&Humblot, 2010), 46).

107 Caroline Walker Bynum, "The Cistercian Conception of Community: An Aspect of Twelfth–Century Spirituality," *The Harvard Theological Review* 68 (1975): 276.

108 As Brian McGuire rightfully points out, the fact that most Cistercians considered friendship and community to be central to the monastic life is not as self-evident as it may seem, as the early eremites whose ideals they claim to restore had rejected friendship, out of fear that it might distract the monks from their spiritual path (Brian McGuire, "Bernard of Clairvaux," in *Medieval Philosophy of Religion: The History of*

as Aelred does, his portrayal of the community of Clairvaux reveal that he considered trust and love among the monks essential for the wellbeing of a monastic community. The concept of 'horizontal learning' seems to apply particularly well to these frameworks.[109] The monks learn from each other through imitation rather than being taught top-down. Those who find themselves in authoritative positions do so because of their spiritual state and not their political status within the order. In the Vita the figure of Bernard exemplifies this more than anyone, as he is an authoritative figure, friend, and servant simultaneously. Of course, this speaks primarily to William's ideals and visions and does not necessarily represent the realities of life at Clairvaux or in other Cistercian communities.

Still, Cistercian model of authority within the community and the larger context of the order differ clearly from the Cluniac conception. Given the external political circumstances at the time of the Cluniac rise, these monasteries relied strongly on centralization and displayed an authoritarian understanding of the spiritual pursuit.[110] The early Cistercian efforts to create a General Chapter of Benedictine abbots and the emphasis on the value of *caritas* in their structural organization could be read as an attempt to avoid the looming threat of an all too powerful and authoritarian Cluny.[111] At least in theory, the Cistercian system aimed to be based not on a self-evident superiority of the powerful but on voluntary subordination and mutual care;[112] this ideal extended both to the organization of the order and the organization of the communities themselves.

Western Philosophy of Religion, ed. Graham Oppy and Nick Trakakis (Slough, Buckinghamshire: Acumen Publishing, 2009), 114).

109   I am using the idea of 'horizontal learning' as it was applied to medieval communities by Micol Long and Steven Vanderputten as "knowledge transmitted and acquired in a context of informal interactions, to which traditional categories such as 'teachers' and 'disciples' do not necessarily apply" (Micol Long and Steven Vanderputten, "Introduction," in *Horizontal Learning in the High Middle Ages*, ed. Micol Long, Steven Vanderputten, and Tjamke Snijders, 9–16. Peer–to–Peer Knowledge Transfer in Religious Communities (Amsterdam: Amsterdam University Press, 2019), 9).

110   Verbaal, "Cistercians in dialogue," 234.

111   Hofmann Berman, *The Cistercian Evolution*, 150. However, as Steven Vanderputten points out, the Cluniac reality might have differed significantly from its Cistercian portrayal, and the role of the abbot of Cluny might not have been as unlimited as Bernard and other reformers made it out to be (Vanderputten, "The First Benedictine 'General Chapter'," 725).

112   Verbaal, "Cistercians in dialogue," 235.

The figure of the abbot thus was conceptualized as a *primus inter pares* and not as being of radically different status. This change of mentality is expressed in William's writings as well. Bernard, for instance, is not described as someone who demands obedience because of his standing within the order. He holds authority because he is loved by his subjects. To the community of Mont Dieu, William suggests a similar model:

> Obedience is a good guardian of our will, whether it depends on a command or a council, desires surrender, or is practiced simply out of love. According to the apostle Peter the sons of obedience purify their heart often more perfectly and more pleasantly if they subject themselves in obedience to the love of their equals or subordinates as if they would subject themselves in obedience to the coercion of a superior. In the first case, only love commands, advises, and obeys. In the other case, it is fear of punishment, or an imperious authority, or fearsome necessity is impending. In one case, obedience deserves more praise, and in the other case, disobedience is threatened with severe punishment.[113]

William acknowledges that there are two different kinds of authority, and he likely witnessed both in contemporary communities. On the one hand, there is an authority that exerts violent power and incites fear in its subjects. It is, as he describes it, an external kind of authority. Obedience to it would not require an internal transformation of the will but merely fear of punishment. William's emphasis, however, lies on the inner desires of the individual monk. While he is well aware that novices might require external structures to progress spiritually, his emphasis lies on the internal transformation of the monk. Through the spiritual process, blind or fearful submissiveness is gradually transformed into joyful and glad obedience.[114] More

---

113 Epistula ad fratres de Monte Dei, CCCM 88, Lib. 2, par. 240: *Bona ergo uoluntatis custos est obedientia, siue imperii illa sit, siue consilii, siue subiectionis, siue solius caritatis. Purius enim ac dulcius saepe, secundum apostolum Petrum, ad pares seu etiam ad minores suos, filii obedientiae castificant corda sua in obedientia caritatis, quam ad maiores subigant per obedientiam necessitatis. In illa enim sola uel praecipit uel consulit et obedit caritas; hic autem poenam uel timet uel minatur imperiosa auctoritas et meticulosa necessitas. Et in illa saepe obedienti maior debetur gloria; in ista uero inobedienti maior semper intentatur poena.*

114 This conception is reminiscent of the observation made by Sita Steckel in regards to the culture of learning from the 9th century onward, when, as she states, "students were encouraged to internalize the values and norms advocated and demonstrated by

than mere compulsion or habituation, perfected obedience is an attitude of freely given love. Stuck in the 'animal' state, the soul is necessarily dependent on external authority, but once it has achieved the 'spiritual' state, it is free to obey of its own volition.[115]

Individuals such as the Vita's Bernard, to whom William ascribes an extraordinary desire "to humiliate himself" (se humiliauit),[116] would be the ones to which authority would be attributed. The Cistercian authorities would derive their claim to power from their alignment with divine authority and are expressions of the latter. It is not a monk's, an abbot's, or a Bishop's status and ability that endows him with power, but his faith.[117] As William says in the Vita: "I cannot possibly question the faith in the faithful".[118]

This notion is also crucial to William's more general understanding of the relationship between ecclesial authority and divine inspiration regarding doctrinal and intellectual questions. Rather than opposing sources of knowledge, he envisions these two aspects as interlinked and dependent on one another. This differentiates William and his contemporaries from many mystics (and their critics) of later centuries. William did not envision a time

---

the master, and to cultivate a loving or friendly relationship with him. The student was considered mature when he possessed enough self-discipline to uphold the community's values on his own, and consequently came to respect the authority of the master. Under these circumstances, voluntary submission to magisterial authority appeared as a symbol of maturity." (Steckel, "Submission to Authority," 74).

115   The aspect of free volition appears several times throughout the Epistle. It is important to differentiate for William between the cell as a 'prison', in which people are forced – which would cause significant harm – and the cell as a 'home of peace'. Only if a monk turns lovingly to God in his cell is he protected from experiencing his recluse as bleak imprisonment (Epistula ad fratres de Monte Dei, CCCM 88, Lib. 1, par. 29). Nicholas Groves describes the process as such: "Grace is necessary for the progression along William's path from a simple willing (which would be possible even in the animal state, by willing to choose a good example) to willing informed by reason (the rational man), and leading to a willing that has been illumined (the spiritual man)" (Groves, "Image–Likeness," 108).

116   Vita Prima Sancti Bernardi, CCCM 89B, Lib. 1, par. 70.

117   In one of the Epistle's passages, William describes the criterion of authority according to the Tree of the Knowledge of Good and Evil (Gen 2,10): An abbot ought to know only that he does not own the critical spirit to judge between good and evil. In a Christian reiteration of the Socratic truth, William states: "His whole wisdom may be that he has no wisdom in this regard" (Et hoc omnis sit eius discretio, ut in hoc nulla ei sit discretio; Epistula ad fratres de Monte Dei, CCCM 88, Lib. 1, par. 51).

118   Vita Prima Sancti Bernardi, CCCM 89B, Prol., pag. 31: [...] quibus fidem non habere nulli fidelium licet (as translated in Costello ed., "The First Life of Bernard," 2.

when monks and nuns would defend outrageous exegetical and doctrinal statements by claiming direct divine revelation. The idea that inspiration would be used argumentatively and even set against established tenets of faith did not occur to him. His understanding is that human testimonies gain or lose their authority according to their spiritual fruit. Any statements inciting sin or promoting a heretical view hence disqualify themselves and can no longer be accepted as divinely inspired.[119]

This thought becomes more complex when applied to William's instructions in the Epistle. While a reader of the *Disputatio* might get the sense that reading Patristic writings and orthodox theology would evoke both faith and virtue, the advice he offers to the novices of Mont Dieu is more nuanced and, at times, even cautious. Theological erudition, he explains, is not necessarily a sign of spiritual advancement. On the contrary: those who believe themselves to be exceptionally knowledgeable might fall prey to pride or incite envy and discouragement in others.[120] Even those most versed in orthodox and Patristic theology might lack the focus they need to pursue perfection; conversely, even those who have achieved spiritual perfection find themselves distracted by "vain, silly, verbose, contentious, curious and ambitious tasks".[121] Although William does not explicitly identify these endeavors as academic or intellectual, it is more than likely that he is here envisioning theological flights of fancy among school-educated monks. The monastic vocation, he stresses at the outset of the Epistle, is not that of a scribe or a scholar, revealing that this understanding was not necessarily self-evident to the communities he was addressing.[122]

While William's critique of Abelard's and William of Conches' approach could suggest at first sight a refusal secular philosophy and its methods, while having no objections to the usage of Patristic texts whatsoever, the Epistle reveals that neither is the case. A novice must first progress to a level of rationality that allows him to use his intellectual faculty appropriately. The differentiation between knowledge and wisdom, a common

---

119 William considers orthodox theology to be the result of a pure heart which in turn will positively affect ethical choices of those who advocate for it (Andrew Lord, "Monastic Wisdom Theology: Insights from William of St Thierry," *Journal of Anglican Studies* 5, no. 1 (2007): 112).

120 Epistula ad fratres de Monte Dei, CCCM 88, Lib. 1, par. 144.

121 Epistula ad fratres de Monte Dei, CCCM 88, Lib. 2, par. 213.

122 It is unclear, however, whether he was implying here the exceptional reputation of Carthusian communities as scribes (see the chapter "6.2. Two Perspectives on Reform").

thread in William's writings, elucidates his skepticism regarding the use of authoritative texts. The 'animal' stage of the spiritual journey requires the novices to acquire basic knowledge. William defines it simply as the 'avoidance of evil' (*abstinemus a malis*).[123] It relies heavily on the persistent practice of spiritual exercises and steady habituation to the solitary life, as described earlier. This kind of negative knowledge, which focuses on what to reject rather than what to pursue, is not wisdom. Wise is the one who loves God and longs for God's knowledge.

That means knowledge can be taught and learned, but wisdom cannot. It has to be experienced or, expressed in William's signature sensual rhetoric, 'tasted' (*sapere*).[124] The novices, yet to be initiated into the mysteries of faith and the experience of divine love, cannot yet differentiate between knowledge and wisdom. Throughout the Epistle and based on the Augustinian scheme, William is cautious not to confuse the different stages of spiritual progress and not to confront the monks who are still confined to the animal stage with demands and expectations that correspond to the more advanced spiritual state. While William does not explicitly forbid the reading of non-biblical texts to the novices, the admonishment he offers to them about the general practice of reading has to be understood in direct reference to the three stages of spiritual advancement:

> The reader who seeks God in their reading receives support from whatever is read to that objective. The senses of the reader are captivated, and any understanding of the text is subjected to the obedience of Christ.[125]

William emphasizes in this passage that the benefit of a particular practice depends on the posture with which the monk approaches it. Whether one is reading texts of Biblical, Patristic or spiritual authority, a soul that has not yet become a lover of God will derive no wisdom from it and even runs the danger of misunderstanding the truth such texts hope to impart. Authority, therefore, changes its role throughout the monk's journey. In the first and most important stage, it guides the monk toward humility. Only once his obedience is perfected does the monk advance through the rational to the

---

123   Epistula ad fratres de Monte Dei, cccm 88, Lib. 2, par. 280.
124   Epistula ad fratres de Monte Dei, cccm 88, Lib. 2, par. 284.
125   Epistula ad fratres de Monte Dei, cccm 88, Lib. 1, par. 124.

spiritual stage. During this period, authoritative figures and their statements begin to nurture the monk's wisdom.

William's multifaceted treatment of authorities for the monastic context is summarized in the very last passages of the Epistle, and it is telling that he ends on this note:

> We are all unable to grasp God, but the one we love forgives. We acknowledge that we can neither speak nor think of God, yet we are called and drawn by God's love and out of love for God's love to speak and think of God. Therefore, the one who thinks ought to humble himself in all things and honor in himself the Lord, his God. He ought to lower himself in the vision of God, subject himself to every human creature in the love of his creator, offer his body as a holy, living, God-pleasing sacrifice as his own rational service.[126]

The passage's almost verbatim resemblance to the most famous statement of 20th-century theologian Karl Barth,[127] while not suggesting any direct influence, nevertheless reveals the astonishing degree of complexity in William's thought. The Christian faith, and the monastic life, in particular, present the individual with significant problems. One of them runs through the Epistle and shapes its fundamental message: on the one hand, human abilities are entirely unable to grasp the divine truth. On the other hand, Christians are called to engage with divine truth, proclaim it, and reach an understanding of it. It is a tension that condenses William's polarized view of authority as both entirely inadequate to 'teach wisdom' and, at the same time, beneficial and comforting to the monk's soul.

William makes the courageous decision to hold these two aspects of faith together in acknowledged tension. Both are equally true and equally exclusive. It is the human struggle with this dichotomy that the faithful soul

---

126   Epistula ad fratres de Monte Dei, CCCM 88, Lib. 2, par. 299–300: *Ad quod cogitandum impares omnino sumus; sed ignoscit quem amamus, et de quo digne nos non posse uel dicere uel cogitare confitemur. Et tamen ut dicamus, ut cogitemus, amore eius uel amore amoris eius prouocamur et trahimur. Cogitantis ergo est in omnibus humiliare seipsum et glorificare in seipso Dominum Deum suum; in contemplatione Dei uilescere se sibi; in amore Creatoris subiectum esse omni humanae creaturae; exhibere corpus suum hostiam sanctam, uiuentem, Deo placentem, rationabile obsequium suum.*

127   Karl Barth, *Das Wort Gottes Und Die Theologie. Gesammelte Vorträge* (München: Kaiser, 1929), 158: "Wir sollen als Theologen von Gott reden. Wir sind aber Menschen und können als solche nicht von Gott reden. Wir sollen beides, unser Sollen und unser Nicht–Können, wissen und eben damit Gott die Ehre geben."

should bring before God as a sacrifice, using even the spiritual difficulties that come with it to honor God. Humility is the attitude that enables the soul to do so without allowing the divine call to reflect and discuss God to incite a prideful attitude, nor letting its limitations stop it from pursuing its calling.

Both human adequacy and human calling are only appropriately understood from a place of humility. It is necessary to subject oneself to authority to acquire the habit of obedience. Yet, once achieved, the soul no longer views authority as an external force or limitation. As the humble and obedient soul progresses, it learns to view humility and obedience as acts of love that do not require the constraints of authority. William's conception of authority in the Epistle is thus a fundamentally dialectical one.

4   Concepts Applied: The Monk's Image-Likeness

The theoretical complexity of William's thought that I have just touched upon is certainly more surprising in a text for novices and monks than it is in a theological treatise or a Biblical commentary. Therefore, I want to take a closer look at how William makes his more theoretical concepts comprehensible to the monks that do not share his education and intellectual talent and are applicable to their everyday lives. I have chosen for this sake a topic already discussed in depth: the interlinked themes of self-knowledge and image-likeness. I have analyzed these themes in the context of William's exegetical *Expositio*[128] and focused mainly on his usage of Patristic tradition and any original contributions. To revisit the theme in the context of a more practically oriented work such as the Golden Epistle provides the opportunity to observe William's versatility on a literary level and to get a clearer understanding of how he brought his intellectual knowledge into the world of the monastery.

As Brian Patrick McGuire valuably remarked, most medieval mystic author "did not live to write about the mystical tradition", but reflect upon their daily life and work.[129] Even the more complex theological texts William wrote were essentially experiential and written for those pursuing the same spiritual journey. His concern was not to think and write adequately

---

128   see the chapter "5.3.'Know Thyself'. William's spiritual anthropology and his understanding of image-likeness".

129   McGuire, "Bernard and the Cistercian Mystical Tradition," 238.

about God but to serve God appropriately. Particular theological themes are not therefore treated explicitly as such but appear implicitly throughout the text, which aims as a whole at guiding its readers through the spiritual journey they have begun. This is the case, particularly with the theme of image-likeness.

As William understands it, achieving the state of image-likeness is the objective of any spiritual progress. It is the telos that accompanies the monks in all of their practices and at every stage of their journey. It is, therefore, a pervasive theme in the Epistle, a work distinctly dedicated to the monks' spiritual progress. While William does explicitly discuss the theme and offers Biblical and theological explications for it, it is important to note that it underlies the entire text and is not to be disentangled from William's more practical advice.

However, the definition of the state of image-likeness as the ultimate goal to achieve stands in contrast to the fact that the Epistle is addressed primarily to novices, who have yet to go a long way. The dynamic between anticipation of fulfillment and frustration over one's remaining inadequacies is the Epistle's common thread and a significant aspect of William's piety. The faithful monk finds himself in a constant transition between seeking and receiving, petitioning and thanking God. While the state of image-likeness is truly understood only once perfection is achieved, the concept and the steps that lead to its consummation have to be explained and taught. William seems aware of this tension when he assures his readers that God will go on to provide the understanding of the things he now relays to them.[130] Referring to 2 Tim. 2:7, he implies that his words require contemplation and will be further enlightened by divine inspiration. It is clear to him that certain aspects of what he discusses are not suited to be intellectually grasped, but to be trusted, reflected upon, and prayed about. Therefore, he offers a combination of intellectual and experiential knowledge.

In the Epistle, just as in the *Expositio* on the Song of Songs, the two theological concepts of image-likeness, and self-knowledge are closely intertwined. The human soul is able to know God because it is made in the image of God and thus resembles its maker. However, the exact nature of such a resemblance is complex to define, particularly in contrast to innate human sinfulness. William goes to great lengths to explain it more

---

130 Epistula ad fratres de Monte Dei, CCCM 88, Lib. 1, par. 24: *Intelligitis quae dico. Dabit enim Dominus uobis intellectum.*

pragmatically for the pastoral context. A fundamental notion he employs is the reception and enjoyment of divine love:

> The love of God, or the love that is God, the Holy Spirit, infuses the human love and spirit and appropriates it. As God loves Himself in a person, God unites the person – both their spirit and their charity – with Himself. Just as the body receives life only from its spirit, the affection of a person, called love, does not actually live or love God if not through the love of the Holy Spirit.[131]

The soul resembles God because God has claimed it. The work of the Holy Spirit allows for such a likeness and that unifies the human and the divine spirit. This enables a monk to witness his growing image-likeness directly. The more he experiences love for God, the more evident it is that God loves Himself within the human soul. William illustrates in a concrete way that the state of image-likeness is achieved once the monk relates to God in the same way God relates to Himself. Through a series of tangible examples, the concept becomes experiential. The monk's authentic self is found, for instance, in his enjoyment of God – an expression of divine enjoyment itself. Growing into likeness means recognizing the way in which one is recognized by God, embracing God as God has embraced oneself.[132] Essentially, it is the ability to see one's own created soul through the eyes of its creator. This is the satisfaction of seeing God 'face to face': the monk sees himself in God, and God sees Himself in him.[133]

More so – although it is present in most of William's works – it is not the metaphor of sight that is most prominent in the Epistle but that of taste. The monk's experience in solitude is one of savoring God and being savored by God. To some extent, the imagery used in the Epistle is the fulfillment of the promise William made in the *Expositio*. The Augustinian Neoplatonic

---

131   Epistula ad fratres de Monte Dei, CCCM 88, Lib. 1, par. 170: *Amor enim Dei, uel amor Deus, Spiritus sanctus, amori hominis et spiritui se infundens, afficit eum sibi; et amans semetipsum de homine Deus, unum se cum efficit et spiritum eius et amorem eius. Sicut enim non habet corpus unde uiuat nisi de spiritu suo, sic affectus hominis qui amor dicitur non uiuit, hoc est non amat Deum, nisi de Spiritu sancto.*

132   Epistula ad fratres de Monte Dei, CCCM 88, Lib. 1, par. 93: [...] *apprehendere sicut apprehensus est, et cognoscere sicut et cognitus est.*

133   Glenn E. Myers says about this passage: "The Intra–Trinitarian communion between the Father and Son expresses itself in the human spirit, and the human person thereby participates in this relationship of divine Persons" (Myers, "William's Legacy," 214).

framework, within which William unfolds his ideas, necessitates that God's qualities can only be recognized and received where they are already present.[134] That essentially means, for William, that only the person formed in the *imago* is able to grasp whose image it is and only truly understands the qualities of its maker, in which it participates. This notion is a cornerstone of Western mysticism. Through the use of sensual imagery, William can visualize this truth. The state of image-likeness, he claims, allows the soul to develop spiritual 'senses', or rather a sensory for the divine. Thus perfected, the soul can taste the divine sweetness and feel divine warmth within itself.[135]

Theologically, William is speaking of a full transformation of the spirit. In the more pastoral language of the Epistle, however, he focuses primarily on a transformation of the will. In one of the most explicit passages, he states that the state of image-likeness is synonymous with the state of willing God's will.[136] Therefore, his focus on the will is not only ontological, but also pedagogical. Intimate understanding of one's spiritual nature is a significantly more abstract notion than awareness of one's will and wishes. An emphasis on the latter allows William to offer unambiguous and systematic instructions for his readers rather than overexerting them with grand intellectual concepts.

In the *Expositio*, William mainly discussed self-knowledge regarding the soul and the spirit as a whole. In contrast, in the Epistle, he guides the monks in discovering their desires. Rather than presenting them simply with the assignment of 'knowing themselves', he explains the concrete steps they are called to take. Likeness, he makes clear, is not achieved from one day to another or in some singular moment of ecstasy.[137] It is a steady process that requires dedication and the willingness to honestly investigate one's motivation for even the most minor acts of every-day life. Achieving self-knowledge is possible through daily and disciplined self-examination.

---

134   Groves, "Image–Likeness," 105.

135   Epistula ad fratres de Monte Dei, CCCM 88, Lib. 1, par. 112: [...] *scabendo spiritum nostrum donec incalescat, ambiendo ad memoriam abundantiae suauitatis Domini, donec ipse in cordibus nostris dulcescat.*

136   Epistula ad fratres de Monte Dei, CCCM 88, Lib. 2, par. 258: *Velle autem quod uult Deus, hoc iam Deo similem esse est.*

137   William does consider individual ecstatic moments to be possible, albeit rare. Yet he is clear that likeness will not be achieved in its ultimate fulfillment until the hereafter (Bell, "The Mystical Theology," 88).

The novices are called to contemplate, precisely question, and thoroughly
study the workings of their will:

> If what one wants entirely is God, one must examine first to what ex-
> tent and in which way one desires God; whether one desires God to
> the disdain of oneself and all things that are or could be, and do so not
> only through the judgment of reason but through the loving inclina-
> tion of the heart. The will ought to be more than will: longing love
> (*amor*), selfless love (*dilectio*), divine love (*caritas*), and unity of spirit
> (*unitas spiritus*).[138]

A monk ought to carefully take inventory not only of the object of his longing but also its extent and its particular expression. The process is therefore
described as taking inventory of the roots and the consequences of desire.
In this specific passage, William assumes the existence of a positive desire
for God. A monk who experiences such desire is confronted with a set of
questions: is it all-consuming? What is he willing to sacrifice for it? Is it simply an intellectual desire, or does it affect every aspect of his soul? William
seems to be aware of the readiness with which desire for God and God's will
is proclaimed, especially in the monastic context. To request that *thy will be
done* is an essential part of the daily prayer practice of every monk. Yet William's directive reads like a warning, an admonition that formal confessions
are not good enough. A desire for God is to be expressed as a burning and
dedicated love.

However, the Epistle does not focus exclusively on examining one's positive longing for God but also discusses examining the will insofar as it strays
from God.[139] The monk is to dissect his sinful wishes and desires to let go of
them progressively. As is the case so often in William's works, Paul serves
here as the moral example for this practice:

---

138   Epistula ad fratres de Monte Dei, CCCM 88, Lib. 2, par. 256: *Si quod in totum uult, Deus
      est, discutiendum est ei, Deum quantum et quomodo uelit, utrum usque in contemptum
      sui ipsius omnium que quae sunt uel esse possunt; et hoc non tantum ex iudicio rationis
      sed etiam ex affectu mentis, ut iam uoluntas plus quam uoluntas sit, ut amor sit, ut dilec-
      tio sit, ut sit caritas, sit unitas spiritus.*
139   It is however important to note that this 'sinful will' is not substantial in itself, but
      marked by its deficiency. William's hamartiology is in line with the Augusinian con-
      ception that understands sin as unlikeness (Groves, "Image–Likeness," 106).

Take care, servant of God, lest you appear to judge those you do not want to imitate. I want you to do, while you are still ill, what the one who was the healthiest did when he said: "Jesus Christ has come, to sinners of whom I am the first". Paul did not say this in an impetuous lie but out of true self-knowledge. Whoever recognizes himself in sincere examination believes that no other sin compares to his because he knows no other sin but his own.[140]

Two things are remarkable in this passage. Self-knowledge is described here as a true and intimate knowledge not only of one's innate resemblance to God but also of one's sinful nature and more so of one's personal sin. First, this marks the introduction of a *via negativa* into the spiritual journey. The assumption of likeness to the divine can only be achieved by rejecting what is not divine. Second, the passage reveals that William does not call for the contemplation of the human and the divine state per se but the concrete acknowledgment of one's past and present sinful thoughts and behavior. In a psychologically astute observation, he notes that a person can only ever know their particular reality. Self-knowledge within such a framework is not as much the attainment of an abstract good but an individual self-reflection. The necessary rejection of sinfulness cannot be externalized. Judging others' behavior and repudiating them as deterrent examples does not actually benefit one's spiritual growth if one's inner thoughts are not seriously addressed.

This is especially important within the context of the monastic community, where the temptation of comparison is ever-present. William's careful differentiation between the three stages of spiritual progress allows him to warn the monks against undue comparisons and expectations from others. Simply because another monk has not yet advanced to one's own spiritual stage should not entice a monk to regress in his journey. William proposes a daily self-assessment to the monks:

Every order consists of three kinds of people. Just as they can be distinguished according to their names they can also be recognized

---

140 Epistula ad fratres de Monte Dei, CCCM 88, Lib. 1, par. 19: *Caue etiam, serue Dei, ne quoscumque imitari non uis, damnare uidearis. Volo hoc facias in aegritudine adhuc tua, quod cum sanissimus esset faciebat qui dicebat: Venit Christus Iesus peccatores saluos facere, quorum primus ego sum. Neque enim hoc dicebat Paulus mentiendi praecipitatione, sed aestimandi affectione. Qui enim perfecte examinando semetipsum intelligit, suo peccato nullius peccatum par esse aestimat, quod non sicut suum intelligit.*

according to the nature of their pursuits. All sons of the day [1 Thess
5,5] ought to carefully examine every day what they lack, where they
come from, how far they have come, and on what stage of progress
they find themselves on a given day or hour according to their self-
knowledge.[141]

This passage reiterates the idea that self-knowledge is achieved and expressed differently in each person. The advancement from the animal to the
spiritual stage is, therefore, not a linear process that takes place at a set
pace. Not only does the process require active discipline from the monks
but also their continual reflection. The demands placed on them, either by
themselves or their superiors, are directly dependent on their current spiritual state. A regular and honest assessment is therefore vital, not only for
the individual monk but also for the resulting relationships within the
community.

Self-examination is an essential tool for the development of divine likeness, but it is not the only one that is at the monks' disposition. Without
indicating precisely what kinds of exercises or practices he refers to, he explains that 'performing heavenly things' (*caelestia actitantur*) will transform
them; doing things that are akin to what God does will allow their souls to
resemble God as well.[142] In a different passage, he speaks particularly about
purity, both of the hands and the heart (*per innocentiam manuum et mundi-
tiam cordis*),[143] and therefore more about refraining from certain acts rather
than carrying them out. In any case, however, William makes it clear that
the monks' motives are of higher importance than their behavior in and of
itself. While actions are subjected to human judgment, the reasoning and
motivation behind them are subjected to divine judgment:

> As long as both kinds of people perform the same act simultaneously,
> people perceive the same acts. But God distinguishes between wishes
> and intentions. When one goes into oneself, one feeds the conscience

---

141   Epistula ad fratres de Monte Dei, CCCM 88, Lib. 1, par. 42: *Et cum ex his tribus homi-
       num generibus constet omnis status religionis, quae sicut propriis nominibus distinguun-
       tur, sic etiam dinoscuntur ex suorum proprietate studiorum, debent omnes filii diei, in
       die qui est, diligenter semper perspicere quid desit sibi, unde uenerint, quousque perue-
       nerint, et in quo proficiendi statu singulis diebus uel horis, sua se aestimatio
       deprehendat.*

142   Epistula ad fratres de Monte Dei, CCCM 88, Lib. 1, par. 32.

143   Epistula ad fratres de Monte Dei, CCCM 88, Lib. 1, par. 26.

with the fruits of one's intention. Yet both do not return to their conscience in the same way. Nobody likes to return to their action if the action was not fulfilled with the right intention.[144]

Although it is ultimately God who evaluates human behavior according to its intent, the monk can participate in his spiritual progress by trusting his conscience. William's usage of the term *conscientia* is complex and does not always follow clear terminological guidelines.[145] As Thomas x. Davis has determined, the conscience "becomes the matrix for self-knowledge", encompassing perceptive, cognitive, and moral functions.[146] The conscience allows him to ensure that his will is appropriately aligned with God's, both in retrospect and in anticipation of certain actions. It thus allows a monk to assess his own position on the spiritual ladder. While the memories of past transgressions will easily tempt the conscience of someone still tied to the sensual world, the conscience of a perfected spiritual mind will feel a deep hatred in response to such recollections.[147] The visceral reaction of the conscience to sin is the most accurate indicator of likeness or a lack thereof. It is the monk's central tool for the process of self-examination.[148]

William's emphasis on intentionality, rather than the behavior itself, allows him to reevaluate the role of monastic routine, a particularly important task in the context of the reform orders' strong accentuation of discipline. Discipline, he explains, is more than the sum of one's actions. It is not as

---

144 Epistula ad fratres de Monte Dei, CCCM 88, Lib. 1, par. 61: *Hi utrique quamdiu simul in actu sunt, homines uident similes actiones; Deus autem uoluntates discernit et intentiones. Cum uero unusquisque redit in sua, unumquemque ex fructibus intentionis suae pascit conscientia sua. Nec tamen ab utroque aeque ad conscientiam reditur, | quia nemo ad eam redire amat post actionem, qui recta intentione ad agendum ab ea non proficiscitur.*

145 Bell, "The Mystical Theology," 107.

146 Davis, "The Trinity's Glorifying Embrace," 136.

147 Epistula ad fratres de Monte Dei, CCCM 88, Lib. 1, par. 62: *Qui uero iam concupiscentiam uicit, quamdiu tamen ueri boni maior concupiscentia uel maior delectatio mentem eius non obtinuerit, cum exosa quadam uoluptate gestorum, uisorum, auditorum patitur imaginationes.*

148 What is reflected in William's emphasis on self-examination is the high degree of individuality that is granted in Cistercian communities. Rozanne Elder has put this in very practical terms when she compared the 12th-century Cistercian communities to "a modern Montessori school" that offered "personal freedom to grow at one's own rate" (Elder, *Formation for Wisdom*, 198). William shows in the Epistle that no one monk's journey toward self-knowledge looks alike, as every monk's conscience will reveal different deficiencies and qualities.

much fruit as it is root. The spirit with which one pursues one's tasks is what determines their ultimate value. Comparing the role of chores to the Pauline subordination of women to men (1 Cor 11,9), William claims that the physical execution of tasks is necessarily secondary to their spiritual fulfillment.[149] Likeness is not bodily but spiritual. Even though he speaks of 'heavenly actions' and dismisses some actions as entirely unsuitable for spiritual application,[150] he makes it clear that no actions are heavenly in and of themselves. Their actual purpose depends entirely on a person's soul and willingness to recover their lost likeness to God. Even the human disposition for artistry (*ingenio ars*) – as much as William rejects it in Cluniac architecture – is originally intended to reveal the inherent divine resemblance to humankind.[151] Yet, only the humble and the spiritually fervent can comprehend this intended usage for what it is and implement it in kind.

When William differentiates between the proud and the humble, however, it is especially important to keep in mind that his understanding of likeness encompasses both. There are two different kinds of likeness.[152] One of them is foundational: it is the likeness naturally embedded in human nature. Every soul participates in it, regardless of the individual's decision to do so or not. This kind of likeness, William boldly claims, is worthless in the eyes of God (*nullius est momenti apud Deum*).[153] Being proud of this natural likeness, the created *imago*, is pointless. The likeness that matters most is the one that is actively pursued; one that the human will, desire, and effort strive for. William's definition of true likeness as a likeness of will is not the result of his theoretical thought about the nature of God but of his pastoral interest: he hopes to inspire and encourage his monks rather than simply assuring them of their natural state – something that might incite laziness or complacency.

---

149   Epistula ad fratres de Monte Dei, CCCM 88, Lib. 1, par. 85: *Non enim uir propter mulierem, sed mulier propter uirum; non spiritualia exercitia sunt propter corporalia, sed corporalia propter spiritualia.*

150   Epistula ad fratres de Monte Dei, CCCM 88, Lib. 1, par. 85: […] *non tamen in hoc semper aeque conuenire uidentur omnia corporalia exercitia, sed quae cum spiritualibus propiorem habere uidentur similitudinem et affinitatem propiorem* […].

151   Epistula ad fratres de Monte Dei, CCCM 88, Lib. 1, par. 55.

152   William states that there are three types of likeness, the third of which is the unitas spiritus, which I will discuss. Yet, I would argue that the *unitas* is not a different kind, as David N. Bell seems to suggest (Bell, "The Mystical Theology," 88) but rather a different degree of likeness.

153   Epistula ad fratres de Monte Dei, CCCM 88, Lib. 2, par. 260.

The monastic calling, as he defines it, is that of enjoyment. The striving for likeness, too, is therefore tied to the role of enjoyment in the monks' individual journey. The soul that truly desires to approach and resemble God does so voluntarily,[154] out of freely offered love. The process of perfection, first and foremost, involves surrendering the heart to God. Love is inextricably linked with the purity and strength of will.[155] This means, in consequence, that the monk is to release all of the objects of his love that are not God. A will that is likened to the divine cannot desire anything other than God.[156] To direct the will towards God in such an exclusive way, both human effort and divine support are required.[157] William explains that there are two alternating aspects to the monk's spiritual journey. The vision of God that teaches the soul to discern what purity means (*intelligit puritati eius non conuenire immunditiam suam*)[158] on the one hand, and the eager purification of one's own heart (*qui uult uidere cor mundet*),[159] on the other. God wants to be enjoyed and imparts knowledge of His enjoyability to the soul. The task of preparing oneself for the enjoyment itself is the individual's responsibility.[160] That is what William believes to be the true purpose of the solitary and reclusive life. Both the preparatory effort and the divine graciousness can then work together to restore the soul to its original state.

---

154   Epistula ad fratres de Monte Dei, CCCM 88, Lib. 2, par. 261: *Sed est alia Deo magis pro-pinqua, in quantum uoluntaria, quae in uirtutibus consistit; in qua animus, uirtutis mag-nitudine, summi boni quasi imitari gestit magnitudinem, et perseuerante in bono constantia, aeternitatis eius incommutabilitatem.*

155   Epistula ad fratres de Monte Dei, CCCM 88, Lib. 2, par. 259: *Et ideo huic perfectioni nutrienda est semper uoluntas, amor praeparandus; uoluntas cohibenda, ne in aliena dissipetur; amor seruandus, ne inquinetur.*

156   Epistula ad fratres de Monte Dei, CCCM 88, Lib. 2, par. 262: *Super hanc autem et alia adhuc est Dei similitudo; haec de qua iam aliquanta dicta sunt, in tantum proprie prop-ria, ut non iam similitudo, sed unitas spiritus nominetur; cum fit homo cum Deo unus spiritus, non tantum unitate idem uolendi, sed expressiore quadam ueritate uirtutis, sicut iam dictum est, aliud uelle non ualendi.*

157   Groves points out, the "need to emphasize that this grace is by no means some mecha-nistic force, working on a nature that is ruined", but that William stresses the "cooper-ation" between the residual human virtue and divine grace (Groves, "Image–Likeness," 109). Rozanne Elder has importantly remarked that William had intensified his empha-sis on grace after his conflict with Abelard, and his refutation of Abelard's thoughts on free will (Elder, "William and the Renewal of the Whole Man," 119).

158   Epistula ad fratres de Monte Dei, CCCM 88, Lib. 2, par. 298.

159   Epistula ad fratres de Monte Dei, CCCM 88, Lib. 2, par. 296.

160   Epistula ad fratres de Monte Dei, CCCM 88, Lib. 2, par. 296.

The monk's life is fundamentally collaborative. Ideally, it unfolds like a love affair, alternating between active pursuit and passive indulgence. William's explanations reveal that his usage of the Song's language of bridal love and union is more than simply allegorical. It is the supreme expression of the intensity and the dynamic nature of the love between the soul and its God. William's identification of the monks with the yearning bride of the Song goes far beyond a narrative or visual approximation. The disappointment, the longing, the push and pull of desire – William finds that his emotional experiences are accurately reflected in the Scriptural language through which he expresses his spiritual journey. It is thus unsurprising that he interprets the consummation of marital love in a more proverbial way than most of his contemporaries. For likeness, he explains, is not the soul's ultimate goal. Its love culminates in union:

> This is called unity of spirit, not just because the Holy Spirit causes it or because it seizes the human spirit, but because this unity is the Holy Spirit itself: God, [who is] love (*Deus caritas*), who is the love of the Father and the Son, their unity and their sweetness, their goodness and their kiss, their embrace and what they have in common. In this highest unity of truth and truth in unity, the person receives the same in regards to God that the Son receives in regards to the Father, and the Father in regards to the Son, in their consubstantial unity. The blessed awareness is found in the midst of the embrace and kiss between the Father and the Son. When a person of God earns in an unspeakable and unthinkable way, not to become God but to become what God is, then this person is through grace what God is through nature.[161]

This passage is among the most explicit in the Epistle and possibly William's entire corpus. Much has already been said about William's concept of the

---

161 Epistula ad fratres de Monte Dei, CCCM 88, Lib. 2, par. 263: *Dicitur autem haec unitas spiritus, non tantum quia efficit eam, uel afficit ei spiritum hominis Spiritus sanctus, sed quia ipsa ipse est Spiritus sanctus, Deus caritas; cum qui est amor Patris et Filii, et unitas et suauitas, et bonum et osculum, et amplexus et quicquid commune potest esse amborum, in summa illa unitate ueritatis et in ueritate unitatis, hoc idem fit homini suo modo ad Deum, quod consubstantiali unitate Filio est ad Patrem uel Patri ad Filium. Cum in osculo et amplexu Patris et Filii mediam quodammodo se inuenit beata conscientia; cum modo ineffabili et incogitabili, fieri meretur homo Dei, non Deus, sed tamen quod Deus est: homo ex gratia quod Deus est ex natura.*

unitas spiritus, and my aim is not to reiterate it but to contextualize it.[162] Rather than a theological idea, the image of union is an expression of his practiced spirituality. It is an individual experience, a personal hope: hope for a time when no more sinful thought or corporeal reality has the power to distract and distance the soul from God any longer,[163] a time when the soul has been transformed according to the nature of divine love so that nothing of a different, lesser nature can have any hold on it.[164]

While William's concern in describing the state of *unitas* in such a way is certainly guided by the pastoral interest to encourage the monks of Mont Dieu, the aforecited passage also reflects his theological concepts. On the basis of the Epistle, Tyler Sergent has asserted that the *unitas spiritus* is for William what the idea of deification is for Christian tradition.[165] However, as with many expressions of deification, doctrinal uncertainties arise. Several scholars have defended William against possible accusations of heresy and have especially emphasized that William's *unitas* is, at best, a *unitas similitudinis* – a unity of likeness.[166] William's complex thought on the various stages of unity and his consistent emphasis on the human dependence on divine grace has been crafted with much doctrinal care.[167]

However, William's definition of unity in the Epistle pushes the envelope of orthodoxy. Especially since the Epistle is addressed, among others, to novices, who by and large will not have enjoyed the exceptional theological education that William has, it is questionable whether the distinction between 'being God' and 'being what God is' (*non Deus, sed tamen quod Deus est*) might not have been too subtle. William's strong condemnation of potentially heretical beliefs in the past makes it highly unlikely that he would have been simply careless in his phrasing. Tyler Sergent, in his study on the theme of *unitas spiritus* in William's sources and his texts, has shown

---

162 Notable are among others F. Tyler Sergent, "Unitas Spiritus and the Originality of William of Saint–Thierry," in *Unity of Spirit: Studies on William of Saint–Thierry in Honor of E. Rozanne Elder*, ed F. Tyler Sergent, Aage Rydstrøm–Poulsen, and Marsha L. Dutton, Cistercian Studies 268 (Collegeville, MN: Cistercian Publications, 2015); Bell, "The Mystical Theology," and McGinn, *The Growth of Mysticism*, 260–267. I referred to the concept already in the earlier chapter "5.4. Love. An Intellectual Principle."

163 Sergent, "Unitas Spiritus," 169.

164 Bell, "The Mystical Theology," 90.

165 Sergent, "Unitas Spiritus," 167.

166 Bell, "The Mystical Theology," 88.

167 Bell, "The Mystical Theology," 86. Rozanne Elder argues similarly that William's understanding of *participatio*, the human participation in divine being, "was neither unique in the West nor heterodox" (Elder, "The Renewal of the Whole Man," 126).

convincingly that among his contemporaries, only Guerric of Igny (ca. 1070–1157) had used the concept in a similar way as William does – namely as a union between God and the human soul – and that William has likely inspired Guerric in doing so.[168] It is thus clear that William's understanding of the idea was not conventional in the context of 12th-century monasticism. All these things considered, William was daring by letting the hope for *unitas spiritus* take center stage in his deliberations on spiritual progress.

This courage, I believe, is mainly expressive of the Epistle's genre and main intention. Other than is the case in such theological tractates as *De natura et dignitate amoris*, for instance, the Epistle's purpose is not to explicate theoretical ideas. Instead, William is interested here in the way doctrine becomes experience. Both the notion of image-likeness, self-knowledge and the idea of the *unitas spiritus* are vapid if they remain thought rather than lived. The spiritual journey that William presents to his readers is, as Nicholas Groves puts it, "one of paradox, contrast, and humor."[169] It is the lived drama between the Song of Song's two lovers, who find themselves passing from sorrowful yearning to excited anticipation and the intense embrace of union. Love, he believes and desires to teach to the monks of Mont Dieu, is inherently dynamic and transgresses boundaries. Whether they are boundaries of doctrine, authority, or conceptual consistency: the monk's will is never to be as concerned with any of them as with God.

---

168   Sergent, "Unitas Spiritus," 169–170.
169   Groves, "Image–Likeness," 111.

Conclusion to Part 3

In the first two parts of this book, I have discussed William's thought as arising from the area of tension between the intellectual innovations taking place in the 12th century and the concern for faithful transmission of truth according to authority. In this last part, I intended to contextualize William's position regarding these contemporary controversies as grounded in his aspiration for monastic reform and his pastoral concern for the emerging reform communities. I argue that his affiliation with the Cistercian reform movement and its ideals is not simply one aspect of his work but reflects his fundamental motivation. His 'Vision for Life in the Monastic Community' – the title I have set for this discussion – is simultaneously the basis of his vision for Christian scholarship and the church as such. This observation reinforces what Brian McGuire has rightfully stressed: "The pragmatic and work-oriented everyday life of the Cistercians seeking to follow Benedict's Rule was the main concern for virtually all monks".[1] The theological concepts with which William operates in his exegetical works and his treatises are not abstract. While describe the human condition and the anthropological possibility of entering into an intimate relationship with the divine, they are also a concrete reflection of obedience to the Benedictine rule and the sensually experienced liturgical life of the monastery.

I have shown that William considers the monastic pursuit the pinnacle of the Christian life, a conception that marks William as decidedly Cistercian. At the same time, however, his ideals clearly transcend the boundaries of the Cistercian community; they are meant to be universal ideals of piety. They hence apply as much to the Carthusian community of Mont Dieu as they do – or should, according to William – apply to any other monastic community. This claim of universality arises from the close interconnectedness between ethics and epistemology within William's framework. The ideas of humility as a prerequisite for insight and love as an intellectual principle reveal themselves particularly fruitful in the monastic context of lived spirituality. Thomas Davis has developed a definition of wisdom, as it

---

1 McGuire, "Bernard and the Cistercian Mystical Tradition," 238. A very similar observation was made by Berger and Nord in their analysis of William's prayers, where they stated that "even where William speaks dogmatically, he remains the abbot and pastoral caretaker of his monks" ("Denn Wilhelm ist auch dann wenn er dogmatisch redet, immer der Abt und Seelsorger seiner Mönche"); Christiane Nord and Klaus Berger, eds., "Einführung." In *Meditationen und Gebete* (Frankfurt: Insel Verlag, 2001), 8.

is represented in the Golden Epistle: "Wisdom is a piety that is the worship of God. Piety here is to be understood not in the context of pious devotions, a more contemporary connotation. Rather, piety is a fierce, selfless devotion; an authentic, steadfast love for God that brings about likeness to God since love has taken on the qualities of charity, the selfless charity that is God."[2] This understanding expresses precisely the dependence of theological endeavors on concrete practice and spiritual pursuit; more so, it represents, once again, the reciprocal effect of faith and knowledge, which I have identified as a running theme in William's thought.

Furthermore, my discussion of 'horizontal authority' as a model of leadership within the monastic community reveals that spiritual growth, dependent on such principles as humility and charity, is also considered determinative of a community's hierarchic structure. William's complex relationship with abbatial responsibility is reflected in how he integrates the necessity for personal contemplation into every aspect of the concrete interpersonal relationships of the monastery as well. It is the 'faith of the faithful' that cannot be questioned. Thus, it is also by the individually faithful, who value their spiritual progress above all else, that a monastic community should be led and guided. I have underlined that there are striking parallels between the way Patristic and Scriptural authorities, on the one hand, and concrete ecclesial authority, on the other, are conceptualized in William's work. These parallels are not coincidental but grounded in his basic conception that guidance depends on wisdom, which is the fruit of spiritual devotion. Whether it is the figure of Paul or Bernard, it becomes clear that what William values as authoritative is not their status nor their intellectual abilities but the human–divine intimacy they each were blessed to have experienced.

William's emphasis on authority, particularly Patristic authority, ought not to be viewed merely within the context of proto-scholastic developments but within the context of reform and renewal of monastic structure. Changing this perspective allows us to view William's defense of orthodoxy according to authority not as a conservative attempt to preserve old structures but as a courageous attempt to revive what he believed to have become stale and empty. Ian P. Wei has noted in his study on medieval intellectual culture that it would be a mistake to view the monastic world of the 12th century as 'static' compared to the highly innovative context of the urban schools, for it was clearly defined by dynamic change as well.[3] Indeed,

---

2   Davis, "The Trinity's Glorifying Embrace," 152.
3   Wei, "Intellectual Culture," 52.

the figure of William exemplifies this notion particularly well: the belief in the catholic faith as transmitted through a history that had become authoritative led him to believe not that change was impossible but rather inevitable. His admiration for the great Christian figures of the past necessarily had incited in him a passionate desire for renewal and restoration.

Through the Lens of Prayer. Concluding Thoughts

In the introduction, I presented the three parts of this book as distinct contexts that provide different perspectives on the person and work of William of Saint Thierry. In the course of these explorations, however, there was one perspective in particular that has proven to be the lens through which to view all others: William's concern for the individual soul's experience of God. It infuses the intentionality, methodology, and content of all of his reflections. For this concluding chapter, I will retrace some central roles that authority and original authorship play in William's understanding of personal devotion. Few of his works represent this aspect with as much honesty, nuance, and care as his *Meditativae Orationes*, William's prayers, and meditations.[1] Written in the form of a *lectio divina* on Psalms, they offer an echo of the liturgical space of the Cistercian monastery, and exemplify the ways in which monastic reform did not intend to reduce role of the psalmody, but to imbue it with new spiritual significance. Read as a hermeneutical key to William's oeuvre and theology, they also represent how William consistently used Scriptural exegesis as a foundation for personal monastic spirituality.

Within the Cistercian context, prayer is not simply repetitive practice. Even in the context of the liturgical office, it is considered an essential part of personal formation. As I have shown in my analysis of William's literary self-representation and his conception of Christian authorship, it is also an epistemological starting point; an attitude with which to approach the pursuit of truth; a fundamental necessity for any relationship between God and the individual. The praying soul knows and worships the source of her knowledge. Prayer, understood as entering the process of growing into likeness to the divine, is the prerequisite for insight. The Christian thinker who relies on prayer demonstrates awareness of the limitations of the human *ratio*, simultaneously asking God to span the vast distance between them and showing gratitude for the grace already received. Given that William, very much in a Cistercian sense, has centered his concept of Christian thought on the attitude of prayer, his concrete prayers are a fertile source for us to find his theoretical notion practically realized.

---

1   William had composed these works over a longer period of time, while he was abbot of
     Saint Thierry (1121–1135), as I discussed in the Introduction.

In the following, I will present three aspects of William's thought, reflected in his prayers. They serve as analogies of the three contexts I have chosen to discuss in this book. I will select only three meditations respectively to revisit each of the three main chapters of this volume: *Meditatio 11*, which will allow me to discuss William's epistemology and the reciprocal role of *ratio* and *auctoritas*; *Meditatio 111*, which will provide the grounds for a reflection on William's core theme of love as an intellectual principle, and lastly *Meditatio VII*, which I will interpret as an expression of William's notion of authority as it relates to monastic living. Through the lens of these meditations and their main themes, I will return to my two initial research questions: the role of authority in William's conception of the Christian task, on the one hand, and the contents and limitations of his reception of tradition, as he displayed it in his spiritual works, on the other hand.

Meditatio 11. The Possibility of Acquiring Knowledge of God

Throughout the *Meditativae Orationes,* William often turns to the literary device of self-reflection. While in dialogue with God, he also shares his thoughts, emotions, and experiences with his readers. William is not a 'visionary' mystic: he rarely discusses moments of ecstasy, visions or particular revelation.[2] Yet, in his prayers, he reveals more about the process of receiving inspired knowledge. In several passages, William speaks of educational and formational encounters with God. Some of them are worth examining here since they could be understood as synoptic accounts of the interplay between divine inspiration and authoritative teachings within one person's soul.

In his second meditation, William poignantly and movingly recounts a period of depression in his life. The state, he explains, is akin to a 'slumber of negligence' (*somno negligentiae*);[3] only ever half-awake, he cannot perceive reality clearly.[4] His heart, he claims, feels already dead (*mortuus a*

---

2 "William's was a more theoretical mind than Bernard's and his works reveal the problems he experienced in balancing his intellectual and his ascetic dispositions. Apparently, he had difficulties bringing his inner voices into harmony. He seemed to compensate for this tension in individual mystic ecstasy" (Verbaal, "Cistercians in dialogue," 239–40).

3 Meditativae Orationes, CCCM 89, Med. 2, par. 10.

4 Meditativae Orationes, CCCM 89, Med. 2, par. 5: *Ego uero usu prauo et stupore nimio obdurui, et didici et assueui contra solis splendorem dormitare, non uidere occurrentia; in mari positus, non audire maris rugitum uel caeli tonitruum, mortuus a corde.*

corde).[5] During this time, William experiences one of the most tragic elements of a monk's life: spiritual isolation. William feels so distanced from God that his daily monastic life becomes futile. Devotion, he cries out to God, has become torture:

> I hear of your great works in the psalms, the hymns, and the spiritual songs. What you have said and done shines to me through your gospels. The examples given by your servants incessantly thrash my eyes and ears. They fill me with terrors and compete with the promises of your true Scripture that constantly pierce my eyes and make my ears go deaf with their strident sound. But I am hardened by perverse habituation and the numbness of the mind.[6]

It becomes clear from this passage that neither Scripture nor tradition offer knowledge of God in an objectively accessible way. Reading Scripture alone does not determine what one derives from it. While one person might be comforted by the stories of the gospel, another might be led deeper into self-hatred. Neither devotional texts nor practice consist of rationally graspable insight alone. Their value reflects the moral state of the person reading, singing, and meditating. William's personal experience exemplifies what we encountered discussing the concept of reader- and authorship arising from the *Expositio super Epistolam ad Romanos*: Biblical texts are not mere documents. Reading them means entering into a relationship with them, their human and their divine author. Whether the truth they contain can be accessed is not a question of rational ability but of the complex interplay between authority and inspiration.

This becomes apparent as William continues to share in his prayer how God eventually makes Himself known to him. The analogy of sleep is central in William's narrative – it is the Holy Spirit who finally wakes him from his destructive state of numbness. Telling him to come to God and let himself be 'enlightened', this pneumatological encounter is, at first, a shock to William's system: his mental senses are now, after having relied for too long on his physical senses alone, overstrung.[7] Yet, once he heeds the Spirit's

---

5 Meditativae Orationes, CCCM 89, Med. 2, par. 5.
6 Meditativae Orationes, CCCM 89, Med. 2, par. 5: *Audio enim in psalmis et hymnis et canticis spiritualibus magnalia tua. Rutilant mihi in euangeliis facta uel dicta tua; uerberant assidue oculos meos et aures exempla seruorum tuorum; concutiunt me terroribus et uellicant promissis scripturae ueritatis tuae, quae se assidue ingerunt oculis meis, et strepitu {suo} contundunt surditatem aurium mearum. Ego uero usu prauo et stupore nimio obdurui* [...].
7 Meditativae Orationes, CCCM 89, Med. 2, par. 7: *Sed cum somnolentos oculos in eum uolo dirigere, reuerberantur, desuefacti luci et assuefacti tenebris.*

instruction and finally turns towards God's aid and habituates his inner eyes to the divine, he is able to perceive God more clearly. He states:

> Suddenly, when I awake from the sleep of negligence, I behold God, about whom the divine law teaches me: "Hear, Israel, the Lord your God is one", and in him, I will be illuminated, whom I will adore and praise, and on whom I have focused the entire intuition of the mind: the Trinity of God appears to me, which the catholic faith, that my parents have invoked in me, that I have memorized in practice, and that you yourself have commended to me through your Doctors, reveals to me.[8]

This passage is, I believe, representative of William's spirituality in many ways. Experiences of God are entirely impossible without the element of divine self-revelation. It is the Holy Spirit who guides – at times forceful, playful, or gentle – the human soul to seek solace in God. Only the soul that turns to God in desperation and humiliation will find enlightenment. As William has presented the transformation of Paul in his Commentary on Romans, he too experiences, in this instance, divine humiliation as a prerequisite for a genuine encounter with God.

Yet, this receptive experience of inspiration is not devoid of an authoritative and doctrinal reconnection: it is through inspiration that William can perceive truth in the traditional dogma. The 'catholic faith' that his parents, his teachers, and the Fathers have imparted to him is essentially the soil in which the Spirit can plant the seed of spiritual transformation. The God the Spirit reveals is consistent with what orthodox tradition states about divine nature. William's prayers are arguably more doctrinally nuanced than those of other contemporaries. Throughout the second meditation, the authority of the church and the Church Fathers is described as a voice harmonious to that of the Spirit, accompanying the inspired faith and protecting the doctrinal contents of its inherent truth.

This occurs, for instance, when William's mind is 'ambushed' by heretical ideas.[9] Whenever such thoughts come up, he explains that "faith

---

8 Meditativae Orationes, CCCM 89, Med. 2, par. 10: *Propter quod, cum a somno negligentiae expergefactus, subito respicio in Deum, de quo me lex diuina instruit dicens: Audi Israel, Dominus Deus tuus Deus unus est, et in eum a quo sum illuminandus, quem sum adoraturus uel oraturus, dirigere omnino habeam mentis intuitum, occurrit mihi Trinitas Deus, quam fides catholica a progenitoribus mihi incantata, usu ipso inculcata, a te ipso tuis que doctoribus commendata mihi demonstrat.*

9 Meditativae Orationes, CCCM 89, Med. 2, par. 11: *Cum haec imaginatio, id est mens imaginans, {etiam} nolens imaginatur [...].*

comes and rejects them, reason judges them through faith and authority condemns them [...]".[10] William is speaking here about views of the Trinity that arise from a specific spiritual practice. As the mind turns to prayer, he claims, the three persons of the Trinity can easily appear distinct from one another. Only through the cooperation of inspired, rational, Scriptural, and ecclesial authority can the praying mind identify this perception as a false fantasy (*imaginatio*).[11] No one of these elements can be used individually in order to override the harmonious voice that arises out of their interplay:

> Even though faith, the ratio, and authority teach me to think of the Father in his own right (*per se*), the Son in his own right, and the Spirit in its own right, it is still not admissible to believe about the Trinity what is temporal, what is local, what establishes a division of substance according to number or what sounds like a confusion of the persons. For the unity of Trinity (*trinitatis unitatem*) is preserved if solitude is removed, and the Trinity of unity (*trinitatem unitatis*), when the divine substance receives no numerical plurality.[12]

This passage demonstrates the complexity of William's epistemological system. While there are rational arguments and even particular authoritative citations or statements of faith that emphasize the particularity of the three divine persons, they nevertheless have to be embedded into a larger framework of Scriptural and ecclesial truth to be interpreted correctly. Both the threefold structure of the Trinity and its unitary character is contained equally in the doctrinal tradition of the church, which is ultimately a perfect and divinely inspired cooperation between Scripture, Patristic observations, and appropriately applied human ratio.

It is difficult not to read in William's accentuation of unanimity and harmony between these different kinds of authority, another implicit critique of dialectic theology. If tradition were not to be taken as an integral

---

10   Meditativae Orationes, CCCM 89, Med. 2, par. 11: [...] *uenit fides et reprobat, ratio per fidem diiudicat, auctoritas condemnat* [...].
11   Meditativae Orationes, CCCM 89, Med. 2, par. 11.
12   Meditativae Orationes, CCCM 89, Med. 2, par. 12: *Nam cum et fides et ratio et auctoritas cogitare me doceant Patrem per se, {Filium per se, Spiritum sanctum per se,} nil tamen in | sancta Trinitate censent admittendum, quod tempore, uel loco, uel numero substantiae faciat diuisionem, uel personarum sonare uideatur confusionem. Sic enim astruunt trinitatis unitatem, ut solitudinem remoueant; sic unitatis trinitatem, ut in deitatis substantia non recipiant numeri pluralitatem.*

consistent body of truth but instead as a collection of statements whose in-dividual validity and weight have to be determined through dialectic dis-cernment, a fragmentation of truth takes place; elements of faith are overstressed, while others are lost. The discussion of the persons of the Trin-ity in their particularity can only be pursued if their unity is affirmed simul-taneously. William fears this would be no longer possible if theological arguments were examined according to their inherent logical consistency rather than their place within the larger stream of revealed and transmitted Christian faith.

The position he seems to hold in his prayers reflects the kind of vision for Christian thought and authorship that we have seen him defend regarding his conflict with Abelard. William appears not as an anti-rationalistic con-servative but as a nuanced spiritual writer who considers it his duty to inte-grate the human intellect into a holistic service of God. Rationality certainly plays a decisive role within this epistemological concept, yet it is not one of discernment and differentiation but of harmonization.

Yet it is, of course, not Abelard he addresses in his prayer. Written both as a self-reflection and pastoral guidance for his monastic community, William addresses the individual monk on his spiritual journey. As we have seen in William's Commentary on Romans and his Golden Epistle, he often pursues a pedagogical concern, and the pastoral accompaniment of the monks' spiritual development is at the heart of William's self-conception as an abbot and monastic writer. His doctrinal and his exegeti-cal deliberations stand in the context of monastic formation: William does not (only) teach his pupils *what* to believe and *what* to think, but more so, *how* to achieve a spiritual state, from which nothing but true faith and thought can spring. Within this framework, Christian thought is but the systematic expression of a soul aligned with God. Spiritual discipline and practice are thus not part of a sphere that is separate from intellectual the-ology. The two are closely intertwined and constitute a common cognitive foundation. William explains these correlations in the following passage of his second meditation:

> [Grace] subjects us to humility, humility to authority, and authority to faith. Faith instructs reason, and reason, nurtured by faith, destroys and discards phantasies.[13]

---

13 Meditativae Orationes, CCCM 89, Med. 2, par. 13: *Ipsa uero subicit nos humilitati, humil-itas auctoritati, auctoritas fidei. Fides instruit rationem; ratio per fidem erudit uel des-truit et abicit imaginationem* [...].

The spiritual process begins, for William, with a divine act of grace. Grace aids the human process of moral formation, allowing the prideful fallen nature to transform into her original state; it is gracious humiliation that William addresses here. Of course, humility is not simply bestowed on the believer. As we have seen in the chapters regarding William's requirements for the monastic life, humility is a virtue that requires patience and diligent practice. This is the case in a twofold way.

In his Commentary on Romans, William presented humility as an epistemological necessity for any theological insight. Pride, he declared, as a mark of ontological unlikeness to the divine, creates a distance between the soul and God that makes intuitive knowledge of God fundamentally impossible. The intellect that misattributes its achievement to itself rather than God forfeits its entitlement to divine truth. Humility, reversely, is the "facilitator of human-divine intimacy".[14] The humble soul is so close to God and the divine virtues that mediated knowledge of God becomes possible. Yet, as William reveals in his more pastoral works, humility is not only a virtuous state of being but a concrete practice of submission to authority. Whether it is in the form of the monastic life, which I have earlier characterized as a life of 'loving obedience', or in the form of content agreement with the doctrinal opinion of the church, humility is a moral requirement for the spiritual journey as such.

Only the mind that, by grace, humbly hands over the responsibility for determining truth to the church can be sure that the content of its faith is aligned with Christian truth; that its beliefs are, in fact, 'faith' (*fide*). Just as humility itself, faith contains for William a more intellectual and more practical dimension. Stating, as he does in the above-quoted passage, that the submission to authority 'leads' to faith, William emphasizes both the corrective and the inspiring element of authority. As I have discussed concerning William's treatment of the Biblical and the Patristic authors, he treats them as "living, breathing companions".[15] Much like the authority figures within a monastic community, the doctrinal authorities of the church are sources of guidance and inspiration. They not only teach the contents of faith but exemplify the experience of a faithful life.

However, human faith in the church's authority does not remain the last stage in the spiritual journey. Faith, in turn, takes on a pedagogical role, as it instructs the human ratio – not in a restricting, but in an empowering

---

14   see the chapter "1.7. Humilitas and the Ideal Reader".
15   see the chapter "2.1. Reading Romans from Two Perspectives".

sense. Rationality is not excluded from the soul's spiritual development but aligned with the purpose the humble and faithful soul pursues. Summarized, what he explains here is the concept of *ratio fidei*.[16] This kind of faith-infused rational ability takes on an important responsibility: it is the human faculty that, in turn, instructs what William calls the 'imagination'. Through the kind of rational reflection that discerns, based on orthodox faith, what is possible or impossible regarding divine truth, the mind can protect itself against sensual mirages.

It is unclear whether William was concerned in this instance with the 'figments' of heresy he had attributed to Abelard or William of Conches, or the kind of doubt and sinfulness, against which he warned the monks in his communities, as well as the Carthusian novices of Mont Dieu. In reality, the distinction might be rather superficial. Within William's framework, which intertwines doctrinal and moral truth, heresy and sinful attachments are symptoms of the same underlying problem: a lack of humility and faith. Making both the potential for knowledge and the potential for moral righteousness dependent on the reception of and the response to divine grace allows William to fundamentally interconnect the different contexts of his life. No problem he addresses appears isolated. The emergence of heretical ideas, then, is inherently connected to a deficient virtuousness of the proponents of Christian thought; defending orthodoxy is not simply a matter of right opinions but of the protection of souls, whose salvation might be endangered by the moral implications of false doctrines.

Meditatio III. The Sensus Amoris

In his third meditation, William grapples again with the question of possible spiritual insight. This time, he centers his discussion on the feeling of longing and the experiences of the heart. There is a certain dialectical tension underlying this text, namely between the intense human desire to know and love God on the one hand and the limitations of the human condition on the other. It is only from a position of prayer that William can hold this tension (albeit not to dissolve it). The theoretical treatment of the topic of knowledge of God becomes here a dialogical one as William enters into a pleading conversation with the 'object' of his yearning. He does so, for instance, in the following passage:

---

16   see the chapter "Interim Conclusion pt. 1".

Forgive, Lord, forgive my inappropriateness and recklessness. We dare as long as we burn. Your fire, which you came into the world to ignite, and which you wanted to see burn so intensely, urges us to do so. I beseech thee, by your omnipotent goodness, by the most lenient patience you always show us, to tolerate that I am still looking for something. Tell me what it is that my soul desires when it desires your countenance.[17]

The idea of a spiritual quest as obtrusiveness appears several times throughout the *Meditativae Orationes*. It expresses the dilemma of the human state, as William describes it: the longing for intimacy with God is simultaneously the central purpose of the human, and more particularly the monastic life, yet a sign of impatience and possibly ingratitude in regards to the divine revelations already received. William is not content with the knowledge he has been bestowed, he claims, but driven by his deep desire, he is still 'seeking something'; still hoping to get closer to what he believes to be the face of God. To take both aspects of this anthropological dilemma seriously, William has to turn to God, confessing his demand for a more profound relationship and, at the same time acknowledging his limited potential to embark on such a journey. Ultimately, he admits, he does not even know precisely what he is looking for.

William's approach in his prayers differs fundamentally from any systematic theology because he not only searches for answers to a clearly defined set of questions – or, more poignantly, *questiones* – but begins his meditation from a place of ignorance, even regarding the content of the questions themselves. Striving to know the face of God has to entail some preliminary knowledge of what the face of God is in the first place. Understanding as much as the question of divine nature, or as William puts it, the question of how God is, exceeds the limitations of the human mind.[18] William does not go into the details of the theoretical issues, such 'theological' questions

---

17   Meditativae Orationes, cccm 89, Med. 3, par. 7: *Ignosce, Domine, ignosce improbitati et importunitati meae. Adhuc audemus, quia ardemus. Ignis tuus urget nos, quem uenisti in terram mittere, et uoluisti uehementer accendi. Obsecro te per omnipotentissimam bonitatem tuam et per mansuetissimam semper in nos patientiam tuam, patere adhuc me aliquid quaerentem, et dic animae meae quid est quod desiderat, cum faciem tuam desiderat.*

18   Meditativae Orationes, cccm 89, Med. 3, par. 7: *Quid ergo est: sicuti es? Hoc uidere supra nos est, quia uidere quod tu es, hoc est esse quod es.*

present, but such passages in the prayers are reminiscent of the limitations he set up for theological inquiry in the *Disputatio* against Abelard.

Referring, in particular, to Ambrose of Milan, William had there defined the boundaries of desire for knowledge. While it is allowed to know in what form God has revealed Himself, it would constitute a transgression of the human state to ask about the *modus operandi* of said revelation.[19]

Theological thought, other than philosophical or scientific deliberations, therefore, must start not from a place of theoretical and rational reflection but with an orientation towards God as the simultaneous telos and source of the knowledge sought. For the monks William addresses in his prayers, this means practically that the first stage of their spiritual journey is to ask God about the nature and the content of their aspirations. Therefore, the principal authority implicated within this aspect of William's methodology is not ecclesial opinion nor communal tradition but divine self-mediation. What does this, in turn, say about William's typology of the Christian thinker? The two main observations are contained in this essential statement: "Yes, [a person can know God] entirely, but not in every way."[20] This means that while William draws up very clear limitations, particularly for the human *ratio*, he nevertheless allows for a strong possibility of seeing and knowing God. He does so by shifting the emphasis away from the rational faculty and its potential and towards the heart, as the 'organ of love'.

In his Commentary on the Song of Songs, William had worked extensively with the Gregorian concept *amor ipse notita/intellectus est*: love is intellect. In my discussion of the concept, I have pointed out that William works with several notions that describe this particular form of the intellect, for instance, the *intellectus spiritualis* or the *sensus amoris*. The human soul, exemplified in the context of his exegesis as the longing bride, develops a new kind of sensory perception. God as Love, William explains, cannot be known with any other faculty but the faculty of love itself. In his prayers, he returns to this theme once again. In less poetic but instead more pedagogical terms, William explains what he means by the *sensus amoris* and why

---

19   Disputatio adversus Petrum Abaelardum, CCCM 89A, cap. 2, pag. 21, linea 145–148: *Quid te quaestionum tormenta delectant? Mihi licet scire de Filio Dei quod natus est, non licet scire quomodo natus est. Item: "Non sunt nuda haec nomina, sed operatricis uirtutis indicia. Non enim ipse Pater qui Filius, sed inter Patrem et Filium generationis est expressa distinctio, ut ex Deo Deus intelligatur".*

20   Meditativae Orationes, CCCM 89, Med. 3, par. 8: *Sic omnino, sed non per omnem modum.*

the heart rather than the rational mind is what enables human knowledge of God:

> The sense of the soul is love, through which it is able to perceive what it senses, whether it is lightly touched or hurt. When the soul extends [this sense] towards something, it is transformed into what it loves. It does not take on its nature but conforms to the affect of the loved object. [The soul] cannot love something good simply because that thing is good, except if it becomes good itself through that good thing.[21]

The heart is the organ that can perceive divine love. In the process, it does not become love itself, but it adjusts to the object of its perception, in the same manner as the eye or the ear, according to William's notion of physical, sensory processing, would turn into the thing that it perceives.[22] The heart then does not love God merely because of God's goodness, but because it has become good itself, through its focus on God. This perceptive transformation is then the basis of what William describes as the process of self-discovery or self-knowledge. What can perceive good has itself become good; only those changed by love into a loving being can perceive love.

In this short passage, William interweaves some of his central concepts regarding the spiritual journey. First, when it comes to knowing God, the intellectual faculty that is able to perceive divine love is the one capable of love. While the *ratio* has its place within the larger spiritual process, as I have discussed in the previous chapter, it is not through rational understanding that the human intellect is able to perceive God but through a likening to the divine nature of love. This leads, second, to the idea of self-knowledge as a cornerstone of William's epistemology. The soul that is transformed into an image of love is able to know God as intimately as it is possible for her in recognizing her likeness to the divine nature. And third, it becomes clear that this type of knowledge of God involves not only the human intellect but the human existence in its entirety. The spiritual process is necessarily also an ethical, sensual, physical, and practical one.

---

21   Meditativae Orationes, CCCM 89, Med. 3, par. 10: *Sensus enim animae amor est: per hunc, siue cum mulcetur siue cum offenditur, sentit quicquid sentit. Cum per hunc in aliquid anima extenditur, quadam sui transformatione in id quod amat transmutatur; non quod idem sit in natura, sed affectu rei amatae conformatur. Vtpote non bonum aliquem amare potest quia bonus est, nisi et ipsa in ipso bono bona efficiatur.*

22   Meditativae Orationes, CCCM 89, Med. 3, par. 9: *Omnis sensus corporeus, ut sensus sit et sentiat, oportet ut quadam sensibili affectione aliquomodo mutetur in id quod sentit.*

What is so fascinating about how William applies and uses his theoretical concepts in his prayers is that they become so accessible to the monastic reader. He does not refer to complex terms, which require extensive Patristic knowledge to understand the passage's meaning, nor does he perform the theoretical labor of explaining how his conceptions relate to one another. He tells, instead, a story; the story of the heart that longs for God's presence; the story of a touched (*mulcetur*) and a broken (*offenditur*) heart.[23] In other words, he tells a story relatable to the monks reading his prayers, even those who do not share his theological education.

The third meditation, in particular, is representative of the approach to Patristic authority that I have attempted to reconstruct from William's treatment of the Song of Songs. The Fathers are undoubtedly influential in providing some of the central concepts on which William centers his exegesis. As we have seen, Ambrose provides William with an ethical legitimization for the erotic language he uses. Gregory the Great, on the other hand, has provided a distinct theological perspective. As William has attempted to reconstruct his voice consistently and harmonically, he has been able to draw from the Gregorian excerpts some central ideas, such as the mentioned *amor ipse intellectus est*. Origen, both through the mediation of Ambrose and Gregory as readers of Origen and through William's knowledge of the Origenist texts, has provided William's larger exegetical framework – a dramatic world, which he could go on to flesh out, embellish and discover for himself. The Fathers have acted as guides and inspirations. Yet what makes William's reading of the Song distinctly his? I believe that it is precisely what he displays in the prayers: he makes Patristic thought applicable, relatable, and pastorally fruitful.

A profound pastoral concern for the individual soul's journey with God underlies all of his works. Rather than introducing entirely new ideas or drastically redefining the concepts he receives from tradition, it is from this place of pastoral spirituality that most of what we consider his 'original' contributions stem. This does not diminish William's intellectual-theological prowess in any way. On the contrary: his anthropological insights, his knowledge of Scripture, and his understanding of Patristic tradition are so extensive that he is able to breathe life into them.

He does so by introducing the element of personal experience. The theoretical concepts he raises should be lived and embodied to prove accurate. William's point of view is a profoundly empirical one. I have observed this,

---

23   Meditativae Orationes, CCCM 89, Med. 3, par. 10.

for instance, discussing William's understanding of the Scriptural senses. Using Origen's fundamental distinction as a foundation, he redefines what Origen had considered the historical sense of Scripture not as one that relates back to the historical circumstances of the text's composition but to the history that unfolds within the reader's own life. "Exploring the historical sense of Scripture", as I have said, "thus means primarily to face one's own part in the larger history between Christ and the *anima christiana*."[24]

The Song of Songs, as the central Biblical text, not only for William but for the generation of Cistercian thinkers that he was a part of, exemplifies this approach. The soul, rather than thinking about God, enters a concrete relationship with the object of its desire; a relationship that consumes the soul entirely until no part of the human life is left unaffected. It is from this place that William also reconceptualizes the notion of a Christian thinker. His model for 'theological' reflection is presented in the following passage:

> To those who meditate, talk and write about you, I beseech thee, offer a sober mind as well as precise and disciplined words and a heart that burns for you, O Jesus, so that we may understand the passage of Scripture that speak of you.[25]

Here, William presents what he considers the fundamental prerequisites for exegetical and theological reflection. A sober mind (*sensus sobrios*), as he calls it, is the foundation of all Christian authorship and theological speech; a longing heart, on the other hand, is a hermeneutic necessity. In other words, the mind is needed to systematize and articulate (with *verba circumcisa* and *disciplinata*) the soul's experiences, while a loving heart facilitates true insight. Exegetical and theological reflection, thus, are grounded in the intimacy of the human-divine relationship. Understanding the complexities of Scripture and transmitted theological thought is a matter of the *sensus amoris*; possible only for those who have been transformed and consumed by spiritual love. William offers in his third meditation a concrete example of the way in which a loving heart can illuminate even the most confusing of theological concepts – the dogma of the Trinity:

---

24   see the chapter "5.2. The Different Senses of Scripture".
25   Meditativae Orationes, CCCM 89, Med. 3, par. 11: *Sed meditantibus et colloquentibus et scribentibus de te, da, quaeso, sensus sobrios, uerba circumcisa et disciplinata, cor ardens de te, o Iesu, in apertionem scripturarum quae de te sunt.*

> If the Holy Spirit envelops the quiet and humble person on whom it rests and transforms them into a different person so that the perceiving sense no longer divides the Trinity and no longer confuses the Unity. The Trinity does not offend the person who piously longs for God. The oneness of [divine] substance does not discourage the love of the one who rejoices in the love of the Father and the Son.[26]

William speaks in this passage of a transformative experience with the Holy Spirit, which allows the human mind to perceive the theological content of the Trinitarian conception in a way that increases rather than diminishes faith. It seems to be William's basic assumption that the notion of a God who is simultaneously three in one is difficult – if not impossible – for the mind to grasp fully. Attempting to understand the workings of a triune divinity, he believes, is unsettling for the reasonable mind, yet not for the soul transformed by divine love. William explains that a heart that longs for and displays a deep desire for God will no longer be deterred by the theological realities of divine nature. Faith, it becomes clear, is increased where divine love is enjoyed rather than rationally deconstructed. Divine inspiration, in turn, does not lead to a better understanding of theological concepts but liberates the heart to desire God more deeply, free from attachment to rational limitations.

One could say that William is avoiding the responsibilities of theological reflection by defining the heart and its capacity for love as the primary setting for spiritual insight. This seems to have been the characterization that Abelard provided of his critics, whom he had considered intellectually incapable of disentangling the web of Christian doctrine. Yet, as I have established, William's criticism of the theological tendencies of the 12th century does not stem from an inability to apply the dialectic method but from a fundamental disagreement with their basic methodological assumptions.

For William, the belief that the human rational faculty could possibly understand something that surpasses it to such a high degree as the inner workings of the divine nature is a symptom of pride – a mark of dissemblance. His complex epistemology is grounded in the notion of the soul's

---

26   Meditativae Orationes, CCCM 89, Med. 3, par. 15: *Sic enim Spiritus Domini quietum et humilem suum super quem requiescit induit repente et mutat in uirum alterum, ut sensum intuentis non diuidat trinitas, non confundat unitas; non offendat trinitas personarum pietatem unum Deum quaerentis; non contristet substantiae unitas caritatem Patris et Filii dilectione gaudentis* [...].

image-likeness to God, that allows for insight through self-knowledge. The heart is not the center of William's theory of cognition by chance or out of romantic sentiment, but because, as the vessel of love, it is the necessary *locus* of likeness. Bypassing this spiritual process to accumulate complex theological knowledge is vanity. As William declared in several of his works, it is precisely not the mark of a sound mind but utter folly (*stultitia*).[27] In the continuation of the above-quoted passage, William returns to this theme once again:

> Neither the oneness nor the plurality can confound [such a person], but the Trinity of the Oneness and the Oneness of Trinity lead them to understand, with a pious and sober intellect, that the incomprehensible majesty of God cannot be understood.[28]

The folly of a mind attempting to rationally harmonize the simultaneous oneness and Trinity of God is contrasted here with the sober intellect of a mind that acknowledges the inaccessibility of its object. The realization of the inherent boundaries of the human condition is not a disappointment within William's framework but the most profound insight the human mind can be granted. Through these words shines the cautious promise that the reader who is humble enough to accept his or her limitations will come to experience and enjoy the object of their desire in a much deeper and more intimate way than through rational understanding; that not only their thirst for knowledge but their longing for divine love itself will be stilled.

Meditatio VII. The Communal Authority of the Saints

William's pastoral concern for the individual spiritual journey is also reflected in his enthusiasm for monastic reform. The concrete expressions of 12th-century monasticism, too, are characterized in the criticism that William raises against them as symptoms of decay in the spiritual development of their individual members. The Cistercian project, as he understands it, is the re-establishment of room for personal spiritual growth within a setting

---

27   see the chapter "1.7. Humilitas and the Ideal Reader".

28   Meditativae Orationes, CCCM 89, Med. 3, par. 15: [...] *in neutro conturbet solitudo uel pluralitas, sed et ad hoc ei ualeant unitas trinitatis et trinitas unitatis, ut pio et sobrio intellectu comprehendat non comprehendendo {maiestatem diuinae incomprehensibilitatis}.*

that has become overly concerned with outward liturgical practice.[29] Personal renewal – the renewal of the 'whole man'[30] – is thus the purpose and the foundation of structural monastic renewal. This interconnection between the micro- and macrocosm of the monastic life, so to speak, is reflected in the way William portrays the role of authoritative figures in the monastic community.

Just as he did in the Golden Epistle, so too in his prayers, he attributes great value to the Early Fathers of Christian monasticism. However, he expresses here the importance of these authoritative figures in a much more personal and experiential way. In his seventh meditation, he discusses their role regarding the monk's state of ignorance and spiritual isolation:

> But, O Lord, you can place hiding places for your countenance in the darkness of our ignorance and the human blindness, but you have set up tabernacles around yourself for your light-bearing saints, who shone and burned with the light and fire of your tents. They illuminated and incited [others] through their words and example, and they proclaimed the phenomenal joy [we will derive] from knowing you in our future life, when we will see you as you are – face to face.[31]

If viewed through the lens of theological concepts, this passage reflects the inherent tension between the reality of a *Deus absconditus* and the potential for human worship. The hidden God reveals Godself through the inspiration of a chosen few. He explains that a person's authoritative status is bestowed on him or her as an extension of divine self-revelation. It is an expression of exceptional 'closeness to God', and a means to facilitate a similarly close relationship with God for others. Those who serve as ethical examples for the communities and whose words contribute to the dissemination of faith can do so on account of their own spiritual experience of intimacy with God.

---

29   see the chapter "7.1. Innovation, Restoration and Renewal", as well as the Introduction to "William's Vision for Life in the Monastic Community".

30   I am referencing here Elder, "William and the Renewal of the Whole Man", 109–130. Gert Melville meanwhile points to this motive as a central part of the early Cistercian *Exordium parvum* (Melville, *The World of Medieval Monasticism*, 137–38).

31   Meditativae Orationes, CCCM 89, Med. 7, par. 10: *Sed, o Domine, licet tenebras ignorantiae nostrae et caecitatis humanae posueris latibulum faciei huius, tamen in circuitu tuo tabernaculum tuum, luminosi illi tui sancti qui aliquando fuerunt, qui de luminis et ignis tui contubernio lucentes et ardentes, uerbo et exemplo ceteros illuminabant et accendebant, et huius superuenientis notitiae tuae solemne gaudium in futura nobis uita denuntiabant, qua uideberis sicut es, uel facie ad faciem.*

This model of *auctoritas* is representative of how William illustrates the figures of authority that shape his thought and the communities he leads. I have presented in this book two vital examples: that of Paul, as an influential figure for the doctrinal and ethical development of the church, and that of Bernard, as a living authority for William's own spiritual development and the establishment of Cistercian communities.

Paul appears not only as an implicit source and reference but as an explicit example of practiced Christian faith in many of William's works. In my juxtaposition of William's and Abelard's respective commentaries on Romans, I have observed that the way William views Paul's impact on the history of the church differs from Abelard's. While the latter understands Paul's thought as a precursor for his own systematic and philosophical approach to theology, William's mental picture seems to be a more holistic one: Paul is characterized as the doctor of grace, not because he had profound intellectual insights into the workings of divine grace, but because he had experienced the abundance of grace. Once consumed by pride and vanity, he was humbled by an encounter with God that allowed him to develop true faith and virtue – the necessary foundation of insight, according to William. Paul's 'words and example' (*verbo et exemplo*) are not separate aspects of his authority but expressions of his profound experience of divine grace that depend on one another.

Just as William defines it in his seventh meditation, Paul's authoritative status rests on both the divine source of his insight and the content of his apostolic mission. It is the enjoyment of God, from which he derives his knowledge, and it is the enjoyment of God that he relays to the communities he serves. Authorities such as Paul have not seen God face to face and thus do not explicate the divine nature in a more accurate way than others do; their exceptional state is not one of full comprehension. Rather, they have been close enough to the divine light that they can anticipate the fact that seeing God face to face will be an experience of inexplicable joy and delight (*supereminentis gaudium*).[32]

William's portrayal of Bernard, particularly in his *Vita prima*, is representative of a similar conception of *auctoritas*. Bernard's great claim to the status he enjoys within his community and beyond is neither a matter of rhetorical ability nor particular exegetical or intellectual talent, as William describes it. It is, instead, a matter of his extraordinary relationship with God. "I cannot possibly question the faith of the faithful" is an assertion

---

32   Meditativae Orationes, CCCM 89, Med. 7, par. 10.

William makes in the *Vita prima*.[33] Read through the lens of William's conception of Christian epistemology and his understanding of the interconnectedness of spiritual intimacy and insight, this is not a statement of blind
deference to authority. It is instead a transparent definition of the role of
authority within communities whose stated purpose is to facilitate the deep-
ening of faith for its members. Figures like Bernard, whose behavior and
practice reveal a profound spiritual connection, are not only able to teach
theoretical truths but to live in truth and lead by example. The 'faith of the
faithful', or as William says in a passage quoted earlier, the 'luminescence of
the light-bearers' is infectious. It incites the longing and enthusiasm William
attributes to the communities pursuing the monastic life and to the individuals who authentically long for God.

William's understanding of the value of authoritative figures for the monastic community, in particular, is rooted in his view of the history of the
church and Christian monasticism. Throughout his works, he displays a
great awareness of the historical contexts in which the Fathers to whom he
refers developed their thoughts. I have highlighted this in particular regarding William's usage of Patristic citations in his *Disputatio* against Abelard.
Categorizing Abelard's theological points of view according to what he understood to be early-church-heresies, he utilized the statements of Fathers
he knew to have addressed them in their own time. He does so, for instance,
with Augustinian anti-Pelagianism and Ambrosian anti-Arianism.[34] Similarly, his florilegia of Ambrose and Gregory in their distinct methodology
reveal an awareness of these Fathers' traditional reputation as the Father of
purity and the Father of monastic reform, respectively.[35] William rarely
chose to apply the authority of authors irrespective of the mission they pursued in their historical and cultural context.

This treatment of historical authority is most pronounced in the figure of
Paul. William's representation of Paul is highly contextual; the themes of
pride and humiliation are not simply abstract anthropological concepts for
William but arise from Paul's direct engagement both with the Roman cultural framework and the relationship between Jewish and Pagan approaches
to the emerging Christian faith.[36] In his Commentary on Romans, William

---

33   Vita Prima Sancti Bernardi, CCCM 89B, Prol., pag. 31: [...] *quibus fidem non habere nulli*
      fidelium licet (as translated in Costello ed., "The First Life of Bernard," 2, as quoted in
      the chapter "7.3. Horizontal Authority and Loving Obedience".
34   see the chapter "2.3. Orthodoxy and Authority in William's Disputatio".
35   see the chapter "4.2.1. Reading between the Lines: Ambrose as a Moral Authority".
36   see the chapter "1.7. Humilitas and the Ideal Reader".

describes the central task of the New Testament authors, such as Paul and the early church Fathers, as the 'defense of grace' against Jewish, Pagan, and Heretic influences of any kind.[37]

Yet, he conceptualizes his own task – or rather, the task of Christian thinkers in his social context – as a distinctly different one. He acknowledges distinctly that the threat of heresy he witnessed in his own time is not to be equated with the situation of the early council period. Since catholicism has experienced a story of success: the formerly pagan territories under Roman reign have been effectively converted, and the church as an institution has developed prosperously. His main concern is, therefore, not that of the ancient authorities – to defend the catholic faith – but to facilitate the spiritual experience of faith for the individual members of the church.[38] His mission is not one of institutional but of spiritual growth. This self-perception, in its contrast to early church authority, is reflected as well in his seventh meditation:

> By now, the flashes of your truth have [through your light-bearers] incited the entire world. These flashes illuminate those who have healthy eyes and rejoice in them. But those who love the darkness more than they love the light are frightened and confused by them.[39]

Rather than describing the task of authorities here as the doctrinal defense of truth, he explains it as an uncovering of truth. The saints and the 'light-bearers' have essentially achieved to proclaim Christian truth and spiritual insight to the entire globe. The self-revelation of God has become – at least in theory – accessible to the large population, as the 'light' of divine truth was made visible to the world. This account is in line with William's description of the church's history since its dawn and the role that particular authoritative figures have assumed in its unfolding.

---

37   see the chapter "1.4. William's Self-Representation in the Praefatio".

38   Expositio super Epistolam ad Romanos (CCCM 86), Praef., linea 21: *Quam in tota epistola hac constantissimus propugnator eius apostolus apostolica auctoritate et prudentia defendit contra Iudaeos; sancti patres ubique contra haereticos; nos autem ad plenae humilitatis affectum et purae deuotionis effectum nostrorum cordibus desideramus inscribi.*

39   Meditativae Orationes, CCCM 89, Med. 7, par. 11: *Interim uero per eos fulgura ueritatis tuae alluxerunt orbi terrae, et illuxerunt coruscationes. Ad quas hilarescunt qui sanos habent oculos, commouentur autem et conturbantur qui diligunt magis tenebras quam lucem.*

Yet again, this passage displays a distinction between the authorities and the saints of the past, and the situation, within which William contextualizes his responsibility and that of his readers. The outstanding task of believers is no longer that of illuminating truth but of enjoying the light it provides. William's concern is one of personal spiritual development. He does not intend to acquaint his readers with the truth of the Christian faith but enable them to see it with 'healthy eyes' and experience its goodness. This understanding is in line with his claim in the Commentary on Romans that he aims to initiate a spiritual journey rather than defend and define its doctrinal parameters, which he makes clear in this passage.

In the seventh meditation, he does not define precisely who he considers the 'light-bearers' of the Christian faith, yet his language is reminiscent of how he talks about the early monastic Fathers in the Golden Epistle or the *Vita prima*. Their authority is not necessarily demonstrated in theological or exegetical works but in their words and their exemplary lives; the fact that their faith, proclaimed and practiced, encourages faith in others is determinative. This does not exclude the Church Fathers, whose authority is defined by the value that ecclesial tradition attributes to their thought – as William considers the genius of these figures to stem from their extraordinary personal faith and practice – but it does include figures whose authority is not confirmed by that same ecclesial status. Authoritative roles, as he defines them, are not limited to a particular era in church history but are dependent on nothing more and nothing less than the spiritual state of a person and community. It is thus that William can boldly state:

> In [this light], your truth manifests in whomever. It is like the sun, whose countenance shines for the just and the unjust, and which remains pure in its nature.[40]

The divine reality remains as it is. Whether or not it is accessible and transmittable is not dependent on a fundamental ontological change in the nature of God or the nature of humanity but dependent on the human soul's ability and willingness to perceive its light. The manifestation of truth can take place not merely for an externally defined elite group, but for anyone whose spiritual state allows for this perception. This understanding has been most prominently exemplified in William's Golden Epistle, where he

---

40   Meditativae Orationes, CCCM 89, Med. 7, par. 11.

attributed an authoritative role to the monks of Mont Dieu. Their faith and practice will, over time, become determinative for their successors.[41]

Intertwining the Threads

William's definition of authority, I have hoped to show, is that of an ongoing process inherently dependent on the personal faith and spiritual development of those who claim an authoritative status. In view of this central observation, William's *oeuvre* cannot be separated into distinct intellectual, spiritual, and pastoral spheres. I have attempted to do so for the sake of a structured exposition, yet the results of my study paint a different picture. Rather than a man torn between his strong aversion to theological innovation and his proclivity for spiritual and monastic renewal, the image of a man whose deep concern for the soul's journey manifests in various genres and contexts. As Brian McGuire has pointed out, "recent work on William has shown him to be more than a spiritual writer and theological polemicist."[42] I agree insofar as it would be a mistake to view these two aspects of his life as mutually exclusive or opposing in any way. My study has provided a shift of focus away from the expressions of William's concrete doctrinal positions and toward the subjacent level of his authorial self-conception.

The interconnectedness of authority and personal faith is crucial in revising some existing representations of William's thought and life. A definition of authority that stresses ecclesial status alone, or carries the assumption of a complete number of authoritative figures, can lead to perceptions of William as a fideistic and conservative writer who does not allow for individual contributions or continued development of tradition. Conceptions like these have mostly overemphasized William's critique of such authors as Abelard or William of Conches rather than discussing it within the framework of his spiritual writing. As I have shown, William's stance on theological innovation is not critical on account of his respect for the Fathers but his more foundational epistemology. The Fathers he consults in response to Abelard's statements are not authoritative *per se*, but they display the kind

---

41   Epistula ad fratres de Monte Dei, cccm 88, Lib. 1, par. 21: *Ex uobis enim, ex uestro exemplo, ex auctoritate uestra, in regione hac pendere habet omnis posteritas ordinis huius sancti. Vos in eo patres, uos in eo institutores, cum debita imitationis reuerentia, appellabimini a successoribus uestris. Quicquid a uobis statutum, quicquid uobis tenentibus et seruantibus in consuetudinem fuerit missum, absque omni retractatione a posteris uestris tenendum erit, et seruandum, nec fas erit ab aliquo immutari.*

42   McGuire, "A Chronology," 22.

of humble attitude in their approaches that allows for spiritual intimacy and insight.

This view of the Patristic authority is substantiated both by William's literary self-reflection and by his theoretical anthropology. The themes of image-likeness, and self-knowledge are not abstract ideas arising from his exegetical treatment of the Song but are explications of William's epistemology. They provide the conceptual connection between William's concern for the soul's spiritual journey and his rejection of overly rationalistic approaches to theology. William's concrete exegesis of the Song of Songs has shown that he is not dependent on Patristic thought for lack of intellectual ability but appreciates the Fathers more profoundly as spiritual guides whose individual relationships with God had endowed them with the kind of insight, for which he longs.

Authorial originality, within this framework, is qualitative rather than quantitative. William is careful not to add or subtract substantial doctrinal content in his discussion of divine truth but considers 'truth' an all-encompassing reality that ought to be meditated, enjoyed, and experienced. This is, in essence, the Christian task, which William exemplified in his exegesis and his spiritual writings. Within this framework, the practice of prayer takes on a particularly crucial role: Prayer, as the exemplification of a receptive and humble *habitus* is the place from which the Christian thinker can access and articulate spiritual insight. Knowledge of God is possible – not in a rationalistic sense, but insofar as it is an experience of love and a steady process towards divine likeness. In that same sense, contributions to the vast Christian tradition remain possible.

Lastly, William's concern for the Cistercian reform movement is not separate from these reflections but likely their most clear expression. Considering William's understanding of the Christian task as one of individual spiritual renewal, his love for the secluded yet communal living that the Cistercian communities provided is to be understood as the external facilitation of his innermost longing. He does not view reform as a political ploy, and his own contributions not as innovation, but the changes in practice that he proposes are, in his eyes, necessary extensions of the parameters he sets for a successful pursuit of truth. His communal definition of authority as loving obedience, therefore, encompasses the different ways in which he utilized authority – Patristic, Scriptural, or ecclesial – throughout his work: it is the submission to a truth that cannot be grasped by the mind but has to be experienced with one's heart.

Bibliography

Manuscripts

S. Bernardus Claraevallensis, Opuscula Selecta, manuscript, *zbs S 231, 15th century*, currently preserved at the Benediktinerkloster Mariastein, https://www.e -codices.unifr.ch/de/list/one/bkm/S-0231 (accessed June 11, 2025).

Theologica und Juridica mit Bezug auf die Karthäuser, manuscript collection, *A VI 14, 1466*, currently preserved at the University of Basel, https://www.e-codices.unifr .ch/en/description/ubb/A-VI-0014/HAN (accessed June 11, 2025).

Cited Works of William of William of Saint–Thierry

Ænigma fidei (PL 180:397–440), 1142–1144.
Guillaume de Saint–Thierry, Deux Traités Sur La Foi. Edited by M.-M. Davy, 24–91. Paris: J. Vrin, 1959.

Brevis commentatio (PL 184:407–36), 1125 (?)
Guillelmi a Sancto Theodorico Opera Omnia, Ii: Brevis Commentatio. Edited by Paul Verdeyen and Stanislaus Ceglar. Corpus Christianorum Continuatio Mediaevalis 87. Turnhout: Brepols, 1997.

De contemplando Deo (PL 184:365–80), 1119–1120.
Guillaume de Saint–Thierry, Deux Traités de l'amour de Dieu. Edited by M.-M. Dav, 31–67. Paris: J. Vrin, 1953.

Guillaume de Saint–Thierry, La Contemplation de Dieu, L'Oraison de Dom Guillaume. Edited by Jacques Hourlier. 2nd ed. Sources Chrétiennes 61 bis. Paris: Les Édi-tions du Cerf, 1959.

Guillelmi a Sancto Theodorico Opera Omnia, Iii: De Contemplando Deo. Edited by Paul Verdeyen. Corpus Christianorum Continuatio Mediaevalis 88. Turnhout: Brepols, 2003.

Disputatio adversus Petrum Abaelardum (PL 180:249–82), 1140.
Guillelmi a Sancto Theodorico Opera Omnia, v: Opuscula Adversus Petrum Abaelar-dum et de Fide. Edited by Paul Verdeyen. Corpus Christianorum Continuatio Me-diaevalis 89A. Turnhout: Brepols, 2007.

Epistola ad domnum Rupertum (to Rupert of Deutz) (PL 180:341–46), 1120–1123.
Guillelmi a Sancto Theodorico Opera Omnia, Iii: Epistola Guillelmi Ad Rupertum Tui-tiensem. Edited by Paul Verdeyen and Stanislaus Ceglar. Corpus Christianorum Continuatio Mediaevalis 88. Turnhout: Brepols, 2003.

Epistola de erroribus Guillelmi de Conchis (to Bernard of Clairvaux) (PL 180:333–40), 1141.

Guillelmi a Sancto Theodorico Opera Omnia, v: De Erroribus Guillelmi de Conchis. Edited by Paul Verdeyen. Corpus Christianorum Continuatio Mediaevalis 89A. Turnhout: Brepols, 2007.

Epistola ad fratres de Monte-Dei (PL 184:307–64), 1144–1145.

Guillelmi a Sancto Theodorico Opera Omnia, Iii: Epistola Ad Fratres de Monte Dei. Edited by Paul Verdeyen. Corpus Christianorum Continuatio Mediaevalis 88. Turnhout: Brepols, 2003.

Epistola ad Gaufridum Carnotensem episcopum et Bernardum abbatem Clarae-Vallensem (Preface to Adv Abl) (PL 182:531–533), 1138.

Guillelmi a Sancto Theodorico Opera Omnia, v: Epistola Willelmi. Edited by Paul Verdeyen. Corpus Christianorum Continuatio Mediaevalis 89A. Turnhout: Brepols, 2007.

Excerpta de Libris Beati Ambrosii super Cantica Canticorum (PL 15:1851–1962), 1128–1130 (?)

Guillelmi a Sancto Theodorico Opera Omnia, Ii: Excerpta de Libris Beati Ambrosii Super Cantica Canticorum. Edited by Antony van Burink. Corpus Christianorum Continuatio Mediaevalis 87. Turnhout: Brepols, 1997.

Guillelmi a Sancto Theodorico Opera Omnia, Ii: Expositio Super Cantica Canticorum. Edited by Paul Verdeyen. Corpus Christianorum Continuatio Mediaevalis 17–133. Turnhout: Brepols, 1997.

Excerpta ex Libris Beati Gregorii super Cantica Canticorum (PL 180:441–74), 1128–1130 (?)

Guillelmi a Sancto Theodorico Opera Omnia, Ii: Excerpta Ex Libris Beati Gregorii Super Cantica Canticorum. Edited by Paul Verdeyen. Corpus Christianorum Continuatio Mediaevalis 87. Turnhout: Brepols, 1997.

Expositio super Cantica Canticorum (PL 180:473–546), 1138.

Guillaume de Saint–Thierry, Exposé Sur Le Cantique Des Cantiques. Edited by Jean-Marie Déchanet. Translated by Maurice Dumontier. Série Des Textes Monastiques d'Occident 8. Sources Chrétiennes 82. Paris: Les Éditions du Cerf, 1962.

Commentaire Sur Le Cantique Des Cantiques. Edited by Robert Thomas. Pain de Cîteaux 9–12. Roybon, France: Abbaye de Chambarand, 1961.

Expositio super Epistolam ad Romanos (PL 180:547–694), 1137.

Guillelmi a Sancto Theodorico Opera Omnia, i: Expositio Super Epistolam Ad Romanos. Edited by Paul Verdeyen. Corpus Christianorum Continuatio Mediaevalis 86. Turnhout, Belgium: Brepols, 1989.

Guillaume de Saint–Thierry, Exposé Sur l'Épître Aux Romains. Livres I–III | Sources Chrétiennes. Edited by Paul Verdeyen. Translated by Yves-Anselme Baudelet. Sources Chrétiennes 544. Paris: Les Éditions du Cerf, 2011.

Meditativae orationes (PL 180:205–48), 1128–1132.

Guillaume de Saint–Thierry, Oraisons Méditatives. Edited by Jacques Hourlier. Sources Chrétiennes 324. Paris: Les Éditions du Cerf, 1985.

Guillelmi a Sancto Theodorico Opera Omnia, Iv: Meditationes Devotissimae. Edited by Paul Verdeyen. Corpus Christianorum Continuatio Mediaevalis 89. Turnhout: Brepols, 2005.

Oraisons Méditées. Edited by Robert Thomas. Pain de Cîteaux. Roybon, France: Abbaye de Chambarand, 1964.

Prière de Guillaume, Contemplation de Dieu. Edited by Robert Thomas. Pain de Cîteaux 23. Roybon, France: Abbaye de Chambarand, 1965.

De natura corporis et animae (PL 180:695–726), c. 1138 (?)

Guillelmi a Sancto Theodorico Opera Omnia, Iii: De Natura Corporis et Animae. Edited by Paul Verdeyen. Corpus Christianorum Continuatio Mediaevalis 88. Turnhout: Brepols, 2003.

De natura et dignitate amoris (PL 184:379–408), 1119–1122.

Guillaume de Saint–Thierry, Deux Traités de l'amour de Dieu. Edited by M.-M. Dav, 69–137. Paris: J. Vrin, 1953.

Nature et Dignité de l'amour. Edited by Robert Thomas. Pain de Cîteaux 24. Roybon, France: Abbaye de Chambarand, 1965.

Guillelmi a Sancto Theodorico Opera Omnia, Iii: De Natura et Dignitate Amoris. Edited by Paul Verdeyen. Corpus Christianorum Continuatio Mediaevalis 88. Turnhout: Brepols, 2003.

Oratio domni Willelmi, 1128–1132.

Guillelmi a Sancto Theodorico Opera Omnia, Iii: Oratio Domni Willelmi. Edited by Paul Verdeyen. Corpus Christianorum Continuatio Mediaevalis 88. Turnhout: Brepols, 2003.

Prologus ad Domnum Bernardum abbatem Claravallis (Prologue to Sac alt) (PL 180:344–45), 1122–1123.

Guillelmi a Sancto Theodorico Opera Omnia, Iii: Prologus [Ad Domnum Bernardum Abbatem Claravallis]. Edited by Paul Verdeyen and Stanislaus Ceglar. Corpus Christianorum Continuatio Mediaevalis 88. Turnhout: Brepols, 2003.

Responsio abbatum auctore Willelmo abbate Sancti Theoderici (to Cardinal Matthew), 1131/32.

Guillelmi a Sancto Theodorico Opera Omnia, Iv: Responsio Abbatum Auctore Willelmo Abbate Sancti Theoderici. Edited by Paul Verdeyen. Corpus Christianorum Continuatio Mediaevalis 89. Turnhout: Brepols, 2005.

De sacramento altaris (PL 180:345–66), 1122–1123.

Guillelmi a Sancto Theodorico Opera Omnia, Iii: De Sacramento Altaris. Edited by Paul Verdeyen and Stanislaus Ceglar. Corpus Christianorum Continuatio Mediaevalis 88. Turnhout: Brepols, 2003.

Speculum fidei (PL 180:365–98), 1142–1144.

Guillelmi a Sancto Theodorico Opera Omnia, v: Speculum Fidei. Edited by Paul Verdeyen. Corpus Christianorum Continuatio Mediaevalis 89A. Turnhout: Brepols, 2007.

Guillaume de Saint–Thierry, Deux Traités Sur La Foi. Edited by M.-M. Davy, 24–91. Paris: J. Vrin, 1959.

Vita prima Sancti Bernardi, Liber Primus (PL 185:225–68), 1145–1147.

William of Saint–Thierry, Arnold of Bonneval, and Geoffrey of Auxerre. The First Life of Bernard of Clairvaux. Edited by Hilary Costello. Collegeville, MN: Cistercian Publications, 2015.

Works by Ancient, Medieval and Early Modern Authors

Aelred of Rievaulx

De Spiritali Amicitia. Centre Traditio Litterarum Occidentalium, CETEDOC., and Brepols (Firm). 2021. Library of Latin texts. Series A. Series A. [Turnhout, Belgium]: Brepols. http://clt.brepolis.net/LLTA/pages/TextSearch .aspx?key=MAERICMo1E (accessed January 10, 2025).

Bernard of Clairvaux

Sermones super Cantica Canticorum. Centre Traditio Litterarum Occidentalium, CETEDOC. Library of Latin texts. Series A. Turnhout, Belgium: Brepols, 2021. http://clt.brepolis.net/LLTA/pages/TextSearch.aspx?key=MBECLSC___ (accessed January 10, 2025).

The Letters of St. Bernard of Clairvaux. Translated by Bruno Scott James. Kalamazoo, MI: Cistercian Publications, 1998.

Opere Di San Bernardo. Edited by Ferruccio Gastaldelli. Vol. VI/2. Milano, 1987.

Bruno of Cologne

"Brief an Radulf Den Grünen." In Quellen Geistlichen Lebens. Das Mittelalter. Edited by Gisbert Greshake and Josef Weismayer, 2:20–28. Ostfildern: Matthias Grünewald Verlag, 2008.

Bonaventure

St. Bonaventure's on the Reduction of the Arts to Theology (English and Latin Edition). Translated by Zachary Hayes. New York: The Franciscan Institute, 1996.

Godfray, Thomas

An epistle of sai[n]t Bernarde, called the golden epistle, whiche he se[n]t to a yo[n]g religyous man whom he moche loued. And after the sayd epistle, foloweth four reuelations of Saint Birget, book, A–C (C8 blank), 1535. Currently preserved at the British Library. https://www.proquest.com/docview/2240870350/citation/ 9DEA5E3DD6E64DEDPQ/1 (accessed January 10, 2025)

Gregory the Great

Moralia in Iob. Centre Traditio Litterarum Occidentalium, CETEDOC. Library of Latin texts, Series A. Turnhout, Belgium: Brepols, 2021. http://clt.brepolis.net/ LLTA/pages/TextSearch.aspx?key=QGREG1708_ (accessed January 10, 2025).

Guigo I

The Consuetudines of Guigo I, 5th Prior of the Carthusian Order. Translated from Latin. Translated by Ugo-Maria Ginex. Canterbury: St. Mary's Hermitage, 2018.

Horace

Satiren / Sermones. Briefe / Epistulae. Edited by Gerhard Fink. Translated by Gerd Herrmann. *Satiren / Sermones. Briefe / Epistulae*. Sammlung Tusculum. De Gruyter, 2011.

Martin Luther

An Kurfürsten zu Sachsen und Landgrafen zu Hessen von dem gefangenen Herzog zu Braunschweig. 1545. Edited by Otto Clemen. *Band 4 Schriften von 1529–1545*. De Gruyter, 2016.

Origen

sec. Transl. Rufini. *Commentarium in Canticum canticorum*. Centre Traditio Litterarum Occidentalium, CETEDOC. Library of Latin texts, Series A. Turnhout, Belgium: Brepols, 2021. http://clt.brepolis.net/LLTA/pages/TextSearch.aspx?key= PORRUA198_ (accessed January 10, 2025).

Peter Abelard

Historia Calamitatum. Centre Traditio Litterarum Occidentalium, CETEDOC. Library of Latin texts, Series A. Turnhout, Belgium: Brepols, 2021. http://clt.brepolis.net/ LLTA/pages/TextSearch.aspx?key=MABAEHICA_ (accessed January 10, 2025).

"Commentaria in epistolam Pauli ad Romanos: Apologia contra Bernardum." In *Petri Abaelardi Opera Theologica I*. Edited by E.M. Buytaert., CCCM XI. Turnhout: Brepols, 1969.

Expositio in Epistolam Ad Romanos: [Lateinisch – Deutsch] = Römerbriefkommentar / Abaelard. Translated by Rolf Peppermüller. Vol. 26, 1–3. Fontes Christiani. Freiburg i. Br.: Herder, 2000.

Sic et Non. Centre Traditio Litterarum Occidentalium, CETEDOC. Library of Latin texts, Series A. Turnhout, Belgium: Brepols, 2021. http://clt.brepolis.net/LLTA/ pages/TextSearch.aspx?key=MABAESINO_ (accessed January 10, 2025).

Sermones. Edited by Lodewijk Jozef Engels and Christine Vande Veire. CCCM 286. Turnhout : Brepols, 2021. http://clt.brepolis.net/llta/pages/QuickResults.aspx? qry=29cf8c75-4ac4-4742-b312-91ef2e780fbd (accessed January 10, 2025).

"Theologia Christiana." In *Petri Abaelardi Opera Theologica II*. Edited by E.M. Buytaert, 71–372. CCCM XII. Turnhout, Belgium: Brepols, 1969.

Peter Lombard

Sententiae in Iu Libris Distinctae. Centre Traditio Litterarum Occidentalium, CETE-
DOC. Library of Latin texts, Series A. Turnhout, Belgium: Brepols, 2021. http://clt.
brepolis.net/LLTA/pages/TextSearch.aspx?key=MPELOSENT_ (accessed January 10, 2025).

Simon of Tournai

Les Disputationes de Simon de Tournai : Texte Inédit. Edited by Joseph Warichez.
Spicilegium Sacrum Lovaniense : Études et Documents 12, 1932.

Matthew of Albano

*Epistula ad abbates OSB Remensis prouinciae de primo capitulo prouinciali Remis a.
d. 1131 habito,* Centre Traditio Litterarum Occidentalium, CETEDOC. Library of
Latin texts, Series A. Turnhout, Belgium: Brepols, 2010. http://clt.brepolis.net/
llta/pages/QuickResults.aspx?qry=d546cc38-fb2e-4caa-a3b9-5ade6a356f32
(accessed January 10, 2025).

Secondary Literature

Adam, André. *Guillaume de Saint–Thierry. Sa vie et ses oeuvres.* Bourg: Impr. du
Journal de l'Ain, 1924.

Ampère, Jacques Antoine. *Histoire Littéraire de La France Avant Le Douzième Siècle.*
3 vols. Paris: L. Hachette, 1839.

Anderson, John D. "Introduction." In *William of Saint Thierry: The Enigma of Faith.*
Cistercian Fathers Series 9. Kalamazoo, MI: Cistercian Publications, 1991.

Anderson, John D. "The Use of Greek Sources by William of St Thierry Especially in
the Enigma Fidei." In *One Yet Two: Monastic Tradition East and West.* Edited by
M. Basil Pennington, Cistercian Studies 29, 242–253. Kalamazoo, MI: Cistercian
Publications, 1976.

Angenendt, Arnold. *Geschichte Der Religiosität Im Mittelalter.* 4th ed. Darmstadt:
WBG (Wissenschaftliche Buchgesellschaft), 2009.

Arblaster, John, and Paul Verdeyen. "The Reciprocity of Spiritual Love in William of
Saint–Thierry and Hadewijch." *International Journal of Philosophy and Theology*
78, no. 1/2 (2017): 39–54.

Asiedu, F. B. A. "The Song of Songs and the Ascent of the Soul: Ambrose, Augustine,
and the Language of Mysticism." *Vigiliae Christianae* 55, no. 3 (2001): 299–317.

Astell, Ann W. *The Song of Songs in the Middle Ages.* Ithaka, NY: Cornell University
Press, 2018.

Astell, Ann W., and Catherine Rose Cavadini. "The Song of Songs." In *The Wiley-
Blackwell Companion to Christian Mysticism.* Edited by Julia A. Lamm, 25–40.
Hoboken, NJ: John Wiley & Sons, Ltd, 2012.

Barrat, Alexandra. "The 'De Institutione Inclusarium' of Aelred of Rievaulx." *The Journal of Theological Studies* 28.2 (1977): 528–536.

Barth, Karl. *Das Wort Gottes Und Die Theologie. Gesammelte Vorträge.* München: Kaiser, 1929.

Baudelet, Yves-Anselme. *L'Expérience Spirituelle Selon Guillaume de Saint–Thierry.* Paris: Les Éditions du Cerf, 1985.

Bell, David N. "Greek, Plotinus, and the Education of William of Saint–Thierry." *Cîteaux – Commentarii Cistercienses* 30 (1979): 221–248.

Bell, David N. "The Alleged Greek Sources of William of St. Thierry." In *Noble Piety and Reformed Monasticism. Studies in Medieval Cistercian History VII.* Edited by E. Rozanne Elder, Cistercian Studies 65, 109–122. Kalamazoo, MI: Cistercian Publications, 1981.

Bell, David N. *The Image and Likeness: The Augustinian Spirituality of William of St. Thierry.* Cistercian Studies 78. Kalamazoo, MI: Cistercian Publications, 1984.

Bell, David N. "The Mystical Theology and Theological Mysticism of William of Saint–Thierry." In *A Companion to William of Saint–Thierry.* Edited by F. Tyler Sergent, 67–92. Brill, 2019.

Bell, David N. "The Vita Antiqua of William of St Thierry." *Cistercian Studies Quarterly* 11 (1976): 246–255.

Bell, David N. "William of St Thierry and John Scot Eriugena." *Cîteaux – Commentarii Cistercienses* 33 (1982): 5–28.

Bell, Nicolas. "Liturgy." In *The Cambridge Companion to the Cistercian Order.* Edited by Mette Birkedal Bruun, 258–267. Cambridge Companions to Religion. Cambridge: Cambridge University Press, 2012.

Benson, Robert Louis, Giles Constable, and Carol Dana Lanham, eds. *Renaissance and Renewal in the Twelfth Century.* Cambridge: Harvard University Press, 1982.

Berndt, Rainer. "Überlegungen Zum Verhältnis von Exegese Und Theologie in 'De Sacramentis Christiane Fidei' Hugos von St. Viktor." In *Neue Richtungen in Der Hoch- Und Spätmittelalterlichen Bibelexegese.* Edited by Robert E. Lerner, 65–78. München: Oldenbourg Wissenschaftsverlag, 1996.

Bhattacharji, Santha, Dominic Mattos, and Rowan Williams, eds. *Prayer and Thought in Monastic Tradition: Essays in Honour of Benedicta Ward SLG.* London: Bloomsbury T&T Clark, 2014.

Bishop, Nadean. "Denial of the Flesh in Origen and Subsequent Implications." *Mystics Quarterly* 14, no. 2 (1988): 70–83.

Borch, Marianne. "The Semantics of Originality as Indicator of the Cultural Paradigm Shift from Medieval to Modern." In *Origins as a Paradigm in the Sciences and in the Humanities.* Edited by Paola Spinozzi, 243–256. Göttingen: Vandenhoeck&Ruprecht, 2010.

Bouchard, Constance Brittain. *Holy Entrepreneurs: Cistercians, Knights, and Economic Exchange in Twelfth-Century Burgundy*. Ithaca, NY: Cornell University Press, 1991.

Bouyer, Louis. *The Cistercian Heritage*. Translated by Elisabeth A. Livingstone. Westminster, MD: The Newman Press, 1958.

Bredero, Adriaan. "William of Saint Thierry at the Crossroads of the Monastic Currents of His Time." In *William, Abbot of St. Thierry: A Colloquium at the Abbey of St. Thierry*. Translated by Jerry Carfantan. Cistercian Studies 94. Kalamazoo, MI: Cistercian Publications, 1987.

Brower, Jeffrey E. "Trinity." In *The Cambridge Companion to Abelard*. Edited by Jeffrey E. Brower and Kevin Guilfoy, 223–257. Cambridge Companions to Philosophy. Cambridge: Cambridge University Press, 2004.

Brower, Jeffrey E., and Kevin Guilfoy. "Introduction." In *The Cambridge Companion to Abelard*. Edited by Jeffrey E. Brower and Kevin Guilfoy, 1–12. Cambridge Companions to Philosophy. Cambridge: Cambridge University Press, 2004.

Burton, Janet, and Julie Kerr. *The Cistercians in the Middle Ages*. Vol. 4. Monastic Orders. Woodbridge, Suffolk: Boydell&Brewer Ltd., 2011.

Burton, Pierre-André. "Aelred of Rievaulx: An Illiterate, or a True Master of Spiritual Teaching?" In *A Companion to Aelred of Rievaulx (1110–1167)*. Edited by Marsha Dutton, 197–220. Brill, 2017.

Buytaert, E. M., ed. "Capitula Haeresum Petri Abaelardi." In *Petri Abaelardi Opera Theologica*, 473–480. CCCM XII. Turnhout: Brepols, 1969.

Cartwright, Steven R. "The Romans Commentaries of William of St. Thierry and Peter Abelard: A Theological and Methodological Comparison." PhD. diss, Western Michigan University, 2001.

Ceglar, Stanislaus. "Introduction." In *Guillelmi a Sancto Theodorico Opera Omnia, Ii: Brevis Commentatio*. Edited by Paul Verdeyen and Stanislaus Ceglar. CCCM 87. Turnhout: Brepols, 1997.

Ceglar, Stanislaus. "The Date of William's Convalescence at Clairvaux." *Cistercian Studies Quarterly* 30.1 (1995): 27–33.

Ceglar, Stanislaus. "William of Saint Thierry and His Leading Role at the First Chapters of the Benedictine Abbots (Reims 1131, Soissons 1132)." In *William, Abbot of St. Thierry: A Colloquium at the Abbey of St. Thierry*, translated by Jerry Carfantan, 34–49. Cistercian Studies 94. Kalamazoo, MI: Cistercian Publications, 1987.

Ceglar, Stanislaus. "William of St.-Thierry: The Chronology of His Life with a Study of His Treatise On the Nature of Love, His Authorship of the Brevis Commentatio, the In Lacu, and the Reply to Cardinal Matthew." Ph.D. diss., Washington, DC: Catholic University of America, 1971.

Chazelle, Celia, and Burton Van Name Edwards. "Introduction." In *The Study of the Bible in the Carolingian Era*, 1–16. Medieval Church Studies 3. Turnhout: Brepols, 2003.

Chenu, Marie-Dominique. *Nature, Man, and Society in the Twelfth Century: Essays on New Theological Perspecitves in the Latin West*. Edited by Jerome Taylor, translated by Lester K. Little. Toronto: University of Toronto Press, 1997.

Clanchy, M. T. "Abelard's Mockery of St Anselm." *The Journal of Ecclesiastical History* 41, no. 1 (January 1990): 1–23.

Colish, Marcia Lillian. "'… Quae Hodie Locum Non Habent': Scholastic Theologians Reflect on Their Authorities." In *Proceedings of the PMR Conference 15*, 1–17, 1991.

Constable, Giles. "Forgery and Plagiarism in the Middle Ages." *Archiv Für Diplomatik* 29, no. JG (1 December 1983): 1–41.

Contreni, John J. *Learning and Culture in Carolingian Europe: Letters, Numbers, Exegesis, and Manuscripts*. Variorum Collected Studies Series. London: Routledge, 2011.

Coolman, Boyd Taylor. "Alexander of Hales." In *The Spiritual Senses: Perceiving God in Western Christianity*. Edited by Paul L. Gavrilyuk and Sarah Coakley, 121–139. Cambridge: Cambridge University Press, 2011.

Coolman, Boyd Taylor. "'Pulchrum Esse': The Beauty of Scripture, the Beauty of the Soul and the Art of Exegesis in Hugh of St. Victor." *Traditio* 58 (2003): 175–200.

Cvetković, Carmen A. "Conflict and Authority: William of Saint–Thierry and Peter Abelard as Readers of Origen." *Open Theology* 7, issue 1 (October 2021): Accessed November 29, 2022.

Dassmann, Ernst. *Die Frömmigkeit Des Kirchenvaters Ambrosius von Mailand: Quellen Und Entfaltung*. Vol. 29, *Münsterische Beiträge Zur Theologie*, Münster: Aschendorff Verlag, 1965.

Davis, Thomas X. "The Trinity's Glorifying Embrace: *Conscientia* in William of Saint–Thierry." In *A Companion to William of Saint–Thierry*. Edited by F. Tyler Sergent, 131–159. Brill, 2019.

Déchanet, Jean–Marie. "Introduction." In *Exposé Sur Le Cantique Des Cantiques*, by Guillaume de Saint Thierry. Translated by Maurice Dumontier. Série Des Textes Monastiques d'Occident 8. Sources Chrétiennes (Paris: Éditions du Cerf, 1962).

Déchanet, Jean-Marie. "Les manuscrits de la Lettre aux Frères du Mont-Dieu de Guillaume de Saint–Thierry et le problème de la «préface» dans Charleville 114." *Scriptorium* 8, no. 2 (1954): 236–271.

Déchanet, Jean-Marie. *Aux Sources de La Spiritualité de Guillaume de Saint–Thierry. Premiére Série d'études*. Bruges: Charles Beyaert, 1940. Originally published as: "Aux Sources de La Doctrine Spirituelle de Guillaume de Saint–Thierry: 1, Saint Grégoire de Nysse." *Collectanea O.C.R. 5* (1938–39): 187–198, 262–278.

Déchanet, Jean-Marie. *Guillaume de Saint–Thierry, Aux Sources d'une Pensees.* Paris: Beauchesne, 1978.

Déchanet, Jean-Marie. *Guillaume de Saint–Thierry, l'homme et Son Oeuvre.* Bruges: Charles Beyaert, 1942.

Déchanet, Jean-Marie. "Guillaume et Plotin." *Revue de Moyen Age Latin* 2 (1946): 246–260.

Del Cogliano, Mark. "A Fresh Look at William of Saint–Thierry's Excerpts from the Book of Blessed Ambrose on the Song of Songs." In *Unity of Spirit: Studies on William of Saint–Thierry in Honor of E. Rozanne Elder.* Edited by F. Tyler Sergent, Aage Rydstrøm-Poulsen, and Marsha L. Dutton, 37–59. Cistercian Studies 268. Collegeville, MN: Cistercian Publications, 2015.

Del Cogliano, Mark. "The Composition of William of St. Thierry's Excerpts from the Books of Blessed Gregory on the Song of Songs." *Cîteaux: Commentarii Cistercienses,* 2007.

Del Punta, Francesco. "The Genre of Commentaries in the Middle Ages and Its Relation to the Nature and Originality of Medieval Thought." In *Was Ist Philosophie Im Mittelalter?*, 138–151, Berlin, Boston: De Gruyter, 1998.

De Lubac, Henri. *Medieval Exegesis: The Four Senses of Scripture.* Vol. 1. Grand Rapids, MI : Wm. B. Eerdmans Publishing Co., 1998.

De Lubac, Henri. *Medieval Exegesis: The Four Senses of Scripture.* Vol. 2. Grand Rapids, MI: Wm. B. Eerdmans Publishing Co., 2000.

Dihsmaier, Monika R. *Carta Caritatis – Verfassung der Zisterzienser.* Schriften zur Rechtsgeschichte 149. Berlin: Duncker&Humblot, 2010.

Dinzelbacher, Peter. *Structures and Origins of the Twelfth-Century "Renaissance."* Monographien Zur Geschichte des Mittelalters. Stuttgart: Anton Hiersemann, 2017.

Döbler, Marvin. "Bernhard von Clairvaux und seine Apologia an Abt Wilhelm zwischen innerchristlichem Pluralismus und Religionskritik." *Zeitschrift für Religionswissenschaft* 15, no. 1 (1 September 2007): 35–51.

Doutre, Jean. "Romans as Read in School and Cloister in the Twelfth Century: The Commentaries of Peter Abelard and William of St. Thierry." In *Medieval Readings of Romans.* Edited by William S. Campbell, Peter S. Hawkins, and Brenda Schildgen. Romans through History and Cultures Series. New York: T&T Clark, 2007.

Dove, Mary. "Sex, Allegory and Censorship: A Reconsideration of Medieval Commentaries on the Song of Songs." *Literature and Theology* 10, no. 4 (1996): 317–328.

Dufal, Blaise. "The Fathers of Scholasticism: Authorities as Totems." In *Individuals and Institutions in Medieval Scholasticism.* Edited by Antonia Fitzpatrick and John Sabapathy, 53–70. University of London Press, 2020.

Duffy, Eamon. *The Stripping of the Altars: Traditional Religion in England; c.1400–c.1580*. New Haven: Yale University Press, 2005.

Dutton, Marsha, ed. *A Companion to Aelred of Rievaulx (1110–1167)*. Leiden: Brill, 2017.

Elder, E. Rozanne. "Bernard and William of Saint Thierry." In *A Companion to Bernard of Clairvaux*. Edited by Brian Patrick McGuire, 108–32. Brill, 2011.

Dutton, Marsha. *Formation for Wisdom, Not Education for Knowledge. Religious Education in Pre-modern Europe*. Leiden: Brill, 2012.

Dutton, Marsha. "The Christology of William of Saint–Thierry." *Recherches de Théologie Ancienne et Médiévale* 58 (1991): 79–112.

Dutton, Marsha. "The Eye of Reason-The Eye of Love: 'Divine Learning and Affective Prayer' in the Thought of William of Saint Thierry." In *Prayer and Thought in Monastic Tradition: Essays in Honour of Benedicta Ward SLG*. Edited by Santha Bhattacharji, Dominic Mattos, and Rowan Williams, 229–42. London: T&T Clark, 2014.

Dutton, Marsha. "The Image of the Invisible God: The Evolving Christology of William of Saint–Thierry." Ph.D. diss., University of Toronto, 1972.

Dutton, Marsha. "The Influence of Clairvaux: The Experience of William of Saint–Thierry." *Cistercian Studies Quarterly* 51.1. (2016): 55–75.

Dutton, Marsha. "William of Saint Thierry and the Greek Fathers: Evidence from Christology." In *One Yet Two: Monastic Tradition East and West*. Edited by M. Basil Pennington, 254–266. Cistercian Studies 29. Kalamazoo, MI: Cistercian Publications, 1976.

Dutton, Marsha. "William of Saint–Thierry and the Renewal of the Whole 'Man.'" In *A Companion to William of Saint–Thierry*, 109–130. Brill, 2019.

Elder, E. Rozanne, and John R. Sommerfeldt, eds. *The Chimaera of His Age: Studies on Bernard of Clairvaux*. Cistercian Studies 63. Kalamazoo, MI: Cistercian Publications, 1980.

Evans, G.R. *The Language and Logic of the Bible*. Cambridge: Cambridge University Press, 1985.

Ferguson, Margaret W. "Saint Augustine's Region of Unlikeness: The Crossing of Exile and Language." *The Georgia Review* 29, no. 4 (1975): 842–864.

Fitzgerald, Allan D., ed. *Augustine Through the Ages: An Encyclopedia*. Grand Rapids, MI: Eerdmans Publishing, 1999.

Frassetto, Michael. "Precursors to Religious Inquisitions: Anti-Heretical Efforts to 1184." In *A Companion to Heresy Inquisitions*. Edited by Donald Prudlo, 41–72. Brill, 2019.

France, James. "The Cistercian community." In *The Cambridge Companion to the Cistercian Order*. Edited by Mette Birkedal Bruun, 80–68. Cambridge Companions to Religion. Cambridge: Cambridge University Press, 2012.

Freeman, Ann. "Theodulf of Orleans and the Libri Carolini." *Speculum* 32, no. 4 (1957): 663–705.

Gabriele, Matthew. "The Last Carolingian Exegete: Pope Urban II, the Weight of Tradition, and Christian Reconquest." *Church History* 81, no. 4 (2012): 796–814.

Gilbert, Bennett. "Early Carthusian Script and Silence." *Cistercian Studies Quarterly* 49 (1 September 2014): 367–397.

Giraud, Cédric. "Schools and the 'Renaissance of the Twelfth Century.'" In *A Companion to Twelfth-Century Schools*. Edited by Cédric Giraud, translated by Ignacio Duran, 1–9. A Series of Handbooks and Reference Works on the Intellectual and Religious Life of Europe, 500–1800 88. Leiden: Brill, 2019.

Giraud, Cédric. "The Literary Genres of Theology.'" In *A Companion to Twelfth-Century Schools*. Edited by Cédric Giraud, translated by Ignacio Duran, 250–71. A Series of Handbooks and Reference Works on the Intellectual and Religious Life of Europe, 500–1800 88. Brill, 2019.

Giraud, Cédric. "Ut Fiat Aequalitas: Spiritual Training of the Inner Man in the Twelfth-Century Cloister." In *Horizontal Learning in the High Middle Ages*. Edited by Micol Long, Tjamke Snijders, and Steven Vanderputten, 65–80. Peer-to-Peer Knowledge Transfer in Religious Communities. Amsterdam: Amsterdam University Press, 2019.

Grabmann, Martin. *Die Geschichte Der Scholastischen Methode*. Vol. 1. Basel: Schwabe, 1961.

Grabmann, Martin. *Die Geschichte Der Scholastischen Methode*. Unveränd. Nachdruck. Vol. 2. Basel: Schwabe, 1961.

Grabois, Aryeh. "The Hebraica Veritas and Jewish-Christian Intellectual Relations in the Twelfth Century." *Speculum* 50, no. 3 (1975): 613–634.

Groves, Nicholas. "Image-Likeness and 'Tathāgatagarbha': A Reading of William of St. Thierry's 'Golden Epistle' and the 'Ratnagotravibhāga.'" *Buddhist-Christian Studies* 10 (1990): 97–117.

Haas, Alois M. "Et Descendit de Caelo Γνῶϑι Σεαυτόν (Juvenal, Satir. XI, 27). Dauer Und Wandel Eines Mystologischen Motivs." *Zeitschrift Für Deutsches Altertum Und Deutsche Literatur* 108, no. 2 (1979): 71–95.

Haas, Alois M. "Christliche Aspekte Des 'Gnothi Seauton'. Selbsterkenntnis Und Mystik." *Zeitschrift Für Deutsches Altertum Und Deutsche Literatur* 110 (1981): 71–96.

Häring, Nicholas M. "The So-Called 'Apologia de Verbo Incarnato.'" *Franciscan Studies* 16, no. 1/2 (1956): 102–143.

Häring, Nicholas M. "Commentary and Hermeneutics." In *Renaissance and Renewal in the 12th Century*. Edited by Robert L. Benson and Giles Constable, 173–200. Cambridge: Harvard University Press, 1982.

Harkins, Franklin T. "Secundus Augustinus: Hugh of St. Victor on Liberal Arts Study and Salvation." *Augustinian Studies* 37.2 (2006): 219–46.

Haseldine, Julian P. "Monastic Friendship in Theory and in Action in the Twelfth Century." In *Friendship in the Middle Ages and Early Modern Age*. Edited by Albrecht Classen and Marilyn Sandidge, 249–394. Berlin, Boston: De Gruyter, 2011.

Haskins, Charles H. *The Renaissance of the Twelfth Century*. Cambridge: Harvard University Press, 1971.

Heil, Johannes. "Labourers in the Lord's Quarry: Carolingian Exegetes, Patristic Authority, and Theological Innovation, a Case Study in the Representation of Jews in Commentaries on Paul." In *The Study of the Bible in the Carolingian Era*, 75–95. Medieval Church Studies 3. Turnhout: Brepols, 2003.

Hessler, Wolfgang. "Auctoritas Im Deutschen Mittellatein. Eine Zwischenbilanz Im Mittellateinischen Wörterbuch." *Archiv Für Kulturgeschichte* 47 (1965).

Heyder, Regina. *Auctoritas scripturae: Schriftauslegung und Theologieverständnis Peter Abaelards unter besonderer Berücksichtigung der "Expositio in Hexaemeron."* Münster: Aschendorff, 2010.

Hofmann Berman, Constance. *The Cistercian Evolution: The Invention of a Religious Order in Twelfth-Century Europe*. Philadelphia: University of Pennsylvania Press, 2010.

Hollywood, Amy. *The Soul as Virgin Wife: Mechthild of Magdeburg, Marguerite Porete, and Meister Eckhart*. Southbend, IN: University of Notre Dame Press, 1995.

Honemann, Volker. *Die "Epistola Ad Fratres de Monte Dei" Des Wilhelm von Saint–Thierry: Lateinische Überlieferung Und Mittelalterliche Übersetzungen*. Vol. 61. Münchener Texte Und Untersuchungen Zur Deutschen Literatur Des Mittelalters. München, 1978.

Honemann, Volker."Eine Neue Handschrift Der Deutschen Epistola Ad Fratres de Monte Dei." In *Überlieferungsgeschichtliche Editionen Und Studien Zur Deutschen Literatur Des Mittelalters. Kurt Ruh Zum 75. Geburtstag*. Edited by Konrad Kunze, Johannes Gottfried Mayer, and Bernhard Schnell, 332–349, 1989.

Honemann, Volker. "The Reception of William of Saint–Thierry's Epistola Ad Fratres de Monte Dei during the Middle Ages." In *Cistercians in the Late Middle Ages*. Edited by E. Rozanne Elder, 5–18. Cistercian Studies 64. Kalamazoo, MI: Cistercian Publications, 1981.

Hourlier, Jacques. "Guillaume de Saint–Thierry et La 'Brevis Commentatio in Cantica.'" *Analecta Cisterciensia* 12 (1965).

Hunt, Richard William. "The Introduction to the 'Artes' in the Twelfth Century." In *The History of Grammar in the Middle Ages: Collected Papers [by Richard W. Hunt]*. Edited by Geoffrey Leslie Bursill-Hall. Amsterdam, 1980.

Hwang, Alexander, Brian Matz, and Augustine Casiday, eds. *Grace for grace: the debates after Augustine and Pelagius.* Washington, D.C.: The Catholic University of America Press, 2014.

Jackson, Sidney L. "The Twelfth Century in the West, Its Libraries, and Hugh of St. Victor's Classification of Knowledge." *The Journal of Library History (1966–1972)* 2, no. 3 (1967): 185–200.

Jacobi, Klaus. "Philosophy of Language." In *The Cambridge Companion to Abelard.* Edited by Jeffrey E. Brower and Kevin Guilfoy, 126–57. Cambridge Companions to Philosophy. Cambridge: Cambridge University Press, 2004.

Jaeger, C. Stephen. *The Envy of Angels: Cathedral Schools and Social Ideals in Medieval Europe, 950–1200.* Philadelphia: University of Pennsylvania Press, 1994.

Johnson, Phillip D. *Arnold of Brescia: Apostle of Liberty in Twelfth-Century Europe.* Eugene, OR: Wipf & Stock, 2016.

Jotischky, Andrew. "Monastic Reform and the Geography of Christendom: Experience, Observation and Influence." *Transactions of the Royal Historical Society, 6th Series* 22 (2012): 57–74.

Kearney, Eileen Frances. "Scientia and Sapientia: Reading Sacred Scripture at the Paraclete." In *From Cloister to Classroom. Monastic and Scholastic Approaches to Truth.* The Spirituality of Western Christendom III. Edited by E. Rozanne Elder, 111–129. Cistercian Studies 90. Kalamazoo MI: Cistercian Publications, 1986.

Kerr, Julie. "An Essay on Cistercian Liturgy." For *Cistercians in Yorkshire.* University of Sheffield, 2004.

King, Peter. "Metaphysics." In *The Cambridge Companion to Abelard.* Edited by Jeffrey E. Brower and Kevin Guilfoy, 65–125. Cambridge Companions to Philosophy. Cambridge: Cambridge University Press, 2004.

Klitzsch, Ingo. *Die "Theologien" des Petrus Abaelardus: genetisch-kontextuelle Analyse und theologiegeschichtliche Relektüre.* Leipzig: Evangelische Verlagsanstalt, 2010.

Knight, Gillian R. "The Language of Retreat and the Eremitic Ideal in Some Letters of Peter the Venerable." *Archives d'histoire Doctrinale et Littéraire Du Moyen Âge* 63 (1996): 7–43.

Knoch, Wendelin. "Der Streit Zwischen Bernhard von Clairvaux Und Petrus Abaelard: Ein Exemplarisches Ringen Um Verantworteten Glauben." *Freiburger Zeitschrift Für Philosophie Und Theologie* 38 (1991): 299–315.

Kouamé, Thierry. "The Institutional Organization of the Schools." In *A Companion to Twelfth-Century Schools.* Edited by Cédric Giraud, translated by Ignacio Duran, 30–48. A Series of Handbooks and Reference Works on the Intellectual and Religious Life of Europe, 500–1800 88. Brill, 2019.

Kramer, Rutger. "Monks on the Via Regia: The World of Smaragdus of Saint-Mihiel." In *Rethinking Authority in the Carolingian Empire,* 123–168. Amsterdam: Amsterdam University Press, 2019.

Landgraf, Artur Michael. *Einführung in die Geschichte der theologischen Literatur der Frühscholastik: unter dem Gesichtspunkte der Schulenbildung.* Gregorius-Verlag, 1948.

LaVere, Suzanne. "From Contemplation to Action: The Role of the Active Life in the "Glossa Ordinaria" on the Song of Songs." *Speculum* 82, no. 1 (2007): 54–69.

Leclercq, Jean. *Recueil d'études sur saint Bernard et ses écrits.* Vol. 3. Rome: Edizioni di Storia e Letteratura, 1969.

Lekai, Louis J. *The Cistercians: Ideals and Reality.* OH: Kent State University Press, 1989.

Linde, Cornelia. "Twelfth-Century Notions of the Canon of the Bible." In *Reading the Bible in the Middle Ages.* Edited by Jinty Nelson and Damien Kempf, 7–18. Studies in Early Medieval History. London: Bloomsbury, 2017.

Lochrie, Karma. "Mystical Acts, Queer Tendencies." In *Constructing Medieval Sexuality.* Edited by Karma Lochrie, Peggy Mccracken, and James A. Schultz. Minneapolis: University of Minnesota Press, 1997.

Lohr, Charles H. "Peter Abälard und die scholastische Exegese." *Freiburger Zeitschrift für Philosophie und Theologie* 28 (1981): 95–110.

Long, Micol, and Steven Vanderputten. "Introduction." In *Horizontal Learning in the High Middle Ages.* Edited by Micol Long, Steven Vanderputten, and Tjamke Snijders, 9–16. Peer-to-Peer Knowledge Transfer in Religious Communities. Amsterdam: Amsterdam University Press, 2019.

Lord, Andrew. "Monastic Wisdom Theology: Insights from William of St Thierry." *Journal of Anglican Studies* 5, no. 1 (2007): 109–121.

Luscombe, David. *The Bible in the Work of Peter Abelard and of his "School". Neue Richtungen in der hoch– und spätmittelalterlichen Bibelexegese.* Edited by Robert E. Lerner. München: Oldenbourg Wissenschaftsverlag, 1996.

Luscombe, David. "St Anselm and Abelard. A Restatement." In *Peter Abelard and Heloise.* London: Routledge, 2018.

Lutter, Christina. *Vita Communis in Central European Monastic Landscapes. Meanings of Community across Medieval Eurasia.* Brill, 2016.

Lynch, Joseph H. *The Medieval Church: A Brief History.* London, New York: Longman, 1992.

Lynch, Joseph H. "The Cistercians and Underage Novices." *Citeaux* 24 (1973): 283–297.

Mann, William E. "Ethics." In *The Cambridge Companion to Abelard.* Edited by Jeffrey E. Brower and Kevin Guilfoy, 279–304. Cambridge Companions to Philosophy. Cambridge: Cambridge University Press, 2004.

Marenbon, John. "Life, Milieu, and Intellectual Contexts." In *The Cambridge Companion to Abelard.* Edited by Jeffrey E. Brower and Kevin Guilfoy, 13–44.

Cambridge Companions to Philosophy. Cambridge: Cambridge University Press, 2004.

Matis, Hannah W. "Early-Medieval Exegesis of the Song of Songs and the Maternal Language of Clerical Authority." *Speculum* 89, no. 2 (2014): 358–381.

Matter, E. Ann. "Anselm and the Tradition of the 'Song of Songs.'" *Rivista Di Storia Della Filosofia* 48 (1993): 551–560.

Matter, E. Ann. *The Voice of My Beloved: The Song of Songs in Western Medieval Christianity*. Philadelphia: University of Pennsylvania Press, 1990.

McGinn, Bernard. *The Flowering of Mysticism: Men and Women in the New Mysticism (1200–1350)*. New York, NY: Crossroad, 1998.

McGinn, Bernard. *The Growth of Mysticism: Gregory the Great Through the 12 Century*. vol. 2. The Presence of God. A History of Western Christian Mysticism. New York, NY: Crossroad, 1996.

McGinn, Bernard. "The Spiritual Teaching of the Early Cistercians." In *The Cambridge Companion to the Cistercian Order*. Edited by Mette Birkedal Bruun, 218–32. Cambridge Companions to Religion. Cambridge: Cambridge University Press, 2012.

McGuire, Brian. "Bernard of Clairvaux." In *Medieval Philosophy of Religion: The History of Western Philosophy of Religion*. Edited by Graham Oppy and Nick Trakakis. Slough, Buckinghamshire: Acumen Publishing, 2009.

McGuire, Brian. "Monastic and Religious Orders, c. 1100-c. 1350." In *The Cambridge History of Christianity: Volume 4: Christianity in Western Europe, c.1100-c.1500*. Edited by Miri Rubin and Walter Simons, 4:54–72. Cambridge History of Christianity. Cambridge: Cambridge University Press, 2009.

McGuire, Brian. "A Chronology and Biography of William of Saint-Thierry." In *A Companion to William of Saint-Thierry*, 11–34. Leiden: Brill, 2019.

McGuire, Brian. "Bernard of Clairvaux and the Cistercian Mystical Tradition." In *The Wiley-Blackwell Companion to Christian Mysticism*. Edited by Julia A. Lamm, 237–50. Hoboken, NJ: John Wiley & Sons, Ltd, 2012.

Friendship & Community: The Monastic Experience, 350–1250. Cistercian Studies 95. Kalamazoo, MI: Cistercian Publications, 1988.

McGuire, Brian. "Sexual Awareness and Identity in Aelred of Rievaulx (1110–67)." *The American Benedictine Review* 45 (1994): 184–226.

McMahon, Clara P. "The Teaching of History in the Twelfth Century." *History of Education Quarterly* 2, no. 1 (1962): 47–51.

Melville, Gert. *The World of Medieval Monasticism: Its History and Forms of Life*. Collegeville, MI: Liturgical Press, 2016.

Mews, Constant J. "Rethinking Scholastic Communities in Latin Europe: Competition and Theological Method in the Twelfth Century." *Medieval Worlds* medieval worlds (2020): 12–32.

Mews, Constant J. "Bernard of Clairvaux and Peter Abelard." In *A Companion to Bernard of Clairvaux*, 133–168. Leiden: Brill, 2011.

Mews, Constant J. "The Council of Sens (1141): Abelard, Bernard, and the Fear of Social Upheaval." *Speculum* 77, no. 2 (2002): 342–82.

Mews, Constant J. "The Schools and Intellectual Renewal in the Twelfth Century: A Social Approach." In *A Companion to Twelfth-Century Schools*. Edited by Cédric Giraud, translated by Ignacio Duran, 10–29. A Series of Handbooks and Reference Works on the Intellectual and Religious Life of Europe, 500–1800 88. Leiden: Brill, 2019.

Mews, Constant J. "The World As Text: The Bible and the Book of Nature in Twelfth-Century Theology." In *Scripture and Pluralism: Reading the Bible in the Religiously Plural Worlds of the Middle Ages and Renaissance*. Edited by Thomas Heffernan and Thomas E. Burman. Studies in the History of Christian Traditions 123. Leiden: Brill, 2005.

Mews, Constant J. *Reason and Belief in the Age of Roscelin and Abelard*. Variorum Collected Studies Series. Aldershot: Routledge, 2002.

Milis, Ludo. "William of Saint Thierry, His Birth, His Formation and His First Monastic Experiences." In *William, Abbot of St. Thierry: A Colloquium at the Abbey of St. Thierry*. Translated by Jerry Carfantan, 9–33. Cistercian Studies 94. Kalamazoo MI: Cistercian Publications, 1987.

Minnis, Alastair. *Medieval Theory of Authorship: Scholastic Literary Attitudes in the Later Middle Ages*. 2nd ed. Philadelphia: University of Pennsylvania Press, 2010.

Monagle, Clare. *Orthodoxy and Controversy in Twelfth-Century Religious Discourse: Peter Lombard's "Sentences" and the Development of Theology*. Vol. 8. Europa Sacra. Turnhout: Brepols, 2012.

Moore, R.I. "Literacy and the Making of Heresy c. 1000–1150." In *Heresy and Literacy 1000–1530*. Edited by Peter Biller and Anne Hudson, 19–37. Cambridge: Cambridge University Press, 1996.

Moritz, Arne, ed. *Ars imitatur naturam. Transformationen eines Paradigmas menschlicher Kreativität im Übergang vom Mittelalter zur Neuzeit*. Münster: Aschendorff, 2010. Morrison, Karl F. The Mimetic Tradition of Reform in the West. Princeton University Press, 1982.

Moritz, Arne. *Tradition and Authority in the Western Church, 300–1140. Tradition and Authority in the Western Church, 300–1140*. Princeton University Press, 2015.

Myers, Glenn E. "Manuscript Evidence of the Golden Epistle's Influence in the Sermons of Johannes Tauler." *Cistercian Studies Quarterly* 48.4 (2013): 479–501.

Myers, Glenn E. "William of Saint–Thierry's Legacy: Progress toward Trinitarian Participation in the Unio Mystica in Johannes Tauler's Sermons." In *A Companion to William of Saint–Thierry*, 196–228. Brill, 2019.

Nelson, Jinty, and Damien Kempf. "Introduction." In *Reading the Bible in the Middle Ages*. Edited by Jinty Nelson and Damien Kempf, 1–5. Studies in Early Medieval History. London: Bloomsbury, 2017.

Neumann O'Neill, Jeanne. "Florus and the 'Commendatio Ad Gloriam' in Horace 'Epistles' 1.3." *Phoenix* 53, no. 1/2 (1999): 80–96.

Nord, Christiane, and Klaus Berger, eds. "Einführung." In *Meditationen und Gebete*, 7–21. Frankfurt: Insel Verlag, 2001.

Ohly, Ernst Friedrich. "Die Kathedrale Als Zeitenraum. Zum Dom von Siena." In *Schriften Zur Mittelalterlichen Bedeutungsforschung*, 171–273. Darmstadt: Wissenschaftliche Buchgesellschaft, 1977.

Olson, Sherri. *Daily Life in a Medieval Monastery*. Santa Barbara: Greenwood, 2013.

Otten, Willemien. "The Texture of Tradition. The Role of the Church Fathers in Carolingian Theology." In *The Reception of the Church Fathers in the West. From the Carolingians to the Maurists*. Edited by Irena Dorota Backus, 1:3–50. Leiden: Brill, 1997.

Pansters, Krijn, and John Green. "The Golden Epistle and the Ladder of Monks: Aspects of Twelfth-Century Carthusian Spirituality." In *The Carthusians in the Low Countries. Studies in Monastic History and Heritage*, 189–216. Miscellanea Neerlandica 43. Leiden: Brill, 2016.

Pelikan, Jaroslav. *The Christian Tradition: A History of the Development of Doctrine, Volume 1: The Emergence of the Catholic Tradition (100–600)*. Chicago, IL: University of Chicago Press, 1971.

Peters, Edward M. "Transgressing the Limits Set by the Fathers: Authority and Impious Exegesis in Medieval Thought." In *Limits of Thought and Power*, 338–362. Varium Collected Studies Series 721. Aldershot: Ashgate Publishing, 2001.

Peters, Nathaniel. "The Eucharistic Theology of William of Saint–Thierry." In *A Companion to William of Saint–Thierry*, 160–195. Brill, 2019.

Pezzini, Domenico. "Aelred's Doctrine of Charity and Friendship." In *A Companion to Aelred of Rievaulx (1110–1167)*. Edited by Marsha Dutton, 221–245. Leiden: Brill, 2017.

Phelan, Owen M. *The Formation of Christian Europe: The Carolingians, Baptism, and the Imperium Christianum*. Oxford: Oxford University Press, 2014.

Ponesse, Matthew. "Standing Distant from the Fathers: Smaragdus of Saint–Mihiel and the Reception of Early Medieval Learning." *Traditio* 67, no. 1 (2012): 71–99.

Posset, Franz. *Pater Bernardus: Martin Luther and Bernard of Clairvaux*. Kalamazoo, MI: Cistercian Publications, 1999.

Pranger, Marinus B. *Bernard of Clairvaux and the Shape of Monastic Thought: Broken Dreams*. Brill's Studies in Intellectual History. Leiden: Brill, 1994.

Reilly, Diane. *The Cistercian Reform and the Art of the Book in Twelfth-Century France. The Cistercian Reform and the Art of the Book in Twelfth-Century France.* Knowledge Communities 5. Amsterdam: Amsterdam University Press, 2018.

Renna, Thomas J. "The Idea of Jerusalem: Monastic to Scholastic." In *From Cloister to Classroom. Monastic and Scholastic Approaches to Truth.* The Spirituality of Western Christendom III. Edited by E. Rozanne Elder, 96–109. Cistercian Studies 90. Kalamazoo, MI: Cistercian Publications, 1986.

Rexroth, Frank. *Fröhliche Scholastik: Die Wissenschaftsrevolution des Mittelalters.* 1st ed. München: C.H. Beck, 2018.

Riché, Pierre, and Guy Lobrichon. *Le Moyen Age et la Bible.* Paris: Beauchesne, 1998.

Ricklin, Thomas: *Einige Hinweise Zu Seinem Verschwinden.* In *The Platonic Tradition in the Middle Ages.* Edited by Maarten J.F.M. Hoenen and Stephen E. Gersh, 139–163. Berlin: De Gruyter, 2002.

Riesenhuber, Klaus. "Der Streit Um Die 'ratio' in Der Frühscholastik." In *Was Ist Philosophie Im Mittelalter? Qu'est-Ce Que La Philosophie Au Moyen Âge? What Is Philosophy in the Middle Ages? Akten Des X. Internationalen Kongresses Für Mittelalterliche Philosophie Der Société Internationale Pour l'Etude de La Philosophie Médiévale, 25. Bis 30. August 1997 in Erfurt.* Miscellanea Mediaevalia 26. Edited by Jan A. Aertsen and Andreas Speer, 460–67. Berlin: De Gruyter, 1998.

Rizek–Pfister, Cornelia. "Die hermeneutischen Pinzipien in Abaelards Sic et non." *Freiburger Zeitschrift für Philosophie und Theologie* 47 (2000): 484–501.

Robb, Fiona. "Intellectual Tradition and Misunderstanding: The Development of Academic Theology on the Trinity in the Twelfth and Thirteenth Centuries." PhD. diss. London: University of London, 1994.

Robertson, Duncan. *Lectio Divina: The Medieval Experience of Reading.* Trappist, KY: Cistercian Publications, 2011.

Roden, Frederick S. "Aelred of Rievaulx, Same-Sex Desire and the Victorian Monastery." In *Masculinity and Spirituality in Victorian Culture.* Edited by Andrew Bradstock, Sean Gill, Anne Hogan, and Sue Morgan, 85–99. London: Palgrave Macmillan UK, 2000.

Rorem, Paul. "Bonaventure's Ideal and Hugh of St. Victor's Comprehensive Biblical Theology." *Franciscan Studies* 70 (2012): 385–397.

Rudolph, Conrad. "Bernard of Clairvaux's Apologia as a Description of Cluny, and the Controversy over Monastic Art." *Gesta* 27, no. 1/2 (1988): 125–132.

Rudolph, Conrad. "Inventing the Exegetical Stained-Glass Window: Suger, Hugh, and a New Elite Art." *The Art Bulletin* 93, no. 4 (2011): 399–422.

Ruh, Kurt. *Geschichte Der Abendländischen Mystik. Bd. 1. Die Grundlegung Durch Die Kirchenväter Und Die Mönchstheologie Des 12. Jahrhunderts.* München: C.H. Beck, 1990.

Rydstrøm-Poulsen, Aage. "The Way of Descent: The Christology of William of Saint–Thierry." In *Unity of Spirit: Studies on William of Saint–Thierry in Honor of E. Rozanne Elder*. Edited by F. Tyler Sergent, Aage Rydstrøm-Poulsen, and Marsha L. Dutton, 78–91. Cistercian Studies 268. Collegeville, MN: Cistercian Publications, 2015.

Rydstrøm-Poulsen, Aage. "The Human Person in the Trinity - William of Saint Thierry's Trinitarian Mysticism." *American Benedictine Review* 61 (2010).

Rydstrøm-Poulsen, Aage. "The Humanism of William of Saint–Thierry." In *A Companion to Medieval Christian Humanism. Essays on Principal Thinkers*. Edited by John P. Bequette, 88–100. Brill's Companions to the Christian Tradition 69. Brill, 2016.

Rydstrøm-Poulsen, Aage. "William of Saint–Thierry on the Soul." In *A Companion to William of Saint–Thierry*. Edited by F. Tyler Sergent, 93–108. Brill, 2019.

Scheck, Thomas P. *Origen and the History of Justification: The Legacy of Origen? Commentary on Romans*. Notre Dame, IN: University of Notre Dame Press, 2008.

Schildgen, Brenda, and Peter S. Hawkins. "Introduction." In *Medieval Readings of Romans*. Edited by William S. Campbell, Peter S. Hawkins, and Brenda Schildgen. Romans through History and Cultures Series. New York: T&T Clark, 2007.

Schrock, Chad. "The Proportion of His Purpose: Peter Abelard's 'Historia Calamitatum' as Sacred History." *Archives d'histoire Doctrinale et Littéraire Du Moyen Age* 77 (2010): 29–46.

Scott, Mark S. M. "Shades of Grace: Origen and Gregory of Nyssa's Soteriological Exegesis of the 'Black and Beautiful' Bride in Song of Songs 1:5." *The Harvard Theological Review* 99, no. 1 (2006): 65–83.

Sergent, F. Tyler. *A Companion to William of Saint–Thierry. A Companion to William of Saint–Thierry*. Brill's Companions to the Christian Tradition 84. Brill, 2019.

Sergent, F. Tyler. "Introduction." In *A Companion to William of Saint–Thierry*. Edited by F. Tyler Sergent, 1–10. Brill, 2019.

Sergent, F. Tyler. "Unitas Spiritus and the Originality of William of Saint–Thierry." In *Unity of Spirit: Studies on William of Saint–Thierry in Honor of E. Rozanne Elder*. Edited by F. Tyler Sergent, Aage Rydstrøm-Poulsen, and Marsha L. Dutton, 144–70. Cistercian Studies 268. Collegeville, MN: Cistercian Publications, 2015.

Sergent, F. Tyler. "William of Saint–Thierry's Sources and Influences: Ratio Fidei and Fruitio." In *A Companion to William of Saint–Thierry*. Edited by F. Tyler Sergent, 35–66. Brill, 2019.

Sergent, F. Tyler, Aage Rydstrøm-Poulsen, and Marsha L. Dutton, eds. *Unity of Spirit: Studies on William of Saint–Thierry in Honor of E. Rozanne Elder*. Cistercian Studies 268. Collegeville, MN: Cistercian Publications, 2015.

Shuve, Karl. *The Song of Songs and the Fashioning of Identity in Early Latin Christianity*. Oxford Early Christian Studies. Oxford: Oxford University Press, 2016.

Signer, Michael A. "Rabbi and Magister: Overlapping Intellectual Models of the Twelfth-Century Renaissance." *Jewish History* 22, no. 1/2 (2008): 115–137.

Smalley, Beryl. *Studies in Medieval Thought and Learning From Abelard to Wyclif.* London: Bloomsbury, 1981.

Smalley, Beryl. *The Study of the Bible in the Middle Ages.* Notre Dame, IN: University of Notre Dame Press, 1964.

Smith, Lesley. *What was the Bible in the Twelfth and Thirteenth Centuries? Neue Richtungen in der hoch- und spätmittelalterlichen Bibelexegese.* München: Oldenbourg Wissenschaftsverlag, 2009.

Solterer, Helen. "Seeing, Hearing, Tasting Woman: Medieval Senses of Reading." *Comparative Literature* 46, no. 2: 129, 2021.

Southern, R. W. *The Making of the Middle Ages.* New Haven, CT: Yale University Press, 1961.

Southern, R. W. "Hugh of St. Victor and the Idea of Historical Development." In *History and Historians. Selected Papers of R. W. Southern.* Edited by R.J. Bartlett, 30–47. Malden, MA: Blackwell Publishing, 2004.

Stammberger, Ralf M. W. "Einleitung." In *Väter der Kirche: ekklesiales Denken von den Anfängen bis in die Neuzeit; Festgabe für Hermann Josef Sieben SJ zum 70. Geburtstag.* Edited by Johannes Arnold, Rainer Berndt, and Ralf M. W. Stammberger, 544–51. Paderborn: Verlag Ferdinand Schöningh, 2004.

Steckel, Sita. "Charisma and Expertise Constructing Sacralized Mastership in Northern and Western Europe, c. 8000–1150." In *Schüler und Meister.* Edited by Andreas Speer and Thomas Jeschke, 641–79. Miscellanea Mediaevalia 39. Berlin, Boston: De Gruyter, 2016.

Steckel, Sita. *Kulturen des Lehrens im Früh- und Hochmittelalter: Autorität, Wissenskonzepte und Netzwerke von Gelehrten.* Köln: Böhlau Verlag, 2011.

Steckel, Sita. "Submission to the Authority of the Masters: Transformations of a Symbolic Practice during the Long Twelfth Century." In *A Companion to Twelfth-Century Schools.* Edited by Cédric Giraud, translated by Ignacio Duran, 10–29. A Series of Handbooks and Reference Works on the Intellectual and Religious Life of Europe, 500–1800 88. Brill, 2019.

Speer, Christian. *Die entdeckte Natur. Untersuchungen zu Begründungsversuchen einer "scientia Naturalis" im 12. Jahrhundert.* Studien und Texte zur Geistesgeschichte des Mittelalters. Leiden: Brill, 1995.

Stirnimann, Heinrich. *Unio-communio: Dimensionen mystischer Erfahrung.* Freiburg, CH: Universitätsverlag, 1995.

Stone, M.W.F. "Augustine and Medieval Philosophy." In *The Cambridge Companion to Augustine.* Edited by Eleonore Stump and Norman Kretzmann. Cambridge Companions to Philosophy. Cambridge: Cambridge University Press, 2001.

Swanson, Robert Norman. *The Twelfth-Century Renaissance*. Manchester: Manchester University Press, 1999.

Sweeney, Eileen. "Rewriting the Narrative of Scripture: 12th-Century Debates Over Reason and Theological Form." *Medieval Philosophy and Theology* 3 (1993): 1–34.

Teeuwen, Mariken. *The Vocabulary of Intellectual Life in the Middle Ages*. Vol. 10. Études Sur Le Vocabulaire Du Moyen Âge. Turnhout: Brepols, 2003.

Tomasic, Thomas Michael. "The Three Theological Virtues as Modes of Intersubjectivity in the Thought of William of Saint–Thierry." *Recherches de Théologie Ancienne et Médiévale* 38 (1971): 89–120.

Valters Painter, Christine, and Lucy Wynkoop. *Lectio Divina: Contemplative Awakening and Awareness*. Mahwah, NJ: Paulist Press, 2008.

Van Asselt, Willem J. van, and Eef Dekker, eds. *Reformation and Scholasticism. An Ecumenical Enterprise. Texts and Studies in Reformation and Post-Reformation Thought*. Grand Rapids, MI: Baker Academic Press, 2001.

Van Dijk, Mathilde van, José van Aelst, and Tom Gaens. "Introduction." In *Faithful to the Cross in a Moving World: Late Medieval Carthusians as Devotional Reformers*, 1–12. Church History and Religious Culture 96. Leiden: Brill, 2016.

Vanderputten, Steven. "The First 'General Chapter' of Benedictine Abbots (1131) Reconsidered." In *Journal of Ecclesiastical History* 66 (October 2015): 715–34.

Van Engen, John. "Rupert of Deutz and William of Saint–Thierry." *Revue Bénédictine* 93, no. 3–4 (1 January 1983): 327–336.

Verbaal, Wim. "Cistercians in Dialogue: Bringing the World into the Monastery." In *The Cambridge Companion to the Cistercian Order*. Edited by Mette Birkedal Bruun, 233–44. Cambridge Companions to Religion. Cambridge: Cambridge University Press, 2012.

Verbaal, Wim. "The Council of Sens Reconsidered: Masters, Monks, or Judges?" *Church History* 74, no. 3 (2005): 460–493.

Verdeyen, Paul. "De Invloed van William van Saint–Thierry Op Hadewijch En Ruusbroec." *Ons Geestelijk Erf* 51 (1977): 3–19.

Verdeyen, Paul. "En Quoi La Connaissance de Guillaume de Saint–Thierry a-t-Elle Progresse Depuis Le Collogue de 1976?" *Revue Des Sciences Religieuses* 73 (1999): 17–20.

Verdeyen, Paul. "La Chronologie Des Œuvres de Guillaume de Saint–Thierry." *Ons Geestelijk Erf* 82, no. 3 (September 2011): 193–203.

Verger, Jacques. *La Renaissance du XIIe siècle*. Paris: Éditions du Cerf, 1996.

Waddell, Chrysogonus. "The Liturgical Dimension of Twelfth-Century Cistercian Preaching." In *Medieval Monastic Preaching*. Edited by Carolyn A. Muessig, 335–349. Brill's Studies in Intellectual History 90. Leiden: Brill, 1998.

Waddell, Chrysogonus. "'Adtendite a falsis prophetis': Abaelard's earliest known anti-Cistercian diatribe." *Cistercian studies quarterly 39* (2004): 371–97.

Walker Bynum, Caroline. *Jesus as Mother.* Vol. 16. Publications of the Center for Medieval and Renaissance Studies. Berkeley, CA: University of California Press, 1982.

Walker Bynum, Caroline. "Did the Twelfth Century Discover the Individual?" *The Journal of Ecclesiastical History* 31, no. 1 (January 1980): 1–17.

Walker Bynum, Caroline. *Fragmentation and Redemption: Essays on Gender and the Human Body in Medieval Religion.* New York, NY: Zone Books, 2002.

Walker Bynum, Caroline. *Holy Feast and Holy Fast: The Religious Significance of Food to Medieval Women.* The New Historicism. Berkeley, CA: University of California Press, 2000.

Walker Bynum, Caroline. "Jesus as Mother and Abbot as Mother: Some Themes in Twelfth-Century Cistercian Writing." *The Harvard Theological Review* 70, no. 3/4 (1977): 257–284.

Walker Bynum, Caroline. "The Cistercian Conception of Community: An Aspect of Twelfth-Century Spirituality." *The Harvard Theological Review* 68 (1975): 273–286.

Wei, Ian P. *Intellectual Culture in Medieval Paris: Theologians and the University, c.1100–1330.* Cambridge: Cambridge University Press, 2012.

Wetzel, James. "The Recovery of Free Agency in the Theology of St. Augustine." *The Harvard Theological Review* 80, no. 1 (1987): 101–125.

Williams, Thomas. "Sin, Grace, and Redemption." In *The Cambridge Companion to Abelard.* Edited by Jeffrey E. Brower and Kevin Guilfoy, 258–278. Cambridge Companions to Philosophy. Cambridge: Cambridge University Press, 2004.

Wilmart, André. "La Série et La Date Des Ouvrages de Guillaume De Saint–Thierry." *Revue Mabillon* 14 (1924): 157–167.

Winterbottom, M., and R. M. Thomson. "Introduction." In *For and Against Abelard: The Invective of Bernard of Clairvaux and Berengar of Poitiers.* Edited and translated by M. Winterbottom and R.M. Thomson, xi–xxxii. Woodbridge: Boydell & Brewer, 2020.

Zerbi, Pietro. "William of Saint Thierry and His Dispute with Abelard." In *William, Abbot of St. Thierry. Translated by Jerry Carfantan,* 181–203. Cistercian Studies 94. Kalamazoo, MI: Cistercian Publications, 1987.

Ziolkowski, Jan M. "Cultures of Authority in the Long Twelfth Century." *The Journal of English and Germanic Philology* 108, no. 4 (2009): 421–448.

Index

If you have any questions regarding this title, please contact:

Koninklijke Brill BV
Plantijnstraat 2
2321 JC Leiden
Email: info@brill.com

Batch number: 08789492